Scottish Literature and World War I

Edited by David A. Rennie

EDINBURGH
University Press

Edinburgh University Press is one of the leading university presses in the UK. We publish academic books and journals in our selected subject areas across the humanities and social sciences, combining cutting-edge scholarship with high editorial and production values to produce academic works of lasting importance. For more information visit our website: edinburghuniversitypress.com

© editorial matter and organisation David Rennie, 2020, 2022
© the chapters their several authors, 2020, 2022

Edinburgh University Press Ltd
The Tun – Holyrood Road
12(2f) Jackson's Entry
Edinburgh EH8 8PJ

First published in hardback by Edinburgh University Press 2020

Typeset in 11/13 Adobe Sabon by
IDSUK (DataConnection) Ltd

A CIP record for this book is available from the British Library

ISBN 978 1 4744 5459 9 (hardback)
ISBN 978 14744 5460 5 (paperback)
ISBN 978 1 4744 5461 2 (webready PDF)
ISBN 978 1 4744 5462 9 (epub)

The right of David A. Rennie to be identified as the Editor of this work has been asserted in accordance with the Copyright, Designs and Patents Act 1988, and the Copyright and Related Rights Regulations 2003 (SI No. 2498).

Contents

Acknowledgements   v
Notes on Contributors   vi

    Introduction: 'A reflection of the contrasts':
    Scottish Literature and World War I   1
    David A. Rennie

Part I: Multi-text Case Studies

1. Scottish Literature, Nationalism and the First World War   21
    Alan Riach

2. 'It Takes All Sorts to Make a Type': Scottish Great
    War Prose   44
    David A. Rennie

3. Unquiet on the Home Front: Scottish Popular Fiction
    and the Truth of War   62
    David Goldie

4. 'One Who Has Sacrificed': The Use of 'High Diction'
    in Women's Correspondence to Scottish Newspapers
    during the First World War   81
    Sarah Pedersen

5. Gaelic Verse   100
    Ronald Black

6. Gaelic Prose   122
    Ronald Black

7. Scottish Philosophy and the First World War   143
    Cairns Craig

Part II: Individual Authors

8. What Next?: Nan Shepherd and the First World War 165
   Alison Lumsden

9. Pagan Modernism: First World War and Spiritual Revival in Lewis Grassic Gibbon's *Sunset Song* and Neil M. Gunn's *Highland River* 180
   Scott Lyall

10. A Bounded Heaven: George A. C. Mackinlay and Great War Pastoral 200
    Randall Stevenson

11. Pastoral as Propaganda in John Buchan's Wartime Writing 218
    Fiona Houston

12. Charles Murray and *A Sough o' War* 238
    Robert Crawford

13. 'But Change, Nothing Abides': *Sunset Song* and the Nature of Change 253
    John Lucas

14. Ewart Alan Mackintosh in Memoriam: Leadership, Patriotism and Posthumous Commemoration 268
    Neil McLennan

Further Reading 286
Index 302

Acknowledgements

Some the essays in this volume developed from papers initially delivered at the workshop 'Scottish Literature and World War I', which was held at Aberdeen University's Research Institute of Irish and Scottish Studies in 2018. The editor would like to thank the Aberdeen Humanities Fund for generously sponsoring that event.

Notes on Contributors

Ronald Black is an Honorary Fellow in the Department of Celtic and Scottish Studies at the University of Edinburgh, having retired as Senior Lecturer in 2001. Among other works, he is editor of *An Tuil: Anthology of 20th Century Scottish Gaelic Verse* (1999) and author of *The Campbells of the Ark: Men of Argyll in 1745* (2017). He is currently co-editing *Galloway: Gaelic's Lost Province*, *John Dewar's Islay, Jura and Colonsay* and *The Edinburgh Biographical Dictionary of Scottish Writers*.

Cairns Craig is Glucksman Professor of Irish and Scottish Studies at the University of Aberdeen, having been previously Professor of Modern and Scottish Literature at the University of Edinburgh. His recent books include *The Wealth of the Nation: Scotland, Culture and Independence* (2018) and *Muriel Spark: Existentialism and the Art of Death* (2019). He is the general editor of the *Journal of Irish and Scottish Studies* and the *Journal of Scottish Thought*.

Robert Crawford's most recent collections of poetry are *The Scottish Ambassador* (2018) and *Strath*, a collection of Scots versions of Song Dynasty Chinese poems with photographs by Norman McBeath (2019). His biography, *Young Eliot: From St Louis to 'The Waste Land'*, was published in 2015. He is Professor of Modern Scottish Literature and Bishop Wardlaw Professor of Poetry at the University of St Andrews.

David Goldie is a senior lecturer in English in the School of Humanities at the University of Strathclyde. He has published extensively on the literature and popular culture of the First World War and is the author (with Roderick Watson) of *The Scottish Poetry of the First and Second World Wars* (2017) and *From the Line: Scottish War Poetry 1914–1945* (2014). He is currently President of the Association for Scottish Literary Studies.

Fiona Houston has a PhD in First World War propaganda from the University of Aberdeen, with a focus on the government-sponsored material written by John Buchan and Ford Madox Ford. She is currently a research assistant at Edinburgh Napier University, looking at the war-books boom of the 1920s and 1930s. Her tracking of the term 'propaganda' in Oxford English dictionaries is published in *Reading World War I Literature 100 Years After: Revista Alicantina de Estudios Ingleses* – Special Issue (2018), no. 31.

John Lucas, author of eleven collections of poetry and six novels, is Professor Emeritus of the Universities of Loughborough and Nottingham Trent. He has produced many critical works, including studies of Dickens, Arnold Bennett and George Crabbe, and has written extensively on English poetry. He has also written a prize-winning account of a year in Athens, a memoir of England in the 1950s and a study of rebels in English cricket. Since 1994 he has run Shoestring Press.

Alison Lumsden is Regius Professor of English Literature at the University of Aberdeen and General Editor of the Edinburgh Edition of Walter Scott's poetry. She has published on many aspects of Scottish women's writing and writing from the north-east of Scotland, including Nan Shepherd and Lewis Grassic Gibbon.

Scott Lyall is Lecturer in Modern and Scottish Literature at Edinburgh Napier University, where he teaches modules on poetry, the modern novel, American literature, and modern Scottish fiction. His research mainly concerns the literature of small-nation revivals in the early twentieth century, especially Scotland and Ireland. He has published extensively on modern Scottish literature, including *Hugh MacDiarmid's Poetry and Politics of Place* and edited volumes on MacDiarmid, Lewis Grassic Gibbon, and *Community in Modern Scottish Literature*.

Neil McLennan is Senior Lecturer and Director of Leadership Programmes (University of Aberdeen), publishing in history and leadership. He is a former History Principal Teacher and President of the Scottish Association of Teachers of History. Neil's great-grandfather was with Ewart Alan Mackintosh when Mackintosh died. Neil's war poetry interest deepened when he was teaching at Tynecastle High School. Wilfred Owen taught there in 1917 as part of 'shell-shock' treatments. Neil led centenary commemorations highlighting Owen's 'Edinburgh Enlightenment' and memorialising war poets across Scotland.

Sarah Pedersen is Professor of Communication and Media at Robert Gordon University, Aberdeen. Her research focuses on women's engagement with the media, particularly for political purposes, using both contemporary and historical sources. Her book, *The Scottish Suffragettes and the Press*, was published in 2017. She is currently working on a study of the politicisation of the parenting website Mumsnet, to be published in 2020. She is Associate Editor of *Women's Studies International Forum* and a Fellow of the Royal Historical Society.

David A. Rennie gained a PhD in American World War I literature from Aberdeen University in 2017. He is the author of *American Writers and World War I* (2020) and co-editor of *F. Scott Fitzgerald: A Composite Biography* (forthcoming). His essays have appeared in *The Hemingway Review* and *The F. Scott Fitzgerald Review*.

Alan Riach is a Poet, and Professor of Scottish Literature at Glasgow University. Born in Airdrie, Lanarkshire, he studied at Cambridge and Glasgow, and worked at the University of Waikato, New Zealand, in 1986–2000, returning to Scotland in 2001. His books include poetry – *The Winter Book* (2017), *Homecoming* (2009) and *Wild Blue: Selected Poems* (2014) – and criticism – *Hugh MacDiarmid's Epic Poetry* (1991), *Representing Scotland* (2005) and (co-authored with Alexander Moffat) *Arts of Resistance: Poets, Portraits and Landscapes of Modern Scotland* (2008), described in the *Times Literary Supplement* as 'a landmark book'.

Randall Stevenson is Emeritus Professor of Twentieth-Century Literature in the University of Edinburgh, and General Editor of the *Edinburgh History of Twentieth-Century Literature in Britain* series. His recent books include *Literature and the Great War, 1914–1918* (2013) and *Reading the Times: Temporality and History in Twentieth-Century Fiction* (2018).

Introduction

'A reflection of the contrasts': Scottish Literature and World War I
David A. Rennie

Conflicting interpretations have been offered regarding the significance of World War I in Scottish writing. Trevor Royle, echoing the earlier sentiments of Colin Milton, argues the vernacular poems of Violet Jacob, Mary Symon and J. B. Salmond 'are harbingers of' the post-war move towards a national school of Scottish literature, spearheaded by Hugh MacDiarmid.[1] Other commentators, however, have argued convincingly that Scottish writing was largely subsumed within wider British literary paradigms, and that little distinctively Scottish literature emerged from the war.[2]

And further divisions exist. Macdonald Daly claims, for John Buchan and Charles Murray, the pastoral expression of 'a distinctly Scottish landscape' forms an apt vehicle to air 'quasi-nationalist difficulties', which can less combatively emerge 'on account of the genre's occlusion of modernity'.[3] Another commentator, however, views Murray's regionalism as one strand in a 'Union [. . .] through which local landscapes are woven into a national *patria*'.[4] Moving to a further matter, one scholar considers Ian Hay's *The First Hundred Thousand* (1915) to convey 'a vital notion of national characteristic' expressive of a renewal of Scotland's 'own national identity'.[5] Another calls Hay's work 'intensely Scottish'.[6] A third, however, identifies in the novel 'a British rather than a specifically Scottish [. . .] cultural identity'.[7]

It seems that part of the difficulty of talking about Scottish writing and World War I arises not just from the idiosyncratic predilections of discussants but also from the inherently fraught question of what it means for literature to be 'Scottish'. As Roderick Watson asks in *The Literature of Scotland: The Twentieth Century*, 'What is

'Scottish literature'? Is it *about* Scotland by anybody, or writing from authors currently living *in* Scotland, or is it literary production about anything by people born in Scotland or of Scottish descent living anywhere?'[8]

These issues are equally pertinent regarding Scottish First World War fiction. What about writers who, though not born in Scotland, nevertheless had strong affiliations with the country? Authors in this category include Boyd Cable (Bangalore, India), Ewart Alan Mackintosh (Brighton, England) and Eric Linklater (Penarth, Wales). Then there are émigrés who spent much of their adult lives abroad, such as Charles Murray (in South Africa), Violet Jacob (in India) and R. W. Campbell (in Australasia). And what of Aberdeen-born Charles Hamilton Sorley, who moved to Cambridge aged five and was educated at Marlborough College and Oxford University? A further issue concerns the relevance of 'modern' historical fiction which reflects on the war, such as Muriel Spark's *The Prime of Miss Jean Brodie* (1961), Bruce Marshall's *The Black Oxen* (1972) and William McIlvanney's *Docherty* (1975). This introduction – and the wider collection – follows Watson's lead in considering '[t]he "literature of Scotland" [. . .] to echo "the matter of Scotland"', rather than attempting a prescriptive definition of Scottishness (although, in the spirit of true inclusivity, contributors are free within their own chapters to disagree with this ethos).[9]

One way we might begin approaching the idea of Scottishness in relation to World War I is G. Gregory Smith's notion of the Caledonian Antisyzygy: that is, the contention Smith offered in his 1919 book, *Scottish Literature: Character and Influence*, that Scottish writing – and the Scottish character it reflects – is 'remarkably varied', amounting to 'almost a zigzag of contradictions'.[10] Ian Brown and Alan Riach contend that this is perhaps an over-familiar term, which nevertheless captures the 'truth', as they have it, of 'the protean, multivalent, multilingual, and multiform nature of Scottish culture'.[11] Rather than 'reduce these many different voices to a single narrative', this collection views Scottish literature as being linguistically, regionally, ideologically and artistically multitudinous.[12] As Catriona Macdonald notes,

> Scottish identity [. . .] was further complicated by its very nature: identity posed as a unifying force when, in reality, it was fragmentary; it posited characteristics peculiar to Scots but, for most Scots, their sense of belonging was an intensely personal 'thing'.[13]

And, as the 2014 independence referendum and 2016 European referendum highlight, this continues to be true of the cultural present from which we retrospectively assess the Great War.

Alastair Niven comments, 'Scottish identity has always been constructed through processes of intercultural exchange arising from the interchange of diverse cultures, through both diaspora and immigration.'[14] Before and after the war, Scots moved to and returned from diverse corners of the Empire. During the war, too, Scots – both those with international backgrounds and those who had never been abroad – interacted with new landscapes and peoples on the Western and Eastern Fronts. A global event, participated in and written about by a geographically mobile cohort of Scots, the First World War produced a body of Scottish writing that was too nuanced, wide-ranging and conditional upon local, international and individual variables to be primarily one thing.

And the complexity of the situation is further enhanced when we concede the existence of views which may not match our own, but which nevertheless have a claim to the matter of Scotland and World War I. Accordingly, this collection of essays examines the nuanced, 'intensely personal' nature of the war experience recorded in Scottish writing. These parameters are sometimes overlooked when wholesale definitions are offered of national characteristics, or even of constituencies of identity which might exist therein.

Scotland at War

After declaring war on Germany in August 1914, it became apparent that Britain's standing army – of just under 250,000 troops – required expansion. On 8 August, Horatio Kitchener, the newly appointed Secretary of State for War, began a recruitment drive to establish a volunteer army, and in little over a month the first 100,000 men had offered their services. Among this cohort were the 10th Argyll and Sutherland Highlanders, whose progression from training in Hampshire to frontline combat Ian Hay relates in his hugely popular novel *The First Hundred Thousand*.[15] Following the repulse of the German advance towards Paris in the First Battle of the Marne (6–12 September), each side struggled to outflank the other in an attempt to win the war swiftly. By Christmas, trench warfare had set in, and what many had envisaged as a short war settled into one of attrition.

In April 1915, the Allies began a campaign in the Dardanelles to open a new front. Storming of the Cape Helles beaches – the main thrust of the offensive – proceeded under the command of Ayrshire-born Major-General Aylmer Hunter-Wilson, whose division contained the 1st King's Own Scottish Borderers and the 1/5th Royal Scots. However, poor communication meant that initial gains were not capitalised on, and the debacle was further exacerbated by the heat and unsanitary conditions. In 1915, Allied attempts to break the stalemate on the Western Front saw Scottish forces participate in the battles of Neuve Chapelle and – in particularly high numbers – Loos (25 September to 15 October). As Trevor Royle writes, 'Loos deserves to be called a Scottish battlefield.' Not since Culloden had so many Scots participated in a military engagement. Half of the seventy-two regiments involved 'bore Scottish titles' and approximately one-third of the 20,598 casualties were Scottish.[16] Among them was Charles Hamilton Sorley, whose seminal war poem 'When you see millions of the mouthless dead' was discovered in his kitbag after his death by sniper on 12 October.

By the end of 1915, Britain's standing army and the 2,466,719 men who volunteered for war service had been decimated by heavy losses. In late December, Edinburgh-born Douglas Haig was appointed successor to John French as Commander-in-Chief of the British Expeditionary Force, and conscription – though long resisted by the government – was introduced with the Military Service Act of 27 January 1916.

Conflict also threatened to break out on home soil. Added to the insult of high wartime rents, skilled workers in Clydeside were concerned that the presence of semi-skilled and unskilled workers would erode the status and higher wages they enjoyed as time-served craftsmen. In February 1916, John Maclean – a Marxist by background who fervently opposed conscription, and Willie Gallacher – head of the Clyde Workers' Committee – and others were arrested on charges of sedition. This resulted in widespread strikes throughout Clydeside in February and March.[17] Open rejection of war service was met with harsh treatment. Repeated arrests weakened Maclean's health and hastened his early death. Conscientious objectors, meanwhile, found themselves sent to punitive Scottish camps at Ballachulish and the notorious, short-lived Dyce encampment, which was closed after a few months following the death of a prisoner from pneumonia.[18]

The Gallipoli campaign finally ended in a mass evacuation in January 1916. This was followed by further disappointment in late April, when British troops – among them men from the 1st Highland Light

Infantry, the 2nd Black Watch and the 1st Seaforths – were forced to surrender to Turkish forces after holding out for 147 days in the siege of Kut-al-Amara. Better – though still disheartening – news came from the navy's performance in the Battle of Jutland (31 May to 1 June 1). Although they sustained more casualties, the numerical superiority of Britain's Grand and Battle Cruiser Fleets – based during the war at Scapa Flow and Rosyth – forced a German retreat, resulting in 'strategic victory' at the price of 'tactical defeat'.[19] Also that year, British forces on the Western Front prepared for the infamous Somme campaign, which sought to use a combination of sustained artillery bombardment and high-volume infantry assault to break the German lines. The 9th and 15th Scottish Divisions, as well as the 51st (Highland) Division, participated in the battle, which lasted from 1 July to 18 November. At the cost of 600,000 casualties, neither the expected breakthrough nor significant territorial gain was achieved.

In April, the 1917 Nivelle Offensive was launched, with British and Canadian forces supplying a diversionary attack at Arras and Vimy Ridge to draw German troops away from the main French assault to the south at Chemin des Dames. Despite early advances, this operation also failed to deliver the hoped-for rout, at the expense of 159,000 casualties – a third of whom were Scottish.[20] That year did, however, see Scottish forces contribute to victories on the Eastern Front. In March, the 1st Highland Light Infantry, the 2nd Black Watch and the 1st Seaforths assisted in the capture of Baghdad, while the 52nd (Lowland) Division participated in the campaign to secure Jerusalem, which came under Allied control in December.

In a final attempt to win the war before American troops arrived in considerable numbers, the Germans launched a new offensive, aimed at dividing the Allied forces. Beginning on 21 March 1918 and codenamed Operation Michael, the advance was initially hugely successful, resulting in 38,000 Allied casualties on its first day. Welsh-born Scot Eric Linklater was caught up in the retreat with the 4/5th Battalion of the Black Watch, which was reduced 'to between thirty and forty men and one wounded second lieutenant'.[21] The Allies withstood the onslaught, however, and – strengthened by continually arriving American troops – were able to counter-attack, forcing a German surrender on 11 November.

Estimates vary as to the exact number of Scots who were killed in the war. Soldiers often died of injuries years subsequent to wounding, and it was possible for those listed as missing to reappear. The number of fatalities is still contested, with debate centring on the claim that Scots' casualties were disproportionately higher than the national average. Niall Ferguson and T. M. Devine have claimed 26.4 per cent of enlisted Scots died.[22] However, this figure, as Hew Strachan notes, 'is actually the proportion of Scottish males [. . .] who volunteered before the end of 1915'.[23] While initial Scottish enlistment figures were higher than in England and Wales, the overall contribution levelled out, and Scottish enlistment rates as a whole were 'only 2.7 per cent higher than that of England and Wales'.[24] Countering Trevor Royle's claim that the figure is likely to be 'higher than the generally accepted 100,000', Strachan 'suggests a maximum of 90,000' and argues 'there is little reason to think that Scottish death rates in the war were massively out of line with those of Britain as a whole'. He clarifies, however, that this estimate 'is not to deny either their scale or their impact'.[25]

E. W. McFarland observes that, broadly characterised by 'economic dislocation, the hardship of trench warfare and spiritual uncertainty', the Scottish war was not 'an experience which was dramatically different in kind from elsewhere'. She notes, however, that the manner in which these pervasive attributes were 'handled in cultural terms' and in their 'impact on Scotland's economy and society were bound to be distinctive'.[26] This is evident, for instance, in the effect of the war on the home front. From 1914 to 1918, Clydeside shipyards produced 481 warships.[27] Meanwhile, sheep farming – the nation's chief agricultural contribution – provided material for uniforms, with the entire Scottish wool production of 1916 being bought by the government. The North British Rubber Company's factory at Fountainbridge in Edinburgh produced 1.2 million pairs of trench boots, while the Dundee jute industry was boosted by high demand for sandbags.

Much home front work was undertaken by women, for whom the war allowed a temporary opportunity to occupy roles that had traditionally been male (though seldom for the equivalent wages). Women worked in munitions factories at Glasgow, Clydebank and Gretna, though they also took positions in the Scottish Land Army and in the Scottish Women's Hospitals under the command of Elsie Inglis. During the war, female employment in Scotland rose from 2.18 to 2.97 million.[28]

On New Year's Eve 1918, a group of veterans from the Western Isles, returning from the war, arrived in Kyle of Lochalsh on the west coast. One of the vessels designated to carry the men home, HM Yacht *Iolaire*, met unexpected bad weather and ran aground within 20 yards of the Stornoway shore, resulting in the death of 201 passengers. The *Iolaire* disaster was commemorated by a memorial erected in 1958 at Holm in Stornoway and a stone pillar has also been fixed on the wreck site.

Memorials to Scots' World War I service – modest and grand – have become a pervasive feature of our rural and urban landscapes. Many commemorate only a few names, such as the simple brass plaque dedicated to the seven war dead which hangs in Reston United Free Church, Berwickshire, or the inconspicuous granite slab recognising the ten fatalities among the employees of the Aberdeen Granite Works which lies recessed in a wall on the city's Constitution Street.

Scots were also commemorated by the graves and monuments erected by the Commonwealth War Graves Commission in cemeteries containing war dead at home and abroad. Individual graves are marked with identically shaped stones recording the name, rank, regiment, age and death date of the soldier. This uniformity of construction stemmed from a desire to maintain parity of quality (since few relatives could afford to construct monuments) and, more controversially, to function as a 'symbol of a great Army and a united Empire'.[29]

Local civic monuments, however, were more idiosyncratic. The Glasgow Cenotaph – designed by Sir J. J. Burnet and unveiled in 1924 – incorporates a representation of the city's patron saint, St Mungo. Dundee's imposing war memorial on the Law is illuminated every night on 25 September to commemorate the local men who died at Loos. Aberdeen's Cenotaph, meanwhile, features a central lion planned by Aberdonian sculptor – and designer of the British War Medal – William MacMillan. Overlooking the town and Dunnottar Castle from Black Hill, Stonehaven's war memorial – designed by local architect John Ellis – takes the form of a deliberately ruinous octagonal temple in an architectural symbol of the lives left wrecked and uncompleted by the war.

It was also decided that a national monument was necessary and Edinburgh Castle – as an ancient military stronghold crowning a central hill within the capital city – was deemed the apt location. The plans of architect Sir Robert Lorimer met with protests that his design valorised militarism and would injure the city's historic skyline. Under Lorimer's revised vision, a Gallery of Honour was incorporated within the walls of an existing barrack at the castle. Inside, eight stained-glass windows illuminate a series of bays displaying regimental colours and rolls of honour. The monument was a collective project, uniting the work of 200 artists. And every effort was made for it to be a truly representative endeavour. Virtually every military rank, branch of service and theatre of war experienced by Scots during the war is referenced, as are the 'Humble Beasts that served and died'.

Scottish Literature and World War I

As part of the centenary, commemorative memorial plaques have been unveiled by Historic Environment Scotland to recognise the contributions of Scotland's World War I writers and artists. Plaques have been dedicated to Margaret Sackville (in Edinburgh's Regent Terrace), to Charles Hamilton Sorley (at Powis Community Centre in Aberdeen), to Joseph Lee (in Dundee's Airlie Street) and to Mary Symon (at Dufftown Town Clock). Applications are under way for J. B. Salmond, W. D. Cocker and R. W. Kerr to receive similar honours. Scotland's war poets have also been accorded a central memorial in the form of a Celtic cross in Makars' Court next to the Scottish Writers' Museum in Edinburgh.[30]

These acts of centennial commemoration reflect the wider status of Scottish World War I literature: a corpus which has belatedly received recognition but whose place in the nation's culture is still being negotiated. The war occasioned a variety of Scottish literary responses – in journalism, poetry, memoirs and novels – from writers using English, Gaelic, Scots and regional dialects. The conflict features in hugely popular contemporary works such as Ian Hay's *The First Hundred Thousand* (1915) and John Buchan's *The Thirty-Nine Steps* (1915) and *Mr Standfast* (1919). It also plays an important role in seminal Scottish Literary Renaissance works such as Lewis Grassic Gibbon's *Sunset Song* (1932) and Nan Shepherd's *The Weatherhouse* (1930). Yet Scottish war writing has been largely excluded from accounts of British World War I literature; nor has Scottish combatant writing traditionally been a central topic in discussions of the country's literature.

The war has, however, been widely acknowledged as a motivating force behind the Scottish Literary Renaissance, particularly in relation to the career of Hugh MacDiarmid. Cairns Craig has made the influential statement that it was following the First World War that Scottish literature emerged 'out of history'. 'In its "historylessness"', Craig writes, nineteenth-century literature suggests that 'the industrial Scotland of before 1914 has taken on the characteristics usually associated in Scottish writing with the Celtic world of the Highlands before the 1745 Rising'.[31] 'The First World War is the focus of so many Scottish narratives', he adds, 'because it is the moment when the historical is reintroduced into the historyless Scottish environment.'[32]

Trevor Royle contends that the war accelerated the move away from the impasse of Kailyard fiction which was already afoot at the start of the twentieth century in George Douglas Brown's *The House with the Green Shutters* (1905), John MacDougall Hay's *Gillespie* (1914) and the vernacular poetry of Charles Murray and Violet Jacob. Discussing the writing of Ewart Alan Mackintosh, Violet Jacob, Mary Symon, W. D. Cocker, Roderick Watson Kerr, Joseph Lee, J. B. Salmond and Gaelic poets Donald MacDonald, John Munro and Murdo Murray, Royle argues these 'war poets are harbingers of [the] change', spearheaded by Hugh MacDiarmid, towards 'a renaissance movement' within Scottish literature.[33] MacDiarmid served with the Royal Army Medical Corps (RAMC) in Greece, Italy and France during the war. Although he wrote little war-related verse, Royle also argues that MacDiarmid's experiences of war heightened his nationalism and spurred his quest 'to lead a cultural revolution'.[34] Patrick Crotty, Karen A. Stewart and Gordon Urquhart, meanwhile, have all pointed to the vivifying effects of the conflict on post-war Scottish literature.[35]

Scottish writing by combatants and first-hand witnesses has not enjoyed the same prestige. Robert Crawford, while praising the poetry of Sorley and Mackintosh, notes that 'battlefield experience produced relatively little outstanding Scottish literature'.[36] David Goldie, meanwhile, maintains that because of Scottish adherence to unionist politics and British literary traditions 'it remains more meaningful to talk about a British rather than a Scottish literature of the First World War'.[37] Similarly, Macdonald Daly has claimed that Scotland produced little 'truly oppositional poetry' because 'Scottish war verse was so dependent on a combination of English literary models and English literary temperament'.[38]

Scottish literature from the conflict has, however, enjoyed greater prominence in recent decades, especially since the centenary. Much of this has been in the form of anthologised Scottish war fiction, including: Trevor Royle's *In Flanders Fields: Scottish Poetry and Prose of the First World War* (1990) and *Isn't All This Bloody?: Scottish Writing from the First World War* (2014); *Scottish Voices from the Great War* (2006), edited by Derek Young; *From the Frontline: Scottish War Poetry 1914–1945* (2014), edited by David Goldie and Roderick Watson; and *Beneath Troubled Skies: Poems of Scotland at War* (2015), edited by Lizzie MacGregor.

Moreover, despite his reservations about the distinctively Scottish properties of the nation's literary response, Goldie's extensive research on Scottish World War I literature has done much to highlight this area of writing. Goldie has illustrated the influence of developing mass media in shaping depictions of the war, noting the role of the popular press in mediating 'factual stories' of the conflict through 'the tropes of' generic romance plots and the sensationalism of New Journalism.[39] In a related approach, he suggests that the increasing popularity of the *Daily Record* and *Mail* and the shift from Scots vernacular to more Anglicised content in *The People's Journal* need not be viewed as the incursion 'of a coercive dominant culture'. Instead, he argues, these developments reflect the way Scottish material culture – including its treatment of the Great War – was implicated in 'a range of mass-market cultural activities'.[40]

Despite the war's undoubted cultural and historical significance, Scotland's World War I literature has largely been omitted from discussions of British World War I writing. Generated in part by the fiftieth anniversary, the formation of the traditional World War I canon – comprised almost exclusively of junior officers such as Wilfred Owen, Siegfried Sassoon and Robert Graves – was avowedly Anglocentric. Key critical texts from the 1960s and 1970s, such as Bernard Bergonzi's *Heroes' Twilight* (1965), Jon Silkin's *Out of Battle* (1972) and Paul Fussell's *The Great War and Modern Memory* (1975), make virtually no mention of Scottish writing. This 'Anglocentric attitude', as Simon Featherstone contends, 'disguises [. . .] the influence of various non-English cultures within Britain'.[41]

Reflecting on the critical reception of World War I writing, James Campbell has identified three main stages of critical activity. Initial scholarship, dating from the mid-1960s to the mid-1970s, he argues, highlighted 'the establishment and defense of a canon' of male poets who 'protest against military and governmental incompetence culminating in endless slaughter'.[42] This first wave was then followed by a 'post-1975 emphasis on gender and sexuality', which focused on 'widening the definition of war literature and on rereading the canonical figures'.[43] Campbell positions Fussell – with his treatment of sexuality – as a bridge to works in this latter category such as Dominic Hibberd's *Owen the Poet* (1986) and Claire Tylee's *The Great War and Women's Consciousness* (1990).

Campbell identifies a third area of criticism which aims to 'put Great War literature in direct relation to more mainstream forms of literary modernism'.[44] Within this phase, Samuel Hynes's *A War Imagined* (1990) points to the way that post-war literature led to the constructed 'Myth' of pervasive post-war disillusionment which, while not necessarily inaccurate, overshadowed a more complex sociocultural reality. Jay Winter's *Sites of Memory, Sites of Mourning* (1995), through his examination of remembrance activities in combatant nations, argues for the existence of continuity – as well as severance – between pre- and post-war cultural practices. Vincent Sherry, meanwhile, in *The Great War and the Language of Modernism* (2003), has argued that the modernism of Pound, Eliot and Yeats is a reaction to the collapse of English Liberal rationalism brought on by the war.

Santanu Das has also pointed to a corrective 'second wave' of scholarship, in the form of studies devoted to 'the recovery of marginalised voices, particularly women, civilians, and of the colonial conscripts'.[45] Texts in this vein include Hew Strachan's *The First World War in Africa* (2004), Richard Smith's *Jamaican Volunteers in the First World War: Race, Masculinity, and the Development of National Consciousness* (2005) and Das's *India, Empire and the First World War* (2018). Reflecting this trend, American World War I literary studies, meanwhile, has also moved away from the idea of a war-disaffected 'lost generation', through an increasing acknowledgement of ethnic, political, ideological and mass media writing.[46]

Although Scottish literature has not traditionally been part of the British canon of World War I writing, much of the scholarly discussion of Scottish works from the conflict is in keeping with the attributes identified by Campbell and Das of increasingly diversified and inclusive 'second wave' scholarship. Through their representation of Scots, Gaelic, home front and female poems, the anthologies edited by Royle, Goldie and Watson, and MacGregor participate in the wider recovery of marginalised voices. Colin Milton has argued for the strength of Doric war poetry, Peter Mackay has published on Gaelic writing from the conflict, and Goldie and David Finkelstein have discussed the influence of mass media on literary depictions.[47]

Historical investigations of Scotland and World War I have also, broadly, worked to highlight the multifaceted nature of the nation's relationship with the war. MacDonald and McFarland's essay collection *Scotland and the Great War* (1999) brings attention to the myriad facets of Scottish culture touched by the war, including regional variations in economic prosperity, increased support for the Independent Labour Party in Scotland during the war, the relationship between recruitment and promises of land to cottars and crofters, and the characteristics of anti-German riots in Scottish localities. Royle's *Flowers of the Forest: Scotland and the First World War* (2007) likewise examines a range of topics, from combatant to home front wartime roles, the domestic economy, Red Clydeside, land reform and conscientious objectors.

Collection Overview

Scottish Literature and World War I proceeds along the broad principles of the 'second wave' to examine the still relatively under-excavated body of Scottish Great War writing. The collection is divided into two sections – the first containing wide-ranging essays which survey literature by topic or genre, and the second taking the form of essays focusing on particular authors. In his chapter, Alan Riach points to the international nature of Scottish literature in the pre-war era. Addressing the war's role in shaping Scottish national identity, Riach notes that '[t]he devastations [. . .] witnessed' by Hugh MacDiarmid 'would underlie the vigour and ruthlessness with which he would pursue his vision for a Scotland regenerated'. Riach, however, recognising patriotic unionist perspectives such as those of Ian Hay and John Buchan, concludes 'that the poly-vocal, multi-media and temporally mutable nature of the Scottish literary response to imperialism and world war cannot be reduced or defined to a single party, moment, poem, book or author'.

Chapter 2 considers the under-scrutinised area of Scottish Great War prose, which has not – in the main – been seen to include a body of 'classic' canonical texts comparable with German, American or English novels such as *All Quiet on the Western Front* (1929), *A Farewell to Arms* (1929) or *The Middle Parts of Fortune* (1929). By looking at key works such as John Reith's *Wearing Spurs* (1966), George Blake's *The Path of Glory* (1929) and Edward Gaitens's *Dance of the Apprentices* (1948), the claim is made that Scotland *did* generate notable prose works comparable to those emerging in other counties, and, furthermore, that at least some of these are not as avowedly unionist in orientation as has been implied. In his chapter, meanwhile, David Goldie challenges the received truth that popular writing deliberately obscured unpalatable wartime realities. Patrick MacGill and Boyd Cable were freely able to publish 'direct and unambiguous' works during the war – perhaps, as Goldie suggests, for the surprising possibility that officialdom felt literary realism might increase public acceptance of the war's seriousness. Sarah Pedersen recovers an overlooked area of Scottish literary response to the war in her chapter on women's letters to the editor published in newspapers. In these letters, ideals of sacrifice and patriotism were 'shaped and reused' to argue for greater financial support for soldiers' families, as well as to criticise conscientious objectors or perceived shirkers. No less than male combatants, Pedersen argues, home front women also saw themselves as making 'sacrifices in a righteous cause'.

In his twin chapters – 'Gaelic Verse' and 'Gaelic Prose' – Ronald Black surveys an impressive range of texts. Black explores Gaelic verse and song but also prose, which has received little recognition. Discussing, among other examples, Murdo Murray's wartime diary, journalism in the periodicals *An Deò-Gréine* and *Guth na Bliadhna*, and fiction by Norman Campbell, Iain MacLean and Roderick Maclean, Black demonstrates the – previously unappreciated – extent and importance of Gaelic writing from the war. The collection then turns to the topic of philosophy in Cairns Craig's chapter. Now overshadowed by the Scottish Enlightenment, it was the idealism of Edward Caird, Craig notes, which was the 'dominant philosophy of the Anglophone world on the eve of the First World War'. The conflict, however, threatened to undermine Caird's 'evolutionary conception of philosophy as an ever closer approach to the understanding of God's presence'. Scottish idealism survived the war – in the work of philosophers such as W. R. Sorley (the father of Charles Hamilton Sorley) – albeit 'maintaining itself in a world which [. . .] had rejected the basis of idealist metaphysics'.

Part II opens with Alison Lumsden's essay on Nan Shepherd, who was a student at Aberdeen University during the Great War. Lumsden discusses the war's oblique traces in *The Quarry Wood* (1928) and Shepherd's more deliberate engagement with the conflict – and post-war social reconstruction – in *The Weatherhouse* (1930). Lumsden discusses the influence of John Macmurray – a philosopher and friend of Shepherd's who posited a rejection of Cartesian separation between intellect and body – on her portrayal of Garry Forbes in *The Weatherhouse*. Looking at numinous relationships with Scottish landscape in Lewis Grassic Gibbon's *Sunset Song* (1932) and Neil M. Gunn's *Highland River* (1937), Scott Lyall also addresses literary engagement with strategies for post-war reconstruction. He suggests that, for Gibbon and Gunn, 'Post war redemption is presented as possible through a return to a pre-Christion autochthonous spirituality connected to the land, not as *patrie*, but as a site of radical political and personal awakening.' In his essay, Randall Stevenson draws attention to the peripheral poetic voice of George A. C. Mackinlay. Like other poets, Mackinlay's channelling of the Georgian pastoral mode was to some extent challenged by the war – resulting in a 'slight harshening of rhetoric in his wartime writing'. More broadly, Stevenson considers the limited propensity of Scottish topography – often more forbidding than 'England's tranquil southern shires' – to offer a pastoral mode which is at once distinctively Scottish but also redolent of the consolatory values embraced (sometimes ironically) by English poets.

Also considering pastoralism, Fiona Houston looks at John Buchan's engagement with the mode in relation to his dual Scottish/British identity. Houston highlights Buchan's use of pastoral tropes such as 'shepherds and birds, neighbourly invitation, the sanctuary of the humble cottage – alongside traditional Scottish literary technique – such as oral folk tales and song – to create an identity that is simultaneously proudly Scottish and proudly British'. Robert Crawford discusses Charles Murray, an Aberdeenshire-born poet who published most of his verse while living in South Africa. Writing in Doric – with a density and nostalgia intensified by his exilic longing for home – Murray produced *A Sough o' War* (1917), which Crawford claims as 'one of the best books of war poetry produced by a Scottish poet during the war'. Although Murray is, certainly from a modern perspective, unpalatably 'committed to imperial militarism', he nevertheless produced enduring works with an 'almost maniacal' sense of connection to the Aberdeenshire countryside.

In his chapter, John Lucas discusses *Sunset Song* and the novel's engagement with temporality and change. Gibbon's novel seems 'unable to resolve the tension' between 'regret for a lost way of life' and 'forward-looking hopes'. Ultimately, Lucas suggests, the character of Chris Guthrie – married to a farmer, Ewan, who brutally rapes her on his return from the front, then scandalously married to the socialist minister Colquhoun – 'embodies a process which absorbs catastrophe into change'. In the final chapter, Neil McLennan looks at the poetry of Ewart Alan Mackintosh, a second lieutenant who won the Military Cross for valorous conduct at Arras and who was later killed at Cambrai in November 1917. Mackintosh, McLennan argues, was a devoted and conscientious leader of men, motivated more by an attachment to Scottish landscape, tradition and loyalty to his comrades than by a hatred of the enemy. McLennan charts the course of Mackintosh's post-war legacy, moving from near-complete obscurity – through a 2004 biography, a monument at the Saint Hubert Chapel in France, anthologisation, and involvement in national centenary commemorations – towards an increasingly central role in the British Great War literary canon. The influence of such acts, McLennan's essay foregrounds, demonstrates the provisionality of the Great War literary landscape which is constantly excavated, extended and redefined by literary and cultural scholarship.

Notes

1. Trevor Royle, 'Literature and World War I', in Ian Brown and Alan Riach (eds), *The Edinburgh Companion to Twentieth-Century Scottish Literature* (Edinburgh: Edinburgh University Press, 2009), pp. 37–49, p. 49. Colin Milton, '"A Sough o' War"': The Great War in the Poetry of North-east Scotland', in David Hewitt (ed.), *Northern Visions: The Literary Identity of Northern Scotland in the Twentieth-Century* (Phantassie: Tuckwell Press, 1995), pp. 1–38.
2. Goldie suggests that the Doric revival 'ran the risk of seeming as much like imperial nostalgia or genteel anthropology as the vivid expression of a live, embattled culture'. See Goldie, 'Scotland for Ever? British Literature, Scotland and the First World War', in Edna Longley, Eamonn Hughes and Des O'Rawe (eds), *Ireland (Ulster) Scotland: Concepts, Contexts, Comparisons* (Belfast: Queen's University Belfast, 2003), pp. 113–20, p. 116.
3. Macdonald Daly, 'Scottish Poetry and the Great War', *Scottish Literary Journal*, vol. 21, no. 2 (1994), pp. 79–96, p. 85.
4. David Goldie, 'Archipelagic Poetry of the First World War', in Santanu Das (ed.), *The Cambridge Companion to the Poetry of the First World War* (Cambridge: Cambridge University Press, 2013), pp. 159–72, p. 170.
5. George Urquhart, 'Confrontation and Withdrawal: Loos, Readership and *The First Hundred Thousand*', in Catriona M. M. Macdonald and E. W. McFarland (eds), *Scotland and the Great War* (Edinburgh: Birlinn, 1999), pp. 125–44, pp. 132, 141.
6. Royle, 'Literature and World War I', p. 41.
7. David Goldie, 'Scotland, Britishness, and the First World War', in Gerald Carruthers, David Goldie and Alastair Renfrew (eds), *Beyond Scotland: New Contexts for Twentieth-Century Scottish Literature* (Amsterdam: Rodopi, 2004), pp. 37–57, p. 51.
8. Roderick Watson, *The Literature of Scotland: The Twentieth Century* (New York: Palgrave-Macmillan, 2007), p. xii.
9. Ibid. p. xii.
10. G. Gregory Smith, *Scottish Literature: Character and Influence* (London: Macmillan, 1919), p. 4.
11. Ian Brown and Alan Riach, 'Introduction', in Ian Brown and Alan Riach (eds), *The Edinburgh Companion to Twentieth-Century Literature* (Edinburgh: Edinburgh University Press, 2009), pp. 1–14, p. 10.
12. Watson, *The Literature of Scotland*, p. xv.
13. Catriona M. M. Macdonald, *Whaur Extremes Meet: Scotland's Twentieth Century* (Edinburgh: Birlinn, 2009), p. 5.
14. Alastair Niven, 'New Diversity, Hybridity and Scottishness', in Ian Brown, Thomas Owen Clancy, Susan Manning and Murray Pittock (eds), *The Edinburgh History of Scottish Literature, Volume 3: Modern Transformations: New Identities (from 1918)* (Edinburgh: Edinburgh University Press, 2007), pp. 320–31, p. 320.

15. Initially serialised in *Blackwood's Magazine*, *The First Hundred Thousand* sold 500,000 copies in 1915. See Patrick Scott Belk, *Empires of Print: Adventure Fiction in the Magazines, 1899–1919* (Oxford: Routledge, 2017), p. 173. Hay's novel was also popular in America, where it topped the *Publishers Weekly* 1917 annual ranking of 'War Books' sales. See Michael Korda, *Making the List: A Cultural History of the American Bestseller, 1900–1999* (New York: Barnes and Noble, 2001), p. 29.
16. Trevor Royle, *Flowers of the Forest: Scotland and the First World War* (Edinburgh: Birlinn, 2007), pp. 85, 92.
17. Ibid. p. 238.
18. Simon Webb, *British Concentration Camps: A Brief History from 1900–1975* (Barnsley: Pen and Sword Books, 2016), pp. 60–1.
19. John Brooks, *The Battle of Jutland* (Cambridge: Cambridge University Press, 2016), p. xviii.
20. Royle, *Flowers of the Forest*, p. 119.
21. Eric Linklater, *Fanfare for a Tin Hat* (London: Macmillan, 1970), p. 65.
22. Thomas M. Devine, *The Scottish Nation 1700–2000* (London: Penguin, 1999), p. 309. Niall Fergusson, *The Pity of War* (London: Penguin, 1998), pp. 298–9.
23. Hew Strachan, 'The Scottish Soldier and Scotland, 1914–1918', in David Forsyth and Wendy Ugolini (eds), *A Global Force: War, Identities and Scotland's Diaspora* (Edinburgh: Edinburgh University Press, 2016). Available at <https://edinburgh.universitypressscholarship.com> (last accessed 15 March 2019), pp. 1–19, p. 15.
24. Ibid. p. 14.
25. Royle, *Flowers of the Forest*, p. 284. Strachan, 'The Scottish Soldier and Scotland, 1914–1918', p. 15.
26. E. W. McFarland, 'A Coronach in Stone', in Catriona M. M. Macdonald and E. W. McFarland (eds), *Scotland and the Great War* (Edinburgh: Birlinn, 1999), pp. 1–11, p. 4.
27. Royle, *Flowers of the Forest*, p. 184.
28. Ibid. p. 208.
29. Sir Frederic Kenyon, *War Graves: How the Cemeteries Abroad Will Be Designed* (London: His Majesty's Stationery Office, 1919), p. 6.
30. Neil McLennan, 'Standing on the Shoulders of Giants: Plaques Commemorating and Creating for Writers Warning About War', Royal Society of Arts, 15 March 2019. Available at <https://www.thersa.org/discover/publications-and-articles/rsa-blogs/2019/03/standing-on-the-shoulders-of-giants--plaques-commemorating-and-creating-for-writers-warning-about-war> (last accessed 12 May 2020).
31. Cairns Craig, *Out Of History: Narrative Paradigms in Scottish and British Culture* (Edinburgh: Polygon, 1996), p. 36.
32. Ibid. p. 48.

33. Royle, 'Literature and World War I', pp. 48–9.
34. Royle, *Flowers of the Forest*, p. 296.
35. Patrick Crotty, 'Swordsmen: W. B. Yeats and Hugh MacDiarmid', in Peter Mackay, Edna Longley and Fran Brearton (eds), *Modern Irish and Scottish Poetry* (Cambridge: Cambridge University Press, 2011), pp. 20–38, p. 21. Karen A. Stewart, *Scottish Woman Writers to 1987: A Select Guide and Bibliography* (Glasgow: Glasgow District Libraries, 1987), p. 31. Urquhart, 'Confrontation and Withdrawal: Loos, Readership and *The First Hundred Thousand*', p. 141.
36. Robert Crawford, *Scotland's Books: The Penguin History of Scottish Literature* (London: Penguin, 2007), p. 353.
37. Goldie, 'Scotland, Britishness, and the First World War', p. 39.
38. Daly, 'Scottish Poetry and the Great War', pp. 79–96, pp. 80, 81.
39. David Goldie, 'Romance by Other Means: Scottish Popular Newspapers and the First World War', in Chris Hart (ed.), *World War I: Media, Entertainments & Popular Culture* (London: Midrash, 2018), pp. 231–58, p. 244.
40. David Goldie, 'The British Invention of Scottish Culture: The First World War and Before', *Review of Scottish Culture*, vol. 18 (2006), pp. 128–48, pp. 143, 144.
41. Simon Featherstone, *War Poetry: An Introductory Reader* (London: Routledge, 1995), p. 87.
42. James Campbell, 'Interpreting the War', in Vincent Sherry (ed.), *The Cambridge Companion to the Literature of the First World War* (Cambridge: Cambridge University Press, 2005), pp. 261–79, pp. 264, 266.
43. Ibid. p. 262.
44. Ibid. p. 262.
45. Santanu Das, 'Ardour and Anxiety: Politics and Literature in the Indian Homefront', in Heike Liebau, Katrin Bromber, Katharina Lange, Dyala Hamzah and Ravi Ahuja (eds), *The World in World Wars: Experiences, Perceptions and Perspectives from Africa and Asia* (Leiden: Brill, 2010), pp. 341–68, p. 343.
46. Following the scholarly revival of female literary responses to World War I, such approaches have highlighted literary representations of: home-front experiences in Mark Van Wienen's *Partisans and Poets: The Political Work of Poetry in the Great War* (1997), Jennifer Haytock's *At Home, At War: Domesticity and World War I in American Literature* (2003) and Karsten Piep's *Embattled Home Fronts: Politics and Representation in American World War I Novels* (2009); racial perspectives in Mark Whalan's *The Great War and the Culture of the New Negro* (2008); the impact of the popular media and periodical fiction in Kimberly Licursi's *Remembering World War I in America* (2018); and a focus on the social consequences of mobilisation in Keith Gandal's *War Isn't the Only Hell: A New Reading of American World War I Literature* (2018).

47. Milton, '"A Sough o' War": The Great War in the Poetry of North-east Scotland'. Peter Mackay, 'Freedom from Judgement Above? Predestination and Cultural Trauma in Scottish Gaelic Poetry of World War I', in Gill Plain (ed.), *Myth, Memory and the First World War in Scotland: The Legacy of Bannockburn* (Lewisburg, PA: Bucknell University Press, 2016), pp. 187–204. David Finkelstein, 'Literature, Propaganda, and the First World War: The Case of *Blackwood's Magazine*', in Jeremy Treglown and Bridget Bennett (eds), *Grub Street and the Ivory Tower: Essays on the Relations Between Literary Journalism and Literary Scholarship* (Oxford: Clarendon, 1998), pp. 91–111.

Part I

Multi-text Case Studies

Chapter 1

Scottish Literature, Nationalism and the First World War
Alan Riach

Introduction

The decade of the birth of C. M. Grieve and the death of R. L. Stevenson, Patrick Geddes's *The Evergreen* and the Mackintoshes' exhibition of their work in the Eighth Secession exhibition in Vienna was the prelude to the twentieth century. The decade which followed takes us from Conrad's *Heart of Darkness* to Charles Ives's *Unanswered Question* and Schoenberg's *Pierrot Lunaire*, Fergusson's *Les Eus* and Cursiter's *Impression of Crossing Princes Street, Edinburgh*. The era from around 1890 to 1914, seen from the distance of more than a century, not only in Scotland but internationally, was a vortex of energies and forms, all wheeling into the First World War.

This sense of something moving towards an unprecedented future is memorably conveyed by Stefan Zweig (1881–1942), writing of his boyhood in late nineteenth-century Vienna in *The World of Yesterday*:

> The truly great experience of our youthful years was the realisation that something new in art was on the way – something more impassioned, difficult and alluring than the art that had satisfied our parents and the world around us. But fascinated as we were by this one aspect of life, we did not notice that these aesthetic changes were only the forerunners of the much more far-reaching changes that were to shake and finally destroy the world of our fathers, the world of security.[1]

There is no single story in which Scottish literature, the growth of Scottish nationalism and the experience of the First World War can be defined. Such stories are often proscribed by their own definition of what their heroes oppose. For Walter Benjamin and Bertolt

Brecht, the principal oppression was capitalism; for Karl Kraus and Joseph Roth, it was, rather, militarism. The bourgeois world was to be condemned for social injustice rather than economic exploitation. For Scottish writers, an imperialism that gathered national identity into British empowerment leading to war was increasingly understood as the enemy; thus the elision of 'British' and 'English' became an infuriation. My point is that all these identifications of necessary resistance were articulating themselves separately, in different ways, creating different forms, in individual writers, political groups, parties and governments, and at different speeds.

It might be argued that these resistances reached a confluence in 1928 with the founding of the National Party of Scotland (NPS) and in 1934 with that of the Scottish National Party, but these too were forming themselves alongside the mobilisation of the Labour movement in the development of the Labour Party. The essential point is that the polyvocal, multimedia and temporally mutable nature of the Scottish literary response to imperialism and world war cannot be reduced or defined to a single party, moment, poem, book or author. The complexities of both incitement and purpose, the impositions and the resistances, have to be appraised with a more careful discrimination in this cradle of social revolution and mortal danger.

And how these resistances were articulated by writers is always affected by the context of the public operation of language. This is why Karl Kraus is a key figure. In Marjorie Perloff's words,

> His argument about the making of World War I is that the public media, in their inevitable reliance on headlines, captions, and sound bytes [*sic*], create an atmosphere in which citizens no longer understand how barbaric and pointless a given policy may turn out to be.

So 'what happens when the media take on a life of their own as they have today, when the "imagination" is itself the product of mediation?'[2]

Kraus's great play, *The Last Days of Mankind*, was not completed until 1922, but the understanding that made it possible had been developing since before the war, and, as Perloff says, it 'is extraordinarily prescient about this situation'. While the most familiar war poets – Wilfred Owen, Siegfried Sassoon and Rupert Brooke, for example – wrote vividly of immediate personal witness, Kraus's play 'uses every device in its poetic arsenal to dramatize the complicity, cravenness, and often inadvertent cruelty, not only of those who make war but also of those who carry it out or remain behind'.[3] The crucial, agonising conjunction and confrontation is not between conflicting ideologies or empires, national ideals or histories, social hierarchies or theologies, but rather between the prevailing language of a culture and the private individual.

The language of any culture helps define how things are seen and understood: it opens the eyes but directs the vision. When its pervasive purpose is to narrow the eyes and foreclose vision, the frontline is occupied by the writers most aware of its practice, and resistant to it, because that language – of media more than anything – is the arbiter of the prevalent attitude towards experience. And there is always more than one attitude seeking expression, and more than one motivation at play.

Internationalism, Industrialisation, the First World War and Modernity

In the period leading up to the First World War, what would become identifiable as modernism can be understood as developing plural possibilities, latent modernisms of various kinds. From at least the 1890s to 1914, in an international cradle, the growth of Scottish national self-awareness developed at different rates of growth. Key figures in this era are Stevenson, Violet Jacob, Marion Bernstein, James Young Geddes, John Davidson, Robert Bontine Cunninghame Graham and Ruaraidh Erskine of Mar.

For Stevenson, the art of the writer – essayist and man of letters, travel writer, writer of children's fiction and genre fiction, a writer for the periodicals – was balanced against the experience of society in different social classes, different geographical, cultural and religious locations. His balance of detachment and sympathy is prophetic of early twentieth-century modernism. In Stefan Zweig's terms, Stevenson speaks more of far-reaching changes than of the security of the world of our fathers.

Both Stevenson in Samoa and Violet Jacob in imperial British India, then South Africa and Egypt and Scotland again, represent locations at different points of the British Empire, geographically and historically, and the roles of women and men moving through different strata within it. Both are opening questions of cultural relativism.

Other poets, and particularly women writing between 1850 and 1900, reflect on and protest about the social conditions of industrialised Scotland. Janet Hamilton (1795–1873), Jessie Russell (1850–?) and Marion Bernstein (1846–1906) directly addressed questions of women's rights and social justice in working-class Glasgow. Male poets writing of alienation in industrialised modernity included James Young Geddes (1850–1913) in Dundee, with 'Glendale & Co. (After Walt Whitman)' and the Nietzschean John Davidson (1857–1909).

So: international provenances and industrial cities developed through the British Empire were the habitations of these writers, each of them prophetic of conflicts to come, colonial, feminist or class-based. Nationality, in complex varieties, is part of their character. None would have declared outright for Scotland's political independence.

But R. B. Cunninghame Graham (1852–1936), like Stevenson and Jacob an international traveller, was also a practising politician, prioritising Socialism, feminist enfranchisement, Scottish nationalism and cultural authority. Along with Keir Hardie, he was a founder member of the Scottish Labour Party (1888), which joined the Independent Labour Party (1895) and later the Labour Party (1906), and also helped to establish the National Party of Scotland (1928), evolving into the Scottish National Party (1934). MacDiarmid met him in the early 1920s, later saying: 'My decision to make the Scottish Cause, cultural and political, my life-work dates from that moment.'[4]

Another key figure in this scene, Ruaraidh Erskine of Mar (1869–1960), advocated a Gaelic confederation of nations within the British Empire, gaining the endorsement of Padraig Pearse in 1906. His support for the Easter Rising in Ireland in 1916 enhanced the association between Irish separatists and Scottish politicians, intellectuals and artists. In contrast to all these writers, George Orwell's contemporaries at an English boarding school in the year running up to and into the first years of the war, offer a very different picture of what 'Scotland' was understood to be.

Orwell attended the fee-paying St Cyprian's boarding school, in Eastbourne, East Sussex, from 1911 to 1916, and in his essay 'Such, Such Were the Joys' (1947), he described the decade before 1914 like this:

> The extraordinary thing was the way in which everyone took it for granted that this oozing, bulging wealth of the English upper and upper-middle classes would last for ever, and was part of the order of things. After 1918 it was never the same again.[5]

Of course, this is only a specific part of England. The point, however, is that there is a direct connection between the ethos thus presented and self-righteousness of the projected image of Englishness perpetrated by increasingly widespread media, including, as the century progressed, screen media. The fictional nature – false consciousness – of this atmosphere is familiar less from the historical account than from the myth elaborated over decades in books, radio, films and television. Orwell summarised the idea of Scotland then taken for granted at such an institution:

> Our picture of Scotland was made up of burns, braes, kilts, sporrans, claymores, bagpipes and the like, all somehow mixed up with the invigorating effects of porridge, Protestantism and a cold climate. But underlying this was something quite different. The real reason for the cult of Scotland was that only very rich people could spend their summers there. And the pretended belief in Scottish superiority was a cover for the bad conscience of the occupying English, who had pushed the Highland peasantry off their farms to make way for the deer forests, and then compensated them by turning them into servants.[6]

Orwell cuts sharply through the delusion to the portentous weight of economic and political power, and forecasts, even if only implicitly, its deployment in the second half of the twentieth century. As clearly as in *Animal Farm* or *Nineteen Eighty-Four*, Orwell allegorises reality and prophesies horrific continuities in the structures of political power.

The defining character of the legacy of the British Empire by which, in Orwell's account, Scotland is a colonial caricature, contrasts starkly with the international and economically realistic awareness in which Scottish writers were increasingly developing self-conscious understanding of national potential.

Patrick Geddes, the Poetry of the First World War and the Scottish Renaissance

When Patrick Geddes published his essay 'The Scots Renascence' in the first issue (spring 1895) of his periodical, *The Evergreen*, he began with the sentence: 'Blackie was buried yesterday.' The first part of the essay is an account of the procession and service at St Giles's High Kirk in Edinburgh's High Street, and reads like a short story, the various mourners 'headed by kilt and plaid', kinsmen, advocates, students and 'the Town itself', and 'working people in their thousands and tens of thousands'. Part II begins:

> From this pageant of Edinburgh it is but one step in thought to that solitary Samoan hill, up which dusky chiefs and clansmen, henceforth also brethren of ours, as he of theirs, were so lately bearing our other greatest dead – the foremost son of Edinburgh and Scotland.

Starting with funeral of J. S. Blackie, professor of Greek at Edinburgh University and prominent advocate of Gaelic literature, and that of Stevenson on the other side of the world, gives Geddes a global provenance for a multifaceted Scottish identity.[7] Geddes embraces Gaelic, Scots and English, universal humanity, priorities of education, language, affection, respect and nationality, defined by the passing of an age of heroes, 'Ossian after the Fianna'. Then his essay turns forward: 'What then – save "Finis Scotiae!" – can remain for us to say?' His answer follows: 'these are the phenomena of Winter, not of Spring – of death, not of life'. Winter slush will not stop the swelling buds and peeping shoots: 'in the long run it even helps'. For, in Geddes's vision, 'year by year, the possibilities temporal and spiritual of the renascent capital return or appear'.

Taking his cue from Allan Ramsay's anthology of older poets from the fourteenth and fifteenth centuries, *The Ever Green* (1724), noting how it urged later regenerations of Scottish literature, Geddes proposes that 'our new "Evergreen" may here and there stimulate some new and younger writer, and hence beside the general interests common to all men of culture' and 'youngest Scottish art, its revival of ancient Celtic design'.

Part III concludes:

> Such is our Scottish, our Celtic Renascence – sadly set betwixt the Keening, the watching over our fathers dead, and the second-sight of shroud rising about each other. Yet this is the Resurrection and the Life, when to faithful love and memory their dead arise.[8]

When the First World War began, the regeneration envisaged went underground. The counterpoint to early enthusiasm for warfare was protest and satirical denunciation. Charles Murray's 'A Sough o' War' registers the determination to fight for the sake of Scotland, but the patriotism was not only tempered and revised as the war went on, but transformed: what might 'Scotland' be said to 'count for' in the longer term?

William Cameron, in 'Speak not to me of War!' (first published in *Forward*, 15 August 1914), was overtly cautionary. As he looks over a 'bloody corpse-strewn plain, / Where man has butchered man', Cameron's scorn is severe: 'Show me the glory there!' And Charles Hamilton Sorley raised this to a searing vision: 'When you see millions of the mouthless dead / Across your dreams in pale battalions go, / Say not soft things as other men have said . . .' The dead are deaf to our laments and praises. Death itself has claimed everything, 'for evermore'.

One of the consequences of war is the polarisation of women and men, and the experience of the home front is as vital as that of the trenches. Eunice G. Murray argues the feminist question in her 'Warrior Women: Should Women Fight?':

> When one reads of the fate that overtakes the civilian population, more especially the horrors that have taken place in Belgium, the burning of houses, the devastation of the land, the imprisonment of the male population, the ruthless orders given to women to retire to their own houses and leave the doors unlocked. When we realize what these things mean there can be but one hope, and that is that warfare is doomed, and that men as well as women, in the words of Adomnan, the Abbot of Iona, 'will stop from things of that kind,' and that reason, not might, will govern the world.

Soldiering itself, though, was the central topic of many of the writers, but not by any means in glorification. Joseph Lee's poem 'The Bullet' reflects: 'Perhaps I killed a mother / When I killed a mother's son.' The bitterness is grim, and is borne out in parody, such as Ewart Allan Mackintosh's 'The Charge of the Light Brigade Brought Up to Date': 'Into the mouth of Hell, / Sticking it pretty well, / Slouched the six hundred.'

Charles Murray himself insisted on the common end of killing, regardless of rank or class, to which 'Staff' and 'six hundred' will come equally, in 'A Green Yule':

> Dibble them doon, the laird, the loon,
> King an' the cadgin' caird,
> The lady fine beside the queyn,
> A' in the same kirkyaird.

And there is remembering. J. B. Salmond writes in 'Twenty Years Ago': 'The boy is dead in all of us, and War's an ugly thing, [. . .] / And there isn't much romance about shell-shock and nervous wrecks.'

The memories can affirm the actions in retrospect, but they might equally give cause to question the worth of it all, and prompt questions about what has been learned from the experience, among those who have survived it.[9]

Poetry in the Scots and English languages is well represented but it would be wrong to overlook the Gaelic poetry of World War I, when so much of Gaelic-speaking Scotland was disproportionately depopulated. This poetry of immediate experience broke across the achievement of song and folklore collectors such as Alexander Carmichael (1832–1912), so while the treasury of Gaelic literature was being recovered and recorded, and the attractions of the 'Celtic Twilight' writers were appealing to a readership eager for sentimentalism, the Gaelic war poets were doing something else, discussed by Ronald Black elsewhere in this volume.

Hugh MacDiarmid, or rather, at this stage, Christopher Murray Grieve, enlisted in the Royal Army Medical Corps in July 1915, spending a year in England before being posted as a sergeant to the 42nd General Hospital in Greece. He published his earliest poems in the local newspaper in the town he came from, the *Eskdale and Liddesdale Advertiser*. These early poems are in tune with those expressing familiar tones of sympathy, encouragement, longing to fight, honouring the fallen. In 'To My Soldier and Sailor School Mates', he writes:

> Honour and glory yours,
> For some the victor's bays,
> But mine – nothing to show
> Through endless days![10]

And in 'To Private John Roddick, Australian Expeditionary Force (Wounded at the Dardanelles)', he writes:

> I wondered if far off beneath the Southern Cross
> Your heart was torn as mine beneath our Scottish sky
> Watching the way my school-mates played their part
> While I all powerlessly stood by.[11]

But in the poem 'June 1915' the tone is different:

> June's golden heart is torn in twain,
> Her glad blue eyes are grey with tears,
> Her radiant face is white with pain,
> For the lost promise of the years
> And the Christ crucified again.[12]

In April that year, Grieve's best friend from before the war, John Bogue Nisbet, had been killed while in the trenches on the Western Front, at the age of twenty-three. Grieve, one year senior, was invalided home in 1918 with cerebral malaria. In 1922, in the first issue of his magazine, *The Scottish Chapbook*, under the name Hugh M'Diarmid, one of Grieve's first published works was a 'conversation piece' entitled 'Nisbet, an Interlude in Post War Glasgow'. Here, the dead soldier and former schoolfriend, gassed to death in France, has returned and is thinking about poetry and sound in the industrial Scottish city, and what might make 'a new insubmersible sort of song'.[13] It is characteristic of MacDiarmid to draw that vision of what the future might bring out of the horror and loss of the past. And Grieve's first book, *Annals of the Five Senses* (1923), was dedicated to John Buchan, 'for the encouragement and help he has given to a young and unknown writer'. His description in this book of the battlefields of France takes a full retrospective view but the book points forward too:

> How would he describe the battle-field of the Somme? A broad road leading through an open country, rising and falling in conformity with the configuration of the ground. A long stretch of that road covered with traffic of all kinds: huge guns being dragged along by heavy tractor-engines; great motor-wagons in an interminable line, carrying food, ammunition, clothing; men marching towards the front, either fresh from their training or returning from rest camps . . . making once more towards the hell of the trenches; others returning from the battle-ground covered with a caking of mud and yet fretted with an odd cheeriness despite the strain through which they had passed and the bitter cold that bit to the bone: long strings of horses . . .
> This was the very heart of the trench-crossed, shell-pitted, mine-caverned battle area. As far as the eye could see on each side of the road there was nothing but desolation. All had been cultivated ground, studded with villages, farm-houses, villas, and here and there a chateau. Pleasant woods had risen up in parts . . . Today a few stumps showed where the woods had been, a few heaps of bricks remained of the villages. Even the piles of bricks were few and far between: in most cases the last vestiges of habitations and of the materials whereof they had been composed had been utterly obliterated. [And] the same desolation had been spread from Riga to the Black Sea . . .[14]

Out of this devastation, a new resolution was rising in MacDiarmid. He wrote of himself in *Annals*: 'He came back with an *idée fixe* – never again must men be made to suffer as in these years of war . . .'[15] As Homi Bhaba puts it in his essay 'Interrogating Identity': 'the state of emergency is also always a state of *emergence*'.[16]

For MacDiarmid, the First World War was the forcing ground of his sense of what the future must ensure. Many poets began in affirmation then increasingly questioned the values and priorities of the war, but characteristically MacDiarmid drove further. The devastations he witnessed would underlie the vigour and ruthlessness with which he would pursue his vision for a Scotland regenerated, politically as much as culturally, seeing both drives as inseparable. The vernacular Scots, the formal legacy of ballad structures and song, the significance of the Gaelic language and the essential questions to do with the virtues of minorities – whether minority languages or small nations – were all in the understanding of what the war had been for, and the authority of imperialist ideals in contest, bringing such destruction upon multitudes, was what he – and by and large the Scottish Renaissance he was soon to initiate – would oppose.

Throughout the First World War, Patrick Geddes had held the Chair of Botany at University College Dundee, from 1888 to 1919, then went to India to occupy the Chair of Sociology at the University of Bombay from 1919 to 1924. In 1925, he was back in Edinburgh, chairing a meeting at Ramsay Gardens beside the Outlook Tower at the top of the Royal Mile, just below the Castle. Reading his poems at the meeting was C. M. Grieve, by this time Hugh MacDiarmid. MacDiarmid's former schoolteacher, the composer F. G. Scott, who was to become a key figure of guidance and authoritative endorsement of the Scottish Renaissance movement, played piano settings of some of MacDiarmid's poems. In other words, precisely the kind of 'Renascence' that Geddes had envisaged in 1895 was being initiated thirty years later, at this meeting. The point is, perhaps, that the war not only had delayed it, but had forced it through, made possible life from the dead ground of its devastation.

According to Geddes's son Arthur, Patrick and he had read MacDiarmid's poems in their home in Montpellier, France, in the French literary periodical *Les Nouvelles littéraires* (which began publishing in 1922), and Patrick had written to MacDiarmid to introduce himself: hence the meeting.[17]

On 19 October, shortly after the reading, Geddes wrote to Grieve:

> More & more there is growing on me the possibility of strengthening all our scattered movements of synthetic & constructive & progressive character – whether regional, literary, scientific, artistic, economic or social etc., by trying to bring them together, & thus increasingly present them as each part of a *synthetic movement*, reaching out beyond the chaos-Babel of current action & thought so apparently predominant.[18]

In his autobiographical book of essays, *The Company I've Kept*, MacDiarmid wrote: 'This reawakening of the vital and the organic in every department undermines the authority of the purely mechanical. Geddes's prime significance lies in the fact that he was one of the greatest prophets and pioneers of this change.'[19]

Literary history has dealt to some extent with the poetry and fiction of the war, but theatre has been less widely understood in the context of the Scottish Renaissance. This is partly because at any given moment there are different theatrical traditions, not all of them coinciding with the visions of MacDiarmid and his contemporaries. David Hutchison has suggested three broad categories for theatre and performance in this era: (1) popular music hall; (2) lightweight comedies and 'entertainments'; (3) high-culture drama.[20]

Dublin's Abbey Theatre was the model for the Glasgow Repertory Company, established in 1909 and suspended in 1914. One of their most significant productions was of Chekhov's *The Seagull* (1909), the first performance of Chekhov in Britain, the play's fin de siècle ethos having a particular bearing in pre-war Scotland. Anthony Rowley's *A Woman's Shuttle* (1910) presents a family firm failing to update their production processes in a way that is reminiscent of the inadequate business skills of Gourlay in George Douglas Brown's *The House with the Green Shutters* (1901), as the railways undermine his dominance. Their early productions included work by George Bernard Shaw and Ibsen, and two Scottish plays of lasting value: Donald Colquhoun's *Jean* (1910), a realistic portrayal of the life of a farming family in hard times, with strong Scots dialogue and powerful characters from different generations; and J. A. Ferguson's *Campbell of Kilmohr* (1915). The latter is set after the Jacobite rising of 1745 and portrays the predicament of a Highlander confronted with the sly duplicity of a Lowlander's military interests.[21] These intensely literary plays and others were written just before the First World War in the national context of commercial theatres, traditions of music hall and pantomime, and a lively tradition of amateur and touring companies, visiting towns and villages throughout the country. A long tradition also attaches to 'Galoshins' (the word is from Galatians – the people from Galatia), a folk version of the Christian resurrection performed by locals and travellers in different parts of Scotland.[22]

Another company, the Scottish National Players, founded around 1920 with the remaining funds of the Glasgow Repertory, produced John Brandane's *The Glen is Mine* (1923), depicting the conflict between development and conservation taking place in the Highlands in the aftermath of the war. They produced early plays by James Bridie (1888–1951) but rejected Joe Corrie's *In Time o' Strife* (1927). Corrie, a working miner, was crossing the boundaries between theatre conventions proscribed by class division. Such challenges were to bear fruit later. Bridie's *The Queen's Comedy* (1950) may be read as a reflection on the wars of the twentieth century, as it presents the Trojan Wars, their gods and generals, with the historical and mythological distance allowing Bridie's satire, insight and questioning much more scope than would have been possible through literalism. The National Players toured Scotland and contributed to BBC Radio in the 1920s, and they were driving towards the establishment of a Scottish National Theatre.

And that drive was being made increasingly in this period. Immediately after the war, the push to establish a National Theatre of Scotland was one of the strands, once again, in the Renaissance movement led by MacDiarmid. MacDiarmid noted in an essay of 1924, 'R.F. Pollock and the Art of Theatre',[23] that an authentic Scottish drama must represent 'the profound differences in psychology between Scots and English'. Pollock himself elaborated on this:

> Plays represented night after night follow a definite plan of exits and entrances. This gives different groupings to present episode and action. By developing the plan to include gesture, facial expression and intonation, the salient features of the Scottish mentality can be faithfully presented on the stage.[24]

MacDiarmid and Neil Gunn both wrote short plays and R. F. Pollock, following Stanislavski, speculated that a drama attentive to distinct aspects of Scots' psychology should begin by acknowledging that one characteristic of many Scots was a terse, restrained, succinct use of language: more goes on below the surface than what is ever seen.

Anglophone modernism is largely understood as engaged with the disruption and fragmentation of the aesthetic priorities of security that characterised the end of the nineteenth century. Eliot's *Waste Land* is made of shards of narratives, Pound's first endeavour was to break the pentameter, Joyce's prose engaged the many internal perspectives of characters alienated from each other. In Scotland, the difference was to reach back through the divided-and-ruled national culture that had been swept into the singular vortex of British imperialism and the First World War, and attempt to bring forward a multifaceted but singular nationality from the violence that war made unavoidable.

Populisms and Specialisms: Fiction, the Blue and the Red

The appeal of the Kailyard novelists in the 1890s was international. Ian McLaren's *Beside the Bonnie Brier Bush* (1894) was snapped up by Queen Victoria and William Gladstone. It was a bestseller in the USA, with 485,000 copies sold by 1908, and 256,000 in the UK. S.

R. Crockett's *The Lilac Sunbonnet* (1894) sold 10,000 copies on the first day of its publication.[25] McLaren and Crockett, both Free Kirk ministers, were key figures in the literary marketplace but their popularity had its political character too. Their counterpoints were the anti-Kailyard novelists George Douglas Brown and John Macdougall Hay, and the dark poets, James Thomson (who used the pseudonym 'Bysshe Vanolis'), in *The City of Dreadful Night*, and John Davidson, with his testaments of lonely outcasts. But beyond the literary, in the realm of political self-identification, it was to Crockett that Stevenson wrote in spring 1888 from Saranac Lake, USA, taking exception to Crockett's self-styled address in a letter: 'Don't put "N.B." in your paper: put "Scotland" and be done with it,' Stevenson wrote. 'Alas, that I should be thus stabbed in the home of my friends! The name of my native land is not North Britain, whatever may be the name of yours!'[26]

In some respects, Stevenson's popularity may have matched that of the Kailyarders, but after the war, Hugh MacDiarmid's book-length poem *A Drunk Man Looks at the Thistle*, published on 22 November 1926 in an edition of 500 copies, had sold only ninety-nine copies by the end of the year.[27] Commercial priorities were now an essential factor in mass literary production, and if that meant political compromise, the priorities of conscience and moral urgency were always going to be at stake. Difficult matters and the worst of human potential brought out in tragic literature might tell truth deeply but these things do not sell easily or quickly. Yet neither do they go away.

Two other writers suggest ways in which the idea of nationalism was forming over the period. Nationalism itself, of course, is one of those woolly words with multiple meanings. With Compton Mackenzie and Ian Hay, we might think of it in terms of what 'Scotland' means, or meant, to people reading their works in the early twentieth century, before, during and after the war. Self-awareness was becoming a different thing, in the context of the UK and Europe, and ideas of imperial assertion and political self-determination.

Mackenzie is familiar for *Whisky Galore!* (1947) but in 1914 his most famous novel was *Sinister Street* (1913), an 800-page *Bildungsroman* centred on the young Michael Fane, growing up in the south of England. He and his sister Stella are scandalously born out of wedlock to rich parents, and Michael travels from school in London to holidays in Cornwall, meets a girl from an Anglo-Indian family and goes to Oxford. It was praised by Henry James, John Betjeman and George Orwell, and noted as a record of the 1910s 'lost generation'.

It anticipates the devastation of the war, like a mirror to Elgar's *Cello Concerto* (1919), which grieves for the loss it looks back on.

In the Foreword to the 1949 edition, Mackenzie tells us it was begun in 1912 and its first volume was to be reviewed in a leader article in the *Daily Mail* but this was decided against when two libraries said they would not circulate the book. Publicity followed: the 'Banned Book' war was quickly superseded by 'the real war', which commenced as Mackenzie was finishing 'the Oxford part' of the novel. 'I can hear now', he wrote in 1949, 'the stillness of that August night before the clock struck twelve, and I can hear now the menacing rumble of the troop-trains and ammunition-trains southward bound all through that August night, until the sun rose and I went to bed.'[28] Mackenzie was sent to Gallipoli (the result of which was his book, *Gallipoli Memories*), and finished volume two in October 1914, travelling to Capri with a copy of the first volume of Proust's *Remembrance of Things Past*, given to him by the critic Edmund Gosse, who suggested it was in 'something of an expression of the same spirit'.[29] Volume two prompted Henry James to write to Mackenzie saying that he had 'emancipated the English novel', but Mackenzie observes that the praise was premature since, in 1915, D. H. Lawrence published *Women in Love*.

Lascelles Abercrombie wrote: 'We seem to be watching that strangest of all modes of evolution, the dissolution of one century's character to make way for the character of another century.' But Mackenzie insisted: 'What no critic has noted is that the scheme of the book demands from the reader that he should identify himself with the principal character through whose eyes he is compelled to look at life.'[30] In this, he anticipates Joyce's *A Portrait of the Artist as a Young Man* (1916), but where Joyce's novel is tightly structured, Mackenzie observed in 1949:

> It will not surprise me to find young people of today, heirs of two mundane wars, impatient of an adolescence of which their own adolescence is riper by a generation, because they will be feeling comparatively so much older and comparatively so much wiser.

Yet the book was still selling 1,000 copies a year. He intended a whole series of sequels to *Sinister Street*, and indeed wrote a number of them, but, he admitted, 'I was compelled to recognise that the First World War had smashed the series of linked novels I intended to call *The Theatre of Youth*. Because I should never be able to escape from it.' He was, he said, 'as impatient of the mood of *Sinister Street* as any man in his thirties should be of his teens'.[31]

In the meantime Mackenzie had been one of the founder members of the NPS in 1928, amalgamating the Scots National League, the Scottish National Movement and the Glasgow University Scottish Nationalist Association. In 1934 the NPS merged with the Scottish Party to form the Scottish National Party. The foundation of the NPS is recorded in a well-known photograph where Mackenzie stands beside the Duke of Montrose, John McCormick, R. B. Cunninghame Graham, C. M. Grieve (Hugh MacDiarmid) and James Valentine. Other founders included the popular 'women's novelist' Annie S. Swan, the folklorist and food writer F. Marian McNeill, the architect Robert Hurd, the party's first leader, and the solicitor Alexander McEwen.

In other words, Mackenzie had moved from being famous as a highly respected author of what we might call society and psychological fiction centred in London, Oxford and the south of England, through working for British Intelligence during the First World War, to being a leading member of the official organisation driving towards political self-determination for Scotland. There is no doubt of his prominence or the publicity he brought to the nationalist movement, though one wonders, given his work for the British government and the violence of the political struggle in Ireland from 1916 through to the 1920s, and the popularity of his writing, whether Mackenzie was not keeping his options open. However, his friendship with MacDiarmid continued for the rest of their lives, as their correspondence shows. On 11 January 1962, Mackenzie wrote to the poet: 'Ours has been a long unbroken friendship.'[32]

A different trajectory was followed by Ian Hay. His work is addressed elsewhere in this book but I want to make a point about his most famous novel, *The First Hundred Thousand* (1915), centring on 'army life under training and in the trenches' and written, as the back cover blurb of the 1985 edition tells us, 'while the author was undergoing the experiences he describes'.[33]

The novel was listed by Edwin Morgan as one of his *Twentieth-Century Scottish Classics*.[34] Morgan says of it:

> The matter-of-fact realities of daily life for the recruits of Kitchener's Army, during that first year of war – drill, kit, food, songs, embarkation for France, dugouts, snipers, zeppelins, grenades, gasmasks, souvenir-mad villagers – give a striking immediacy to this book. Its jaunty, laconic, humorous style may seem curious to a generation brought up on the horrors of Owen and Rosenberg, but salutarily so.

There is a further point to be made, thinking about the book's representation of Scotland in the context of British soldiers at war, and in the wake not only of Owen and Rosenberg but of *Catch 22*. Chapter 11 begins with a list of the 'heavenly host' which 'orders our goings and shapes our ends':

(1) The War Office;
(2) The Treasury;
(3) The Army Ordnance Office;
(4) Our Divisional Office

And goes on to categorise these into three 'departments':

(1) Round Game Department (including Dockets, Indents, and all official correspondence).
(2) Fairy Godmother Department.
(3) Practical Joke Department.

In Chapter 14, we are told to follow 'the golden rule': 'When given an impossible job by a Brass Hat, salute smartly, turn about, and go and wait round a corner for five minutes. Then come back and do the job in a proper manner.'[35]

The humour of these examples is clear enough but there is less bitterness, futility, irony and anger in the tone here than what becomes pressing in work written later in the war. Towards the end of Chapter 20, soldiers in dialogue are considering the question, what is 'the general attitude' of 'the dear old country at large' – by which is meant Britain.[36] The answer is threefold: 'Both sides are trying to drag the great British Public into the scrap by the back of the neck.'[37] One side claims that the British army is desperate for men, the other that 'the personal liberty of Britain's workers' is being 'interfered with by the Overbearing Militarist Oligarchy'.[38] However, the 'country at large' is 'not worrying one jot about Conscription'; its 'one topic of conversation at present is – Charlie Chaplin'.[39] Having dug a new trench before their frontline, the soldiers reflect on what lies ahead for them 'the day after tomorrow': '"If this thing goes with a click, as it ought to do," said Wagstaffe, "it will be the biggest thing that ever happened – bigger even than Charlie Chaplin."' Blaikie replies: '"Yes – *if!*"'[40] Then he says this, bringing the chapter to an end:

> 'Whatever we make – history or a bloomer – we'll do our level best,' replied Blaikie. 'At least, I hope "A" Company will.'
> Then suddenly his reserved, undemonstrative Scottish tongue found utterance. 'Scotland for Ever!' he cried softly.[41]

The next, final, chapter, goes into the present tense as the first person plural narrator tells us: 'We move on again at last, and find ourselves in Central Boyau, getting near the heart of things.' And the novel closes by acknowledging that if the author writes again of 'The First Hundred Thousand', they will still bear that designation but no longer be 'The Hundred Thousand'. As the novel closes, the casualties are only beginning.[42]

Hay's political conservatism characterised his life and his Scottish patriotism was decidedly and continuously unionist, yet the Scottish identity that prevails in the novel perhaps signals more than one thing. Reference to the working-class movement in Glasgow that was to centre on John Maclean, opposing what Hay calls 'the Overbearing Militarist Oligarchy', to the populism of Chaplin, film and mass media, and to the newspapers and other media supporting conscription, gives the exclamation 'Scotland for Ever!' a more poignant, nuanced, ambiguous tone than might have been predicted, and in the twenty-first century it is inevitable that much of Hay's writing can be read with a sensitivity to its unconscious irony, the bitter legacy of its robustness, the ambivalence of its good humour.

Maclean, calling as he did for a Scottish Socialist Republic, was perhaps one source of the representation of the Clydeside 'reds' in John Buchan's novel *Mr Standfast* (1919) but to turn to the text of Maclean's speech from the dock of the High Court in Glasgow, 9 May 1918, we can appreciate his words not only in their historical and political moment but as a lasting masterpiece of literary rhetoric:

> I wish no harm to any human being, but I, as one man, am going to exercise my freedom of speech. No human being on the face of the earth, no government is going to take from me my right to speak, my right to protest against wrong, my right to do everything I can that is for the benefit of mankind. I am not here, then, as the accused; I am here as the accuser of capitalism dripping with blood from head to foot.

The fact that Maclean's life and words had such a long and deep influence on the major poets of twentieth-century Scotland, including Hugh MacDiarmid, Sorley MacLean and Hamish Henderson, testifies to the kind of nationalism that was evolving through the war years. MacDiarmid's poem 'The Innumerable Christ' evokes the blood of the martyr sacrifice, as Christopher Marlowe's *Faustus* did in 1592, and Maclean's similar rhetoric brilliantly works as accusation (capitalism is the bloody business) and his own physical sacrifice in the effort to end it. After sentencing, prison wasted his health and he died only five years later at the age of forty-four.[43]

In his trial for sedition in 1918, in Edinburgh, Maclean himself said this:

> I have taken up unconstitutional action at this time because of the abnormal circumstances and because precedent has been given by the British government. I am a socialist and have been fighting and will fight for an absolute reconstruction of society for the benefit of all. I am proud of my conduct. I have squared my conduct with my intellect, and if everyone had done so this war would not have taken place.

This is a man who did all he could for a Socialist Republic of Scotland, to end the constitutional horror of class, royalty and the creation of wealth for the few through the exploitation of the many and to end the British Empire of the United Kingdom in the only truly progressive way: to take up once again the best of England, which only can be started, seriously, in the good neighbourly company of an independent Scotland.

Edwin Morgan, in his poem 'On John Maclean', quotes the words of the Lenin-appointed Bolshevik consul to Scotland: 'I am not prepared to let Moscow dictate to Glasgow.' Morgan comments: 'it is the firmness / of what he wanted and did not want / that raises eyebrows' and notes that Maclean evidently wanted 'to let them know that Scotland was not Britain' before acknowledging his defeat in a regime of merciless establishment propaganda and force:

> Well, nothing's permanent. It's true he lost –
> a voice silenced in November fog. Party
> is where he failed, for he believed in people,
> not in partiinost' that as everyone knows
> delivers the goods. Does it? Of course.
> And if they're damaged in transit you make do?
> You do – and don't be so naïve about this world!
> Maclean was not naïve, but
>   'We are out
> for life and all that life can give us'
>
> was what he said, that's what he said.[44]

Indeed, patriotic unionism was a matter of self-awareness of distinctive nationality; the endorsement of pacifism, seen by some as the most dangerous 'enemy within', was recognised by John Buchan himself as one quality in *Mr Standfast*, in the character of Lancelot Wake, a rare example of a positive contemporary depiction of the conscientious objector as someone of integrity. He sacrifices himself in battle and, mortally wounded, gets back to the hero Richard Hannay, saying this: '"Funny thing life. A year ago I was preaching peace . . . I'm still preaching it . . . I'm not sorry." I held his hand till two minutes later he died.' Wake's '"I'm not sorry"' refers to his objection to killing but it also justifies the action he has taken, to save the lives of his fellows. Buchan keeps the sense of the character's integrity intact.[45]

Mackenzie, Hay and Buchan remain familiar names and suggest the variety of kinds of writing that were embodying national self-consciousness through the First World War, and influencing the development of particular forms of nationalism in its aftermath. For John Maclean, that influence was directly political and intended to bring about revolutionary social change. Hugh MacDiarmid summarised this:

> The Social Revolution is possible sooner in Scotland than in England. The working-class policy ought to be to break up the Empire to avert war and enable the workers to triumph in every country and colony. Scottish separation is part of the process of England's Imperial disintegration and is a help towards the ultimate triumph of the workers of the world.[46]

But the popularity of the Kailyard writers and the pervasive presence of unionism and militarism in the literary mainstream and the press, and increasingly through mass media (also exemplified in Mackenzie's reference to the 'Banned Books' war of 1913 and Hay's to Chaplin in 1915), clearly indicate the extent to which warfare was and is conducted by more means than one.

The eight-minute film footage of Chaplin and Harry Lauder from 1918 offers strange insight into the appeal of both characters, the 'stage Scot' and the 'little tramp'.[47] Both are performances, the work of actors playing their roles, but where Chaplin's, seen from the twenty-first century, speaks of self-possession, self-conscious playfulness, impishness and cheek, and carries the authority of the poor man with self-respect, Lauder's seems projective of an eccentricity always in thrall and at the service of the greater authority. The truth of this may represent their relationship but it also speaks clearly about the authority of America/Britain/London over Scotland. Lauder's popular Scottishness is discomforting because of its caricature of nationality; Chaplin's speaks of a truth about human dignity in conditions of poverty. When they exchange hats, Chaplin seems to enact Scottishness cheerily, merrily, but Lauder's hopping after Chaplin is curiously repulsive. No wonder MacDiarmid wrote so spitefully about him.[48]

> You've played England's game and held Scotland up
>   To ridicule wherever you've gone,
> Yet it was a different ladder behind the scenes
>   You crawled to knighthood on.[49]

Just as theatre, and later, radio, cinema and television, were to address and influence an increasing number of people, the essential value of literary art was becoming eclipsed, or at least readjusting its co-ordinate points in a world where attitudes to experience were themselves naturally changing and being deliberately manipulated.

Conclusion

Finally, I want to suggest that the centrality of the First World War was only a prelude: the international rise of fascism, the Spanish Civil War, the Second World War, the Cold War and the information propaganda war, increasingly global since 1989, are its sequelae. In 1940, George Orwell wrote this:

> But, after all, the war of 1914–18 was only a heightened moment in an almost continuous crisis. At this date [1940] it hardly even needs a war to bring home to us the disintegration of our society and the increasing helplessness of all decent people.[50]

The metaphor of militarisation was maintained by Hugh MacDiarmid. In an essay of 1942, after praising new work by (among others) Sorley MacLean, George Campbell Hay, Douglas Young, Sydney Goodsir Smith, J. F. Hendry, Nicholas Moore, G. S. Fraser, Norman MacCaig, W. S. Graham (poets and translators), Robert Melville (art critic), Robert MacLellan and Paul Carroll (playwrights), and William Johnstone (artist), MacDiarmid says this (and the bold at the end is in the original text):

> The [Second World] war may thus have acted as a forcing-bed, bringing to somewhat speedier development what was already securely rooted in the circumstances of our nation; and in this sense it may, perhaps, be said later that: '**The Scottish renaissance was conceived in the First World War, and sprang into lusty life in the Second World War.**'[51]

Central to our understanding of this is the context of propaganda generated by the developing technological forms of the press and mass media. The key figure before the First World War was Karl Kraus, whose epic play, *The Last Days of Mankind*, ends with these words: 'This is world war. This is my manifesto to mankind.'[52]

In the major post-Second World War poem by Hugh MacDiarmid, *In Memoriam James Joyce* (1955), Kraus is a critical reference. Quoting from a source by Erich Heller, MacDiarmid makes the point that the Austrian satirist's attention to the detail of press propaganda, the atrocities inflicted on syntax and meaning which Kraus shows up simply by quotation, are the prelude to the increasingly dangerous later twentieth century. MacDiarmid's poem, also structured through quotation and demonstration rather than the projected inspiration of a divinely singular voice, prefigures information technology; however, it is driven neither by commercial priorities nor by chaotic over-supply, but rather by political and ultimately moral priorities. It prophesies the twenty-first century. As Yuval Noah Harari says, 'In the past, censorship worked by blocking the flow of information. In the twenty-first century, censorship works by flooding people with irrelevant information [. . .] Today having power means knowing what to ignore.'[53]

And what to ask, and how to remember.

Notes

1. Stefan Zweig, *The World of Yesterday: Memoirs of a European*, trans. by Anthea Bell (London: Pushkin Press, [1942] 2009), p. 80.
2. Marjorie Perloff, *Edge of Irony: Modernism in the Shadow of the Habsburg Empire* (Chicago and London: University of Chicago Press, 2016), p. 25.
3. Ibid. p. 24.
4. Hugh MacDiarmid, *R.B. Cunninghame Graham: A Centenary Study*, in *Albyn: Shorter Books and Monographs*, ed. Alan Riach (Manchester: Carcanet Press, [1952] 1996), pp. 130–61, p. 132.
5. George Orwell, 'Such, Such Were the Joys', in *Essays* (London: Penguin Books, [1947] 2000), pp. 416–452 (p. 441).
6. Ibid. p. 442.
7. For Blackie, see Stuart Wallace, *John Stuart Blackie: Scottish Scholar and Patriot* (Edinburgh: Edinburgh University Press, 2006).
8. Patrick Geddes, 'The Scots Renascence' (1895), reprinted in *Edinburgh Review*, vol. 88 (1992), pp. 17–22.
9. For the poems, see David Goldie and Roderick Watson (eds), *From the Line: Scottish War Poetry* (Glasgow: Association for Scottish Literary

Studies, 2014); Lizzie McGregor (ed.), *Beneath Troubled Skies: Poems of Scotland at War, 1914–1918* (Edinburgh: Scottish Poetry Library and Polygon, 2015); Andrew Ferguson (ed.), *Ghosts of War: A History of World War I in Poetry and Prose* (Stroud: The History Press, 2016).
10. Hugh MacDiarmid, *A Langholm Lad Goes to War*, ed. Ron Addison (Langholm: Langholm Library Trust, 2014), p. 24.
11. Ibid. p. 25.
12. Ibid. p. 28.
13. Hugh MacDiarmid, 'Nisbet, an Interlude in Post War Glasgow' (1922), in *Annals of the Five Senses and Other Stories, Sketches and Plays*, ed. Roderick Watson and Alan Riach (Manchester: Carcanet, 1999), pp. 104–13 (p. 108).
14. C. M. Grieve, *Annals of the Five Senses* (Edinburgh: The Porpoise Press, 1923), pp. 113–15.
15. Ibid. p. 89.
16. Homi Bhabha, 'Interrogating Identity', in *The Location of Culture* (New York: Psychology Press, 1994). Available at <http://readingtheperiphery.org/bhabha/> (last accessed 4 June 2019).
17. Hugh MacDiarmid, *The Company I've Kept: Essays in Autobiography* (London: Hutchinson, 1966), p. 79.
18. John Manson (ed.), *Dear Grieve: Letters to Hugh MacDiarmid (C. M. Grieve)* (Glasgow: Kennedy & Boyd, 2011).
19. MacDiarmid, *The Company I've Kept*, p. 81.
20. David Hutchison, 'Scottish Drama 1900–1950', in Cairns Craig (ed.), *The History of Scottish Literature. Volume 4: Twentieth Century* (Aberdeen: Aberdeen University Press, 1987), pp. 163–77.
21. John Ferguson (ed.), *Seven Famous One-Act Plays* (Harmondsworth: Penguin, [1937] 1950).
22. See Brian Hayward's *Galoshins: The Scottish Folk Play* (Edinburgh: Edinburgh University Press, 1992).
23. Hugh MacDiarmid, *Contemporary Scottish Studies*, ed. Alan Riach (Manchester: Carcanet, [1926] 1995), pp. 177–82.
24. Ibid. p. 279.
25. Chris Bambery, *A People's History of Scotland* (London: Verso, 2014), p. 133.
26. Robert Louis Stevenson, Letter to S. R. Crockett (Saranac Lake, spring 1888), in *The Letters: Volume Three*, ed. Sidney Colvin (London: Heinemann [Tusitala edn vol. XXXIII], 1926), pp. 185–6, p. 186.
27. Alan Bold, *MacDiarmid: Christopher Murray Grieve: A Critical Biography* (London: Paladin, 1990), p. 257.
28. Compton Mackenzie, 'Foreword to the 1949 Edition', in *Sinister Street* (Harmondsworth: Penguin Books, [1913] 1960), pp. 9–13, p. 10.
29. Ibid. p. 11.
30. Ibid. p. 11.
31. Ibid. p. 12.

32. Manson, *Dear Grieve*, p. 458.
33. Ian Hay, *The First Hundred Thousand* (Glasgow: Richard Drew, [1915] 1985).
34. Edwin Morgan, *Twentieth-Century Scottish Classics* (Glasgow: Book Trust Scotland, 1987), p. 8.
35. Hay, *The First Hundred Thousand*, p. 143.
36. Ibid. pp. 229–30.
37. Ibid. p. 229.
38. Ibid. p. 230.
39. Ibid. p. 230.
40. Ibid. p. 233.
41. Ibid. p. 233.
42. Ibid. p. 256.
43. Henry Bell, *John Maclean: Hero of Red Clydeside* (London: Pluto Press, 2018).
44. Edwin Morgan, 'On John Maclean', in *The New Divan* (Manchester: Carcanet, 1977), p. 82.
45. John Buchan, *Mr Standfast* (Edinburgh: Polygon, [1919] 2014), p. 324.
46. Hugh MacDiarmid, *Lucky Poet: A Self-Study in Literature and Political Ideas*, ed. Alan Riach (Manchester: Carcanet, [1943] 1994), p. 144.
47. This can be seen on YouTube. Available at <https://www.youtube.com/watch?v=jYf7O4kzGJQ> (last accessed 8 June 2019).
48. See David Goldie, 'Hugh MacDiarmid, Harry Lauder and Scottish Popular Culture', *International Journal of Scottish Literature*, vol. 1, Autumn 2006. Available at <http://www.ijsl.stir.ac.uk/issue1/goldie.htm> (last accessed 8 June 2019).
49. Hugh MacDiarmid, 'Sir Harry Lauder', *The Complete Poems*, vol. 2, ed. Michael Grieve and W. R. Aitken (Manchester: Carcanet, 1993), p. 1287.
50. George Orwell, 'Inside the Whale', in *Essays* (London: Penguin Books, 1994), pp. 101–33, p. 131.
51. Hugh MacDiarmid, 'Scottish Arts and Letters: The Present Position and Post-War Prospects', in *The New Scotland: 17 Chapters on Scottish Reconstruction* (Glasgow: Civic Press and the London Scots Self-Government Committee, 1942), pp. 136–51, p. 151.
52. Karl Kraus, *In These Great Times: A Karl Kraus Reader*, ed. Harry Zohn (Manchester: Carcanet, 1984), p. 258.
53. Yuval Noah Harari, *Homo Deus* (London; Harvill Secker, 2016), quoted in Robert Calasso, *The Unnameable Present*, trans. by Richard Dixon (London: Allen Lane, 2019), pp. 77–8.

Chapter 2

'It Takes All Sorts to Make a Type': Scottish Great War Prose
David A. Rennie

The prose of soldiers and non-combatant participants has traditionally been a neglected area of Scottish World War I literary scholarship. Only John Buchan's *Mr Standfast* (1919) and Ian Hay's *The First Hundred Thousand* (1915) appear to have garnered widespread attention. Trevor Royle's 2014 anthology *Isn't All This Bloody?: Scottish Writing from the First World War* has highlighted the widespread body of extant material, but first-hand Scottish Great War prose has never attained anything like the status of works by participants in other belligerent nations.

Why? In Adrian Gregory's opinion: 'The simplest answer may still be the best: that Scottish culture was more patriotic, perhaps even more militaristic, than English.' 'One in six British soldiers of the war were Scottish,' he observes, 'but apparently not a Graves, Sassoon [or] Aldington.'[1] The martial zeal Gregory identifies may be a contributing factor, although this is difficult – as he recognises – to quantify. The numerical consideration he highlights is less ambiguous: there were fewer Scots than English – or, for that matter, American or German – troops to write such works. But why has no Scottish equivalent to the likes of *All Quiet on the Western Front* (1929), *A Farewell to Arms* (1929) or *The Middle Parts of Fortune* (1929) emerged?

Part of the answer to this question, I argue, is that Scots with first-hand wartime experience did actually generate prose comparable to that emerging in other countries throughout the 1920s and beyond, but that this has been somewhat overlooked. John Reith's *Wearing Spurs* (published in 1966 – though written in 1937), David Rorie's *A Medico's Luck in the War* (1929), George Blake's *The Path of Glory* (1929) and Edward Gaitens's *Dance of the Apprentices* (1948) are notable examples – stylistically and thematically – of Scottish writers engaging with the topics of militaristic bureaucracy, the general physical discomfort of army life, and graphic wounding.

By discussing some of these under-studied texts, this chapter will challenge – or at least supplement – the notion that Scottish writing was dominated by North Britons who 'arrived at a defining Scottishness by way of a wider British formation'.[2] The range of emotional and personal response within avowedly unionist Scots literature will also be examined. Here I suggest that support for the Union did not eradicate a whole spectrum of recognisably Scottish cultural markers from appearing in the writing of individual authors.

David Goldie acknowledges that 'distinct local perspectives and practices [. . .] have contributed significantly to the complexities of' Scottish World War I writing, but notes that the picture is more involved than merely being a composite of separate Scottish identities, such as Doric or Gaelic. At play is also 'a different set of identifications – ones that derive not from the regional "below" but from the national and international "above"'. There are, for instance, 'less straightforwardly homogenous' categories of Scots – the diasporic, immigrants and unionists.[3] Moreover, the presence of a 'strongly expressed Scottishness' in the works of Buchan, Hay and Ewart Alan Mackintosh buttresses 'British imperial integration' by promoting 'strength in diversity' which contrasts favourably with 'Prussian monoculture'.[4] Meanwhile, the Anglicisation of the *People's Journal* and the increasing popularity of the *Daily Record* and *Mail* form another intersection with the 'above', but not, Goldie writes, one of British 'cultural imperialism'.[5] Rather it represents changing consumer taste in Scotland through a willing embrace of mass-market culture.

Considering these various strands, Goldie rejects the notion that Scottish identity 'must be one thing':

> It might, I suggest, be more productive to regard national cultures pragmatically, and see them simply as the sum of all current activity taking place in that country or otherwise relating to it: to think less in terms of Scottish Culture and more about the range of cultural activities taking place within Scotland.[6]

This is 'an idea of culture as the product of material and ideological contention'.[7] The notion of interacting 'above' and 'below' influences offers a valuable model through which to conceive the multivalent, contingent flux of variables constituting Scottish identity at the time of World War I. There is, however, the risk that, while building an overall model of complex national identity, the nuances and idiosyncrasies of individuals' reactions are suppressed – especially if they are assigned one vector of identity. If writers such as Buchan and Hay depict 'a Scotland of a British' mind, as Goldie has persuasively argued, it also seems possible that their depictions will be coloured by the 'from below' attributes of their background, individual character and creative choices.[8]

Several Scottish writers of World War I could be considered to represent a double emphasis on 'a distinctive Scottishness and an assimilatory Britishness'.[9] In each instance, however, the type of 'Scottishness' and the manner of assimilation vary markedly. Ian Hay's *The First Hundred Thousand* follows the Bruce and Wallace Highlanders from initial training to frontline combat at Loos. The soldiers become 'less individualistic' and more acquiescent as training progresses, eventually forming 'a cohesive unit of fighting men'.[10] The novel unequivocally states its case that a display of Scottish individuality is compatible with fervent unionism, describing the Highlanders as possessing '[t]he entirely Hibernian faculty of being able to combine a most fanatical and seditious brand of Nationalism with a genuine and ardent enthusiasm for the British Empire'.[11] Hay builds his narrative of assimilation by suggesting parallels between army and school life: 'One's first days as a newly-joined subaltern are very like one's first days at school.'[12] As George Urquhart writes, this choice of 'public school as the metaphoric vehicle with which to comprehend the army life' is apt, given the likely resonance it would have for 'the predominantly middle-class readership novel of *Blackwood's* [*Magazine*]' in which it was initially serialised.[13]

Despite its overwhelming positivity for war and Empire, the work is sensitive to the nuances of Scottish experience. The narrator holds that, given their relative sizes, 'Big England's sorrow is national; little Scotland's is personal.'[14] We also see varying attitudes to war among the men. For Captain Wagstaffe, war 'wipes out all the small nuisances of peace-time'.[15] One soldier, Ainslie, claims enlistment has improved his digestion and sleep; another, Ayling, is grateful to escape his job as a public school teacher; while Hattrick, a struggling doctor in peacetime, is glad of the steady income. As Hay's narrator summarises: 'you find it impossible to generalise. Your one unshakeable conclusion is that it takes all sorts to make a type.'[16]

For Goldie, John Buchan's *The Thirty-Nine Steps* (1915), *Greenmantle* (1916) and – especially – *Mr Standfast* (1919) offer 'a prime example of the adaptation of the colonial adventure to the conditions of wartime'.[17] Indeed, it would be hard to argue that Hannay's epiphanic wonderment at the rural beauty of the Cotswolds constitutes anything else:

In that moment I had a kind of revelation. I had a vision of what I had been fighting for [. . .] It was peace, deep and holy and ancient [. . .] It was more; for in that hour England first took over me. Before my country had been South Africa [. . .] But now I realised that I had a new home.[18]

Goldie is surely in the right when he notes that Buchan is 'constructing an England that is part of an Imperial Britain of the imagination'.[19] Yet Buchan also penned poems in Lowland Scots about the war, such as 'Home Thoughts from Abroad' and 'On Leave' in *Poems Scots and English* (1917). In his memoir *Memory Hold-the-Door* (1940), Buchan admitted that it was his time at Oxford – his exile from his native land – which intensified his interest in the literature and countryside of Scotland. As such, Goldie views Buchan's poetry as being comparable to the attempt in Kailyard literature to 'recover a mid-nineteenth-century Scotland', with the difference that Buchan possesses 'few such memories' and is 'impelled to construct one out of what is effectively a British literary tradition'.[20]

Douglas Gifford, however, has argued that in his earliest fiction, beginning with *Sir Quixote of the Moors* (1895), 'Buchan first began to write in the tradition of Scottish historical fiction' of Walter Scott and Robert Louis Stevenson.[21] And for Macdonald Daly, Buchan's Lowland war poems express 'an aesthetic appeal to a specifically Scottish, as distinct from a British, patriotism'.[22] Perhaps, as Gifford does, it may be more productive to acknowledge in Buchan 'constant movement between his dual Scottish and English identities', 'two different *personae*: the Scottish Buchan remaining in nostalgic memory; the English Buchan changing in voice and manner to adapt to his new identity'.[23]

R. W. Campbell's *Private Spud Tamson* (1915) and J. J. Bell's *Wee Macgreegor Enlists* (1915) are comparable in their focus on the comedic escapades of a central character drawn from the tenements of Glasgow. To the pride of their respective families, Spud and the diminutive Macgreegor enlist without hesitation. Reflecting Macgreegor's initial appearance as a recurring character in stories published by the *Glasgow Evening Times* since 1901, *Wee Macgreegor Enlists* depends largely on the interactions of its quaint characters – Macgreegor's affected aunt, his erudite, playful, on-off girlfriend, Christina, and his ne'er-do-well associate Willie – for its sentimental humour. War and the process of mobilisation are largely peripheral to the will-they-won't-they dynamic between Christina and Macgreegor. Only one of the episodes in the novel concerns active duty, in which, during 'a splendid moment', Macgreegor bayonets a German.[24] Although he is wounded enough to be kept 'out of action for several months', his injuries are more of a narrative ploy to make Christina reconsider her arch rebuffs of Macgreegor than they are an engagement with the human cost of modern warfare.[25]

Private Spud Tamson also draws on the comedic adventures of the Glasgow working class, but Campbell acknowledges the city's darker side. Early in the novel we learn that Spud's father has been to jail for '[k]nockin' lumps aff the auld wife's heid wi' a poker'.[26] His mother later finances 'a spree' for Spud by pawning 'the goods which had been regularly pawned once a week for twenty years'.[27] The men of the Glesca Mileeshy to which Spud belongs – described as 'the scrapings of humanity' – revel in recreational violence.[28] One member deliberately provokes a mass brawl with a rival Perthshire unit: 'then the battle commenced. Skin, hair, and blood went flying.' The concluding thoughts of an observing colonel – who watches with 'a smile in his heart' – sum up the novel's attitude to such behaviour: 'D___ rascals, but d___ good soldiers.'[29] Unlike *Wee Macgreegor Enlists*, Campbell's novel recognises serious social concerns such as domestic abuse, poverty, drunkenness and casual violence. Such issues are sanitised, however, by the novel's contention that these 'brutal qualities essential in war' can be channelled into '[t]he fights for Britain's Glory'.[30] Indeed, Campbell goes as far to claim that the men are suited to this task ideologically as well temperamentally. The Mileeshy men 'are instinctively conservative', every one 'at heart a Tory'.[31] '[D]own like an avalanche swept the sons of Empire,' writes Campbell, as the men charge the Germans in the novel's final scene.[32]

As we compare these examples, various facets of Scottish identity emerge within the works of authors which can be described as patriotic, pro-war and unionist. Hay adopts public school camaraderie aimed at his middle-class audience; Buchan's war tale takes place within the distinctive bounds of the thriller, although he also felt compelled to write poems in Scots; *Wee Macgreegor Enlists* provides a 'sentimental and stylised picture of working-class life in Glasgow'; *Private Spud Tamson*, meanwhile, glancingly recognises profound social issues it then subsumes within a narrative of militaristic enthusiasm.[33] To note these variations is not to dispute the obvious inclination of these texts to unionist politics. However, while aligning with the 'above' of the Union, each of these works has a distinct 'below' – as they represent different aspects of Scottish life, and do so in ways which are shaped by the genre and stylistic choices of the author. Not only was the writing of certain unionist authors highly engaged in the nuances of the Scottish war experience, there exists a body of literature about the First World War by Scots who do not fit this mould. Scottish writers who were apolitical or conscientious objectors also wrote memoirs and novels which lie outwith the pale of 'assimilatory Britishness'.

A liminal figure in this regard is John Reith, known today mainly for his role as the first Director-General of the BBC. Born in Stonehaven, Reith left work as an engineer at the Royal Albert Dock to serve as a transport officer with the 5th Scottish Rifles. He supervised the transfer of the unit's sixty-six horses and twenty-two wagons to France in October 1914 and secured a billet in Erquinghem. Reith was glad to be spared 'the ghastly boredom and discomfort of trench life', but his proximity to ration dumps and the 'traffic to and fro the trenches' frequently exposed him to enemy fire.[34] His imperious character created friction with certain superior officers, and in September 1915 he was transferred to the Royal Engineers, 2/2nd Highland Field Company. Just a few weeks later, on 7 October, Reith's war service ended when he was shot in the face while inspecting trenches at the front.

Reith's wartime memoir, *Wearing Spurs*, was written in 1937. His friends cautioned against publication, however, advising 'It is just what your enemies are waiting for.'[35] Eventually published in 1966, Reith's work is notable for the way it anticipates the highly influential ideas of Paul Fussell, who wrote, in *The Great War and Modern Memory* (1975): 'Every war constitutes an irony of situation because its means are so melodramatically disproportionate to its presumed ends.'[36] While he acknowledged the 'ghastly tragedy of death [. . .] and incapacitation' of war, Reith – applying his penchant for administration and the principles of efficiency from his engineering background – was repulsed by the 'appalling inefficiency' with which the war was conducted. He elaborates:

> Efforts and costs of all kinds in the Great War were utterly disproportionate to results [. . .] What portion of those whose names are commemorated on the hundred thousand memorials which star the land gave their lives, in fact less for God, King, and Country, than simply to stupidity, jealousy, and managerial incompetence.[37]

Adrian Gregory calls *Wearing Spurs* 'the great Scottish war memoir of the 1930s'.[38] Yet, while Reith's stewardship of the BBC has assured him a place in the history of British twentieth-century media studies, his memoir has attracted scant notice within discussions of Scottish literature.[39]

After the war, Reith worked as secretary to London Conservative MPs during the 1922 election. In 1922, he became General Manager of the BBC and from 1927 to 1938 served as its first Director-General. During World War II, Neville Chamberlain appointed Reith Minister of Information and he was found a safe seat in 1940 as MP for Southampton. After Churchill came to power, Reith was moved to Minister of Transport, becoming Minister of Works thereafter. In 1942, he was forced out of government and became Baron Reith of Stonehaven with a seat in the House of Lords.

Figuratively and literally, Reith – who stood at 6 foot 6 – was a gigantic figure in the British establishment. And he was a complex individual. A domineering personality, Reith was devoted to the principles that the BBC should broadcast 'all that is best in every department of human knowledge, endeavour, and achievement' while maintaining 'the preservation of a high moral tone'.[40] Despite his didacticism, Reith also strove to protect the BBC from political interference and rebuffed attempts to make the Corporation 'a propaganda machine' during the 1926 General Strike.[41] The son of the Presbyterian minister of College Church, Glasgow – who later became the Moderator of the United Free Church of Scotland – Reith was also a deeply religious man. These idiosyncrasies colour *Wearing Spurs*.

Reith had just turned twenty-five when war broke out. He recalled his feelings at this time:

> here was something tremendously exciting. In a sense I had been looking forward to war, and for years; now it was coming. It was an entirely personal affair; no thought of what it might mean to home, or country, or civilisation.[42]

Reith had a longstanding interest in the military, having joined the Glasgow Cadet Corps in 1901 and been commissioned in the Scottish Rifles in 1911. Military service appears to have appealed to him as a means of fulfilling or demonstrating his potential: allowing him the opportunity to command, display his capacity as an administrator, and pursue distinction. The main thread of *Wearing Spurs* centres on the friction generated by Reith's partially justified self-belief and the inevitable resentment this stirred in his superior officers.

Running alongside his highly developed sense of personal destiny, his profound religiosity also shaped Reith's identity. *Wearing Spurs* is written in fluid, confident prose containing Latin phrases and French dialogue. Virtually the only references to literary texts, however, are theological. Along with multiple quotations from the Psalms, Reith quotes texts such as John Greenleaf Whittier's 'The

Eternal Goodness' and John Keeble's *The Christian Year*. Reith described himself as possessing:

> strong religious convictions; certain that only a practical application of Christian principle in affairs national and international could ever bring peace and prosperity to the world. No party affiliations; only vaguely Liberal.[43]

Behind this religiousness looms the influence of Reith's upbringing as the son of a Presbyterian minister in Glasgow – one he repeatedly returns to in *Wearing Spurs*.

Reith's ambition of military service was epitomised by the imagined image of him 'returning unexpectedly from war and going up the aisle of College Church in Glasgow – but always and essentially to the ring of spurs'.[44] The night he was informed that his battalion was 'proceeding overseas at once', Reith's thoughts were not only 'of Mother and Father' but also of his urge to attend a service at 'College Church', aware he 'might never have the chance again'.[45] Prior to Easter Day 1915, twenty-two of Reith's nominally Presbyterian Transport Division members elected to 'join the Church' officially at a special service held by a minster in an *estaminet*. Pleased to see his men 'brought into this new relationship with God', Reith wrote to inform his father; all twenty-two names are recorded in *Wearing Spurs*.[46] The following service on Easter Day prompted Reith to reminisce on the proceedings of 'Communion services in College Church'; afterwards, he halted his party of men to add that 'if we can't carry the significance of [the service] into our work, then we shall be making a farce of it'.[47]

Reith was able to fulfil his 'silly (or splendid) fantasy' of returning to his father's church from war 'to the ring of spurs'. His account of the episode may explain the significance of his conflation of church and army in this anticipated moment. Reith was early infatuated with 'the sight and sound and superiority' of spurs.[48] Furthermore, as he notes, '[i]n churches in Scotland the Manse pew is usually at the front, and its occupants are not only observable, but very much observed'.[49] Thus the experience of wearing spurs in his home church unites two of the things most important to Reith: faith and the visible demonstration of his superiority. Andrew Boyle describes Reith as 'an instinctive patriot', but there is little discernible engagement with the war as a means to defend the Empire or uphold the Union in *Wearing Spurs*.[50] Instead, Reith's memoir showcases a confirmed individualist facing the challenges of the Great War – steeled by 'the intuitive certainty that he was predestined by a God [. . .] to carry out some important task in life'.[51]

David Rorie's *A Medico's Luck in the War* (1929) forms another high-quality, yet under-studied text. Born in Edinburgh in 1867, Rorie spent his childhood in Aberdeen, before returning to the capital to gain M.B. and C.M. degrees from Edinburgh University. He pursued various roles before moving in 1894 to serve as a 'medical superintendent for a group of collieries' in Auchterderran, Fife, and from 1905 to 1933 worked as a GP at Cults outside Aberdeen. A highly energetic figure, Rorie published two books of poetry – *The Auld Doctor and Other Poems and Songs in Scots* (1920) and *The Lum Hat Wantin' the Croon and Other Poems* (1935) – and was joint editor of the *Caledonian Medical Journal* from 1911 to 1937. He was also a noted folklorist, whom David Buchan describes as the first in Scotland 'to record the culture of an industrial community: that of the Fife miners'.[52]

Aged forty-seven in 1914, Rorie was mobilised as part of the Territorial Force's 1st Highland Field Ambulance. He arrived at Le Havre in May 1915 and remained in service six months beyond the armistice. In his memoir, Rorie also has recourse to Latin phrases and incorporates French dialogue, but his referential palate is more expansive and secular than Reith's. Rorie compares the detailed relation of his journey through France to the geographical exactitude of Xenophon.[53] At Béthune, 'once the adventure country of "The Three Musketeers"', Rorie wonders what Dumas's heroes would make of 'rum in a tin mug' or 'four years of trench warfare'.[54] *A Medico's Luck in the War* is littered with references to Dickens, Shakespeare, Brueghel, Hogarth and various classical deities.

Yet Rorie maintains a constant focus on Scottish identity. Quotations from the poetry of Allan Ramsay and William Dunbar appear alongside anecdotes of Scots servicemen. For example, one Royal Army Medical Corps (RAMC) private is asked if he wears the '*courte jupe*'. '"Ach! The Kilt!" he replied: "Na, na: owre muckle bendin' aboot oor job, wifie! Compree?"'[55] Another Scottish RAMC man, Corporal Charlie – 'one of the best known characters in our unit' – blusters his way through the language barrier when addressing German prisoners:

> '*Nine*, ye gommeral? It's nae nine: it's twal' o' ye! C'wa noo! Look slippy! *You*, Nosey!' (indicating a gentleman endowed in this way by nature). 'An' *you*, Breeks!' (to another, the seat of whose trousers was severely damaged by barbed wire).[56]

These comedic vernacular episodes could be viewed in the same vein as the Scottish characters in *The First Hundred Thousand* and *Private Spud Tamson*: a celebration of Scottish individuality within a cheerful endorsement of the Union and Empire. Yet would Rorie, as a Scottish folklorist and vernacular poet, be likely to view these episodes in such a way?

Rorie's poem 'The Pawky Duke' is a satirical rebuff to the stereotypical image of the Scot 'known to the Southron': 'pawkiness and pride of race; love of the dram'. Rorie's Duke:

> [. . .] dined each day on the usquebae [whisky]
>   An' he washed it doon wi' haggis. [. . .]
> For that's the way that the Heelanters dae
>   Whaur the foamin' flood an' the crag is![57]

Rorie's playful disdain of the caricature of the Scot held by English audiences calls into question whether his depictions of Scots in *A Medico's Luck in the War* are formed along the lines of an assimilatory Britishness. Further examples from his memoir strengthen this impression:

> the true *liaison* between the British and French armies was the Scottish troops. This statement is curiously true – for two reasons. One is that many of the English had never got away from the 'd– foreigner' idea of the Napoleonic Wars: the other, that sentiment of the 'Auld Alliance' persisted strongly amongst the French, both military and civilian.[58]

This Franco-Scots bond is exemplified in a later episode when a local civilian learns that Rorie is Scottish. The Frenchman 'started off at once on Marie Stuart': 'For the Scots, yes – you are our ancient allies! But the English [. . .] Of course, they too are our allies and we must love them; but for me it is difficult!'[59] Rorie's memoir points to an understated – but unmistakable – feeling of solidarity among the Auld Alliance, one that is not matched by the members of the Union.

Without there being any obvious animosity between the Scottish and English forces, there are subtly – but clearly defined – expressions of discrete national characteristics. When an Englishman complains of some Americans, who have butchered and eaten a pig he had been saving for his own table, Rorie cites the example of St Serf from the *Chronicle* of Andrew Wyntoun (c.1350–c.1425). In this episode, the guilt of a thief who has stolen one of St Serf's sheep is revealed, somewhat grotesquely, when the digested 'sheep then bleated in his wame [belly]'. Unsurprisingly, this obscure reference does not register: 'Never heard of the blighter! Damn these gum-chewers, anyway!'[60] Rorie's cultural in-joke suggests a level of Scottish autonomy within the British army, one reinforced by his interlocutor's exemplification of the English disdain for foreigners identified earlier in the narrative.

Wearing Spurs and *A Medico's Luck in the War* are examples of highly readable memoirs which do not fall comfortably within the parameters of a North British perspective of the Great War. Similarly, there are at least two outstanding novels reflecting first-hand experiences of the conflict by Scots which – as far as I can tell – have not been widely appreciated as war texts. George Blake (1893–1961) was born in Greenock and interrupted his legal studies at Glasgow University to serve in Gallipoli. Blake drew on these experiences in *The Path of Glory* (1929). The novel centres around Col Macaulay, a twenty-year-old from Benbecula in the Outer Hebrides, who has emigrated to the shipyards of Clydeside. Described as one of 'the Highland tinkers, slow and hazy of mind', Col's sole interest is his 'deep inarticulate love for the art of the bagpipe'.[61] Following the outbreak of war, he enlists as a piper alongside his friend John Macleod and their paternal co-worker, Deveney. Posted to Cults farm for training, Col encounters the promiscuous Kirsty Galbraith, whom he begins dating and soon marries. Shortly afterwards, Kirsty gives birth to a child fathered by another man.

At Devonport, Col's company board – to their joy – the Clyde-built *Alsatia* and sail, via Gozo and Lemnos, to Cape Helles on the Gallipoli Peninsula. As Col's battalion makes its way into the lines, their enthusiasm is tempered as they begin to perceive the absence of any clear idea – throughout the chain of command – as to the strategy and goals of the manœuvres they participate in. These men of the shipyards follow a 'boy officer' who is 'not at all clear as to the fate of the battalion': 'It was often like that in the field – as if [. . .] a trench-system was really an affair beyond human control, as if the Staff trusted largely to luck. There seemed to be no taut plan about it all.'[62]

After their guide loses his way, the men are directed to dig a new trench in the open; they are discovered and come under fire from 'rifles and machine-guns blazing fire and lead'.[63] The men then leave the trenches and are ordered to a gully, where they are forced to wait – apparently forgotten – for an entire day without water. Deveney complains to a junior officer about this oversight: 'The subaltern smiled cynically and shrugged his shoulders. It was none of his business. It was always the business of somebody in authority. The chain of responsibility ran on and on – till it passed out of sight.'[64]

To his distress, Col is made a runner and is unable to join John and Deveney when his comrades attack the Turkish positions. Believing his friends have been killed, Col – disobeying his orders – goes in search of them. When he finds the corpse of Deveney lying over a trench parados, a passing stretcher-bearer observes: 'That poor bloke's copped it all right. Ope they get 'im buried before 'e stinks.'[65] Refusing medical attention for a shrapnel wound in his wrist, Col sneaks into no-man's-land and reaches the enemy trenches. There he is shot in the back and lies in his own blood until he is taken into a Turkish ambulance. Col is then deposited at a roadside, where he finds himself in view of the sea and the hills of Asia. As he lies dying, the view recalls to Col 'the hills of Scotland in the sweet summer', and he imagines himself 'back again in the Isles'.[66] Though poignant, Blake undercuts any sentimentality in this scene with the concluding line: 'It did not matter very much that Col Macaulay at length lay dead under the alien stars.'[67]

As Jenny Macleod writes, *The Path of Glory* possesses 'several features of the soldiers' tale, such as confused battle descriptions and strange incidents' – not least its ironic title.[68] Yet Blake is careful to make the point that, though they may be fighting a war they cannot understand, these men of Clydeside are proud of their readiness to serve. Though, as skilled workers, they are offered the chance to leave their unit and join the munitions effort, none does so. Deveney even offers to 'knock the flakin' heid aff any man that says he's going back'.[69] At the front, a soldier's self-inflicted wound damages 'the pride of the Company', while John and Deveney are 'hard put to it' to console Col after he is excluded from a combat role.[70] It is possible, of course, that such feelings would subside during and after the war. The novel, furthermore, is forthright in its suggestion that these men deserve better leadership. But a strength of *The Path of Glory* lies in its avoidance of a laboured didactic indictment of the establishment. Blake's direct, understated ending resonates with a poignant sense of the purposeless loss of young lives during the war.

Edward Gaitens (1897–1966) was born in Glasgow and served two years in Wormwood Scrubs during World War I for his beliefs as a conscientious objector – experiences which inform his 1948 novel *Dance of the Apprentices*. Beginning in Glasgow's notorious Gorbals district in the years prior to World War I, Gaitens's novel unflinchingly depicts the squalor, drunkenness and poverty which appear in a sanitised, comedic vein in the opening chapters of *Private Spud Tamson*. Some of Gaitens's characters hope to transcend the circumstances they have been born into, however. To young Socialist Eddy

Macdonnel, the deprived environment of alcoholism and domestic violence in which he has been raised is a direct result of poverty generated by the capitalist system. For him, 'Poverty made brutes and wastrels of human beings. Socialism would bring plenty and freedom for all mankind.'[71]

The novel follows the effect of the war on the lives of Eddy, his two Socialist friends – Neil and Donald – and three other Macdonnel brothers – John, Francie and James. Eddy conceives of the war along the lines of political idealism: to enlist is merely to volunteer oneself as 'cannon-fodder to the Juggernaut of Mammon and Militarism'.[72] He, Donald and Neil each hold to their socialist principles and refuse to fight in the capitalist war. Also passionately opposed to the conflict, Francie ignores his calling-up papers, but by some clerical error is never called up again. The novel, however, accommodates a spectrum of views on the war. For Jimmy, enlistment represents a means of escape from the position of being 'unemployed, unloved and deeply out of tone with life'.[73] John, though free from conscription because of his skill set as a Worker of National Importance, is pressured into enlistment by his sweetheart's reluctance to date a shirker.

H. Gustav Klaus writes that the 'longing' Eddy, Neil and Donald display 'for beauty, knowledge, and truth is serious, if not free from conceit and self-importance'.[74] In Gaitens's novel, war is the supreme – and in the end, insurmountable – test of such youthful idealism. James is killed on active service with the 7th Cameronian Scottish Rifles. John survives the war to become a dyspeptic town councillor trapped in a staid marriage to a socially ambitious wife. Donald serves an eighteen-month sentence at a Government Work Centre in Dartmoor; afterwards, 'his nerves [. . .] slowly gone to pieces with long unemployment', he attempts suicide for a second time.[75] After his release from prison, Neil struggles to find employment and becomes trapped in a marriage with 'a dull commonplace woman'; grimly, he observes that '[l]ife as expression and development was ending for him'.[76] Eddy, meanwhile, having refused to work at a government camp in the Highlands, serves a two-year sentence, including solitary confinement of a three-month duration which he earns for attempting to incite a rebellion amongst his fellow objectors. In his cell, depressed and isolated, Eddy concedes that his 'gesture' of attempting to 'suffer as much for pacifism as soldiers were suffering for patriotism had been one of mere vanity'.[77]

Klaus observes: 'These apprentices in social idealism have all been failures in one sense or another'.[78] There is, however, some ambiguity as to why the apprentices' ideals fail. Are they conditional on a youthful zeal which cannot survive into adult maturity? Or are the apprentices bound to failure, given their resistance to forces they cannot possibly overpower – in which case there is a redemptive nobility in their dearly bought gestures of protest? Rather than offering a definite assessment, *Dance of the Apprentices* explores the costs and limitations of idealism, as the wartime experiences of Eddy, Donald and Neil erode their faith in the possibility of achieving a fairer world.

Several of the characters in Gaitens's novel find the war morally unconscionable and hold to those beliefs at steep personal cost. *The Path of Glory* starkly addresses the poignant human cost of the conflict and – like *Wearing Spurs* – points to serious shortcomings in the manner in which it was fought. First World War literary studies, however, has long moved away from viewing the literature of the conflict as primarily reflecting a pervasive revulsion with the means and ends of war. Samuel Hynes summarised this reductive, yet indelible, paradigm as the widespread belief that

> a generation of innocent young men, their heads full of high abstractions like Honour, Glory, and England, went off to war to make the world safe for democracy. They were slaughtered in stupid battles planned by stupid generals. Those who survived were shocked, disillusioned and embittered by their war experiences, and saw that their real enemies were not the Germans but the old men at home who had lied to them.[79]

The main purpose of this chapter has been to point to the existence of a body of Scottish Great War prose – albeit relatively small, though one which may be expanded by further research – which is comparable to more recognised works by Hemingway, Remarque and Manning. This is not to say, however, that the relevance of these Scottish texts simply emanates from their adherence to the 'Myth of the War', as summarised by Hynes.

Today it is more common to recognise that, in the words of Ian Isherwood, '[r]ather than affirming any particular zeitgeist, war books instead reflected a broad spectrum of interpretations of the Great War, most somewhere in the middle of the wide gulf between abject disillusionment and propagandist patriotism'.[80] Furthermore, as David Taylor notes, individual writers often combined 'an undoubted awareness of the suffering caused by the war and often a profound anger' alongside 'widespread humour, a continuing faith in the rightness of the cause and little general disillusionment'.[81] The work of Reith, Rorie, Blake and Gaitens lies somewhere within this reconfigured understanding of

World War I literature: that is, writing which is forthright about the war's destructive capacity and critical of its leadership and presumed aims, while also accommodating more redemptive or commendable aspects of warfare, such as fortitude, pride in service, and camaraderie.

More than just presenting a multifaceted view of war, these works convey aspects of a specifically Scottish war experience which are not necessarily subsumed within a wider British identity. Reith, a Presbyterian individualist, is more absorbed in his own destiny than that of the nation. In Rorie's memoir, Scottish servicemen feel a sense of fellowship with the French, rather than English, forces. In *The Path of Glory*, John and Col go to war 'mad with pride' to carry on the tradition of the music they love by serving as pipers.[82] The most immediate motivation of the men in Blake's novel seems to be loyalty to the battalion whose 'pride' and 'repute' they guard fiercely: there is seldom any consciousness of wider motivation.[83] Gaitens's novel depicts with profound realism the effects of the war on a Gorbals family, all of whom experience the war differently: as a means of escape, a role acquiesced through social pressure, and an impermissible capitalist outrage.

Perhaps the ubiquitous association of poetry with the First World War in Britain – and the greater ease with which it can be anthologised – has contributed to the relative neglect of these texts. They demonstrate, to some extent at least, the existence of writers whose accounts drew on aspects of Scottish identity – religion, music, politics, intra-battalion loyalties, vernacular humour and social realism – without any apparent sense of belonging to – or serving – a wider unionist or colonial identity.

Notes

1. Adrian Gregory, *The Last Great War: British Society and the First World War* (Cambridge: Cambridge University Press, 2008), p. 83.
2. David Goldie, 'The British Invention of Scottish Culture: The First World War and Before', *Review of Scottish Culture*, vol. 18 (2006), pp. 128–48, p. 131.
3. Ibid. p. 128.
4. Ibid. pp. 138, 139.
5. Ibid. p. 143.
6. Ibid. pp. 143, 144.
7. Ibid. p. 144.
8. Ibid. p. 132.

9. David Goldie, 'Scotland for Ever? British Literature, Scotland and the First World War', in Edna Longley, Eamonn Hughes and Des O'Rawe (eds), *Ireland (Ulster) Scotland: Concepts, Contexts, Comparisons* (Belfast: Queen's University Belfast, 2003), pp. 113–20, p. 114.
10. Ian Hay, *The First Hundred Thousand* (Edinburgh: William Blackwood and Sons, 1915), pp. 17, 149.
11. Ibid. p. 174.
12. Ibid. p. 37.
13. George Urquhart, 'Confrontation and Withdrawal: Loos, Readership and *The First Hundred Thousand*', in Catriona M. M. Macdonald and E. W. McFarland (eds), *Scotland and the Great War* (Edinburgh: Birlinn, 1999), pp. 125–44, p. 126.
14. Hay, *The First Hundred Thousand*, p. 50.
15. Ibid. p. 120.
16. Ibid. p. 171.
17. David Goldie, 'Scotland, Britishness, and the First World War', in Gerald Carruthers, David Goldie and Alastair Renfrew (eds), *Beyond Scotland: New Contexts for Twentieth-Century Scottish Literature* (Amsterdam: Rodopi, 2004), pp. 37–57, p. 45.
18. John Buchan, *Mr Standfast* (London: Thomas Nelson and Sons, [1919] 1954), p. 23.
19. Goldie, 'Scotland, Britishness, and the First World War', p. 46.
20. Goldie, 'The British Invention of Scottish Culture: The First World War and Before', p. 132.
21. Douglas Gifford, 'The Roots that Clutch: John Buchan, Scottish Fiction and Scotland', in Kate Macdonald and Nathan Waddell (eds), *John Buchan and the Idea of Modernity* (London: Routledge, 2016), pp. 17–33, p. 17.
22. Macdonald Daly, 'Scottish Poetry and the Great War', *Scottish Literary Journal*, vol. 21, no. 2 (1994), pp. 79–96, pp. 80, 81, p. 83.
23. Gifford, 'The Roots that Clutch: John Buchan, Scottish Fiction and Scotland', pp. 18, 28.
24. J. J. Bell, *Wee Macgreegor Enlists* (Edinburgh: Birlinn, [1915] 1993), p. 202.
25. Ibid. p. 207.
26. R. W. Campbell, *Private Spud Tamson* (Edinburgh and London: William Blackwood & Sons, 1915), p. 4.
27. Ibid. p. 80.
28. Ibid. p. 88.
29. Ibid. p. 76.
30. Ibid. pp. 71, 8.
31. Ibid. p. 269.
32. Ibid. p. 289.
33. Trevor Royle, *The Macmillan Companion to Scottish Literature* (London: Macmillan Press, 1983), p. 26.

34. John Reith, *Wearing Spurs* (London: Hutchison, 1966), p. 69.
35. Ibid. p. 11.
36. Paul Fussell, *The Great War and Modern Memory* (Oxford: Oxford University Press, 1975), p. 7.
37. Reith, *Wearing Spurs*, pp. 34–6.
38. Gregory, *The Last Great War: British Society and the First World War*, p. 83.
39. Passages from *Wearing Spurs* have been excerpted in two anthologies edited by Trevor Royle. See *In Flanders Fields: Scottish Poetry and Prose of the First World War* (Edinburgh: Mainstream, 1990), pp. 248–55, and *Isn't All This Bloody?: Scottish Writing From the First World War* (Edinburgh: Birlinn, 2014), pp. 227–40. Reith's memoir is also discussed in Brian Bond's *Survivors of a Kind: Memoirs of the Western Front* (London: Continuum, 2008), pp. 45–58, and in John Broom's *Fight the Good Fight: Voices of Faith from the First World War* (Barnsley: Pen and Sword Military, 2015).
40. John Reith, qtd in Robert S. Fortner, *Radio, Morality and Culture: Britain, Canada and Culture, 1919–1945* (Carbondale: South Illinois Press, 2003), p. 202.
41. Thomas Gibbons, '"Club Government" and Independence in Media Regulation', in Monroe E. Price, Stefaan Verhulst and Libby Morgan (eds), *Routledge Handbook of Media Law* (London: Routledge, 2013), pp. 47–65, p. 50.
42. Reith, *Wearing Spurs*, p. 13.
43. John Reith, *Into the Wind* (London: Hodder and Stoughton, 1949), p. 80.
44. Reith, *Wearing Spurs*, p. 15.
45. Ibid. pp. 42–3.
46. Ibid. p. 154.
47. Ibid. p. 159.
48. Ibid. p. 15.
49. Ibid. p. 131.
50. Andrew Boyle, *Only the Wind Will Listen: Reith of the* BBC (London: Hutchinson, 1972), p. 53.
51. Ibid. p. 73.
52. David Buchan, 'Introduction', in *Folk Tradition and Folk Medicine in Scotland: The Writings of David Rorie*, ed. David Buchan (Edinburgh: Canongate Academic, 1994), pp. 1–16, p. 11. Rorie took an active interest in the miners, becoming 'a member of the Parish Council [. . .], chairman of the Auchterderran School Board, and a Justice of the Peace'. He also wrote to the *British Medical Journal*, calling for the universal 'legislative enactment' of accident stations in collieries. See Buchan, 'Introduction', in *Folk Tradition and Folk Medicine in Scotland: The Writings of David Rorie*, p. 2.
53. David Rorie, *A Medico's Luck in the War* (Aberdeen: Milne and Hutchison, 1929), p. 4.

54. Ibid. p. 48.
55. Ibid. p. 20.
56. Ibid. p. 109.
57. David Rorie, *The Auld Doctor and Other Poems and Songs in Scots* (London: Constable, 1920), p. 6.
58. Rorie, *A Medico's Luck in the War*, p. 19.
59. Ibid. p. 231.
60. Ibid. p. 181.
61. George Blake, *The Path of Glory* (London: Constable, 1929), p. 10.
62. Ibid. pp. 154, 158.
63. Ibid. p. 163.
64. Ibid. p. 168.
65. Ibid. p. 213.
66. Ibid. p. 223.
67. Ibid. p. 224.
68. Jenny Macleod, *Reconsidering Gallipoli* (Manchester: Manchester University Press, 2004), p. 172.
69. Blake, *The Path of Glory*, p. 109.
70. Ibid. pp. 181, 191.
71. Edward Gaitens, *Dance of the Apprentices* (Edinburgh: Canongate, [1948], 1990), p. 19.
72. Ibid. p. 108.
73. Ibid. p. 106.
74. H. Gustav Klaus, 'Individual, Community and Conflict in Working-Class Fiction, 1920–1940', in Scott Lyall (ed.), *Community in Modern Literature*, (Leiden: Brill, 2016), pp. 43–60, p. 58.
75. Gaitens, *Dance of the Apprentices*, p. 192.
76. Ibid. pp. 221–2.
77. Ibid. p. 252.
78. Klaus, 'Individual, Community and Conflict in Working-Class Fiction, 1920–1940', p. 58.
79. Samuel Hynes, *A War Imagined* (London: Pimlico, [1990] 1992), p. x.
80. Ian Isherwood, *Remembering the Great War: Writing and Publishing the Experiences of the Great War* (London: I. B. Tauris, 2017), p. 4.
81. David Taylor, *Memory, Narrative and the Great War: Rifleman Patrick MacGill and the Construction of Wartime Experience* (Liverpool: Liverpool University Press, 2013), p. 80.
82. Blake, *The Path of Glory*, p. 42.
83. Ibid. pp. 95, 107.

Chapter 3

Unquiet on the Home Front: Scottish Popular Fiction and the Truth of War
David Goldie

Ever since C. E. Montague's account of wartime disillusionment, *Disenchantment* (1922), it has been common to believe that the popular press in the First World War played a part in effectively silencing soldiers: representing the actions in which they were involved in vague euphemistic terms; relying heavily on either outright lies or an outdated and inappropriate vocabulary of heroism, glory and honour to render the experience of wartime unrecognisable to the soldiers themselves; forcing a cognitive chasm between servicemen and credulous civilians across which meaningful communication was no longer possible. These are the arguments that underpin Paul Fussell's analysis of the corrosive ubiquity of wartime euphemism in *The Great War and Modern Memory*.[1] They underline, too, Samuel Hynes's diagnosis of an 'unbridgeable gap' between soldier and civilian with its consequent debauching of the currency of language, and contribute to Randall Stevenson's characterisation of the First World War as an 'unspeakable war'.[2]

The aim of this chapter is not to refute such interpretations but to qualify them – particularly as they relate to the part played by popular fiction and film in the war. There can be no doubt that many soldiers were embittered by the failure of civilians to understand their experiences fully, and there is ample evidence to suggest that much popular culture was complicit in perpetuating the kinds of damaging euphemism of which literary historians complain. Aspects of that culture will be explored below, but so too will other strands of popular fiction that were much more direct and unambiguous in their representations of the war. These not only challenge assumptions that popular writing about the war was uniformly evasive and misleading, but also raise additional and awkward questions about where the responsibility lay for the breakdown in communication between soldiers and their civilian counterparts.

I.

The most trenchant post-war critic of the damage done by the war to free, accurate expression was C. E. Montague – a journalist on the *Manchester Guardian* who had played a part in the war's news management as an officer in military intelligence. His disaffected polemic *Disenchantment* (1922) was written out of frustration at having seen his own and others' good intentions compromised by the many evasions, half-truths and occasional outright lies necessitated by war. In a chapter tellingly titled 'You Can't Believe a Word You Read', he vented a long-suppressed anger at the complicity between the General Staff and war writers in betraying the experience of the ordinary soldier:

> 'Our casualties will be enormous', a General at G.H.Q. said with the utmost serenity on the eve of one of our great attacks in 1917. The average war correspondent – there were golden exceptions – insensibly acquired the same cheerfulness in face of vicarious torment and danger. In his work it came out at times in a certain jauntiness of tone that roused the fighting troops to fury against the writer. Through his despatches there ran a brisk implication that regimental officers and men enjoyed nothing better than 'going over the top'; that a battle was just a rough, jovial picnic; that a fight never went on long enough for the men; that their only fear was lest the war should end on this side of the Rhine. This, the men reflected in helpless anger, was what people at home were offered as faithful accounts of what their friends in the field were thinking and suffering.[3]

Philip Gibbs, the official war correspondent of the *Daily Chronicle*, *Daily Telegraph* and *Glasgow Herald*, and perhaps the war's most highly regarded journalist, had reported under Montague's censorship.[4] But he shared Montague's low opinion of the relationship between a complacent military and complaisant press. In *Realities of War* (1920; published in the United States as 'Now It can be Told'), Gibbs recalled General Hague's rather limited estimation of the role and capabilities of the press and his encouragement to journalists 'to get hold of little stories of heroism, and so forth, and to write them up in a bright way to make good reading for Mary Ann in the kitchen, and the man in the street'. Gibbs demurred, but still found himself content to accept wartime censorship and make his accounts within its constraints, even though, as he said, 'I had to leave out something of the underlying horror of them all, in spite of my continual emphasis, by temperament and by conviction, on the tragedy of all this sacrifice of youth.'⁵ Gibbs came out of the war with a pride in having done a decent job in difficult circumstances, but also (and perhaps like Montague) a nagging worry at having been complicit in shielding the newspaper-reading public from the worst of the war's horror and the occasional incompetence of those who managed it. He also emerged with the realisation that wartime censorship had been driven less by a concern about offering comfort to the enemy than by suppressing dissent at home: 'it was', as he put it, 'fear of their own people, not of the enemy, which guided the rules of censorship, then and later'.⁶

Daily and evening newspapers were the principal means of conveying information from the front, and the work of intelligence officers such as Montague and compliant official correspondents like Gibbs meant that such information was often limited in its scope and detail. Access was restricted and news managed – sometimes for honourable reasons, as well as dishonourable ones – and as a consequence most reporters could do little other than serve up the information from the front in a manner palatable to the military and civil authorities.

The conditions for other forms of coverage, particularly those of reportage or fiction, which placed a higher premium on colour and atmosphere than on matters of strategy and fact, were, however, considerably less restrictive. From the very beginning of the war, readers in Scotland, as elsewhere in the UK, looked to supplement the bare facts of newspaper coverage with more vivid tales of frontline experience from other sources. One ready supply came in the weekly papers, which had a long tradition of employing features and fiction to supplement their commentaries on the news of the day. The most significant of these, and easily the best-selling in Scotland at the time, was the *People's Journal*.

The *Journal*'s characteristic slant on the hostilities, especially in the war's early stages, can be seen in a feature titled 'The Gunners' Last Stand', which it published in November 1914. The story is ostensibly a piece of factual reporting that details a recent action in which two members of the Royal Field Artillery have won Victoria Crosses. The piece's veracity as reportage is somewhat compromised by the stylistic choices it makes – preferring, for example, to use the omniscient narration of fiction rather than the subjective perspective of an identifiable eye-witness, and quoting implausibly long sections of direct speech. The piece's unashamedly tabloid style – with its descriptive prose, hackneyed metaphors and historical references, and its formulaic characterisations of valour – makes it seem the epitome of General Hague's 'little stories of heroism' for 'Mary Ann in the kitchen, and the man in the street':

> Nelson's face was ghastly; his lips were blue and his teeth chattered as though with bitter cold. But in his eyes there burnt a spirit dauntless as that of his immortal namesake of Trafalgar.
> 'You've done your bit,' said Captain Bradbury. 'You aren't fit to go on fighting, Nelson; it's time you retired from the fighting line.'
> He gave orders for him to be carried to the rear.
> But Nelson laughed grimly. Not if General French himself was to bid him retire would he obey while that German gun remained unbeaten, he declared.
> Captain Bradbury was about to remonstrate once more. There was a momentary lull in the firing, and Nelson had a chance to get to the rear which might not come again.
> 'I'm staying here,' gasped Nelson. 'I may be useful yet.'
> As the words left his lips there came the scream of a shell. They felt the wind on their faces. It was the best-aimed shell that had come as yet, and as it struck the earth and burst, they were half-paralysed for a moment by the shock of the explosion. Brown whirling earth: green choking fumes blotting out everything next moment. The green fumes curled away, and revealed the shattered body of Lieutenant Campbell.
> 'Fight on Boys!' he gasped; then he crawled under a limber and died.[7]

The bridge that such an article makes between factual reporting and magazine fiction is one that many fictional war stories and books were also happy to make – larding ostensibly factual tales of military experience with the familiar tropes of popular fiction. A common factor in these was the winning of the Victoria Cross. Stories in popular magazines were quick to adapt their formulae to accommodate this honour as the acme of manly endeavour, as were novels arriving at the fag end of the Kailyard tradition. The story 'Ian Stuart V.C.: A Hero of the War', in the *People's Friend*, was one of very many magazine stories to give this heroic, military twist to the boy-wins-girl formula common to women's magazines.[8] J. L. Dickie's tales of the couthy country folk of 'Glengollach', collected in *Peter Tamson: Elder o' the Kirk and Sportsman* (1915), similarly bent its serio-comic schtick in this direction, having its hero enlisting at the improbably advanced age of 55 (with the help of a London theatrical wig-maker) and winning the highest honour in saving the life of a young subaltern.[9]

Many popular works by serving soldiers (almost always officers) saw a similar tendency towards what Montague characterised as a casual 'cheerfulness in face of vicarious torment and danger' and a 'jauntiness of tone' that betrayed the true nature of the conditions under which the war was being fought. R. W. Campbell's highly popular series of novels featuring the reformed reprobate Spud Tamson (a Catholic-Irish son of Glasgow's Saltmarket, who discovers his life's purpose in military, and later imperial, service – and another fictional winner of the Victoria Cross)[10] reduces military life to a series of quirky humorous adventures, along the way peddling the deceit noted by Montague that our men enjoying nothing more than 'going over the top':

> 'Fix bayonets prepare to charge,' was the next order flashed along the line. The clicking of the steel rings on the bayonet standards was a cheerful sound to all.
> 'Charge!' A wild hurrah was heard from seven thousand men. Seven thousand bayonets gleamed in the now sparkling sun. And down like an avalanche swept the sons of Empire. Words can never depict a charge. It is wild, almost insane, yet glorious [. . .] And this was an Imperial charge a charge of willing volunteers, who loved the Motherland.
> The stupefied Germans were horror-struck. Seven thousand fresh and lusty warriors struck terror into their hearts. And those bayonets! Well, who wouldn't run! They fled like hares on a frosty morning, pursued by the yelling and stabbing multitude.[11]

What edge there might be here, in the portrayal of the awful terror of a bayonet charge, is somewhat blunted by the amiable, colloquial tone ('And those bayonets! Well, who wouldn't run!) and the depiction of Germans, like something out of Surtees, fleeing like hares on a frosty morning. In many ways, both thematic and stylistic, the war is being rendered here, as Montague had feared, as a kind of 'rough, jovial picnic'.

Similar qualities can be seen, too, in Ian Hay's best-selling *The First Hundred Thousand* (1915).[12] Like Campbell, Hay was a popular writer turned military officer, and his account of military life and warfare is similarly softened by the good-humoured patronage his narrator extends to his 'humorously-pathetic' men, lauding both the cheerfulness and the resolve of these 'sturdy, valiant legions' even as they face the horrors of the Battle of Loos.[13]

It appears clear, then, that Montague's denunciations of the wartime press for misrepresenting the experience of the conflict might also be applied to the works of supposed reportage and fiction appearing in wartime magazines and popular books. Works like Hay's and Dickie's had appeared first as serialised contributions to magazines, as had other works of their ilk, such as Thomas M. Lyon's *In Kilt and*

Khaki books and Lachlan MacLean Watt's *In France and Flanders with the Fighting Men*.[14] The determination of such coverage to stay within the conventional boundaries of popular magazine journalism, most notably through its use of stereotypical characterisation, a non-confrontational approach to class and social difference, and a persistent tone of ameliorative optimism, appears to bear out the claims of Fussell and Hynes that journalism and popular culture had a deadening effect on the war's participants: alienating servicemen who knew the whole truth, and insulating civilians who were denied knowledge of the less agreeable facts of the war.

II.

But this is only part of the story. For there were other witnesses to the war who wrote troubling accounts of action for readers on the home front. One of these, also present at the Battle of Loos, was Patrick MacGill. MacGill was an Irish immigrant to Scotland, who had risen before the public eye as the author of graphic accounts of the appalling poverty of working-class Scotland in his autobiographical novels *Children of the Dead End* (1914) and *The Rat-Pit* (1915). He had already published two lightly fictionalised accounts of his experiences of the war in *The Amateur Army* (1915) and *Red Horizon* (1915) before describing his experiences of the Battle of Loos in his third, *The Great Push* (1916). This book offered a noticeably grimmer take on the battle than that offered by Hay and Campbell. In one episode, for example, MacGill finds himself struggling across the battlefield at night:

> At that moment I tripped on something soft and went headlong across it. A dozen rats slunk away into the darkness as I fell. I got to my feet again and looked at the dead man [. . .] Buffeted by the breeze, battered by the rains it rotted in the open. Worms feasted on its entrails, slugs trailed silvery over its face, and lean rats gnawed at its flesh. The air was full of the thing, the night stank with its decay.[15]

The tone here is markedly different to the jovial stoicism of Hay or Campbell, which, like the story of the Gunners in the *People's Journal*, tend to keep the intimacies of death and wounding at arm's length, obscured in a fog of metaphor and euphemism. Here the facts of death and the slow rotting of the body are inescapable, lying exposed in the open to be bumped into and tripped over by narrator and reader alike. Also markedly absent from MacGill's account is a sense of wider purpose, of a necessary sacrifice. His litany of the battle's devastating aftermath is noticeably scant of consolation in its descriptions of the trenches

> fringed with dead; dead soldiers in khaki lay on the reverse slope of the parapet, their feet in the grass, their heads on the sandbags; they lay behind the parados, on the levels, in the woods, everywhere. Upwards of eleven thousand English dead littered the streets of Loos and the country round after the victory, and many of these were unburied yet.
>
> A low-lying country, wet fields, stagnant drains, shell-rent roads, ruined houses, dead men, mangled horses. To us soldiers this was the only apparent result of the battle of Loos.[16]

If, as Gibbs asserted, the greatest concern of those prosecuting the war was how to ensure that the public were not overly unsettled by graphic representations of warfare, it might be reasonable to expect that accounts like his would be suppressed. MacGill was a serving soldier under military discipline, after all, and even as his book was going through the press in early 1916 the authorities were stamping down on dissent among munitions workers on the Clyde – closing down briefly the Glasgow Independent Labour newspaper *Forward* and permanently the Socialist *Vanguard*, while exiling members of the Clyde Workers Committee from Glasgow.[17]

But, in fact, MacGill's work met no impediment and instead received considerable backing from its publisher and from reviewers, quickly selling 50,000 copies in its first six months. Reviewers were quick to note and to praise the book's rawer qualities – one fearing that its 'realism at times is almost too graphic', and another describing it as 'very painful reading' for its presentation of 'all the terrible aspects of the struggle'.[18] *The Scotsman*'s reviewer similarly hesitated over MacGill's 'almost morbid tendency to dwell upon the more painful aspects of the struggle for existence', but hailed *The Great Push* for offering an 'extraordinarily vivid idea of the psychical and physical experiences of the individual soldier'.[19] So the book was widely welcomed. And this welcome extended to his employers in the military, who did not simply allow the book to be published but actively assisted in its promotion. They granted MacGill time to give public recitals from it with his wife, as he did in charity readings at London's Aeolian Hall in February 1916 and Dundee's King's Theatre and Edinburgh's Freemasons' Hall in November 1916, and allowed a band from the Royal Scots to accompany the performances.[20]

Part of the reason for this, as it turns out, was because MacGill had been recruited in early 1916 into an obscure branch of the Intelligence Services, MI 7b (1), a unit dedicated to literary propaganda in whose service he remained until the end of the war.[21] This was not a covert attempt to co-opt and suppress MacGill – he continued to maintain a high profile as a public lecturer and writer, going on to pen another three books about the experiences of Irish, American and Australian soldiers in the war, and then in 1921 a strongly anti-war novel *Fear!*[22] So what purpose did military intelligence have in mind in supporting MacGill's graphic, soldier's-eye accounts of the realities of warfare?

One suggestion can be found in another officially backed work aimed at a popular audience, Geoffrey Malins's and John McDowell's film *The Battle of the Somme* (1916). This was easily the most-watched film of the war and is, in Nicholas Reeves's view, 'arguably the most successful British film of all time'.[23] Purporting to be a straightforward documentary, but in fact incorporating staged combat scenes and footage of troops in training, the film promised a highly detailed account of the preparations for the battle, as well as scenes of actual fighting and its consequences. Scottish audiences, like others across the UK, flocked to it. The film was showing in Scotland from 28 August 1916, a mere eight weeks after the battle's beginning and while it still raged, with the press reporting on the 'tremendous crowds' of unprecedented sizes attending screenings in Glasgow and Edinburgh, with continuous screenings from 11 a.m. to 10.30 p.m.[24] It was billed as an Official War Film and was advertised with endorsements from Lloyd George, then Secretary of State for War, so there was a strong implication that it was both authentic and authoritative.[25] Given this, it is a surprise to see its unsparing treatment of the consequences of battle. Early parts of the film show the impressive logistical preparations for the battle, displaying mountains of accumulated materiel and cheerful columns of marching soldiers. But the aftermath is less innocently reassuring, as the film displays scenes of material devastation, wounded soldiers being carried back to a dressing station and a field of British corpses driven over by the guns and limbers of a field artillery unit. The film's fifth and final section is especially disturbing, as the camera pans across German corpses lying contorted in a shell hole with others spread haphazardly along the bottom of trenches and shell holes. Shocking, even to a modern audience, is the lingering shot of a British corpse bent double at the bottom of a trench – almost, it might seem, as if asleep but for the unnatural stillness and the telling sight of his pendent hand black with livor mortis.

III.

Cinema audiences and readers were, then, not as wholly insulated from the grimmer realities of war as has sometimes been suggested. They did not have to look too hard to find detailed instances of the horror of war, exacted on British as well as German troops. Such examples were also found in abundance in one of the most popular Scottish fiction writers of the war, Boyd Cable. Hailed by *Punch* as 'one of the prose Laureates of the War' for his unparalleled ability to capture 'vividly the noise, the squalor, the terror, the high courage, the self-sacrifice, and again the nerve-shattering noise that make up the fierce confusion of trench fighting', he has been long neglected and is now almost wholly forgotten.[26]

Cable, born Ernest Andrew Ewart and educated at Aberdeen and Banff Grammar Schools, had been an itinerant worker and occasional writer before the war, travelling extensively in Europe and Australasia.[27] He enlisted on the outbreak of war as an artillery officer and began to publish stories of the frontline in the *Cornhill Magazine* and *Westminster Gazette*, which were collected as *Between the Lines* (1915). The book met with immediate success, selling over 100,000 copies in its first year; it was republished in the USA, and translated into French in 1917.

The book's main selling point was its purported authenticity – these were stories told by a soldier within earshot of the guns (a fact Cable was keen to emphasise) and which appeared to offer unmediated accounts of frontline experience. This directness was reinforced by the structure of the stories – each having as an epigraph the bland words of an official despatch above a graphic and detailed account of the grim realities that underlay them. The intention, it seems, was to generate the kind of exasperated irony at official euphemism that Fussell describes as the defining mode of serving soldiers: the irony that would be exploited by Erich Maria Remarque in titling his epic novel of suffering and loss, *All Quiet on the Western Front*.[28]

The technique is seen in the collection's first story, 'The Advanced Trenches'. This begins with the terse communiqué: '*Near Blank, on the Dash-Dot front, a section of advanced trench changed hands several times, finally remaining in our possession.*'[29] The story that follows describes the reality cloaked by these seemingly innocuous words:

> Supports poured out to their assistance, and for a full five minutes the fight raged and swayed in the open between the trenches and among the wire entanglements. The men who fell were trampled, squirming,

underfoot in the bloody mire and mud; the fighters stabbed and hacked and struck at short arm-length, fell even to using fists and fingers when the press was too close for weapon play and swing [. . .] The British flung in on top of the defenders like terriers into a rat-pit, and the fighters snarled and worried and scuffled and clutched and tore at each other more like savage brutes than men. The defence was not broken or driven out – it was killed out; and lunging bayonet or smashing butt caught and finished the few that tried to struggle and claw a way out up the slippery trench-sides.[30]

'The Advance' similarly starts with the anodyne words of an 'Official Despatch': *'The attack has resulted in our line being advanced from one to two hundred yards along a front of over one thousand yards.'*[31] And again, Cable is unsparing in confronting the reader with the brutalities that underlie the easy words, talking of attackers exterminating and being 'exterminated'; of 'shooting, stabbing, flinging hand grenades' and of being 'intent only on the business at their own bayonet points, to kill the enemy facing them and push in and kill the ones behind':

When their ammunition was expended they used rifles and cartridges taken from the enemy dead in the trench; having no grenades they snatched and hurled back on the instant any that fell with fuses still burning. They waged their unequal fight to the last minute and were killed out to the last man.[32]

Cable's book was published in 1915, before the introduction of conscription, and as such its depictions of extreme violence could be construed as a discouragement to volunteering – as antithetical to the message of moral responsibility fostered by Kitchener's 'Your Country Needs You' poster. Such accounts, though, might attract a different sort of volunteer – one avid for war's adventure and its loosening of moral constraints – and this is an impulsion that perhaps ought not to be underestimated. Philip Gibbs would later talk of the 'call of the wild – the hark-back of the mind to the old barbarities of the world's dawn' as a motivating factor for a number of volunteers, noting the manner in which 'some instinct of a primitive savage kind for open-air life, fighting, killing, the comradeship of hunters, violent emotions, the chance of death, surged up into the brains of quiet boys, clerks, mechanics, miners, factory hands'.[33] A reviewer in the urbane *Punch* noted such attractiveness in Cable's extreme realism. While remarking that Cable was an exception to the many 'war chroniclers' who 'deal only sparingly with the absolute killing and being killed that are at the heart of the whole hideous business', the reviewer highlighted the power and popular appeal of his approach – praising a representation

> so vivid that at times the roar and reek, the whole terrific nerve-wracking tension of trench warfare seems to leap out at you from the pages. It is a terrible and thrilling glossary that will be read and re-read in countless homes.[34]

As Cable's wartime career developed, however, it became clear that there was another reason for the explicit violence of his narratives besides simply thrilling readers and feeding fantasies of violence and revenge, and another reason why the authorities would continue to back his work in the way they supported MacGill and *The Battle of the Somme*. This relates to his role as an artillery officer, and in particular to his anxieties about the lack of ordnance finding its way to the frontline in the early stages of the war.

Between the Lines was being written in the middle of the so-called Shell Crisis of 1915, the shortage of munitions that was often cited – especially by the Northcliffe papers – as the main factor in the disaster of the British offensive on Aubers Ridge in May and the devastating losses of the Battle of Loos in the autumn. The scandal, whipped up as it was by interested parties in the press, led directly to the promotion of Lloyd George to a new Ministry of Munitions in 1915 and, ultimately, to the Premiership the following year. A further complication of the crisis was industrial unrest in the munitions industry, arising from the bullish, peremptory attitude of the new Ministry and the resistance of workers to changes in their working practices and protected status. Glasgow was a particular problem. There had been a successful rent strike in the city earlier in 1915, and Lloyd George considered it one of the 'worst districts' for industrial disruption on account of the organisation of munitions workers by shop stewards and the Clyde Workers' Committee.[35] When Lloyd George came to the city to face down the workers on Christmas Day, 1915, he was subjected to sustained heckling and interruption from the floor. The consequence of this affront to a Minister of the Crown was the temporary suppression of newspapers like *Forward* and the forced removal of key shop stewards mentioned earlier.[36]

Between the Lines addresses the shell shortage and attendant industrial unrest both implicitly and explicitly, not least in its second story, 'Shells'. This begins, like the others, with the words of an official despatch: '*to the right a violent artillery bombardment has* been in progress'.[37] The reality is, needless to say, quite different. The Allied forces are not engaged in violently bombarding the enemy at all but are rather endangered by, and frustrated at, the inability of their artillery to respond adequately to the German guns. A Scottish voice is heard in the trenches questioning why the Allied forces are not counter-bombarding the Germans – a question that raises the wrath of the story's central character:

> He turned angrily at last on one man who put the query in a broad Scots accent,
> 'No,' he said tartly, 'we ain't tryin' to silence their guns. An' if you partickler wants to know why we ain't – well, p'raps them Glasgow townies o' yours can tell you.'
> He went on and No. 2 Platoon sank to grim silence. The meaning of the gunner's words were plain enough to all, for had not the papers spoken for weeks back of the Clyde strikes and the shortage of munitions? And the thoughts of all were pithily put in the one sentence by a private of No. 2 Platoon.
> 'I'd stop cheerful in this blanky 'ell for a week,' he said slowly, 'if so be I 'ad them strikers 'ere alongside me gettin' the same dose'.[38]

This frustrated sense of the imaginative distance from the trenches to the homeland animates *Between the Lines* (it closes with one soldier plaintively saying to another 'what I wants to know – an' there's a many 'ere like me – is why don't somebody let 'em know about it ; let 'em really know') and offers the key to the book's insistent depiction of the grim realities of the frontline experience.[39] Cable is clearly attempting to bridge a cognitive gap between soldier and civilian reader, to undeceive the home population forcefully and ensure that the suffering of soldiers is properly acknowledged. But it is plain that he also harbours a more contentiously political intention – to display the horrors of frontline experience as a means of shaming workers into complying with the national armaments strategy.

Cable acknowledged such an intention in the Preface to his next book, *Action Front* (1916). Addressing those 'who complained that my last book was in parts too grim and too terrible', he retorted that not only is it 'impossible to write with any truth of the Front without the writing being grim', but 'I felt it would be no bad thing if Home realised the grimness a little better'.[40] Like MacGill, Cable found himself increasingly encouraged in this by the authorities and was drawn into the realm of propaganda not because he had written evasively or amelioratively about the war, but because he had confronted it directly and abrasively.

This encouragement was seen in another Cable book of 1916, *Doing Their Bit*, a book intended to depict the war industries from the soldier's point of view, and for which he was seconded by the War Propaganda Bureau and the Ministry of Munitions to the factories whose workers he had criticised. His secondment offered Cable the opportunity not only to explain the work of the munitions factories to the troops, but also to take to their workers the message of *Between the Lines* and 'tell them what a shortage of shells meant to the Front'. Cable recounts lecturing the workers on the frustrations felt by soldiers over:

> the squabbling amongst munition workers and their haggling over *8d.* or *8½d.* an hour pay, or Saturday half-holidays, or double overtime for Sunday, while the men in the trenches suffered a hell of shell-fire, and soaked in knee-deep gutters, and lost their limbs and lives from frost-bite, and put in six or sixteen-day spells, as need be, with no half-holiday and a shilling a day pay for time and overtime.[41]

In hectoring workers who haggled over their pay and supposed perks Cable did not spare the grim details. His intention was explicitly to 'make these men understand what it means to see a line of infantry hung up by barbed wire', to

> watch the line dwindle and wither and melt away to heaps and clumps of dead lying still in the mud or squirming in the clutch of the wire entanglements, to scattered figures crawling and rolling and dragging their broken limbs and shattered bodies back across the shell- and bullet-swept ground in a last struggle to reach shelter.[42]

Like MacGill, Cable was not hindered in this by the authorities but rather actively supported. Following *Doing Their Bit* and *Action Front*, he published two more accounts of trench warfare, *Front Lines* (1918) and *Grapes of Wrath* (1917) – a work of opportunistic propaganda aimed at American supporters of the war, along with a book, *Airmen o' War* (1918), which was commissioned by the Royal Flying Corps. His work received explicit official sanction – *Doing Their Bit* appeared with a Preface by Lloyd George – and was published and serialised in many magazines and newspapers. The *Post Sunday Special*, for example, which hailed Cable as 'The Greatest Scottish Writer Discovered by the War', serialised *Between the Lines* in early 1917, not stinting on reprinting the more graphic passages; these included, on 4 February, the story quoted earlier, 'The Advanced Trenches', in which British soldiers are depicted as terriers in a rat-pit, snarling, worrying, scuffling, and clutching and tearing at each other, 'more like savage brutes than men'.[43] Like MacGill, Boyd was also in demand for public lectures to a variety of audiences. In October 1917, he addressed a fashionable audience in the West End of London, chaired by his 'warm friend and admirer' Lord Cowdray.[44] In March 1918, he exhorted an audience of West of Scotland munitions workers that 'extra energy at home by war workers meant the saving of lives at the front, and the shortening of the war'.[45]

IV.

The examples of Cable and MacGill demonstrate that the military and civilian authorities were not wholly concerned with suppressing or disguising the less savoury facts of wars, but might at times be content to allow them to be spelled out and amplified. To some home readers the gruesome realities of war might be off-putting, but to many others they might act as a reminder of the terrible existential seriousness of the war and as a spur to the increased endeavour that would lead to victory.

This is consistent with other measures taken by the military authorities in seeking to acquaint a wide audience with conditions at the front. A significant part of Montague's labour in working for military intelligence, as it had been for John Buchan, had been comprised of conducting civilian visitors on tours of the frontline. Such visitors were often politicians, dignitaries and opinion formers, but they also included delegations of workers, particularly those representing trades unions. Cable, in fact, describes such a visit of trades unionists in the concluding story of *Front Lines*, ironically titled 'The Conquerors'.[46] The book's Preface gives an indication of the likely tenor of this encounter, with its statement that the 'workers at home' are 'either woefully ignorant still of what the failure of their fullest effort means to us, or, worse, are indifferent to the sufferings and endurings of their men on active service', adding the by now characteristic Cable barb that they 'are unpatriotic, narrow, selfish enough to put the screw on the nation for their own advantage'.[47] Needless to say, Cable's overweening trades unionists are suitably humbled by the conditions at the front and the arguments of the soldiers they meet.

However cosmetic or superficial such trench visits might have been, they were hardly consistent with an official policy of hiding or disguising the truth in order to preserve industrial stability and social peace of mind. Not only was information available for those who sought it, but at least some of those involved in intelligence and propaganda saw the advantages in making it widely available. The fact that MacGill and Cable were actively encouraged in their writing – offering trench visits of a different kind – suggests a different, and perhaps more disturbing, anxiety troubling those responsible for ensuring public morale: not so much that civilians needed to be protected from the truth, but that they were increasingly less interested in hearing that truth.

This is perhaps borne out by the experience of the war's other predominantly popular medium, cinema. From early in the war it was becoming apparent that soldiers preferred not to read accounts of war action, finding attempts to portray the realism of the trenches paradoxically 'horrible' and discomforting.[48] An official report on wartime cinema habits noted their dislike of dramatic film and their particular aversion to films about military action.[49] American film director Bennet Molter visited cinemas in the war zone and remarked on soldiers' preference for westerns over war pictures – in Molter's view 'a real picture', a dramatic feature, would fall flat, as the soldiers 'don't want to have to think'.[50]

The fact of the huge success of *The Battle of the Somme* might appear to prove that such arguments did not hold in their application to civilian audiences, and it is certainly true that these audiences showed a healthy appetite for war-related films in the early stages of the conflict. But it is also true that *The Battle of the Somme* was the high point of popular cinematic interest in the war. Three more full-length official films followed *The Battle of the Somme*, but each attracted less interest than its predecessor. *The Battle of Ancre* (1917) was, according to the Scottish section of the *Bioscope* film magazine, withdrawn from cinemas two days early because of its lack of business at the box-office.[51] Malins's *The Battle of the Arras*, filmed in April 1917, only eight months after his *Battle of the Somme*, was a failure and prompted the ending of full-length official war films. Lord Beaverbrook, soon to become the First Minister of Information, observed that 'the present style of films is played out. The public is jaded and we have to tickle its palate with something more dramatic in the future.'[52]

In an attempt to save this situation in 1917 and to ensure that war documentary continued in cinemas, the War Office Cinematograph Committee set up an official newsreel, the War Office Topical Budget. But this, too, failed to capture the public imagination, with the *Glasgow Herald* noting its shortcomings in 1918.[53] Towards the end of the war, the War Office's films were screening regularly in only 150 cinemas across Britain (this at a time when there were one billion cinema attendances annually in the UK), and according to audiences lacked 'human interest' and 'cohesion'. The resistance of exhibitors and commercial audiences was such towards the end of the war that the Ministry of Information was experimenting with methods of screening, including touring units, that would bypass the commercial cinema entirely.[54]

It had been a similar story with dramatic films of war – the visual equivalents of the stories of Campbell and Hay, and those of the *People's Journal*. As early as January 1915, the *Bioscope* was commenting on the outpouring of war dramas, and reporting a 'growing opinion that the public is being given quite enough, if not too much, war topics', suggesting that audiences were instead looking for 'relaxation and encouragement in its daily tasks'.[55]

The difficult truth faced by the cinema, amply demonstrated by its audience, was that civilians were weary of the war and would much rather be diverted from it than forced to confront it in what little time they had for leisure. It seems reasonable to assume that the magazine- and fiction-buying public were little different and that they were content, once their initial curiosity about the war had been satisfied, to shift their attentions elsewhere. It was just such a lack of attention and empathy that enraged Cable and prompted him to his graphic depictions of the war's horrors – to shock into realisation that mass of civilians he described as 'indifferent to the sufferings and endurings of their men on active service'. And in attempting to drive the hard truths of the war home, he was, like MacGill, helped rather than hindered by the popular publishers who printed and distributed his work and by the military establishment that employed him. Given this, it seems inadequate simply to blame the breakdown in communication between combatants and non-combatants on the press, or the military authorities, or on the failure of language to be able to represent the truth of the war satisfactorily. This was not so much a problem with transmission as with reception. The outlets were there for those who wanted to speak, but the conclusion that might be drawn is that there were disturbingly few people willing to listen.

Notes

1. Paul Fussell, *The Great War and Modern Memory* (Oxford: Oxford University Press, 1975), pp. 155–90.
2. Samuel Hynes, *A War Imagined: The First World War and English Culture* (London: The Bodley Head, 1990), p. 116. Peter Buitenhuis describes a similar 'unbridgeable' gap in his *The Great War of Words: Literature as Propaganda 1914–18 and After* (London: Batsford, 1989),

p. 179. Randall Stevenson, *Literature and the Great War 1914–1918* (Oxford: Oxford University Press, 2013), pp. 1–61. See also Hazel Hutchison, *The War That Used Up Words: American Writers and the First World War* (New Haven, CT: Yale University Press, 2015).
3. C. E. Montague, *Disenchantment* (London: Chatto & Windus, 1922), pp. 97–8.
4. Philip Gibbs, *The Pageant of the Years: An Autobiography* (London: William Heinemann, 1946), p. 166. See also his *Adventures in Journalism* (London: William Heinemann, 1923), pp. 240–1. Like the other four official war correspondents, Gibbs was knighted for his wartime service in 1920.
5. Philip Gibbs, *Realities of War* (London: William Heinemann, 1920), p. 24.
6. Ibid. p. 58.
7. 'The Gunners' Last Stand', *People's Journal, National Edition* (21 November 1914), p. 5.
8. M. C. Ramsay, 'Ian Stuart V. C.', *People's Friend* (23 November 1914), pp. 450–1.
9. J. L. Dickie, *Peter Tamson: Elder o' the Kirk and Sportsman* (London: Country Life, 1915), pp. 110–19.
10. See R. W. Campbell, *Private Spud Tamson* (Edinburgh and London: William Blackwood & Sons, 1915); *Sergeant Spud Tamson, V. C.* (London: Hutchinson, 1918); and *Spud Tamson Out West* (London and Edinburgh: W. & R. Chambers, 1924).
11. Campbell, *Private Spud Tamson*, pp. 289–90.
12. In its first year the book sold 115,000 copies in Britain and the colonies, and 350,000 copies in the USA. See Gordon Urquhart, 'Confrontation and Withdrawal: Loos, Readership and *The First Hundred Thousand*', in Catriona M. M. Macdonald and E. W. McFarland (eds), *Scotland and the Great War* (East Linton: Tuckwell, 1999), pp. 125–7.
13. Ian Hay, *The First Hundred Thousand: Being the Unofficial Chronicle of a Unit of 'K (1)'* (Edinburgh and London: William Blackwood & Sons, 1915), p. 342. See also his *Carrying On: After the First Hundred Thousand* (Edinburgh: William Blackwood & Sons, 1917).
14. Hay's books were serialised in *Blackwood's Magazine* and Dickie's in *Country Life* and *Scottish Field*. Lyon's books, *In Kilt and Khaki: Glimpses of the Glasgow Highlanders in Training and on Foreign Service* (Kilmarnock: Standard Press, 1915) and *More Adventures in Kilt and Khaki: Sketches of the Glasgow Highlanders and Others in France* (Kilmarnock: Standard Press, 1917) were published serially in the *Kilmarnock Standard*. The stories in MacLean Watt's *In France and Flanders: With the Fighting Men* (London: Hodder & Stoughton, 1917) first appeared in *The Scotsman* and *Chamber's Journal*.
15. Patrick MacGill, *The Great Push: An Episode of the Great War* (London: Herbert Jenkins, 1916), pp. 210–11.
16. Ibid. pp. 221–2.

17. See Iain McLean, *The Legend of Red Clydeside* (Edinburgh: John Donald, 1983), pp. 49–62.
18. 'Literature of the Day', *Belfast News-Letter* (3 August 1916), p. 3; 'A Literary Letter: "The Great Push" by Patrick MacGill', *The Sphere* (29 July 1916), p. 22.
19. 'New Books', *The Scotsman* (19 June 1916), p. 2.
20. See 'Rifleman MacGill's Story of Loos', *The Times* (11 February 1916), p. 3, and '"The Great Push" Recital in Kings Theatre: Full House will Greet Patrick and Mrs MacGill', *Dundee Courier* (15 November 1916), p. 4.
21. See the MI 7b (I) Farewell Magazine, *The Green Book*, no. 1 (January 1919), reprinted in facsimile in D. J. L. Arter, *MI 7b: The Discovery of a Lost Propaganda Archive from the Great War* (Jeremy Arter, 2013). The Scottish writer Frederick Sleath, author of *Sniper Jackson* (1919), was another soldier serving in the unit.
22. *The Brown Brethren* (1917), *The Dough Boys* (1918) and *The Diggers* (1919). David Taylor quotes several reviews of *The Brown Brethren* which suggest that it maintained MacGill's reputation for uncompromising realism. See David Taylor, *Memory, Narrative and the Great War: Rifleman Patrick MacGill and the Construction of Wartime Experience* (Liverpool: Liverpool University Press, 2013), pp. 11–12. For a view that MacGill sold out and remained effectively a propagandist, see Jonathan Atkin, *A War of Individuals: Bloomsbury Attitudes to the Great War* (Manchester: Manchester University Press, 2002), pp. 168–9. It is perhaps worth noting, too, the opinion of the *Edinburgh Evening News* that in later works like *The Brown Brethren* MacGill 'is somewhat more restrained in his style and descriptions than in his earlier work'. See 'The Brown Brethren', *Edinburgh Evening News* (5 September 1917), p. 2.
23. Nicholas Reeves, 'Official British Film Propaganda', in Michael Paris (ed.), *The First World War and Popular Cinema: 1914 to the Present* (Edinburgh: Edinburgh University Press, 1999), p. 31.
24. S. D. Badsey, 'Battle of the Somme: British War Propaganda', *Historical Journal of Film, Radio and Television*, vol. 3, no. 2 (1983), p. 108. 'Cinema Chit-Chat', *Entertainer*, vol. 2 (September 1916), p. 5.
25. Though it was later acknowledged that the film's battle scenes – which included British soldiers falling as though shot – were, in fact, filmed during training exercises.
26. 'Our Booking-Office', *Punch, or the London Charivari* (14 March 1917), p. 176.
27. 'Obituary', *Daily Commercial News and Shipping List* (1 November 1943), p. 2.
28. In fact, Cable anticipates Remarque here. His story 'Nothing to Report' begins with the ironic epigraph from an official despatch '*On the Western Front there is nothing to report. All remains quiet.*' Boyd Cable, *Between the Lines* (London: John Murray, 1917), p. 84.

29. Ibid. p. 1.
30. Ibid. pp. 7, 10.
31. Ibid. p. 130.
32. Ibid. pp. 143–5.
33. Gibbs, *Realities of War*, p. 58.
34. 'Our Booking-Office', *Punch, or the London Charivari* (1 December 1915), p. 459.
35. David Lloyd George, *War Memoirs of David Lloyd George*, vol. 1 (London: Odhams Press, 1938), p. 187.
36. For accounts of the event by Lloyd George's antagonists, see William Gallacher, *Revolt on the Clyde* (London: Lawrence and Wishart, [1936] 1940), pp. 77–99; David Kirkwood, *My Life of Revolt* (London: George G. Harrap, 1935), pp. 110–12.
37. Cable, *Between the Lines*, p. 12.
38. Ibid. p. 21.
39. Ibid. p. 272.
40. Boyd Cable, *Action Front* (London: Smith, Elder, 1916), p. vii.
41. Boyd Cable, *Doing Their Bit: War Work at Home* (London: Hodder & Stoughton, 1916), pp. 62–3.
42. Ibid. p. 128.
43. 'Between the Lines', *The Post Sunday Special* (4 February 1917), p. 3.
44. 'Boyd Cable's New Role', *Aberdeen Evening Express* (6 October 1917), p. 2.
45. 'Lecture to War Workers', *Airdrie and Coatbridge Advertiser* (30 March 1918), p. 2.
46. Boyd Cable, *Front Lines* (London: John Murray, 1918), pp. 295–306.
47. Ibid. p. viii.
48. For an account of such attitudes to 'horrible realism' see Stevenson, *Literature and the Great War 1914–1918*, pp. 84–92.
49. *The Cinema. Its Present Position and Future Possibilities: Being the Report of and Chief Evidence Taken by the Cinema Commission of Inquiry Instituted by the National Council of Public Morals* (London: Williams & Norgate, 1917), p. 228.
50. Molter, quoted in Kevin Brownlow, *The War, the West, and the Wilderness* (London: Secker & Warburg, 1978), p. 46.
51. *Bioscope* (15 February 1917), p. 737. Quoted in Nicholas Reeves, 'Cinema, Spectatorship and Propaganda: "Battle of the Somme" (1916) and Its Contemporary Audience', *Historical Journal of Film, Radio and Television*, vol. 17, no. 1 (1997), p. 12.
52. Quoted in 'The Power of Film Propaganda – Myth or Reality?', *Historical Journal of Film, Radio and Television*, vol. 13, no. 2 (1993), p. 194.
53. 'Germany and Film Propaganda', *Glasgow Herald* (24 May 1918), p. 5.
54. Nicholas Reeves, *Official British Film Propaganda During the First World War* (London: Croom Helm, 1986), p. 240. See also 'The Power of Film Propaganda', pp. 181–201.
55. 'The Topical "War" Drama', *Bioscope* (21 January 1915), p. 205.

Chapter 4

'One Who Has Sacrificed': The Use of 'High Diction' in Women's Correspondence to Scottish Newspapers during the First World War

Sarah Pedersen

This chapter uses as source material women's letters to the editor published in Scottish newspapers during the First World War. Newspapers are a particularly important resource in accessing the otherwise unrecorded voices of ordinary men and women, and are becoming much more accessible to the historian via the many on-going digitisation projects of newspaper archives. In particular, it investigates letters written to the newspapers by correspondents using familial pen names by which the writer claimed to be the mother, wife, daughter or widow of a combatant. The chapter investigates the types of issue that roused such women to write – anonymously – to their local newspaper during the war, the power of such a pen name, and the language used in their correspondence. In particular, it investigates the use of the 'high diction' of sacrifice and heroism in the letters of women correspondents, many of whom were working-class; how such language was used to frame the war experiences of both the soldiers and their female family members; and how the use of 'high diction' changed during the war as women reworked it for their own purposes.

A Righteous War?

Paul Fussell's *The Great War and Modern Memory*[1] posits the First World War as the point at which the lofty idealism of the nineteenth century was replaced by a new age of irony and cynicism, forged in the mud and death of trench warfare. The myth of war as noble and chivalric – defined in such 'high diction' terms as 'sacrifice', 'honour' and 'just' – was, according to Fussell, destroyed by the realities of twentieth-century warfare. A heroic view of warfare through education, religion and literature had been inculcated into both the Edwardian élites who led the troops and the soldiers themselves, on both sides of the conflict. At the outbreak of war in 1914, the speeches of politicians, sermons of the church and words of newspaper editors framed it as a righteous war, and the soldiers' personal sacrifice worthwhile and necessary. However, according to Fussell, the ideal of a valorous and Christian warriordom was one of the early casualties of the war, blown away by the shelling of 1915. In his book he refers particularly to writers such as Wilfred Owen, Siegfried Sassoon, Robert Graves and Edmund Blunden. In recent years, some cultural historians have started to question the total disappearance of 'high diction' and its concomitant values by the later years of the war. Jay Winter, for example, argues that other soldier–writers continued to use more traditional motifs throughout the war and afterwards.[2] Alexander Watson and Patrick Porter agree that, for some officers and men, the ideal of sacrifice continued throughout war and might even exacerbate the violence.[3] While they agree that the use of 'high diction' declined, they argue that, for most soldiers, the conflict remained a just and necessary war of self-defence and that there was a strong conviction of the rightness of the struggle and the worth of individual sacrifice. Similarly, Bell argues that 'sacrifice' was the dominant trope throughout the war, and that language developed in which making the 'supreme sacrifice' – that is, dying in battle – was not described as a passive act but as the product of a conscious decision to follow a path, such as enlisting in the army or taking a particular action in battle, that might lead to death.[4]

This 'high diction' of Sacrifice and a Just War was a product of a pre-war imperialist and Christian concept of patriotism and nationhood promulgated by the church, schools, and high and popular literature. Bell points out that the education of both the officer class and the men serving under them would have included frequent experience of religious worship, Bible reading and hymns, and that a particular use of militaristic language was exemplified in hymns such as *Onward Christian Soldiers* and *Soldiers of Christ, Arise*. Watson and Porter agree that the ideals of sacrifice, suffering and redemption borrowed heavily from a Christian vocabulary, but also from a popular appetite for heroic tales. Authors such as H. Rider Haggard, Anthony Hope and Arthur Conan Doyle, plus hundreds of other pulp-fiction writers, flooded the late Victorian and Edwardian market with adventure stories in which the superiority of the British Empire and its white, male heroes was celebrated. Thus on the outbreak of war, appeals for national unity and volunteers were framed in terms of patriotism and the moral validity of a Just War, supported by the church, while the ideology of sacrifice became shorthand for 'a diffuse body of values, concepts and themes extolling the laying down of your life for a greater good'.[5]

In her study of popular responses to the outbreak of war in 1914, Pennell argues that ordinary people employed the same language about the war as found in official publications, using words such as honour, justice, defence and righteousness in order to justify British involvement in the war.[6] Robb notes that, throughout the war, British journalists used euphemistic language and formulaic expressions, such as soldiers offering 'splendid resistance' and 'brilliant counter-attacks', thus elevating the most ordinary and squalid engagements to the realm of myth and chivalry.[7] He argues that journalists resorted to the use of such 'high diction', and the language that had been educated into a whole generation through adventure stories and the poetry of Tennyson and Bridges, in their careful and censored reports of action at the front. Thus there is growing agreement that, whilst they might be less articulate, the common soldiery were just as likely to be embued with a heroic understanding of the war as their public-school officers at the start of the war and that, although there was a decline in the use of 'high diction', it did not entirely disappear.

As Darrow points out, this was above all a male myth of war experience.[8] War was noble, chivalric and masculine, while women were frequently framed as anti-militaristic, pacifist or even spies. She suggests that one of the few ways in which women could lay claim to some part of the war experience was to volunteer as nurses, although such war service was seen as a personal, rather than an abstract, national, service. While the soldier served the nation, the nurse served the soldier. The same romantic literary tradition found in the letters and diaries of officers can be seen in the similar output of middle-class nurses,[9] and Watson notes that volunteer nurses were often compared to volunteer soldiers in popular patriotic literature, although she makes a distinction between the 'service' of middle-class volunteers and the paid 'work' of working-class women.[10] Thus some women could aspire to a vision of war service framed in the chivalric terms of sacrifice and valour. They could even be heroes, as the death of Edith Cavell showed, although Robb points out that, in the framing of her death, Cavell, a fifty-year-old unmarried principal of a nursing school, was consistently represented as a delicate 'girl' and powerless victim.[11]

However, what of women who did not perform such specific war work as nursing or working in the munitions factories? How did they perceive their role in the war, and did they make use of the 'high diction' of sacrifice and patriotism to frame either the parts played by their menfolk or themselves during the wartime emergency? An analysis of women's letters published in Scottish newspapers during the war suggests that they not only made use of such language, but also adapted it to suit their own ends, particularly to justify criticism of the conduct of others during the war emergency, including the government.

The Role of the Press

Mass-circulation newspapers started to appear in Britain during the 1890s, and soon surpassed older newspapers in terms of sales because of their lively and sensationalist reporting style, and use of interviews, photographs, massed headlines and introductory paragraphs to offer 'stories' rather than merely a straightforward retelling of events. This new type of newspaper was exemplified in Scotland by the *Daily Record*, which was established in Glasgow by Alfred Harmsworth in 1895. Key to this new journalism was the encouragement of readers to become involved in news-making, through a variety of mechanisms for sharing their opinions, including correspondence columns. Despite the introduction of censorship imposed by the Defence of the Realm Act in August 1914, newspapers were still seen as an important source of information during the war, and a thirst for news meant that sales continued to increase, with over 6 million newspapers sold every day.[12] Newspapers were also used for propaganda purposes, such as encouraging men to volunteer and, as noted above, frequently used 'high diction' and euphemistic language in the reporting of military action. In Lewis Grassic Gibbon's novel *Sunset Song*, set in rural Kincardineshire during the First World War, it is the 'right fierce' urging of the newspaper editors that leads Socialist crofter Chae Strachan to enlist: 'Chae Strachan came up to Blawearie one night with a paper in his hand and a blaze on his face, and he cried that he for one was off to enlist.' Gibbon mockingly suggested: '*Man, some of those editors are right rough creatures. God pity the Germans if they'd their hands on them!*'[13]

As Pennell notes,[14] newspapers can provide an excellent foundation for establishing popular reactions to the war, although they need to be used critically. Individual newspapers might contain political bias and inaccuracies, but the use of correspondence columns from a variety of Scottish newspapers can help to identify issues that stimulated public debate and the types of rhetoric used to discuss them. Letters to the editor offer the opportunity to access the opinions of ordinary readers who might have left no other written record of their thoughts, and there is evidence to suggest that the opinions of letter-writers can be considered broadly representative of non-writers who read the same newspaper.[15] The letters discussed in this chapter were accessed via the use of digitisation projects such as *The Scotsman Digital Archive* and the *British Newspaper Archive*. Both allow advanced searches enabling the researcher to focus on material published during a particular time period in one country (Scotland), a particular region or even a specific newspaper. Correspondence columns were searched for letters from women using familial pen names. In the case of some newspapers whose archives have not been digitised, such as the *Aberdeen Free Press*, hand-searching of the newspaper archives was undertaken.

Scottish newspapers published several different types of letter within their pages. The letters of serving soldiers were eagerly consumed and could be found in both national newspapers like *The Scotsman* and more local newspapers, which often featured columns of frontline soldiers' correspondence, although such letters might be subject to censorship.[16] Newspaper correspondence columns were also employed by the vast array of official and semi-official organisations that blossomed during the war and used letters to newspapers to communicate with the public. Such correspondents included lady organisers fundraising for charities, arranging the collection of comforts for the armed forces, and highlighting opportunities of war work for women.[17] Their letters are valuable as sources for a history of the involvement of women in the organisation of the war effort, and the increasing militarisation of the home front. The letters discussed here, however, are not those submitted for publication by charities or other women's organisations. Instead, this chapter focuses on the letters from individual women, whose letter to a local newspaper might be their first, or indeed only, step into the public sphere. In particular, it makes use of letters from women who requested publication under familial pen names associated with male members of their family serving at the front. The focus is therefore on the writing of ordinary women readers. These are women whose voice is little heard in the history of the war: women who left no diaries or reminiscences and who are otherwise not represented in official archives – the wives of working men, crofters, farm labourers and soldiers and sailors. The majority of work that has been undertaken on the role of women in wartime Britain has focused on those who became involved in war work, such as nursing, land work, employment in the munitions factories or – by the last year of the war – as part of the new women's armed services. As Hughes and Meek note, the history of women's engagement in the war has mainly been evaluated through their entry into what had been considered men's jobs and in their role in the medical and nursing professions.[18] This chapter instead investigates the writing of women who were unable or unwilling to undertake such war work and whose main contribution to the war was perceived to be the support of their menfolk in the armed services and in keeping the home fires burning.

Mothers of Soldiers

There is little evidence of editorial gatekeeping in the Scottish newspapers of the period.[19] Letters might be held over for a day because of a lack of space and editors published apologies for this practice, but otherwise letters seem to have been published as soon as possible after they had been received. As the war continued and paper rationing was introduced, editors requested correspondents to limit the length of letters, but there is little evidence that these requests were heeded. Letters were published as long as the correspondent supplied their name and address – but they could choose to remain anonymous in print through the use of a pen name.

Pseudonyms that depicted the writer as a soldier's mother were particularly popular – 'A Soldier's Mother', 'Lad's Mother', 'A Prisoner's Mother' or 'Widowed Mother of an Only Son Lying Ill in France'. Even if the writer was the wife of a soldier the choice of pseudonym frequently emphasised her maternal role: for example, listing how many children she had – 'Mother of Three', 'Mother of Four', 'Mother of Eleven' and even 'Mother of Nineteen'. Such correspondents used their identity as mothers to legitimise their criticism of the organisation of the war effort as it impinged on themselves and their families. This criticism might be levelled at individuals, such as the 'very fussy person who calls herself a "lady" visitor';[20] the government itself; bodies that were in charge of separation allowances and pensions; or landlords who refused to rent to soldiers' wives and families.

The letters were written in aggrieved tones, and the use of a maternal pen name legitimised these grievances by drawing upon the trope of the patriotic mother, who had given her sons for the good of the nation: for example, the mother who wrote to the *Dundee Evening Telegraph* in November 1914, 'I have only one son, a soldier in the Black Watch, but if I had six I would say "Yes, with a mother's blessing."'[21] The patriotic mother was a well-known and admired image in British iconography during the war, and women who did not wish to reveal their identity to the newspapers' readers used their motherhood to justify their recourse to the press. Their motherhood bestowed on them the right to question or complain about some aspect of army or government policies that affected themselves or their sons. It legitimised their concerns and gave them a status without which they might not have had the courage to write to the press. Writing such a letter, and thus raising the issue in the public sphere, was also frequently seen as the utmost such a woman could do – a recurring theme in such letters was: 'Hoping someone with more education than I will take the matter up'[22] or 'Trusting someone in authority will take this matter in hand'.[23] Others wrote in the hope that their letter would stimulate more correspondence on the subject from others in the same situation, like 'Distracted Mother' who trusted that 'some other poor sorrowing mothers may have the courage to back me up'.[24]

High Diction and Sacrifice

The 'high diction' of sacrifice is very much to the fore in these letters – throughout the war period. This is particularly seen in women correspondents' descriptions of dead or injured soldiers: A 'Soldier's Widow' described the death of her husband – 'he made the supreme sacrifice over a year ago'[25] – while 'Yvonne' described the son of the local manse having made 'the great sacrifice'.[26] Both of these letters were written in 1917, demonstrating that the concept of the supreme sacrifice remained a useful shorthand throughout the war. Watson and Porter argue that the ideology of sacrifice survived and remained relevant in determining how men interpreted their experiences throughout the war. It is clear that was also supposed to help the interpretations of loved ones left behind at home. In Gibbon's *Sunset Song*, the death of Chris Tavendale's husband is described by several of those attempting to support her as 'fine': 'he's died like a man out there, your Ewan's died fine', 'he'd died fine, for his country and his King he'd died'.²⁷ Ironically, as we find out later in the novel, Ewan Tavendale was actually killed by a firing squad for desertion. However, Chris was not supposed know this.

Women were expected to support the war effort by stoically sending their men to war.²⁸ In a letter to the *Dundee Courier* in 1917, 'A Mother' described how it is 'the bravest women who bid Godspeed to their men. Though their hearts are breaking, they control eye and lip till their dear one is out of sight.'²⁹ The death or injury of a soldier might also be framed by correspondents as the woman's sacrifice, almost suggesting that the choice to join the army was made by his mother or wife rather than by the man himself. The death of a loved one was therefore framed as both his sacrifice and that of his wife or mother. 'Soldier's Mother' wrote to the *Aberdeen Daily Journal* of 'the sacrifice the mother has made in letting her son to join the colours',³⁰ while a correspondent to the *Edinburgh Evening News* noted: 'I, too, have been called upon to make that great sacrifice.'³¹ As Robb explains, 'the Christian ideal of self-sacrifice gave the war a deeper meaning for soldier and civilian alike. They spontaneously employed an idealised vocabulary, without any prompting from above.'³² Thus the concept of heroic sacrifice could be applied to the mother or wife, as well as to the soldier. A correspondent who explicitly described herself as 'One who has Sacrificed' wrote to the *Dundee Evening Telegraph* in 1917 stating: 'I have voluntarily given dependents out of my home to the army – two of my sons in August 1914 and my husband and remaining dependents in the first months of 1915.'³³

The sacrifice a woman made not only was related to the death of her husband and son, but might also be seen in the impact of the war on her lifestyle. 'A Soldier's Widow' recounted:

> Before the war my husband had a good wage, and we were comfortable. He left his work and answered his King and country's call at the outbreak of war without a penny from his employer, and without waiting for a call from Lord Derby. He made the supreme sacrifice over a year ago. I get 10s a week having no family.³⁴

In Support of Home Front Women

The women who used familial pen names in letters to the newspapers often wrote in complaint about the impact the war had had on their lives. One thread that runs throughout wartime correspondence columns relates to the policing of working-class women's lives and morals. The letters make it clear that, while their male relatives were away at the front, these women perceived themselves as being monitored in a variety of official and non-official ways and were aware that their standard of living might depend on their perceived standards of morality. Writing in support of a widow complaining about the size of her pension, 'A Soldier's Wife' argued, 'A widow and her children are required to live a respectable life, but without a respectable sum they cannot possibly do so.'[35] The women had learned that their claims to better housing and sufficient funds to feed and clothe themselves and their children depended to some extent on whether they were judged to be deserving. This is made very clear in letters about the allowances and pensions paid to wives of soldiers and sailors, a topic that stimulated frequent letters throughout the war.

The question of how to support the families of enlisted men was a new problem for the wartime government. Before 1914, the vast majority of ordinary soldiers had not been officially permitted to marry at all, although many had unofficial wives and families. However, with the need for volunteers at the beginning of the First World War, followed by the introduction of conscription in 1916, it became impossible for the army to continue to disregard army wives and widows. In 1885, the Soldiers' and Sailors' Families Association (SSFA) had been founded to assist both official and unofficial wives and families. On the outbreak of war, Asquith announced provisions extending the minimum level of separation allowances and war widows' pensions to unofficial wives and the wives of all volunteers, and the government turned to the SSFA for assistance in administering these. However, as Lomas points out, although soldiers' families were in theory entitled to compensation for the temporary or permanent loss of the main wage-earner, the use of a charity's volunteers as administrators meant that servicemen's families were dependent on the personal judgement of these volunteers, who were used to judging cases – and withholding funds – on moral issues.[36] Hints of these attitudes can be found in the many letters of complaint sent to Scottish newspapers throughout the war. For example, a series of letters in the *Aberdeen Daily Journal* complained about the way in which officials attempted to bargain down the allowance:

> Under the new scale of allowance, the mother of a soldier would be entitled to 12s 6d if there were no children; but the official comes and asks if 8s or 9s would do. If a protest is made to the effect that the sacrifice the mother has made in letting her son to join the colours entitles her to

more, the officer advances the proposed allowance of 10s. On the mother remarking that that is not much coming into a house from which the breadwinner has gone, it is said she may be offered 11s, and obliged, as, it is said, others have been, to accept this curtailed payment.[37]

This letter was signed 'Soldier's Mother'. The correspondent was supported by several other letters from women using the same pen name. While the bureaucracy of the war machine became far more organised in later years of the war, complaints about allowances, and in particular the need for increases in the sums awarded in the face of rising food and housing costs, continued throughout the war. In 1916, 'Still Another Tommie's Wife' argued, 'The way we "Tommie's wives" are treated is a disgrace to our country and an insult to our men,'[38] while 'A Soldier's Daughter', who had been unable to find employment and relied on the allowance made to her mother, admitted: 'I am painfully aware of the struggle to make ends meet.'[39] As the war continued, similar letters of complaint appeared from widows in reference to pensions. In the *Edinburgh Evening News*, 'Soldier's Widow' complained about her access to a pension from the Tramway Company:

> Well, my husband had 15 years' service as conductor, and he was killed in Gallipoli two years ago. I was left with 11 children, nine of them dependent on me. My husband was among the first of the men to pay to this fund every month and I have never received any relief from it.[40]

'A Tommy's Loved One' wrote bitterly: 'We are told it is an honour to be a soldier's widow. I fail to see where the honour comes in.'[41]

Honour and Horror

Chivalric concepts such as honour, gallantry and knighthood are evident throughout the women's correspondence, even in the later years of the war. Women were concerned with their own honour, that of their husbands, or the wider honour of nations. Writing about the possibility of the introduction of conscription, a nurse wrote 'for the sake of Nurse Cavell, let us all do our best to keep the blot of forced service off our country's escutcheon',[42] a chivalric term for a shield bearing a knight's coat of arms. A letter to the *Dumfries and Galloway Standard* in August 1914 referred to 'our gallant soldiers, Regular or Territorial'.[43] For a correspondent to the *Aberdeen Daily*

Journal, Serbia was gallant, with 'loveable qualities and fine ideals', while Austria was treacherous and cruel.[44] Writing to the 'married shirkers' who had not yet joined up, 'A working man's wife' urged them to 'make a bold attempt to don the khaki, and accomplish some heroic deed' before they died.[45] Another correspondent felt that those who did not join up were 'a disgrace to Scotland'[46] while 'Girl War Worker' described the words of a conscientious objector as 'utterly unworthy of a Scotsman'.[47]

The framing of Edith Cavell as a young female victim has already been mentioned. Soldiers themselves were often referred to as innocent 'boys' or the more colloquial 'laddies'. A letter to the *Edinburgh Evening News* from 'Scot', complaining about the behaviour of women who turned out to cheer soldiers as they marched through the city, stimulated an indignant reply from 'Territorial's Mother'.[48] This correspondent defended the actions of women like herself, who liked to think of her own son as she cheered on the marchers and suggested that 'Scot' was a 'sour old maid'. She described the Territorials' 'pure simple conversation' and referred to their officers as 'refined gentlemen', suggesting that 'Scot' 'should be thankful that our dear boys, the Territorials, are doing all in their power to guard her. Otherwise she might be carried off by a German officer as the poor Belgian women were.' This reference was to propaganda that had started circulating early in the war about German troops' treatment of Belgian women and children. Such stories also had the useful effect of offering a more human justification for Britain's entry into war rather than treaties and border disputes, and made it a matter of honour in the face of the inhumane torture of women and children. Thus 'A Simple Woman' stated in a letter of 1915 that the cause of the war was 'because a little country had been trampled by a mighty tyrant'.[49]

It is clear that the stories about the horrors perpetrated on Belgian women had a deep impact on Scottish newspaper correspondents. The fate of the Belgian women was in the mind of 'Scots Mother' when she suggested 'it would be a good plan for as many women as possible to learn how to shoot, especially after reading of the horrible manner in which the brave Belgians have been treated',[50] but was also used as a threat by 'Stir Up' who wrote to the *Dundee Evening Telegraph* urging young men to join up: 'Think of it seriously, men, I implore you for the love of your country, and for the love of the kiddies. You don't want to see your mothers and sisters sharing the fate of our poor Belgian sisters.'[51] In *Sunset Song*, Long Rob of the Mill refers to the newspapers' reports of the Germans 'raping of women and their gutting of bairns'.[52]

The fate of Belgian women was also used as a warning in 1916 when 'Girl War Worker' warned that women in Scotland might be subjected to the 'same shameful treatment as were our poor Belgian sisters' if conscientious objectors were allowed to refuse to serve.[53] Pennell argues that such stories were not just a clever method of vilifying the enemy but also provided a language in which women could express some of their fundamental reactions to the outbreak of war, particularly the fear of invasion.[54] However, it may also be that – as with some of the uses of the story illustrated above – the Belgian atrocities were used as a way to control women and make them fall into line. Women were threatened with similar treatment if they did not support the war effort or if their menfolk did not 'do their bit'.

Christianity

It is also clear that, to many correspondents, the war was a just one. As Bell points out, on the declaration of war Britain was perceived as the new Israel, with God on her side, and physical and spiritual war were conflated in the speeches of politicians and the sermons of clergymen.[55] In *Sunset Song*, the minister Gibbon 'had fair become a patriot' at the outbreak of war. He preaches a sermon denouncing German sympathisers and suggesting that men who have not yet joined up are 'tinks and traitors' and 'a shame to Kinraddie'.[56] In Nan Shepherd's *The Weatherhouse*, set in wartime Aberdeenshire, Garry Forbes, a soldier home on leave to recover from his terrible experiences in the trenches, can still argue: 'I believe we are in some way fighting the devil. Have you no belief in the sanctity of a cause?'[57] Similarly, correspondents to the Scottish newspapers made associations between Christianity and the righteousness of the war. In April 1915, just before the second battle of Ypres, 'Minister's Wife' took it upon herself to write to the *Aberdeen Daily Journal* to answer what she claimed to be a constant 'parrot cry' asking 'Is Christianity a Failure?' Her letter made explicit a connection between the sacrifice of the soldier and that of Christ:

> To our brave young heroes who are going forth at this Easter season, I would say that, in following the example of their Lord, in offering their young lives for their religion, their King and their country, they will be forever absolved from all stains of the past, for, 'without shedding of blood there is no remission'. And in that agony of loneliness which each one hides in his heart, under cover of brave smiles – that agony which is

worse than death itself – may it comfort them to remember, when all else fails, that they are sharing in that most awful agony of Gethsemane, and may this remembrance be indeed 'an angel sent to strengthen them'.[58]

Whilst this correspondent's role as a minister's wife would, of course, lead her to such public sentiments, she was not the only letter-writer to make this connection. 'A Simple Woman', writing to the *Dundee Telegraph* the following October, clearly saw the war as between good and evil:

> War is because there is evil, and so long there is evil there will be war. Nothing but Christianity can make matters better. Rather die honourably than live a laggard and a dastard. Up, men, every one who can join the ranks and sing 'Onward, Christian Soldiers' – not only against our enemies, but against the devil!ial[59]

The enemy was not only in the ranks of the opposing forces. Writing to the *Aberdeen Daily Journal* in April 1916 about an encampment of conscientious objectors at Dyce near Aberdeen, 'A Soldier's Lass' used the Biblical denunciation of false prophets: 'By their deeds ye shall know them.'[60] Such letters demonstrate a growing trend amongst women correspondents to Scottish newspapers as the war went on – while the use of 'high diction' and religious imagery did not disappear, it was repurposed to criticise or attack groups other than the enemy, such as conscientious objectors, those who refused to enlist or the government. Thus, in 1918, 'A Wife and Mother' wrote to the *Dundee Courier*: 'The miserable inadequacy of the sum granted by the Government to the dependents of our gallant soldiers makes my "woman's soul" burn with righteous indignations',[61] while 'Distracted Mother' could demand of *Hawick News*, 'if the winning of this awful war depends on our poor 18 year-old boys to finish it, where are our manly men? In the name of the freedom and righteousness for which we are fighting, save our boys!'[62]

Our Brave Sons

The continuance of the language of sacrifice throughout the war does not, however, mean that a more realistic appreciation of the horrors of war did not also appear in women's correspondence. Descriptions of 'our brave sons up to the waist in mud and water and suffering untold hardships'[63] or 'boys lying quietly in France, with nothing to mark their resting-place but a little wooden cross'[64] demonstrate a clear understanding of some of the realities of war. Accounts of dealing with men broken by the war were often more brutally phrased, since here women were writing of their own experiences. A mother wrote to the *Dundee Evening Telegraph* in November 1916 to describe her own situation:

> I gave my only son to my King and country soon after the war started. After being in the army about nine months he was invalided home and given his discharge. He has been under the doctor's care since coming home. I have had to feed him, dress and wash him, as he is not able to help himself.[65]

Another correspondent worried that '[t]he glamour of war and the admiration of every true girl for a boy in khaki or blue' led too many girls to a hasty marriage and warned that the 'warrior may return perchance maimed for life, helpless burden to himself, and in the long run to his wife'.[66] In such letters, 'high diction' phrases such as 'warrior' and concepts of 'giving' your son to King and country were enmeshed in darker messages about the price such families might pay in long-term care for once-healthy men.

Such bitterness frequently led to criticism of men who had not volunteered, either because of their conscience or because they were in reserved occupations such as farming. In some of these letters another type of mother emerged – the woman who refused to allow her son to enlist. As Suzan Zeiger points out, this was the negative side to the image of the 'patriotic' mother.[67] The patriotic mother sacrificed her sons willingly to the army, but the unpatriotic mother was 'selfish' and overly – probably unhealthily – attached to her children. Such a mother was described in a letter to the *Aberdeen Free Press* by 'One Who Has Given Each of Her Sons':

> I regret to say, there have been mothers so utterly selfish that they have put their trifling individual interests in the balance against a nation's. They said – 'My boy cannot join; it would interfere with his studies or his ambitions in life.'[68]

'A Farmer's Wife' wrote in March 1916 that she was proud of her sons, who had enlisted, but many of their contemporaries claimed to be indispensable because of their work. Had her sons acted in such a way, she remarked, 'in my secret soul I should have been ashamed of them'.[69]

The Military Service Act of January 1916 introduced conscription for men aged 18 to 41, although men employed in essential work could not be conscripted. Farmers were exempt from conscription, but their sons and labourers were not. The government left it up to local tribunals to decide what was and was not essential work – a system that was open to abuse. As 'Widowed Mother of an Only Son Lying Ill in France' pointed out bitterly, it was not surprising that farmers and their sons were being given 'wholesale exemption' by the tribunals in Aberdeenshire, 'seeing they are as to three-fourths composed of farmers, with factors as chairmen'.[70] Caroline Dakers reports that some farmers 'ostensibly retired from business and announced that their sons had taken over the farm' in order to persuade the tribunals that theirs was essential work.[71] Not only were farmers' sons less likely to be conscripted, but they were not even even working hard on the farms. 'A Soldier's Wife' asked:

> Why should the young bucks of farmers be allowed to trot about as they do, clothed in fine linen, when the only son of a poor widow is in khaki and fighting hard for life and for his country's liberty?[72]

Perhaps because of such criticism some farmers volunteered for war service despite their exemptions. In *Sunset Song*, Ewan Tavendale joins up because he was 'sick of it all, folk laughing and sneering at him for a coward'.[73]

It is noteworthy that few farmers or their sons dared to write to defend their behaviour. Instead, letters of defence were written by their womenfolk. 'A Farmer's Daughter' pointed out that farmers were 'putting forth all their energies to keep their bushels brimming to feed their country',[74] while another 'Farmer's Daughter' wrote to the *Aberdeen Free Press* in December 1917 with a long list of all the sons sacrificed to the war by farmers in the Banffshire area.[75]

Conclusions

While the majority of research that has investigated the use of the language of sacrifice and a just war during the First World War has focused on the writing of male combatants, women also made use of such language. Work on the writing of nurses at the front has established that these middle-class volunteers used similar language as their officer equivalents – influenced by a similar education and the popular literature of the period. Recent work has also established the use of such language by the common soldier. However, little work has been undertaken on these soldiers' womenfolk, mainly because of the lack of evidence – these women rarely left diaries or published works. Letters to the editors of local newspapers, however, allow us a glimpse of the concerns of working-class women on the home front, and the language that these women used to phrase their complaints.

The mothers, wives, widows and daughters of male combatants during the First World War used a variety of linguistic tropes to frame their experiences in their letters to Scottish newspapers. The majority of the letters published from such women were complaints about the situation in which they found themselves. They felt that, as the families of men on active service, they deserved better treatment by the state, its officials, and their fellow members of the home front.

The women mostly chose to use pseudonyms in their correspondence with the press – for many of them this would have been the first time they had stepped so clearly into the public sphere and they were happy to use the convention of pen names in order to preserve their anonymity. However, by presenting themselves as the wives and mothers of members of the armed forces, their chosen pen names became more than a shield of anonymity and instead augmented and amplified their right to be heard. Some correspondents chose names that were more than simply statements of their relationship to a soldier. Pen names such as 'One Who Has Sacrificed', 'Widowed Mother of An Only Son Lying Ill in France' and 'One Who Has Given Each of Her Sons' carried within the signature deeper messages intended to influence the reader and stir their emotions. Such names – and many of the letters discussed in this chapter – made use of what has been termed 'high diction'.

The contents of these letters also use 'high diction' terms such as sacrifice and concepts of a righteous war. Their menfolk are conceived as pure heroes, young men sacrificing their lives for the good of the nation. However, the women also frame themselves in this way in their letters – they too have sacrificed, whether that is in sending their sons and husbands to the war or in reducing household income and concomitant standards of living. Thus the language of sacrifice was applied to the home front as well as the trenches, and women claimed their own experiences as part of a righteous and even holy war. As the war continued, this language was also used by the women correspondents to justify their criticisms of those who were perceived as internal enemies – whether that was conscientious objectors, shirkers or even officials of the government who were not working to support the families of fighting men. In their use of this 'lofty vocabulary',[76] women correspondents demonstrated both their internalisation of the tropes of a just war, but also their abilities to reshape and reuse such tropes for their own ends. Women on the home front saw themselves as making their own sacrifices in a righteous cause. Theirs, however, were less acknowledged and certainly perceived as lesser sacrifices than those of their menfolk, and did not become part of the official record of the war.

Notes

1. Paul Fussell, *The Great War and Modern Memory* (Oxford: Oxford University Press, 1975).
2. Jay Winter, *Sites of Memory, Sites of Mourning: The Great War in European Cultural History* (Cambridge: Cambridge University Press, 1998).
3. Alexander Watson and Patrick Porter, 'Bereaved and Aggrieved: Combat Motivation and the Ideology of Sacrifice in the First World War', *Historical Research*, vol. 83, no. 219 (2010), pp. 146–64.
4. Stuart Bell, '"Soldiers of Christ Arise": Religious Nationalism in the East Midlands During World War I', *Midland History*, vol. 39, no. 2 (2014), pp. 219–35.
5. Watson and Porter, 'Bereaved and Aggrieved', p. 147.
6. Catriona Pennell, *A Kingdom United: Popular Responses to the Outbreak of the First World War in Britain and Ireland* (Oxford: Oxford University Press, 2012).
7. George Robb, *British Culture and the First World War* (London: Macmillan International Higher Education, 2014).
8. Margaret H. Darrow, 'French Volunteer Nursing and the Myth of War Experience in World War I', *The American Historical Review*, vol. 101, no. 1 (1996), pp. 80–106.
9. Christine E. Hallet, *Veiled Warriors: Allied Nurses of the First World War* (Oxford: Oxford University Press, 2014).
10. Janet S. K. Watson, *Fighting Different Wars: Experience, Memory, and the First World War in Britain*, vol. 16 (Cambridge: Cambridge University Press, 2004).
11. Robb, *British Culture and the First World War*.
12. Ibid.
13. Lewis Grassic Gibbon, *A Scots Quair* (Edinburgh: Canongate, 1995), p. 192.
14. Pennell, *A Kingdom United*.
15. Lee P. Ruddin, 'The "Firsts" World War: A History of the Morale of Liverpudlians as Told through Letters to Liverpool Editors, 1915–1918', *International Journal of Regional and Local History*, vol. 9, no. 2 (2014), pp. 79–93, p. 80.

16. Pennell, *A Kingdom United*.
17. Sarah Pedersen, 'Ladies "Doing their Bit" for the War Effort in the North-East of Scotland', *Women's History: The Journal of the Women's History Network*, vol. 2, no. 2 (2015), pp. 16–20.
18. Annmarie Hughes and Jeff Meek, 'State Regulation, Family Breakdown, and Lone Motherhood: The Hidden Costs of World War I in Scotland', *Journal of Family History*, vol. 39, no. 4 (2014), pp. 364–87, p. 365.
19. Sarah Pedersen *The Scottish Suffragettes and the Press* (London: Palgrave Macmillan, 2017).
20. 'Mrs C.', *Edinburgh Evening News* (14 November 1917), p. 4.
21. 'Stir Up', *Dundee Evening Telegraph* (4 November 1914), p. 2.
22. 'A Soldier's Mother', *Aberdeen Evening Express* (15 March 1915), p. 4.
23. 'A Worried Mother', *Aberdeen Daily Journal* (10 January 1916), p. 2.
24. 'Distracted Mother', *Hawick News* (17 May 1918), p. 3.
25. 'Soldier's Widow', *Dundee Evening Telegraph* (5 February 1917), p. 2.
26. 'Yvonne', *Fife Free Press and Kirkcaldy Guardian* (10 November 1917), p. 3.
27. Gibbon, *A Scots Quair*, p. 235.
28. Jonathan Rayner, 'The Carer, the Combatant and the Clandestine: Images of Women in the First World War in *War Illustrated* Magazine', *Women's History Review*, vol. 27, no. 4 (2018), pp. 516–33.
29. 'A Mother', *Dundee Courier* (2 May 1917), p. 2.
30. 'Soldier's Mother', *Aberdeen Daily Journal* (12 March 1915), p. 3.
31. 'Mrs C', *Edinburgh Evening News* (14 November 1917), p. 4.
32. Robb, *British Culture and the First World War*.
33. 'One Who Has Sacrificed', *Dundee Evening Telegraph* (5 February 1917), p. 2.
34. 'Soldier's Widow', *Dundee Evening Telegraph* (5 February 1917), p. 2.
35. 'A Soldier's Wife', *Aberdeen Evening Express* (12 December 1917), p. 6.
36. Janis Lomas, '"Delicate Duties": Issues of Class and Respectability in Government Policy Towards the Wives and Widows of British Soldiers in the Era of the Great War', *Women's History Review*, vol. 9, no. 1 (2000), pp. 123–47.
37. 'Soldier's Mother', *Aberdeen Daily Journal* (12 March 1915), p. 3.
38. 'Still Another Tommie's Wife', *Aberdeen Evening Express* (2 December 1916), p. 4.
39. 'S.M.L.', *Aberdeen Evening Express* (2 December 1916), p. 4.
40. 'Soldier's Widow', *Edinburgh Evening News* (6 August 1917), p. 2.
41. 'A Tommy's Loved One', *Edinburgh Evening News* (28 August 1917), p. 2.
42. 'T. E. MacWilliam', *Aberdeen Daily Journal* (25 October 1915), p. 2.
43. 'Isabel Hutcheon', *Dumfries and Galloway Standard* (26 August 1914), p. 5.
44. 'Dorothy Grierson Jackson', *Aberdeen Daily Journal* (29 March 1915), p. 6.

45. 'Working Man's Wife', *Dundee Courier* (18 March 1916), p. 4.
46. 'Widowed Mother of an Only Son Lying Ill in France', *Aberdeen Daily Journal* (14 April 1916), p. 3.
47. 'Girl War Worker', *Aberdeen Daily Journal* (18 April 1916), p. 7.
48. 'Territorial's Mother', *Edinburgh Evening News* (2 February 1915), p. 4.
49. 'A Simple Woman', *Dundee Evening Telegraph* (13 October 1915), p. 2.
50. 'Scots Mother', *Daily Record* (4 September 1914), p. 5.
51. 'Stir Up', *Dundee Evening Telegraph* (4 November 1914), p. 2.
52. Gibbon, *A Scots Quair*, p. 192.
53. 'Girl War Worker', *Aberdeen Daily Journal* (18 April 1916), p. 7.
54. Pennell, *A Kingdom United*.
55. Bell, 'Soldiers of Christ Arise'.
56. Gibbon, *A Scots Quair*, p. 195.
57. Nan Shepherd, *The Weatherhouse* (Edinburgh: Canongate, [1930] 2010), p. 169.
58. 'Minister's Wife', *Aberdeen Daily Journal* (5 April 1915), p. 7.
59. 'A Simple Woman', *Dundee Evening Telegraph* (13 October 1915), p. 2.
60. 'A Soldier's Lass', *Aberdeen Daily Journal* (19 April 1916), p. 3.
61. 'A Wife and Mother', *Dundee Courier* (5 August 1918), p. 4.
62. 'Distracted Mother', *Hawick News* (17 May 1918), p. 3.
63. 'A Soldier's Mother', *Aberdeen Daily Journal* (19 September 1916), p. 3.
64. 'A Soldier's Wife', *Aberdeen Daily Journal* (4 November 1916), p. 3.
65. 'Montrose', *Dundee Evening Telegraph* (9 November 1916), p. 2.
66. 'Kathryn', *Aberdeen Evening Express* (4 October 1916), p. 4.
67. Susan Zeiger, 'She Didn't Raise her Boy to be a Slacker: Motherhood, Conscription, and the Culture of the First World War', *Feminist Studies*, vol. 22, no. 1 (1996), p. 6.
68. 'One Who Has Given Each of Her Sons', *Aberdeen Free Press* (11 February 1916).
69. 'A Farmer's Wife', *Aberdeen Daily Journal* (7 March 1916), p. 3.
70. 'Widowed Mother of an Only Son Lying Ill in France', *Aberdeen Daily Journal* (14 April 1916), p. 3.
71. Caroline Dakers, *The Countryside at War* (London: Constable, 1987), p. 138.
72. 'A Soldier's Wife', 'Letters to the Editor', *Aberdeen Daily Journal* (4 November 1916), p. 3.
73. Gibbon, *A Scots Quair*, p. 213.
74. 'A Farmer's Daughter', 'Letters to the Editor', *Aberdeen Daily Journal* (11 October 1917), p. 4.
75. 'Farmer's Daughter', *Aberdeen Free Press* (14 December 1917).
76. Bell, 'Soldiers of Christ Arise'.

Chapter 5

Gaelic Verse
Ronald Black

The tragedy of the war fell disproportionately upon the people of the Highlands and Islands. The shock of it was so great that Gaelic society – in the sense of a complete set of Gaelic-speaking cohorts embracing all social classes – collapsed. Not counting Culloden and the Clearances, it was the second of two cultural body-blows, the first being the Education (Scotland) Act of 1872, which had swept away the charity and church schools in which Gaelic was taught without making alternative provision for the language. This meant that of the 200,000 Gaelic speakers in 1914 (roughly 1 in 20 of the Scottish population), none under fifty years of age had been educated in their native language. The war removed all the confidence that was left, and it has taken a long time to get some of it back.

By January 1916 it was estimated that the number of Gaelic-speaking soldiers in the fighting line was 6,000.[1] To these we may add something like 4,000 in the navy (including the reserve). By doubling the total to 20,000 we may reach an approximation of the number of Gaelic speakers in the armed services during the war as a whole – that is to say, about one-tenth of the Gaelic-speaking population. It may have been far more than that, but is unlikely to have been less. They served in all the main theatres in which the British were involved, including the Western Front, Italy, Macedonia, the Dardanelles, Palestine, Mesopotamia, the Battle of Jutland, and the Atlantic or Mediterranean convoys. All of these have left their mark on Gaelic verse.

One other 'theatre' falls to be mentioned, however, which may be less familiar to non-Gaelic readers. Early in the morning of 1 January 1919, HM Yacht *Iolaire* sank on *Biastan Thuilm* (the 'Beasts of Holm' at the entrance to Stornoway Harbour) with the loss of 201 men out of 280, mostly sailors returning home to Lewis and Harris from the war. As the total population of Lewis and Harris was only about 35,000, the impact of this disaster can well be imagined. Its memory remains vivid to this day, and it features almost as prominently in the Gaelic verse of Lewis and Harris as the war itself. A very fine book, *The Darkest Dawn*, was published to mark the centenary in 2019. It includes a dozen songs and half a dozen poems – none by survivors, but several by close relatives. The best song is a late one (1979) by Kenneth Smith, Earshader, Lewis, who lost his father. It is critical of the negligent seamanship that led to the disaster, and is one of those rare Gaelic songs that contain, in their words, all the light, colour and magnificence of a cathedral. Also notable is one by Norman MacLeod, Harris:

> *Nuair shaoil leotha a bhith sàbhailte*
> *Bho gach gàbhadh agus pian,*
> *Sann ghoid a-staigh am bàs orra –*
> *'S neo-bhàidheil a bha Bhiast.*

> 'When they reckoned they were safe
> From all danger, and all pain,
> Death stole in and took them –
> How merciless was the Beast.'[2]

There is double irony here, as in all the other Gaelic songs of the period (as we will see) the 'Beast' is the Kaiser. Most of the songs and poetry are readily available with English translations. All the translations in what follows are by myself, and may therefore vary slightly from what has been published.

The Songs

The Gaelic song tradition was still in full flow in 1914–18. Every community in the West Highlands and Islands had its songmakers, many of whom served in the armed forces. The tradition was basically oral, but around 120 Gaelic songs relating to the war have reached print. About half of these were composed in 1914–18; the other half are a mixed bag, consisting of at least fourteen laments for individuals killed on active service, perhaps a dozen songs about the *Iolaire*, and over thirty composed since then, down to the era of Runrig.[3] Typically, such songs contain five elements – a piece of ballad-style narrative, a passage of personal praise or dispraise, a lyrical description of what the poet sees, hears and feels, and an expression of longing for the person or place that is gone (or is far away), ending with pious sentiments and a hope-filled prayer. Dispraise was always of Kaiser Wilhelm II, and is remarkably robust, though he disappears almost completely from verse composed after 1918. The songs of 1914 are full of British patriotism and the bravery of Highland regiments; those of 1915–18 are uglier; those of peace in 1918–19 are subdued. Women's songs are less predictable than men's. Perhaps one should say 'even less predictable', because this is not a courtly tradition but a popular one, in which there is always the chance of coming across something brilliant, striking, unexpected or thoughtful.

At the very core of the material are songs made by servicemen or those who have lost a loved one, though sometimes it is impossible to know whether a song is by a man on active service or not.[4] The core of the core is provided by Donald MacDonald, *Domhnall Ruadh Chorùna* from North Uist (1887–1967), who, in a remarkable series of thirteen compositions, described exactly what it looked, felt, sounded and even smelt like to march up to the front, lie awake on the eve of battle, go over the top, be gassed, wear a mask, and be surrounded by the dead and dying remains of his comrades.[5] His 'Òran Arras' ('The Song of Arras') is his most anthologised piece, and rightly so, but all his work is imbued with dramatic tension.[6]

Songs of this kind offer different forms of realism. A soldier serving in the trenches describes comrades without heads or feet. Another speaks of 'Jack Johnsons', the army's nickname for heavy German artillery shells: Jack Johnson (1878–1946) was world heavyweight boxing champion. A sailor hints at racism in the navy by declaring 'that England won't deracinate me', *nach dean Sasainn Gall dhiom*. Yet in some ways the outstanding songs of the war were those composed long afterwards by Murdo MacFarlane (1901–82), who was too young to be called up. 'Naoi Ceud Deug 's a Ceithir Deug' ('Nineteen Fourteen') has a filmic quality. And in 'Chan fhada gu Madainn' ('Not Long until Dawn') he puts himself into the mind of a soldier to be shot for falling asleep on sentry duty.[7]

Some examples of striking imagery may be cited. Hector MacKinnon, Berneray, back from duty in the navy, used an extraordinary metaphor to express the closeness of the contest: *Na teudan cho teann 's an t-sreang a' fulang, / Toirt srann le tuilleadh 's a' chòir.* 'The harpstrings so tight that the gut suffers, / Humming with intensity.' In one of the *Iolaire* songs (by John MacLeod, Lewis) we are told, in a mood of resignation: *Am fear as tréin' cur cath a' bhàis / Chan fhearr na 'm fionnan-feòir.* 'He who most bravely fights death's battle / Is no better than the grasshopper.' And one of the strongest recurring images involves dead sailors and the shore. Catherine Morrison, Lewis:

> *Nuair a théid mi chun an dorais*
>   *Oidhche ghealaich 's i 'na h-àirde,*
> *Cianalas a' tighinn air m' inntinn*
>   *Nuair a chluinn mi fuaim na tràghad.*

> 'Any time I go to the door
>   On a night when the moon is full,
> Longing is what comes to mind
>   When I hear the sound of the shore.'

Margaret MacLeod, Lewis:

> *Nuair bhios càch 'nan cadal, cha bhi mise 'na mo thàmh,*
> *D' uaigh 's i cho fada bhuam 's nach stad mi anns an àit';*
> *Nam faighinn dhan an ùir thu 's ciste dhùint' ort, a ghràidh,*
> *Gun tugadh sin dhomh saorsa, gun mo shùil bhith air an tràigh.*

> 'When others are at rest, I can't get a wink of sleep,
> As your grave's so far away that I can't stay where I am;
> If I had you in the ground safe and sound in a coffin, love,
> That's what would give me freedom, no more staring at the shore.'[8]

Jean Martin, Harris:

> *Nuair a thig mi gon a' chladaich 's a chì mi tonn air thonn*
> *'S a chuimhnicheas mi, Chaluim, gur e siud banaltram do chinn . . .*

> 'When I go to the shore and see wave upon wave
> And I remember, Calum, that they are nursing your head . . .'[9]

With the *Iolaire* the searching of the shore was a literal fact, as in the case of John Campbell, Lewis, looking for his brother:

> *Mi fhìn a' falbh, gad iarraidh, 's mi sileadh sìos gu làr,*
> *Ach ò, Ailig, cha robh sgeul ort, a-muigh ri cliathaich caladh tàmh.*

> 'I went along, seeking you, weeping all the time,
> But oh you weren't there, Alick, out beside a tranquil bay.'

Yet here again Murdo MacFarlane seems to surpass them all. In 'Raoir Reubadh an *Iolaire*' ('Last Night the *Iolaire* was Torn') he says:

> *O nach tug thu dhuinn beò iad,*
> *A chuain, thoir dhuinn bàtht' iad.*

> 'Since you didn't give us them live,
> Ocean, give us them drowned.'[10]

The songmakers' opinions may be ranged across a right–left spectrum. Murdo Morrison, Lewis, directs all his hatred at Germany, claiming that the only thing Britain has done wrong is break the Sabbath. Roderick MacKay, North Uist, devotes a verse to the Germans' low, cowardly tricks (referring presumably to gas and submarines, also used by the British). And he claims that Highland troops kept the Germans from invading England. John Morrison, origin unknown, claims that the troops were fighting 'for Scotland and her reputation' (*air son Alb' 's a cliù*). Rachel Ferguson, Taransay, points out helpfully that according to the Bible there will be war everywhere before there is everlasting peace. But at this point in the spectrum, dualities creep in. Anon., Lewis, declares that the Germans will come to the Highlands and destroy all the houses if they win, then complains about how the Highlands are already being treated:

Riamh o thàinig sgoilean Gallda
Dhubhadh a-mach cainnt ar màthar;
Iomradh air Sir Cailean Caimbeul?
Cha chluinn mi ach 'English Army'.

'Since we were saddled with Lowland schools
Our mother tongue has been put in the bin;
Mention of Sir Colin Campbell?
All I hear is "English Army".'

But he ends by blaming the Kaiser for everything anyway. Roderick MacKay, North Uist, straightens out this kind of confusion: he states sarcastically that although Highland soldiers will fight bravely and loyally as they should, they can certainly expect no reward. William MacKenzie, Glenelg, lays out exactly what the soldiers want – to boot out landowners, put livestock on the land and fish freely for salmon.[11] John MacCormick, Mull, complains that the belligerents are 'Fighting for a cause / Which a pen could have fixed' (*Dian-chogadh mu adhbhar / D'am foghnadh am peann*).[12] Donald MacKay, Lewis, roundly condemns all world rulers, while Donald John MacDonald, South Uist, points out that the evil empires include England's:

Tart cumhachd gus dìreadh
  Air na h-ìompairean gràineil:
Riaghladh Shasainn a' cìsneadh
  Bhochdan, ìslean is ànraich,
Shnàmh suas i gu ìre
  Tro fhuil phrìseil a bràithrean.

'Thirst of power's on the rise
   Upon loathsome emperors:
England's government taxes
   The poor, the humble, the exile,
She's swum up to where she is
   Through her brothers' precious blood.'[13]

Throughout the war, Germany was a military dictatorship run by Hindenburg and Ludendorff. The prominent place given to Wilhelm II in the Gaelic verse of the period is due to the emphasis placed on him by British propaganda, the fact that Kaiser (if pronounced Kay-ser) is a homophone for Gaelic *Ceusar* 'Crucifier', and ill-founded stories in the press about the crucifixion of captives. 'I don't hesitate', sang Margaret MacLeod, Lewis, 'to call the beast *Ceusar* / For he's ripped up many hearts that were brave on their departure.' (*Ò cha b' fhair' orm Ceusar a thoirt air a' bhéist mar ainm – / 'S iomadh crìdh rinn e reubadh a bha glé threubhant' a' falbh.*) Similarly, a song by Neil MacLean, Tiree, contains the word-play *Thoill do ghnìomhairan breuna do cheusadh gu bàs* 'For your stinking deeds you deserve crucifixion'.[14] Following the 'Rape of Belgium' in 1914, a songmaker called Kenneth MacLeod – presumably the Reverend Kenneth MacLeod (1871–1955), Marjorie Kennedy Fraser's collaborator – offered an alternative nickname, the *Feòladair* ('Butcher'). His satire on the Kaiser begins:

Mosglaibh, a chlann,
Á clos na sìth-shàimh,
   Tha chorc ann an làimh an Fheòladair;
Le lasgar 's le gaoir,
A' saltairt nan gaoth,
   Tha casgairt nam maoth air tòiseachadh.

'Awaken, children,
From quiet or silence,
   The knife's in the hand of the Butcher;
With crashing and banging,
Trampling the winds,
   The slaughter of the innocents has started.'[15]

A lengthy attack on the Kaiser by Angus Morrison, Lochbroom, was first published in 1916 as a pamphlet entitled *Oran a' Cheasar*, price 3d, proceeds to the Red Cross.[16] And Malcolm MacKay, Lewis, declared that Wilhelm and his son should be burnt in pitch and tar.[17] As a result of all this, *Ceusar* has become the spelling of choice for 'Kaiser' in twenty-first-century Gaelic novels.

A couple of the songs published in the magazine *Deò na Gréine* deserve recognition as literary curiosities. *Deò* (as we may call it for short) informs us that 'An Cath-Ghairm' ('The Battle-Cry'), by the Reverend Angus M. MacFarlane, United Free Church minister of Dores and Bona, is suitable for a children's choir. In it, a thrush sings of heroes who are ordered overseas

> 'N aghaidh naimhdean borb neo-bhàidheil,
> Gearmailtich làn foill is àrdain,
> Bulgharaich fhuilteach 's Turcaich ghràda.
>
> Trian, cha mhór, de'r n-òigridh àlainn
> Reubta, marbht', no 'n làimh an nàmhaid
> No an grunnd a' chuain iad bàthte . . .
>
> Rìgh nan Dùl thoirt dhachaigh sàbhailt'
> 'Chuid tha beò dhiubh air am fàgail
> 'N déidh dhoibh buaidh thoirt air gach nàmhaid.

'Against fierce unmerciful foes,
Germans full of deceit and pride,
Bloody Bulgarians and ugly Turks.

Almost a third of our handsome young men
Are wounded, killed or in enemy hands
Or drowned at the bottom of the sea . . .

May God of the Elements bring home safe
Those of them who are left alive
Once they have beaten all our foes.'

And an anonymous contributor responded to the Armistice with 'Ceol-Chomhraidh', a 'Musical Conversation' between two lovers, one of whom is a returning soldier. Racist in tone, it mocks the Germans for surrendering by repeatedly using the word *Kameràd*.[18]

The Poetry

By this is meant verse intended for reading, not singing. We should begin with the most promising Gaelic poet of the new century, Father Allan McDonald (1859–1905). In his short poem 'Ceum nam Mìltean' ('The March of Thousands'), he wrote:

> Tha fuaim 'nam chluais 's 'nam cheann
>   A tha fàgail geilt air mo chridhe,
> Mar cheum nam mìltean ag imeachd san ùr-shneachd
>   Dol gu gleac ás nach till iad.

'There's a sound in my ear and head
   That's leaving dread upon my heart,
Like thousands marching through fresh snow
   Going to strife they won't come back from.'

Early commentators thought that this might be a premonition of the Great War, but it was written in 1882–93, too early to reflect the military build-up of the Great Powers, which did not begin until 1898. Still, enough had happened by the 1880s to make Father Allan imagine the wars of Napoleon – still vivid from the reminiscences of veterans in his father's tavern – having to be fought all over again. When war came in 1914, the truth was to be worse than his worst nightmares, but he did not live to see it.[19]

In an editorial of April 1919 entitled 'A Bheil na Baird Ghaidhealach 'nan Cadal?' ('Are the Highland Poets Asleep?'), the editor of *Deò*, Donald Macphie, wrote:

Shaoileamaid ma bha srad de spiorad na bàrdachd ri fhaotainn air Gaidhealtachd, gun taisbeanadh se e fein an dàin no cumha a ghlacadh cridhe na dùthcha air mhodh shònraichte, oir tha 'n call a thachair nas truime na na thachair aig Cùil Lodair.

'One would think that if there were a spark of poetic spirit in the Highlands, it would reveal itself in poems or a lament that would seize the country's heart in a particular way, for the losses that have been inflicted upon us are heavier than those of Culloden.'[20]

It is possible to understand where Macphie was coming from, because one or two of the verse contributions to *Deò* in this period were intellectually challenged. In a long poem entitled 'Spiorad nam Beann' ('The Spirit of the Mountains'), for example, Colonel John MacGregor showed that the Highlands had been turned into a desert, but were threatened by Germans 'who would leave every dwelling-house wretched, enslaved' (*a dh'fhàgadh gach fàrdach gu dìblidh, fo bhann*), so the war was necessary.[21] One seeks in vain for a hint of irony. Despite this sort of stuff, it is the present writer's contention that, in general terms, the poets of the Great War pass Macphie's 'Culloden test' with flying colours.

The two leading exponents of the genre who served in the trenches were the friends John Munro (1889–1918) and Murdo Murray (1890–1964), both from Lewis. Munro's best surviving poem, 'Ar Gaisgich a Thuit sna Blàir' ('Our Heroes who Fell in Battle'), is notable for its words 'plant the standard / firm and high / on the Glorious Hill of Good Peace' (*cuir a' bhratach an sàs / daingeann ard / air*

Sliabh Glòrmhor Deagh-Shìth). The concept of a 'good peace' was fundamental to those who thought seriously about the purpose of the conflict. It meant redistribution of wealth and land, freedom from oppression for all peoples, and an end to all war. Munro died for it at Ypres on 16 April 1918.[22]

Murdo Murray was the author of the diary described in Chapter 6.[23] His best-known poem, 'Luach na Saorsa' ('The Value of Freedom'), queries the Calvinist doctrine of predestination. Stopping a speeding bullet for a moment, he politely asks its opinion. Taking the Calvinist view of its mission, the bullet helpfully points out that death brings victory and freedom.[24] In light of this, it is worth pointing out that in his diary for 1915 Murray has a great deal to say about stray bullets (I give the following in translation only). On 5 March that year, he speaks of 'J. A. M. keeping bullets off with his spade'. On the 11th, 'a bit of shrapnel hit me in the coat'. His full entry for the 16th, after a short spell away, runs: 'Fine day – getting ready for the trench. We went up Kemel way about 7 p.m. We had a lovely afternoon for coming to trenches h2, h3 and h4. First bullet.' He must have been grazed. On the 23rd he remarks: 'A bullet nearly castrated Gardan!' There are serious bullet problems while filling bags with soil on 15 April:

> Bang! Away went my glasses, and the soil stained my face. It hit the bag in front of me. But then my friend Murdie hit a slender bullet[25] with his spade, deflecting it. Unfortunately it went towards Isaac Iain an Tàileir, then out of here towards Lt. Watson. Isaac on his knees while I threw his shirt around his head. Even so, there was no sign of the bullet-hole. But then we found a little red pimple like a fleabite – that was Isaac's wound. Work started again.

On 6 May, 'J. F. Knowles was killed (11 p.m., 5.5.15) coming in from the communication trench, trying to run away from death while death ran after him.' That one could have been shrapnel or a firebomb, of course, but there is no doubt about this (13 June): 'M. A. Cumming was killed by a bullet inside the dugout. For a bullet to hit him, there was only one way for it to come. And it came that way.'

In September 1915, at the Battle of Hooge, Murray was wounded in the head and back. It was the very month that saw the publication of his prose-poem 'Air an Raoin' ('On the Field'), a dream of women, children and music in the style then being encouraged by An Comunn Gaidhealach.[26] It begins, as the title claims, 'on the field':

> *B'i madainn Di-Dòmhnaich a bh' ann. Bha sinn uile gabhail ar tàimh air an raoin, oir bha 'n oidhche seachad, agus àm a' chunnairt – cailleamachadh an latha a' lasadh suas gu maise na maidne samhraidh. Tro norradh beag luaineach bhruadair mi ...*

'It was Sunday morning. We were all resting on the field, as the night was over, and the time of danger – dawn brightening into the beauty of the summer's morning.'

And when the dream is over:

Thàinig an eubh orm; chaidh sin uile air falbh 'na sgleò, ach fad na maidne bha 'n ceòl a chuala mi a' ruith air cùl m' inntinn. A dh'aindeoin oidhirp, chan fhaighinn greim air, ach saoilidh mi gun robh na focail rudeigin mar seo:
  Ò, falbhaidh mi gu m' dhachaigh fhìn,
  Ò, gu m' dhachaigh fhìn – o-hò,
  Falbhaidh mi gu m' dhachaigh fhìn,
  Och a Rìgh, ciod thàinig oirnn!

'I was called; it all faded away, but throughout the morning the music I'd heard was echoing in the back of my mind. Although I tried, I couldn't catch hold of it, but I think the words were something like this:
  "Oh I'll go away to my own home,
  Oh to my own home, oh ho,
  I'll go away to my own home,
  Oh my God, what's happened to us!"'

Following hospitalisation and recuperation, Murray returned to the trenches, this time as an officer; he was wounded again in 1918, but survived, married, settled down as a country schoolmaster in Strathpeffer, and wrote a number of Gaelic essays and poems.[27]

In his thesis on the importance of the war to the history of Gaelic Scotland, Niall Bartlett explains that comparing Munro's two surviving poems from 1916 with his single composition of 1918, 'Air Sgàth nan Sonn' ('For the Sake of the Warriors'), led him to believe at first that these showed how an individual soldier went from idealism to disillusionment. Then he discovered what Murray had said about Munro in 1957:

An déidh dha a bhith aig an tigh air fòrlagh, sgrìobh e thugam ann am mìos na Màirt, 1918, ag innse mar a chòrd a thurus dachaigh ris, ach gu robh e toilichte a bhith air ais ann am poll nan trainnsichean agus – ged nach dubhairt e anns na briathran sin e – na h-uiread r' a dhèanamh: an còrr cha b' urrainn e innse.

'After being at home on leave, he wrote to me in March 1918 telling me how he had enjoyed his visit home, but that he was glad to be back in the mud of the trenches when – though he didn't say it in so many words – there was so much to be done: the rest he couldn't say.'

Bartlett concluded from this that Munro was not disillusioned at all.[28] This fails to take account of the realities of war. Munro had been serving in the trenches for three and a half years. When he led Murray to understand that there was 'much to be done', his friend knew what he meant. He had scores to settle. He was similar to a young man described by Angus Campbell:

> 'Sann an déidh tighinn air tìr an Steòrnabhagh air an t-slighe dhachaidh air fòrladh ás an Fhraing a chuala 'Hero' á Dail-o-Dheas gun deach an treas fear de bhràthraibh a chall. Leis nach leigeadh meud a bhròin agus a chlaoidh spioraid leis aghaidh a chur air an dachaidh, 'se tilleadh an oidhche sin air ais dha'n trainnse a rinn e.

'After coming ashore at Stornoway on his way home on leave from France, "Hero" from South Dell heard of the loss of yet another of his brothers, the third. As he couldn't bear to go home, given the enormity of his grief and depression, he turned round that same night and went back to the trenches.'[29]

One of the foremost Gaelic poets of the home front is another Lewisman, Thomas Donald MacDonald (1864–1937). Born on the Galson estate, he held managerial posts in places like Bristol, London, Ottawa, Glasgow and Stirling, served as secretary of An Comunn Gaidhealach and then retired to Oban.[30] In 1918 he published thirty-two original poems of high quality, carefully constructed in traditional metres, and arranged in such a way as to provide a thoughtful commentary on the evolution of the war; he also threw in a spirited rendering of 'It's a Long Way to Tipperary' with *Tobarmhoire* (Tobermory) in place of Tipperary. For 1914–15 there is enormous pride in 'Trusadh nan Gaidheil a Tìrean Céin' ('The Gathering of the Gael from Foreign Lands'). For 1916, 'Am a' Chogaidh is 'na Dhéidh' ('Wartime and Afterwards') ends in hope that the soldiers will get their rights, which he describes as:

> *Sìth is pailteas maille ruinn*
> *Is seilbh leinn air gach raon,*
> *Sitheann ga toirt ás a' bheinn*
> *Is bradain á Loch Bhraoin.*

'Enjoying peace and plenty
  With possession of the fields,
Taking venison from the hill
  And salmon from Loch Broom.'

At Christmas 1916 he uses the phrase *cogadh breun*, 'stinking war'; he deploys it twice more before the conflict is over. For 1917, 'Imcheist a' Chogaidh' ('War Worries'), an outstanding poem which makes very skilful use of Gaelic vocabulary, is a graphic depiction of the war and its purpose.

> *Toitean nimheil a' tachdadh nan sonn*
>   *Mur bi iad fo chidh'sean deagh-ghléidhte,*
> *Milleadh air bhailtean is tolladh air fhonn –*
>   *Is neònach an cùrs' e gu réite.*

> 'Poisonous clouds are choking our heroes
>   Unless they wear well-maintained gas-masks,
> Towns are destroyed and land's filled with holes –
>   It's a strange way to reach an agreement.'

The German people, he says, have been corrupted by the enemies of peace. 'Ann an Taigh-Eiridinn' ('In a Hospital') is a graphic account of a soldier dying of his wounds, watched over by a nurse. It is an important poem in which we should note the dying soldier's 'desire to return to the fight with his blade' (*a dhéidh air bhith tilleadh dhan chòmhraig le lann*). As we have seen, this emotion is not unique. 'An Àiteigin san Fhraing' ('Somewhere in France') is a powerful lament in four verses, the beginning of each serving as a refrain: *An àiteigin san Fhraing* ('Somewhere in France'), *An àiteigin fon mhuir* ('Somewhere under the sea'), *An àiteigin an cridhe* ('Somewhere in the heart'), *An àiteigin bidh sgrìobht'* ('Somewhere will be written'). It is the beginning of memorialisation.[31]

There is a graphic immediacy in MacDonald's poems for 1917 that makes one wonder why. 'Dìlseachd 'n Am a' Chruaidh-Chàs' ('Loyalty in Time of Crisis'), for example, is subtitled 'Nì a thachair air raon a' bhlàir' ('Something that happened on the battlefield'). The scene is one of horror. The narrator spends an entire night holding his wounded comrade's head out of the water and mud which are filling the trench up to their waists. The poor man seems to have died in the morning, but the narrator speaks twice of the gratefulness in his eyes. The use of the first person arguably raises questions about MacDonald's biography, and it may be speculated that the narrator was his son Robert. This is by no means the only poem in which Macdonald experiments with voice: elsewhere he adopts the personae of a blinded soldier, a dreaming soldier, a wounded soldier, Freedom, the past, and finally a mother, in which her tender feelings for her son in the trenches are interspersed with brutal reality. Could this be MacDonald's wife?[32]

For 1918, 'Leasan a' Chogaidh' ('The Lesson of the War'), which was published in the magazine *Guth na Bliadhna* early that year, begins with a powerful picture of the Highland poor rotting in the slums. The war opens their eyes to injustice, and the lesson is that when peace is achieved, people will strive to throw off their chains and be 'free from the power and greed / Of the minority of the people' (*saor bho smachd is sannt / A' bheag-chuid dhen an t-sluagh*). The longest poem in the book, though not the best, is 'Deireadh a' Mhàirt 1918' ('The End of March 1918'), which presumably refers to the Battle of the Somme. The war is utterly senseless, he says, and he rejects racism, which leads him to express hope that out of the 'ghastly furnace' (*fuirneis oillteil*) will come a better world. 'An Céin-Àit 'na Chadal tha Donnchadh nan Òran' ('Sleeping Abroad is Duncan of the Songs') is a powerful lyric on the theme that the Highland people, personified as the great poet Duncan Ban Macintyre (1724–1812), have died in Flanders. It is essentially about rights to the land. The fact that (as is well known) the real Duncan of the Songs died in his bed in Edinburgh, and is buried in Greyfriars, adds weight to the conceit. 'An Lon-Dubh san Fhraing' ('The Blackbird in France') is another powerful lyric. And 'A' Ciùineachadh an t-Sluaigh' ('Calming Down the People') is a call for moderation as peace approaches.[33]

MacDonald's response to the peace of 1919 is contained in a long poem 'An Déidh a' Chogaidh' ('After the War').[34] Under the same title, and dated 6 December 1921, is an interesting little item in three stanzas beginning:

> 'N déidh seachd ceud bliadhna, thàinig Éirinn gu 'saors',
> Rinn Sasainn rithe géilleadh, 's tha crìoch air a daors',
>   Ged 's iomadh nì fuathaicht' a rinn i san t-srìth,
>   Bha a misneachd làn bhuadhach, is bhuannaich i 'n t-sìth.

> 'After seven hundred years, Ireland's come to her freedom,
> To her England has yielded, her enslavement has ended,
>   Though she's done many loathsome things in the struggle,
>   Her courage has triumphed, and she has won peace.'

He pays tribute to Lloyd George (*Leòid Deòrsa*), the Celt who 'made England bend' (*Thug e lùbadh air Sasainn*), and ends by saying that this gives 'encouragement to Gaelic and the company of the poets' (*misneachd don Ghàidhlig 's do chuideachd nam bàrd*), the latter being an old-fashioned phrase meaning all that Gaelic poets stand for throughout Ireland and Scotland. This is MacDonald's usual moderate voice: he does not say that the Gael of Scotland are trapped in the wrong country, nor does he call for Scottish home rule.[35]

The view of the war put forward by the Reverend Donald MacCallum (1849–1929) in his epic poem 'Domhnullan' is essentially romantic. He places beauty above truth, and his aims are moral and didactic. His work has verve, humour, variety, lyric power and philosophical integrity. This is not true of the so-called *English Translation of the First Canto of Domhnullan*, however, which is a disgrace – not because it is not a translation, but because it is doggerel. On perusing either version, innocent readers will gain the impression that the war (the subject of the First Canto) was fought entirely with swords. They will find the word 'trenches' twice in the alleged English translation, but they will seek in vain for its Gaelic equivalents, *trainnsichean* or *claisean*, in the original. This is an example of the grip of 'panegyric language' on the older Gaelic poets of the day. Curiously, the section 'Treubhantas' ('Valour'), which deals with Domhnullan's martial exploits, is missing from the *English Translation*. In it, MacCallum states explicitly that his purpose is not to describe the goriness (*gaoirealachd*) of the war.[36]

Another of the leading Gaelic poets of the period was Donald Sinclair from Barra (1885–1932), whose work as an essayist is described in the chapter 'Gaelic Prose'. He spent the war working in Manchester and Wembley as an electrical draughtsman for Metropolitan Vickers, a 'reserved occupation', and the reticence in his work in matters pertaining to the war is exemplified by a line in his poem 'Slighe nan Seann Seun' ('The Way of the Old Spells'). Hugh MacDiarmid translated *A làithean sin a thriall le ial-luchd àis mo shluaigh* as 'O days that departed with the time-store of the wisdom of my people'.[37] But the poem resurfaced in 1954 with *ùir* in place of *àis*, which allows a translation 'O days that took away a whole new generation of my people'.[38]

As a professional in the munitions industry, Sinclair must have signed a contract which forbade him to write about public affairs, but there may be more to it than that. The earliest evidence of codification comes in his long poem 'Là nan Seachd Sìon' ('The Day of the Seven Elements').[39] It is a description of a gale in the islands, but includes the following:

> *Bha slochdan an aodann an talmhan*
>   *'S an d' amhlaig an dearg-theine 'theas*
> *'S mar thaisbhalt air ùthachd na beathrach*
>   *Gum b' ùr-sgàinte aghaidh nan creag.*
> *Bu lìonar ceann taighe bha rùisgte*
>   *'S cabar dubh smùide bha dis,*
>   *Gun tughadh, gun sgrath is gun sìoman,*
>   *Lom-nochda, tur-spìonte, gun riob'.*

> 'There were pits in the face of the earth
>   Where the 'red fire' had buried its heat
> With the face of the rocks freshly split
>   As proof of the thunderbolt's suicide.

Many houses were roofless, revealing
    Black, smoke-stained, teetering timbers
Without thatch or divots or anchors,
But naked, plucked bare, without ropes.'[40]

The *slochdan*, 'pits', sound like shell-craters. The last lines of the poem are:

Bhuail coileach na sìthe a sgiathan,
    A' salmadh am fianais gach pòir,
'O cliù dhuits' Aon-Dé na Trianaid
    A ghiùlain tro sheunaibh sinn beò!'

'The cockerel of peace beat its wings,
    Announcing before every people,
"O be praised, One God of the Trinity
    Who brought us alive through enchantments!"'[41]

Note the poet's choice of *sìth* 'peace' in preference to *fèath* 'calm' or *turadh* 'dry weather'. Did 'Là nan Seachd Sìon' begin as a description of a storm and end as a description of the harm that war does to the poor?

Sinclair's poem 'Gairm Dùsgaidh' ('Awakening Cry', 1917) is a call to spiritual values, leading to the concluding phrase *Tìr nan Òg* ('the Land of the Young', the Celtic paradise). The war is not mentioned, but capitalism is – and, by implication, those such as the board and shareholders of Metropolitan Vickers who were profiting hugely from it.

Ò, cuimhnich fòs nach e do shalchar-mhaoin
A mheasas Eòlas agus Oilean naomh.
    Ò, tuig gu ceart seo, nach e tòic na feòl'
No cnàimh de d' cholainn ach an spiorad beò
    A sheasas cùirt nan àl.

'Oh, remember still that it isn't your wealth-dirt
That Knowledge and Learning will see as holy.
    Oh, get this right, that it's not the swelling of flesh
Or a bone of your body but the living spirit
    That will triumph in history's eyes.'

Salchar-mhaoin, 'wealth-dirt', 'filthy lucre', is an expression worth remembering.[42]

Sinclair's love poem 'Ròs Àluinn' ('Lovely Rose', 1917) brings us still closer to the heart of the matter. It was presumably addressed to his sweetheart from Barra, Margaret Campbell, whom he married in 1918.

Neo 'n e aon de chlann na sgéithe
Gheibh do ghaol mar mhil do chléibhe?
Ò, mas è – car son nach fheudadh
　　Mise fhéin a bhith den àl sin?

'Or will it be one of the "sons of the shield"
Who'll capture your heart like your bosom's honey?
Oh, if it is – why couldn't I
　　Myself be one of those people?'

Guilt, then, that he was not at the front. And in fact, 'Gaol-Mhulad' ('Love-Sadness', also 1917) is a prose-poem which corresponds so closely in style to Murray's 'Air an Raoin' that it could have been modelled on it. It is full of language like: *Chunnaic mi 'san chòmh-thràth seana chraobh nan caogad Samhuinn a' smìdeadh le a meòirean ioma-luasgach ris a' chuan shiar.* 'I saw in the half-light the old tree of fifty Hallowe'ens waving to the western ocean with its ever-moving branches.' It is a vision that might well be seen by a wounded soldier, although Sinclair would never have been so crass as to make such a claim, nor to pretend to set it in the trenches. Its setting is a place where the poet can sit on a hillock surrounded by bracken, and observe fishermen bless themselves before going down to the sea with their *bonnach-cuain* ('ocean-bannock') under their oxter – in a word, Barra.[43]

Sorley MacLean (1911–96), the foremost Gaelic poet of the twentieth century, devotes two passages of his work to the Great War. The first is in his long political poem from the 1930s, 'An Cuilitheann' ('The Cuilinn').

Dé nì siud do ar n-eilean,
Festubert eile is Loos eile,
　　is barrachd ainmean na dh'fhóghnas
　　air cloich Phort Ruigh'dh fo thòin an leómhainn?
Se diabhlaidh beag a bha gur mealtainn
ged ghabh sibhse Beaumont-Hamel;
　　's ma bhios sibh beò a-rithist, chì
　　sibh garraich eile le O.B.E.
is cailleachan beairteach an Sligeachan suilbhir
ag ithe 's a' faicinn a' Chuilithinn.

'What good will another Festubert
and another Loos do to our island
　　when there are more than enough names already
　　under the lion's bum on the Portree monument?
Athough you captured Beaumont-Hamel
you got precious little pleasure from it,

>   and if you come alive again, you'll see
>   other gannets who have the OBE
> with their rich wives in cheerful Sligachan
> dining and gazing upon the Cuillin.'

It is in rhyming couplets, of which the rhyme *chì* : *O.B.E.* (also reflected in the English version) is particularly amusing. As throughout this poem, the poet stands upon the Cuillin, a position taken up to represent the cumulative experience of all who ever lived in Skye, to guard the island, to defend its future, and to look out questioningly over the whole world, its heroes and its villains, to try to work out what is right and what is wrong. Firstly, another war will do no good. The Portree War Memorial features a lion perched on a granite column, the lower parts of its anatomy clearly visible from below; it is the British lion, of course, and the poet implies that those from the island who fought in the Great War were treated like excrement.

Festubert, Loos and Beaumont-Hamel were all battles fought by men of the Cameron Highlanders from Skye. For centuries, taking a town in battle had been synonymous with plunder and enrichment, not to mention rape; for these men there was nothing, even if anything had been left of the town. Why the poet should say 'other gannets' is puzzling until one remembers that men in the trenches were often left three or four days without rations. There is a contrast, then, between ravenous men in the trenches who have nothing, and ravenous men in Sligachan who have the Order of the British Empire and are merely fat. The reference to their rich wives implies that they have married into wealth and are themselves contemptible: as MacLean's editors point out, these lines are 'veined with class hostility'. For all the Skyemen's sacrifice, then, their once-happy land, symbolised here by an alliterative toponym (*Sligeachan suilbhir*), is occupied, the irreverent interlopers gorging themselves while gazing blankly upon MacLean's *mons sacer*. Did the men of Skye pay with their lives to make their island a holiday playground for the rich?[44]

'Festubert 16/17.v.1915' is one of MacLean's latest poems, first published in 1992. It is dominated by doors. There is no obvious reason why these should provide the dominant image of a poem about a battle in the Great War, other than that Festubert must have been connected with doors in one of the poet's childhood memories. The clue to that is the prominence given to the children of Skye in the heart of the poem.

> *Dorsan gam fosgladh gu sàmhach*
> *agus gan dùnadh mar a dh'fhosgladh:*
> *gille no nighean, no dithis no triùir,*
> *gan toirt a-mach á rumannan sgoile,*

agus iad ri dhol dhachaigh
sìos an Drochaid Mhór,
gu meadhan a' bhaile,
no deas gu na h-Acraichean . . .

'Doors opening quietly
and shut as they were opened:
boy or girl, or two or three,
taken out of the schoolrooms,
having to go home
down by the Big Bridge,
to the middle of the town,
or south to Lots . . .'

And so he continues, listing the different parts of Portree, stressing (by repetition) the figure of thirteen dead from the town in one day, then listing other parts of Skye and the Highlands that suffered losses at Festubert.

MacLean was born on 26 October 1911. On 17 May 1915 he was three years and 204 days old: not old enough to go to school, but exactly old enough for the strange word 'Festubert' to be associated in one of his earliest memories with doors.

Doors are important to a child of that age. They are large. Something bad can come through them. They can make a frightening noise. They can hurt you. If you suffer from separation anxiety, a closed door between you and your mother can make you cry. But if you are very clever, you can drag a chair up to a door, climb up and open it for yourself.

Doors are also relevant to Great War armaments. The pillboxes that protected the great guns on both sides of the front had steel doors on their loopholes. These opened up, belched death and closed again. The poem begins:

Stararaich nan gunnachan beaga
is dairirich nan gunnachan móra,
dorsan troma gan dùnadh
le sgailc is stairnich na doininn;
sian is miolaran nan sligean
mu Fhestubert a' phuill 's na fala:

dorsan móra troma dùnadh
air ioma òigear làidir treun.

'The rattle of the little guns
and the roar of the big guns,
heavy doors being shut

with the blast and crash of the storm;
the whizz and whine of the shells
around Festubert of the mud and the blood:

big heavy doors shutting
on many brave strong warriors.'

We speak of the doors of the mind too, and the shutting of doors on 'brave strong warriors' can signify madness or death. Both apply. There is a contrast with the quiet doors of school and home in the passage already quoted. And at the end, following the litany of Highland place-names, all of the doors come back.

Dorsan gam fosgladh 's gan dùnadh
gu sàmhach ann an ioma taigh
agus a' chlann a' dol dhachaigh
gu còineadh no gu tost.

Dairirich nan gunnachan móra,
sgailc dhorsan troma a' dùnadh
mu bhailtean eile san Fhraing
agus feadh na Roinn Eòrpa,
is dorsan gam fosgladh gu sàmhach
gu fàrdaichean a' bhristeadh-chridhe.

'Doors being opened and closed
quietly in many a house
and the children going home
to weeping or silence.

The roar of the big guns,
the crash of heavy doors closing
about other towns in France
and all over Europe,
and doors being opened quietly
to dwellings where the heart is broken.'

There is every kind of door here: of the house, of the school, of the mind, of the pillbox, of politics, of military strategy, and of the coffin lid as it is slowly closed and nailed down. Thanks no doubt to the power of memory, MacLean has created a remarkable artefact out of a simple word.[45]

In his poem 'Bàs Baile' ('The Death of a Township'), the Reverend John MacLeod (1918–95), whose father was lost on the *Iolaire*, said memorably of the war: *Bha 'm murt ud laghail.* 'That murder was lawful.' And verse was still being made to the war a century after it began. It is of particular interest when the poet can be seen as one of its victims: for example, through the loss of his grandfather and the effect this had on his mother. I am thinking here of the comedian and writer Norman Maclean (1936–2017). This sort of chain effect, the long-remembered shock of a loved one's death, is synthesised by the Lewis poet Maletta MacPhail in two short lines: *Cha tàinig Uilleam dhachaigh tuilleadh. / Cha tàinig na Oighrig.* 'William never returned. / Neither did Oighrig.'[46]

Notes

1. *Deò*, vol. 11 (1915–16) (January 1916), p. 61.
2. Malcolm Macdonald and Donald John MacLeod, *Call na h-Iolaire: The Darkest Dawn, The Story of the Iolaire Tragedy* (Stornoway: Acair, 2018), pp. 330–4, 410–13; Dòmhnall Alasdair Moireasdan (ed.), *The Going Down of the Sun: The Great War and a Rural Lewis Community/Dol Fodha na Grèine: Buaidh a' Chogaidh Mhòir – Nis gu Baile an Truiseil* (Stornoway: Acair, 2014), pp. 112–15, 259; Jo NicDhòmhnaill, Annella NicLeòid and Dòmhnall Iain MacLeòid (eds), *Cuimhneachan, Remembrance: Bàrdachd a' Chiad Chogaidh, Gaelic Poetry of World War One* (Stornoway: Acair, 2015), p. 362.
3. NicDhòmhnaill et al., *Cuimhneachan*, pp. 261–335 (laments), 343–77 (*Iolaire*), 420 (the Runrig song).
4. For example, 'Bruadar an t-Saighdear' by 'Daileach', a dream of home with a lyrical battlefield scene, sounds authentic. It was published with music in *Deò*, vol. 12 (1916–17) (September 1917), p. 185.
5. Fred MacAmhlaidh (ed.), *Domhnall Ruadh Chorùna: Òrain is Dàin le Domhnall Domhnallach a Uibhist a Tuath* (Lochmaddy: Comann Eachdraidh Uibhist a Tuath, 1995), pp. 1–63; cf. Ronald I. M. Black (ed.), *An Tuil: Anthology of 20th Century Scottish Gaelic Verse* (Edinburgh: Polygon, 1999), p. xxiv.
6. Black, *An Tuil*, p. 122; NicDhòmhnaill et al., *Cuimhneachan*, p. 56; David Goldie and Roderick Watson, eds, *From the Line: Scottish War Poetry 1914–1945* (Glasgow: Association for Scottish Literary Studies, 2014), p. 39; Lizzie MacGregor (ed.), *Beneath Troubled Skies: Poems of Scotland at War, 1914–1918* (Edinburgh: Scottish Poetry Library and Polygon, 2015), p. 86.
7. Murchadh MacPhàrlain, *An Toinneamh Dìomhair* (Stornoway: Stornoway Gazette, 1973), pp. 62–4, 81–2; Black, *An Tuil*, pp. 236–40; NicDhòmhnaill et al., *Cuimhneachan*, pp. 92, 104, 144, 226–8, 398–402.
8. NicDhòmhnaill et al., *Cuimhneachan*, pp. 124, 270, 332, 350.
9. Mòrag NicLeòid (ed.), *Bàrdachd Scalpaigh* (Tarbert: Adhartas na Hearadh, 2014), pp. 192–3.

10. MacPhàrlain, *An Toinneamh Dìomhair*, pp. 68–9; NicDhòmhnaill et al., *Cuimhneachan*, pp. 346, 376; Macdonald and MacLeod, *Call na h-Iolaire*, p. 398.
11. NicDhòmhnaill et al., *Cuimhneachan*, pp. 24–6, 34, 44, 78, 162, 240–6, 328, 330.
12. *Deò*, vol. 14 (1918–19) (January 1919), p. 58; NicDhòmhnaill et al., *Cuimhneachan*, p. 222.
13. NicDhòmhnaill et al., *Cuimhneachan*, pp. 276, 384.
14. Ibid. pp. 160, 250.
15. *Deò*, vol. 10 (1914–15) (November 1914), p. 21. For MacLeod see Black, *An Tuil*, pp. 720–2.
16. *Deò*, vol. 11 (1915–16) (July 1916), p. 159; NicDhòmhnaill et al., *Cuimhneachan*, pp. 230–6.
17. NicDhòmhnaill et al., *Cuimhneachan*, p. 82.
18. *Deò*, vol. 12 (1916–17) (March 1917), p. 88, and vol. 14 (1918–19) (February 1919), p. 70.
19. Ronald Black (ed.), *Eilein na h-Òige: The Poems of Fr Allan McDonald* (Glasgow: Mungo, 2002), pp. 288, 426.
20. *Deò*, vol. 14 (1918–19) (April 1919), p. 99.
21. *Deò*, vol. 14 (1918–19), pp. 60–1, 73–4.
22. Murchadh Moireach, *Luach na Saorsa* (Glasgow: Gairm, 1970), pp. 87, 88; Black, *An Tuil*, p. 216; NicDhòmhnaill et al., *Cuimhneachan*, p. 134.
23. Moireach, *Luach na Saorsa*, pp. 11–51.
24. *Deò*, vol. 10 (1914–15) (May 1915), p. 126; Moireach, *Luach na Saorsa*, pp. 73–4; Black, *An Tuil*, p. 220; Goldie and Watson, *From the Line*, p. 68; MacGregor, *Beneath Troubled Skies*, p. 32.
25. *Peilear caol*, a cliché of Gaelic verse.
26. *Deò*, vol. 10 (1914–15), pp. 180–1, cf. Black, *An Tuil*, pp. xxiii–xxiv.
27. Black, *An Tuil*, p. 749.
28. Murchadh Moireach, 'Iain Rothach (1)', *Gairm*, no. 19 (An t-Earrach, 1957), pp. 262–5, p. 265; Moireach, *Luach na Saorsa*, pp. 83, 87–8; Black, *An Tuil*, p. 218; Niall Somhairle Finlayson Bartlett, 'The First World War and the 20th Century in the History of Gaelic Scotland: A Preliminary Analysis' (unpublished M.Phil. thesis, Glasgow, 2014), pp. 13–14; Moireasdan, *The Going Down of the Sun*, p. 164.
29. Aonghas Caimbeul (Am Puilean), *Suathadh ri Iomadh Rubha* (Glasgow: Gairm, 1973), p. 63.
30. Lachlan Macbean, *The Celtic Who's Who* (Kirkcaldy: Fifeshire Advertiser, 1921), pp. 90–1; *An Gaidheal*, vol. 32 (1936–7), pp. 150–1; Black, *An Tuil*, p. xxviii; NicDhòmhnaill et al., *Cuimhneachan*, pp. 468–9; public records.
31. T. D. MacDhomhnuill, *Dàin agus Dealbhan-Fhacail an Am a' Chogaidh* (Glasgow: Archibald Sinclair, 1918), pp. 12–13, 14–16, 21–2, 25, 26, 27, 29, 30, 35.

32. Ibid. pp. 19–20, 23, 32, 33, 34–5, 36, 49. Robert John MacDonald was born in Ottawa in 1896. He was at school in Glasgow in 1911, according to that year's census. What happened to him subsequently is as yet unknown.
33. *Guth*, vol. 15 (1918), pp. 81–2; MacDhomhnuill, *Dàin*, pp. 37–8, 42–3, 46–8, 50, 51.
34. T. D. MacDhomnuill, *An Déidh a' Chogaidh* (Glasgow: Archibald Sinclair, 1921), pp. 11–29, see Black, *An Tuil*, pp. xxviii–xxix.
35. MacDhomnuill, *An Déidh a' Chogaidh*, p. 3.
36. An t-Urr. Domhnull Mac Chalum, *Domhnullan, Dàn an Ceithir Earrannan* (Glasgow: A. Mac-Labhruinn, 1925), pp. 10–11; Rev. Donald MacCallum, *English Translation of the First Canto of Domhnullan* (Glasgow, 1927), pp. 13, 16; Black, *An Tuil*, p. xxviii.
37. Hugh MacDiarmid (ed.), *The Golden Treasury of Scottish Poetry* (London: Macmillan, 1946), p. 18.
38. Anna NicIain, 'Baird a' Bhaile Againn', *Gairm*, no. 7 (An t-Earrach, 1954), pp. 221–5, p. 225; Black, *An Tuil*, p. 737.
39. *Guth*, vol. 12 (1915), pp. 310–14, 425–33, and vol. 13 (1916), pp. 108–12, 180–9.
40. Lisa Storey (ed.), *D.M.N.C: Sgrìobhaidhean Dhòmhnaill Mhic na Ceàrdaich* (Inverness: Clàr, 2014), p. 59.
41. Ibid. p. 62.
42. Ibid. p. 68.
43. Ibid. pp. 73, 387–90.
44. Somhairle MacGill-Eain/Sorley MacLean, *Caoir Gheal Leumraich/White Leaping Flame, Collected Poems in Gaelic with English Translations*, ed. Christopher Whyte and Emma Dymock (Edinburgh: Polygon, 2011), pp. 78–81; Somhairle MacGill-Eain/Sorley MacLean, *An Cuilithionn 1939 and Unpublished Poems*, ed. Christopher Whyte (Glasgow: Association for Scottish Literary Studies, 2011), pp. 56–7, 176–7.
45. MacGill-Eain, *Caoir Gheal Leumraich*, pp. 338–41, 460, 476–8; NicDhòmhnaill et al., *Cuimhneachan*, pp. 416–19.
46. Black, *An Tuil*, p. 414; NicDhòmhnaill et al., *Cuimhneachan*, pp. 432, 442.

Chapter 6

Gaelic Prose
Ronald Black

Although the Gaelic verse of the war has received substantial attention,[1] little or none has been paid to the prose. The present chapter is a first attempt to remedy this. It is a rewarding field because it includes a number of subliterary categories, and Gaelic writing tended to avoid the torch-beam of censorship.

Due to space constraints, quotations are given in translation only. The translations are by the present writer.

The Diary

The most remarkable Gaelic document to emerge from the war is a diary kept by Murdo Murray (1890–1964), a shoemaker's son from Lewis.[2] Graduating from the University of Aberdeen in 1913, he taught successively in Lewis, Uist and Sutherland before joining the Gordons at the outbreak of war.

The diary covers the periods February to November 1915 and April to June 1917. The first few entries introduce us to the routine of the trenches: mud, shells, watching aeroplanes, inspections by brigadiers and generals, the sound of the pipes, variable weather, digging, and a frequently noted activity which Murray always calls, in English, 'bomb throwing'. Presumably it means taking the pin out of a grenade and throwing it into an enemy trench – clearly a specialisation, hence the use of English. We meet the same phenomenon in the war memories of the Reverend Malcolm Morrison – to epitomise a true soldier he says: 'Se *bomb-thrower* a bh' ann.' ('He was a bomb-thrower.')[3]

The reader is struck by a succession of 'firsts': the first letter from home, the first mention of death, the first longing for home, the first mention of gas, the first elegiac tone, the first instance of culture-clash with English soldiers, the first criticism of a general, the first mention of God. One day in March 1915, Murray writes: 'A letter from home and another from S.' He notes no more letters from home, but many from 'S'. Not until May 1917 does he reveal her name – *Sìne*, Jean (Macinnes, from Skye).

At various points we note: eagerness to escape the trench and get at the Germans; a startling emphasis on painterly beauty; sensitivity to sound; graphic descriptions of the ruined towns of Ypres and Arras; regular (roughly week-on, week-off) rotation away from the trenches;[4] days of exquisite joy. Some examples will not go amiss. The entry for 14 April 1915 includes an extraordinary contrast:

> Lovely with full sun, the whole world joyful. The chirping of the birds, a sweet flowing note. But we had cause to grieve. James Orr Cruickshank was wounded through the head – his forehead was dashed to pieces; despite all that could be done, his blood spilled to the ground and his life petered out.

On 27 April, Murray notes laconically that twenty-two men out of twenty-six have been killed in J trench 'by Jack'; this is Jack Johnson (1878–1946), heavyweight boxing champion of the world, the army's nickname for a heavy German artillery shell. On 8 June, sandwiched between reports of deaths and shelling, he says: 'Lovely misty morning, the sun a red flame behind the trees – gorgeous to behold – the mist rising multicoloured from the surface of the ground on this side of the row of trees – as beautiful a sight as I've ever seen.' On 17 June, he writes in English: 'The wounded came streaming across the road, some with smashed minds, arms, legs, crawling along. Piteous scenes – brave, plucky fellows. What blood.' His switches to English are variously provoked by a speech from a general, the mechanical horror of the Battle of Ypres, or a dogfight in the sky – new technology.

There is also the unexpected. On 1 August, Murray tells how his platoon had been out digging the night before while a tremendous bombardment went on.

> At Krunstat the shells were getting too close, so we stopped. I hadn't been there long when I saw a horseman galloping along, knocking sparks off the road, making an opening for a six-horse shell-carriage. I'll never forget the struggling and rattling of the horses. Three like that went by, as they were needed somewhere. Tide waits for no man.

Then on the 7th the only entry is: 'Reading Ossian. A minute now and again.'

At the Battle of Hooge in September, Murray was wounded in the head and back. When he came home on leave next month, all mention of his family is absent, though he has had plenty to say of Jean. He speaks only of scenery. When he returned to the trenches it was as an officer in the Seaforths. How he spent 1916 we do not know, but by 1917 he had more time for thinking and reading, comparing the Gaelic and English New Testaments for example, and it struck him as ironic that Christianity calls man the 'highest being', although he wreaks such destruction. When he meets an old Frenchman who had been in the Franco-Prussian War, he remarks: 'His son was seriously wounded. He's seen a lot of war. This made me think – every generation in France blooded defending their country! What's wrong?'

There is no diary record for the serious arm wound which Murray received in 1918. He married Jean in 1921, and they settled down as country schoolteachers in Strathpeffer. They had no family.[5] Murray made a modest name for himself as a poet and essayist, but his war diary is his outstanding achievement. It is remarkable for its revelation of joy, colour and beauty in the midst of appalling ugliness.

The *Iolaire*

Early in the morning of 1 January 1919, HM Yacht *Iolaire* sank on *Biastan Thuilm* (the 'Beasts of Holm' at the entrance to Stornoway Harbour) with the loss of 201 men out of 280, mostly sailors returning from the war. There have been several books about the disaster, only one of them in Gaelic. *Call na h-Iolaire* by Norman Malcolm Macdonald (1927–2000) is a work of non-fiction, but Macdonald was a playwright and poet.[6] In Chapter 1 he describes the chaotic situation at Kyle of Lochalsh on 31 December, as hundreds of servicemen pile off the trains and the naval authorities look for a way of getting them to Stornoway. Two vessels are available, the *Sheila* and the *Iolaire* (it is Gaelic for 'eagle', but the sailors, unaccustomed to their language receiving any respect, assumed it had something to do with *Iolanthe*). Macdonald dramatises or imagines the conversations, and the chapter ends:

> 'The glass is rising,' said Mason. 'And it looks like being a fine night.'
> 'What speed do you do?'
> 'Ten knots.'
> 'Happy New Year.'
> The *Iolaire* sailed.

Chapter 2 consists solely of quotations from the survivors, arranged in order of events. This fulfils the dramatist's urge to tell the story through the characters' words. Firstly, there is the voyage across the Minch, the men looking forward to being home. What comes next is the most chilling moment of all to readers who have travelled on a CalMac ferry, and have moved towards the door leading down to the car-deck as their destination comes into view.

> Then I said to Calum, 'We're nearly in.' So we put on our oilskins and went up to sit at the bow, ready to step out of her. And I turned to him and said, 'Oh, Calum' (I was always joking with him), 'we're nearly on the shore here!' 'Aha,' says he, 'but you're from Harris.' He was always pulling my leg.

Next, in quotation after quotation, we have first-hand accounts of the awful noise the ship makes on striking the Beasts, the steep list to starboard, the pitch darkness, men jumping (or tumbling) into the agitated sea, the stern swinging into the rocks, the officers doing little or nothing, lifeboats being smashed by the waves, men trying to leap on to the rocks, rockets going up, and John Finlay MacLeod's memorable account of how he brings a rope ashore. Some men get across it, while others fall into the sea. One man who fell says: 'I felt sea filling me up inside. I don't think there's any death as easy as that. It's like falling asleep. And I lost consciousness until I found myself vomiting brine on land.'

Some of the men who get ashore stumble as far as a house. The *Iolaire* drifts out a little, lists further to starboard, the funnel crashes down, and several men climb up the masts, but only one survives till morning, by which time the masts are the only part of the *Iolaire* that can be seen. The chapter ends with an irony-laden quotation of just fifteen words. 'Peace had been declared: it was our last journey.'

The creative heart of *Call na h-Iolaire* is Chapter 5. It is poignantly prefaced with the text of a sermon preached by the Reverend Kenneth Cameron on the first Sabbath after the disaster, *Bithibh sàmhach, agus tuigibh gur mise Dia* . . . (Psalms 46: 10). In the King James Bible this is: 'Be still, and know that I am God.' In Gaelic, however, it means: 'Be quiet, and know that I am God.' The first page is extraordinary. In style, as its paragraphs become shorter and shorter and disappear finally into ellipsis, it resembles the sinking of a ship. The chapter follows the experiences of some of the survivors, and some of those who were waiting in various townships to greet their loved ones. We meet the beginnings of memorialisation, as in: '"Sheshader has been drowned," they'd be saying.' Sheshader is not a person but a place. Towards the end of this superb piece of writing the author says:

> What was it anyway but the loss of two hundred more men after a war that had killed millions? What was it but something that had happened up there far away amongst those people, worthless as they were, who lived in the Highlands?

A very fine book, *The Darkest Dawn*, was published to mark the centenary. Mostly in English, it contains the recorded memories of five survivors and ten of those who were awaiting the men's return. Perhaps the most dramatic of the recordings is one in which Donald Morrison, 'the Patch', tells how MacLeod brought the rope ashore and how he himself spent the night on the mast.[7]

The Essays

During the war there were two Gaelic periodicals, *An Deò-Gréine* ('The Sunbeam') and *Guth na Bliadhna* ('The Voice of the Year'). We may call them *Deò* and *Guth* for short. Both contained articles in English as well as Gaelic, but the present discussion will consider only Gaelic material. *Deò* was the monthly magazine of An Comunn Gaidhealach, right-wing, unionist, pietist, frequently racist, fond of printing songs with music, effectively a tabloid. *Guth* was an independent quarterly, left-wing, nationalist, internationalist, strongly inclined towards irony and sarcasm, fond of printing serious poetry, effectively a broadsheet. *Deò* was edited by Donald Macphie, a country schoolmaster, and the Gaelic in it was generally good, seldom outstanding. *Guth* was edited by a Fabian member of the gentry, Roderick Erskine of Mar, and the Gaelic in it varies from poor to excellent. Neither said a single word about the *Iolaire*; the reason for this is a matter for further research.

Between these two periodicals, the outstanding journalist was Angus Henderson from Ardnamurchan. His articles in *Guth* display a vivid turn of phrase, a fearless approach to controversy, and an impressive grasp of economics and geopolitics. Articles in *Guth* were frequently unsigned, in which case they may have been the product of teamwork. Leading articles in *Deò* were always unsigned but were presumably Macphie's work.

Guth argued consistently for pacifism and the self-determination of peoples. It always referred to what we now call the UK as *na Trì*

Rìoghachdan, 'the Three Kingdoms', and to the dominant force in the UK as *Sasunn* ('England') or *Iain Buidhe* ('Yellow John', John Bull). In 1910, it presented cogent arguments against the arms race, speaking of Armageddon and how a spark could light it. It pointed out that all countries were now interdependent through trade, and that the trade per capita of small countries was bigger than that of big ones. 'Big nations boast of empire, strength and race, small nations of better things.'[8]

By 1912, Henderson was warning that 'the barometer is steadily falling in every European capital'. Wars are caused by the rich and idle; the rich and educated start wars, but do not fight in them. Setting out the geopolitical situation from the German point of view, he found that Germany's aspirations, such as the use of a coaling port on the Mediterranean, were reasonable. The greatest danger to peace, he claimed, was England's love of empire. England's difficulty was Scotland's and Ireland's opportunity; both the latter kingdoms were ready for home rule, but always looked at everything through English eyes. 'When Iain Buidhe unsheathes his sword, Scotland and Ireland go battle crazy.' For militarism in the Gaelic world Henderson blamed poets from Ossian to John Campbell of Ledaig (1823–97). Scotland, he said, needed a leader.[9]

The beginning of the war produced an outstanding essay, almost certainly also by Henderson, 'Neo-Phàirteachd na Flandrais' ('The Neutrality of Belgium'). If Germany had not invaded Belgium, the British or French would have done so. England, he said, was not fighting for Belgium but for herself, and 'It's news to us indeed to hear that our friend is a protector of countries weaker than herself . . . Supporting small states! How then did she build up her empire, on which the sun never sets?'[10]

As the war dragged on, both *Guth* and *Deò* became reluctant to discuss anything but peace. This meant tackling the land issue, however, which an anonymous writer in *Guth* did head-on, attacking landlordism in general and the then Duke of Sutherland in particular. More than once he declared that 'the wages of war are the eviction notice'. Everything was taxed except land, he said, because the élite owned it. He also attacked An Comunn Gaidhealach, while praising the soldiers and Keir Hardie. 'Let the returning soldiers demand the land.'[11]

The end of the war produced the interesting comment, perhaps by Erskine, that 'the only thing to come out of it that we can be proud of is the Russian Revolution'. This resulted in his having to defend himself from critics on his own side, and in his injunction: 'Irishmen, commit murder and rapine for England on foreign soil, and you will get your birthright.' After that, it was time for a full assessment. During the war, found *Guth*, the government had paid shipowners ten times the value of their vessel if sunk. 'The state is generous when it gets a chance to hand over millions and scores of millions to financiers.' Huge numbers of men had fought and died for two promises: that peoples would have self-determination, and that it was to be 'the last of all wars'. Both had been broken. The latter notion had been rubbished already by 'Churchill, an Englishman from Dundee', Haig having agreed that they must get ready for the next conflict. The new world that men fought for was just a *bruadar faoin* – a vapid dream. 'The main result of the war', declared *Guth*, 'is that the whole of society has been left at the mercy of capitalists.' And for Germany, submitting meekly to the Treaty of Versailles was a bad idea. Next year, they said it again, speaking of the soldiers:

> They turned a deaf ear to the history of their country . . . They knew that nothing was ever got from England in time of war but sweet words (*beul bòidheach*) and broken promises . . . Nevertheless, they willingly joined the army.

The cause of war, said *Guth*, is capitalism. And years afterwards, the theme was taken up by a writer called John Campbell: 'How we will be mocked by Germans who read about Highlanders thrown into prison for ploughing a bit of land in their own country!'[12]

Turning now to *Deò*, the beginning of the war was marked by a ferocious editorial entitled 'Uilleam-gun-Chèill – Plàigh na Roinn Eòrpa' ('Mad Willie – the Plague of Europe'). Macphie describes how women and children were raped in Belgium by invading German armies, and how our brave Highland soldiers responded with their bayonets: 'At the first thrust, the enemy would be squealing like piglets.' He made much use of the words *brùid* ('brute') and *brùidealachd* ('brutality'), portraying the war as a struggle between right and wrong, and stating that young men who failed to join up were cowards – anyway, 'the more soldiers there are, the sooner it will finish'. January 1915 brought New Year wishes to 'our soldiers, our sailors, the Highlands and Britain'. Obviously responding to reasoned arguments, he stated that 'the navy saves us money' and that it was wrong to mention the Clearances because 'everyone must do his duty to the kingdom', at which sticky point he changed the subject and attacked the Kaiser instead. On one occasion, however, he took the risk of giving voice to the opposition, in the form of a man who had told him: 'Scotland might as well be under German rule, the way things are going!' He couched his answer in religious terms, praying that those who came back from the war would have the place in their own land that they deserved. He also accused *Guth* of treason, remarking that his competitor was in line for the Iron Cross. Then in October 1915, he discussed the cost of the conflict and the need to save money, concluding that if it led to abstinence, the war would have been a blessing.[13]

Editorials of 1919 proposed weak and vague solutions to the land problem in which landlords were not mentioned. A view of the class system was expressed, using the past tense because, in the editor's view, the war had put such things to one side:

> People were divided into classes according to wealth – upper, middle, lower. The upper classes were spending their lives as if in a world of their own. Those in the middle were striving to go higher, with an eye to the top of the roost. Those below were moaning and muttering, and blaming everyone but themselves . . . The lower classes have given the only wealth they had, their lives.

Clearly he had spotted the weakening of the class system; like everyone else, he recognised that change was coming, but the only basis he could see for change was Christianity.[14]

Macphie's editorial on the Armistice focuses on grief, hatred of Germany and rebuilding (the land question). Despite writing a paragraph filled with hate, he ends: 'One virtue above all others will resolve tricky issues, and that is Brotherly Love.' His editorial on the Treaty of Versailles is equally anti-German. Slightly more subtle is 'Plàigh an Ama' ('The Plague of Our Times'). The plague is no longer the Kaiser but dissatisfaction and uncertainty, Macphie preferring joy. In a gentler way than *Guth*, however, he shows that he knows that the problem is 'a swarm of swindlers everywhere under the guidance of the king of profit – people who are indifferent to the state of their fellow creatures as long as they themselves heap up riches which they could never aspire to before'.[15]

Arguably, the leading Gaelic essayist of the period was Donald Sinclair from Barra (1885–1932), whose work as a poet is described in the chapter 'Gaelic Verse'. There is a reticence in his work in matters pertaining to the war, and it is not because he was a reticent man – in 'A' Ghàidhlig agus a Muinntir' ('Gaelic and its Speakers', 1916) he remarks of Gaelic speakers that there is not 'as much as an atom of moral courage in our people'. As a professional in the munitions industry, he will have signed a contract which forbade him to write about public affairs. However, 'A' Ghàidhlig agus a Muinntir' ends:

> The races of Europe are currently thrashing each other, fighting for their survival as races, and my hope is that we won't let slip this opportunity any longer to put ourselves and our rights on a better and more appropriate footing amongst the peoples of the world.[16]

In 'Innis-na-Bréige' ('The Isle of Lies', 1918) Sinclair at last tells us exactly what he thinks of the war.

> Today the world, yes, the human race, has gone blazing red mad with thirst for conflict and dog-rage of blood, flesh and sinew, people insatiable with hunger to destroy each other's lives, blind drunk with the intoxicating drink of demons – for the sake of Honour and Truth! – on behalf of Justice and Freedom!

Then after conflict come ... statistics. 'During four years of war,' he writes in 'Litir Dhachaidh' ('Letter Home', 1924), 'they killed or murdered a total of millions of each other, yes, for the sake of a drop of oil, for the sake of coal, iron and other metals.' And he gives more room to the war in 'Cogais Nàiseanta' ('National Conscience', 1927–30) than in any previous essay, measuring the cost not in blood but in pounds sterling. He had found out that it had cost £8 million per day.

> Eight million a day! If the boards of agriculture or fisheries had had eight million for just one day, instead of the wretched pittance they get between them each year, wouldn't that be of some use to increase happiness and prosperity instead of all the evil and misery that blight our country?

He also raises the land question.

> We're in the habit of saying that they stood up for *their* country, but until we get proof that the country was *theirs*, we can't use language of that sort. The Highland people, as they have done so often, stood up for the name without the benefit. They stood up as no other people on earth have done, for a country that was theirs in name only. But tonight, in the place where they were reared, the owl and the otter know the truth, and those to whom they will never return have the anguish of knowing the truth as well.[17]

The Recordings

The first book in Gaelic to commemorate the war since 1921 was *An Cogadh Mór* of 1982. Concentrating on the experiences of men from the Western Isles, it consists of tape-recorded memories backed up by contemporary photographs. Both are graphic. Subsequent publications have reused many of the memories, often with English translation. One reads them now with a sense of déjà vu: they have become a literary canon.[18]

Of course, the word 'literary' should be used with caution. One definition of literature might be 'well-constructed narrative in print'. Some such narratives are not well constructed. When William Murray, Lewis, speaks of his ship going down in the Mediterranean, he explains:

> She was torpedoed during the night, and everyone was shouting and screaming. Not many were saved. She went down so fast – broken in two halves. I was saved at least, but not many of those fished out were alive. We were so long in the sea. I don't remember what the ship was called . . .

Then he searches audibly in his memory for the name of the ship and of the company that owned it.[19] It is a record of dreadful events, but is it literature?

On the other hand, there are countless examples of well-constructed narrative. We find superb descriptions of the trenches themselves ('like a freshly-opened peat-bank'), trench warfare ('the Black Watch spent the night killing wounded Germans, most of them were out of their minds'), the astonishing effect on the soldiers of the sound of the pipes, the 'Friendly Armistice' of Christmas 1915, gas attacks and hunger ('I was wounded in the morning as I served breakfast, four people around the loaf – and that after having nothing for three days'). The war at sea yields stories of the armed trawlers that accompanied Atlantic convoys. John MacLeod, Lewis, explains that the west of Ireland was full of islands: 'Whenever night fell we'd land with the boat and steal a wedder. I was the butcher, but then I'd been a butcher here before I ever went to war.' Kenneth MacLeod, Lewis, tells how he was washed up from a sinking lifeboat on the coast of Sutherland, then brought to a house where the doctor declared, wrongly, 'This man's finished.' Murdo Murray, Lewis, who had served as a soldier in the Middle East (not he of the diary), told a similar story of the 2nd Battle of Gaza, 7 November 1917. 'I was left for dead on the field – the sergeant who was with me – the lads leapt to help me when I was wounded, but he said, "Leave him alone, he's finished anyway."'

There are also good accounts from the home front, one highlight being a war-related instance of the second sight.[20]

The recorded memories of the Reverend Malcolm Morrison (1894–1987) are substantial, and have a cerebral feel, as one would expect from a man who had since become a minister of religion. He uses fewer English words than the others, and better Gaelic ones, like *rathad-beathachaidh* for the ammunition belt of a machine-gun. Summing up the trenches, he says: 'The main things I noticed that affected me a lot were the dirt, the hunger, the cold, the lack of sleep, death and other troubles.' He describes his experience of the Spanish 'flu. He tells how he asked a man what he thought about when he was stuck in No Man's Land. And he gives his opinion of the war. 'I was saying to myself, "I don't think there's much sense in any of this."' His biggest fear was of being taken prisoner, given what he had heard. When word came of the Armistice, 'we were gathered in an orchard, and it was lovely, the fragrant scent of the apples restoring us, and it was so strange to come across something like that'. Yet his feelings were dead. He and his companions were as dumb and emotionless, he said, as clods of earth. They had got used to feeling that it was never going to stop, that they were all going to die, that that was all there was. They could not grasp the concept of peace, and he found it difficult to go home.

> My parents were both alive, and I wondered how hard it would be for me to meet the parents of the lads who had been lost . . . I thought something was saying to me, 'Och, you shouldn't be alive either.'

Later, when there was an 'awakening' in his native parish, he was converted, but to his own surprise the war had nothing to do with it – not bullets, nor filth, nor hunger, nor cold, all of which had hardened his heart, but the small calm voice in the Gospel.[21]

The classic Gaelic tale from the war, in the sense of a developed non-fictional narrative sustained over the length of a short story, is 'Bleith leis a' Bhrathainn ann a Sailoiniga' ('Grinding with the Quern in Salonika'), recorded from Peter Morrison, North Uist, in 1966. He speaks first of how supplies were brought in on ox-carts, with the Bulgarians shooting at them. If bread arrived at all, it was in bits.[22] Reduced to foraging, the men find plenty of grain in the girnels, and also quern-stones, which are very familiar to Peter. The highlight of the story is his description of how he sets up the quern and gets it going. The men begin to queue up for porridge with their mess-tins, and soon the officers appear as well. After that an old wood-fired steam-driven mill is discovered, repaired and set in motion. They try distilling whisky but fortunately it is a failure, so Peter turns his hand to baking scones, which are a success. The narrative includes snatches of conversation and touches of light humour, all threaded through with the names of Gaelic-speaking comrades, a feature of the genre. 'And there you have the story,' concludes Peter, 'of the Salonika grinding.'[23]

The Autobiographies

The only Gaelic autobiography of a man who had served in the war is that of a songmaker from Point in Lewis, John MacLeod ('Suileabhan', 1889–1956). The book was actually written for him following extensive interviews by a neighbour. He tells how he joined the Militia, the means by which thousands of young men and boys were prepared for war. One day, at age 14, he saw an army captain home on leave who 'looked as smart as anything you could buy in James's shop – and me in my guernsey, my fisherman's trousers and my boots, covered in fish-scales and guts, like something thrown up by the sea'. So he got a book about the Militia through the post, and signed up.[24]

All Suileabhan tells us about his actual war experiences is this:

> I was at home at the end of the First World War – me and the old men and the other wounded who were being sent home crippled. The war was a horror-show, as everyone knows, with news of death coming to the townships every week. There wasn't much for anyone to do but sit at home lamenting the boys who were being murdered – friends who would never come home.

When attending a wake he heard about a cask of rum hidden in the Geodha Mhòr, and he tells how he stole some and was chased for it, though when he claims to have been told that 'it would be easier for you to go through the Maginot Line than to get near the Geodha Mhòr', he is confusing Maginot with Hindenburg.[25]

The first Gaelic autobiography to be published was by Angus Campbell (1903–82) from Ness in Lewis. Campbell combines childhood memories with trenchant opinions. He begins with the lust of European rulers to assert their power, remarking that the people of Lewis were in favour of the war at first, for servicemen's families received a 'separation allowance' which brought in much-needed cash. Things speedily went wrong, of course. 'Every day the post office received a telegram with news of the war. A copy of it was read at the letter-box in our village during school playtime, and we seldom missed it.'[26]

Campbell discusses the statistics of loss. Some families, including his uncle's, lost three sons. Due to the *Iolaire*, the loss of sailors was perhaps greater than that of soldiers. Some communities lost eight in a hundred, but there was no condemnation, for it was seen as God's will. 'Weren't they fulfilling their duty to king and country,' says Campbell, 'a country and government that had banished, plundered and violated their people and fathers?' This brings him to the role of propaganda, which turned soldiers into heroes who would get justice when they came back. 'Those promises proved completely empty.' War was glorified in the school history books of the day, and the children – who saw them at their lunchtime, because that was when the post-van left – viewed departing soldiers not as sacrifices but as heroes.[27]

Always scornful of élites, Campbell points to the pernicious role played by certain clergymen, especially the Reverend Duncan MacDougall of Cross.[28]

> Some evangelical ministers taught that this valley of death guaranteed an open door to paradise. One of these was our Free Church minister in Ness. When they began raising men against their will up to the age of 45, there was a schoolmaster in Cross, a widow's only son. The minister offered to take his place, so William was released from his calling and plucked off to the war. He was lost on the *Iolaire*. Who couldn't deny that his life had been shortened by the mistaken zeal and wayward opinion of one man?

After describing life in rural Lewis during the war, Campbell makes the point that it was only in the 1960s that historians had begun drawing attention to the incompetence of the generals involved. Then, as is his style, he tells a series of funny stories: for example,

> There was a man in the navy who wrote home to his wife telling her he'd been landed and sent to hospital with a swollen neck, and that he'd had an operation. The poor soul nearly called a wake when she read, 'They put me over the side and then they cut my throat.'[29]

Campbell's memories of the war were subsequently taped and a transcript published. At first he follows his autobiography, then he tells the story of a Nessman in the navy who had three fortuitous escapes.

In the last of these, he was aboard the *Iolaire* at Kyle when a friend gave him an army greatcoat so that he could come aboard the *Sheila* in the guise of a soldier.[30]

The autobiography of the Right Reverend Thomas M. Murchison (1907–84) was published in 2011. He had been brought up on his father's croft at Kylerhea in Skye. Of twelve Kylerhea men who went to war, nine came back. One of the fallen was only 20 years old; another was his own uncle. He also speaks of a man who had been injured by a bomb at Archangel, and had an artificial arm. It was the most marvellous thing the children had ever seen.

Kylerhea was a fishing community, cut off from the rest of Skye but linked to the world by the Sound of Sleat. A permit was needed to go out and fish, or even to go to Kyle for supplies. Every day someone went over to Glenelg, however, where news of the war was displayed on the post office window. The sound was full of ships avoiding the waters further west for fear of submarines, and the waves they created were a danger to small boats. Now and again bodies were washed ashore, or strange lights were seen. Ships in difficulty sometimes jettisoned cargoes that benefitted the community – coal, usually, but on one occasion, to young Thomas's delight, a model ship.[31]

There is a curious moment in Murdo Beaton's autobiography of 2018. Born in 1941, Beaton is an ex-policeman and schoolmaster from Skye. He tells how he helped his school with trips to Flanders, and speaks of his mother's brother, Alasdair, lost aged twenty-four at Aubers Ridge in April 1915. Finally, he lists the names of Skyemen on the monuments at Le Touret, Thiepval and Ypres, beginning with the line 'Pte Norman MacAskill, Geary, Seaforths'. These lists stand out from Beaton's text because they are in English. They have the qualities of poetry. Each of the eighty evocations is different yet the same, like a poem in regular metre with its refrain.[32]

The Letters

Letters from serving soldiers and sailors were not normally written in Gaelic, partly for fear they would not pass the censor, partly because Gaelic had not been taught in schools since 1872. Servicemen who could not speak or write English had their letters written for them. Nevertheless there are a couple of small exceptions. In a lament for Charles MacLeod, Lewis, killed in France on 15 November 1914, aged twenty-one, we are told: 'I got your letter on Friday / With one side of it in Gaelic.' And Roderick Murray, Lewis, regularly signed off his letters *Slan lat*, the Gaelic for 'Goodbye'. Writing from Mesopotamia on 13 October 1917, he ends (this is not a translation): 'Give my best respect to my mother Brothers and sisters and to all cosuns and frinds to Mordo M glan dall [*Glen Dell*] closen [*closing*] Rody keep the horse prisk till I get home next spring slan lat.' He was killed on 5 November.[33]

The war memorial in Paddington Station, London, is a sculpture of a soldier standing reading a letter. In 2014, the BBC invited listeners to suggest what he was reading, and the Gaelic version of the project resulted in a published book. Shrugging off the narrow parameters of the original proposition, the participants produced four kinds of letter: family-member/sweetheart writing to soldier/sailor; soldier/sailor writing to family-member/sweetheart; soldier/sailor writing to other soldier/sailor; and the living writing to the dead. One writer reminds us that each war comes on top of a previous one.

> Your father says how afraid he was himself during the first weeks he was in the Transvaal. But that he got over it. He said the worst thing for him wasn't the noise of the shells but looking at those around him – the fear in their own eyes. Some of them even crying. Please don't cry, my love – even if truly in your heart and body you're screaming. Don't let them see you weeping.

Different opinions are expressed about the brutality of the war. One soldier's parents tell him they are 'proud that you were, as a young boy fresh out of school, going voluntarily to fight for your country against an enemy that's uncivilised and merciless'. But to another his sweetheart says: 'Don't harden your heart against the enemy. Every one of them is a mother's son. The killing you're doing is no nobler than the killing they're doing.'

The causes of the war are different in the eyes of different people. One man wrote: 'The big question for me, your brother's grandson, is . . . why, why, why?' And another:

> I wonder if it's worse to be fighting and dying in a war without much obvious reason for it than to be, say, a soldier in a war that took place for reasons that were easy to understand on both sides, like the American War of Independence, or the War of Freedom in Ireland.

But a female listener has no doubts. 'One thing that's certain is that our world is the freer, the safer and the better for your heroism.'

The letters also emphasise that some people did not ask why. One woman to her brother in the trenches: 'With the Lord's help we'll get through it. The Bible passage that's often in my thoughts is – "Here is the way, and walk therein". We just have to accept it.' (The passage is from Jeremiah 6: 16.) Another writes to her son from a Lewis township: 'Oh, it will pass – no matter who it takes away. All they say here is that we've got no choice but to fulfil our destiny and that we've got no control over that.'

In literary terms, two letters stand out. The first is to a pair of nameless soldiers, one of whom put 'the gun in your own mouth that night amongst the rats and lice', the other of whom refused to go over the top and was treated to 'a dozen British bullets at dawn, though they gave you a cigarette first'. The second is a gentle one written in the guise of a soldier who shows how surreal the world of the trenches is, without saying anything that will frighten the family or fall foul of the censor. Almost his first words are: 'Tell Mam I left the lid of the churn under the bench . . .'[34]

The Fiction

Gaelic fiction about the war emerged smoothly from fact in the shape of Norman Campbell's short story 'Am Bucach' ('The Buckie Man'). Campbell begins by recalling how his mother used to count the numbers of dead by going through the townships in her head. 'Twenty-four, isn't it? I think so . . .' This sounds very like the twenty-seven men killed out of ninety-four from Campbell's own township of South Dell in Lewis.[35] He describes the ceilidh-house where stories were told and songs sung every night, presumably in the years around 1950. He wishes he could be there again to ask about Mesopotamia, the place whose name he remembers best. This brings him to Alasdair Mhurchaidh Thormoid, the Bucach, a regular visitor to the family. Norman and his brother Alasdair would ask him for stories about the war, and he would oblige. Following a Turkish attack, he said, he once spent a night in a trench with his cousin's dead body and a wounded madman, who kept putting his head above the parapet. Twice he loaded his rifle to finish the madman off, but he died in the morning. He buried them both. 'My tunic was as stiff as cowhide with Tormod Dhoilidh's blood.' Then there was a story from France about the arrival of an eighteen-year-old recruit from Stornoway with his smart, clean uniform. One bullet got into the trench that night, and suddenly the lad lay dead at his feet. 'What did you do?' said the boys. 'I ate his bully beef.'

The Bucach embarrassed the boys by talking about women. In cafés, some men would sing 'Pack up your Troubles' and 'Tipperary', when the Bucach and his friends sang Gaelic songs the girls would flock around and the kissing would start. He was wounded in Mesopotamia. In a shower of bullets, he was marvelling at how he had never been hit when one entered his back and came out the other side. That was when the nurses 'got their chance with me', as he put it, and 'I was never so happy as I was with them.' But the last story is about how he carried a wounded Nessman called Niall Thormoid Sheumais to a casualty station on his back. Many years later, in Lewis, he was trudging home one night from his work as a stonemason when a bus stopped and the driver said, 'Want a ride?' He hopped in, and the driver said, 'There was a time when you gave me a ride.' It was Niall Thormoid Sheumais.

The Bucach plays a cameo role in another of Campbell's stories, 'Na Bodaich' ('The Old Men'). One of these was Seòras Ruadh, who had been a sergeant in France. He told the boys what it was like.

> Yon lice ... we'd never seen lice as big, they had horns on them. We wore kilts, bloody things. The pleats were alive with them, we had to go into the burns in our underwear to get them clean. You should have seen Alasdair Mhurchaidh Mhòir cursing them – the first time, he yelled and ran! You had to claw them away in heaps. Even the enemy wasn't so bad.

But when the war was over, the boys found that Seòras Ruadh could not stand the sound of the pipes, for it made him weep. 'All the ones who were lost,' he'd say. 'All the ones who were lost.'[36]

The Bucach was Alexander Morrison, South Dell. These and other war stories were subsequently told elsewhere, with an English translation and a picture of the Bucach in his kilt.[37]

Angus Peter Campbell's *An Oidhche mus do Sheòl Sinn* ('The Night before We Sailed') is an ambitious novel, set mainly in South Uist and Spain, that follows a cast of characters through the twentieth century. From the fictitious township that provides its wellspring, we are told that only two out of twenty individuals come back from the Great War. One of them has lost a leg, the other his mind. But the author concentrates on Alasdair, who, he says, wins a lot of medals, marries an Englishwoman, settles in Brighton and never comes home at all. There are parties, concerts and conversations, such as one where a major says, 'Of course, they're all bloody well blaming us now, as if we could have done anything about the mud and the rain.'

At which we are told: 'Alasdair would remember, in those moments, Aonghas Iain's blood spurting out of him at the Aisne.'

Aonghas Iain is his late brother, and the chapter turns into an examination of the reasons for the war. For suddenly into his comfortable life there erupts his little sister in a leather jacket, getting off her motor-cycle to examine the motives for which he survived and prospered, and for which her other brother died. She tells him of the family, and of the telegram about Aonghas Iain's death that destroyed their mother. Against the background of a cornet launching into 'Free and Easy' at a party, Alasdair weeps for shame, then she explains the reason for her visit: she is going to war too now, not an imperialist war or a commercial one, and she wants to see 'the shifty eyes of glory' before sacrificing herself. She is off to Spain, she says, 'to sweep aside the Fascists and the likes of you, the petit bourgeoisie, in the name of freedom and justice'. Then she revs up her motor-cycle while Alasdair entertains his friends to 'Cead Deireannach nam Beann' ('The Last Farewell to the Bens'), a song by Duncan Ban Macintyre which speaks sadly of a landscape devoid of people, a hunting-ground for the rich, the triumph of those who have money over those who have nothing but anger.[38]

The setting of Iain MacLean's novella *Cogadh Ruairidh* ('Roddy's War') is the Battle of the Somme. Roddy is a hero. He makes his way through showers of bullets to the German trenches, knocks out three machine-guns and comes back alive. The action and the horrors are well described; the problem is the ending. The author could have decided to show how Roddy's breakthough ended the war, or he could have had Roddy accept a medal then put a bullet in his own head out of guilt for surviving, or he could have sent him all the way home to fall into his sweetheart's arms. But no. On reaching Inverness station, 'He bought a bottle of rum, and started making his way home, at last.' What does that mean?[39]

The most recent Gaelic literary commentary on the war is in Ruairidh Maclean's *Còig Duilleagan na Seamraig* ('The Five Leaves of the Shamrock'). Set in Wester Ross, London and Ireland during 1896–1922, the novel is about the struggle for Irish independence; as such, it is shot through with references to the Great War, of which the first comes in Glasnevin Cemetery when Patrick Pearse makes his oration on 'the fools, the fools – they have left us our Fenian dead, and while Ireland holds these graves, Ireland unfree shall never be at peace'. The hero, Donald Mackenzie, a policeman from Wester Ross, becomes personal bodyguard to Lloyd George, who trusts him, as a fellow Celt, with secret missions to Ireland. Mackenzie is an attractive figure, a combination of James Bond and Kevin Costner's character in *The Bodyguard*, but a good deal more intellectual than either. And his conversations in Ireland make him think about the contempt in which the Gael are held in Scotland: they were praised only when they 'fell in the trenches or sank to the bottom of the sea with their lungs full of brine in the cause of the Empire', yet they toasted the king and saluted the Union Jack. But here now were their neighbours, 'proud to be Gaelic' and 'showing a way ahead for Scotland too'. Later in the novel, Donald repeats the same sentiments in direct speech.

> Ireland is showing us all the way ahead . . . Out of the Empire, out of the United Kingdom, Scotland making its own way in the world. As a republic in which power lies with ordinary people, not the gentry. And women as well as men.

Elsewhere he thinks to himself, when confronted by the monarchistic sentiments that prevailed amongst his own kinsfolk, 'How long will it be before desire for an independent republic awakens in the hearts of the Scottish people?'

So Maclean traces the line of political thought that leads from the Great War through the struggle in Ireland to Scottish independence.[40]

Notes

1. See especially Jo NicDhòmhnaill, Annella NicLeòid and Dòmhnall Iain MacLeòid (eds), *Cuimhneachan, Remembrance: Bàrdachd a' Chiad Chogaidh, Gaelic Poetry of World War One* (Stornoway: Acair, 2015).
2. Murchadh Moireach, *Luach na Saorsa* (Glasgow: Gairm, 1970), pp. 11–51.
3. Dòmhnall Alasdair Moireasdan (ed.), *The Going Down of the Sun: The Great War and a Rural Lewis Community/Dol Fodha na Grèine: Buaidh a' Chogaidh Mhòir – Nis gu Baile an Truiseil* (Stornoway: Acair, 2014), p. 137; see 'The Recordings' below.
4. For rotation see also Moireasdan, *The Going Down of the Sun*, pp. 106, 144.
5. Ronald I. M. Black (ed.), *An Tuil: Anthology of 20th Century Scottish Gaelic Verse* (Edinburgh: Polygon, 1999), pp. 749–50.
6. Tormod Calum Domhnallach, *Call na h-Iolaire* (Stornoway: Acair, 1978).
7. Malcolm Macdonald and Donald John MacLeod, *Call na h-Iolaire: The Darkest Dawn, The Story of the Iolaire Tragedy* (Stornoway: Acair, 2018), pp. 330–4; Moireasdan, *The Going Down of the Sun*, pp. 112–15, 259.

8. *Guth*, vol. 7 (1910), pp. 253–71.
9. *Guth*, vol. 9 (1912), pp. 6–21, 400, 403.
10. *Guth*, vol. 11 (1914), pp. 399–411.
11. *Guth*, vol. 12 (1915), pp. 1–19, 369–86, and vol. 17 (1920), p. 259.
12. *Guth*, vol. 15 (1918), pp. 21, 217–18; vol. 16 (1919), pp. 104–5, 233–9, 294–5, 388–9; vol. 17 (1920), pp. 259–61; vol. 19 (1923–4), pp. 58–9.
13. *Deò*, vol. 10 (1914–15), pp. 1–3, 34, 50, 62, 162, and vol. 11 (1915–16), pp. 1–3.
14. *Deò*, vol. 12 (1916–17), pp. 161–2, and vol. 14 (1918–19), pp. 49–51, 81–3.
15. *Deò*, vol. 14 (1918–19), pp. 49–51, 161–2, 177–8.
16. Lisa Storey (ed.), *D.M.N.C: Sgrìobhaidhean Dhòmhnaill Mhic na Ceàrdaich* (Inverness: Clàr, 2014), pp. 320, 331.
17. Ibid. pp. 73, 354, 369, 370, 387–90, 423.
18. Dòmhnall Iain MacLeòid et al. (eds), *An Cogadh Mór 1914–1918: The Great War* (Stornoway: Acair, 1982); Moireasdan, *The Going Down of the Sun*, pp. 93–171; Macdonald and MacLeod, *Call na h-Iolaire*, pp. 317–53.
19. Moireasdan, *The Going Down of the Sun*, p. 143.
20. Ibid. pp. 98, 101, 102, 103, 106, 108, 128, 144, 168.
21. Ibid. pp. 131–41, 349.
22. For this see also ibid. p. 125.
23. Pàdruig Moireasdan, *Ugam agus Bhuam* (Stornoway: Acair, 1977), pp. 85–90.
24. Calum MacFhearghuis, *Suileabhan* (Glasgow: Gairm, 1983), p. 37; cf. Moireasdan, *The Going Down of the Sun*, p. 100.
25. MacFhearghuis, *Suileabhan*, p. 75.
26. See also Moireasdan, *The Going Down of the Sun*, pp. 161, 315.
27. See also ibid. pp. 14, 162.
28. For MacDougall see also ibid. p. 32.
29. Aonghas Caimbeul (Am Puilean), *Suathadh ri Iomadh Rubha* (Glasgow: Gairm, 1973), pp. 55–66.
30. Moireasdan, *The Going Down of the Sun*, pp. 160–5.
31. Dòmhnall Eachann Meek (ed.), *Mo Là gu Seo: Eachdraidh mo Bheatha le Tòmas M. MacCalmain* (Glasgow: Scottish Gaelic Texts Society, 2011), pp. 55–6, 59–62.
32. Murchadh Peutan, *Sùil air Ais anns an Sgàthan* (Inverness: Clàr, 2018), pp. 46–55.
33. Moireasdan, *The Going Down of the Sun*, pp. 181, 190, 403.
34. Lisa Storey (ed.), *Litir chun an t-Saighdeir gun Ainm* (Inverness: Clàr, 2016), pp. 23, 27, 33, 41, 49, 58, 79–80, 98, 131.
35. Moireasdan, *The Going Down of the Sun*, p. 14. For his mother's memories of the war see ibid. pp. 166–70.
36. Tormod Caimbeul, *An Naidheachd bhon Taigh* (An Teanga: Cànan, 1994), pp. 86–92, 94–6.

37. Moireasdan, *The Going Down of the Sun*, pp. 151–2.
38. Aonghas Pàdraig Caimbeul, *An Oidhche mus do Sheòl Sinn* (Inverness: Clàr, 2003), pp. 94–104.
39. Iain Mac Ill Eathain, *Cogadh Ruairidh* (Dingwall: Sandstone, 2009), p. 89.
40. Ruairidh MacIlleathain, *Còig Duilleagan na Seamraig* (Inverness: Clàr, 2019), pp. 127–8, 135, 146–7, 149, 178, 235, 236, 240, 265.

Chapter 7

Scottish Philosophy and the First World War
Cairns Craig

David Hume's *Treatise of Human Nature* may, in his own words, have 'fallen still-born from the press' but philosophers have been among Scotland's most successful writers, even if the success is achieved only slowly and over a long period of time. Hume, of course, achieved success with his essays and with his *History of England* but the *Treatise* is still in print, as are the works of his great antagonist, Thomas Reid, with new editions appearing in North America, backed by the Liberty Fund, and much scholarly effort being harnessed for the production of the Edinburgh Edition of Thomas Reid. In the nineteenth century, it was writings on German philosophy and German literature that established Thomas Carlyle as a significant literary presence, and a spoof philosophical work – *Sartor Resartus* (1833) – that catapulted him to international success. In the twentieth century, the works of John Macmurray were promoted for a general audience in paperback by Faber & Faber, and Macmurray's major philosophical works – the two volumes of *The Form of the Personal* – are still in print. In addition, in 1996 a compilation of his writings was edited by Philip Conford – *The Personal World: John Macmurray on Self and Society* – and published with a foreword by Tony Blair. In *The Democratic Intellect* (1961), George Elder Davie argued that the role of philosophy, as the common element studied by all Scottish university students, had been at the core of Scotland's distinctive culture – and cultural distinction – in the eighteenth century and through the first half of the nineteenth, but that the educational reforms of the 1870s and 1880s, designed to bring the Scottish universities in line with English ones, had eroded that centrality. Ironically, however, it was in the period after 1870 that Scottish philosophy became a central component in university curricula throughout the Empire and was the dominant philosophy of the Anglophone world on the eve of the First World War.

A few years before the War, the Gifford Lectures in Glasgow were given by John Watson, Professor of Logic, Metaphysics, and Ethics at Queen's University, Kingston, in Ontario, Canada. Watson had been appointed in 1872 after completing his degree at Glasgow University, and his nomination as a Gifford Lecturer was important because he was the first Canadian to deliver the annual lectures which had been funded by a bequest from Adam Gifford and which had become a centrepiece of Scottish philosophical and theological life. Watson's nomination was a recognition of how important Scottish philosophy was in the 'settler colonies' of the Empire and, as a former student of Edward Caird's at Glasgow University, how significant was the influence of Caird in those colonies. An obituary of Caird in the *Harvard Theological Review* estimated that twenty-five of his students held chairs in philosophy or theology in British universities and that at least a further nineteen held chairs across North America, India and the British territories of the southern hemisphere.[1] This period of Scotland's philosophical eminence has now been eclipsed by the rise to international prominence of the thinkers – and, indeed, the phenomenon – of the Scottish Enlightenment. It is worth recalling, however, that it was not those who were first regarded as the luminaries of the Scottish Enlightenment – David Hume and Adam Smith – who had the greatest impact in Scotland and across the world. Hume's scepticism and possible atheism made him an unacceptable mentor to a still-believing age, and Smith's economics were regarded by the early nineteenth century as quaintly antiquated. It was Thomas Reid, who made the greatest international impact, his philosophy of 'common sense' being widely taken up in both North America and in France.

Indeed, Garry Wills has set a trend in the analysis of the framing of the American constitution that makes Reid – rather than Locke or Hobbes – the dominant intellectual force in the new, post-revolutionary state. James Wilson, who was, along with James Madison, the principal architect of the Federal Constitution in 1787, had been a student at St Andrews, his political principles formed by the philosophy of Thomas Reid. He wrote:

> This philosophy will teach us that first principles are in themselves apparent; that to make nothing self-evident is to take away all possibility of knowing anything; that without first principles there be neither reason nor reasoning . . . Consequently, all sound reasoning must rest ultimately on the principles of common sense.[2]

Madison, in turn, was one of the first graduates of John Witherspoon's tenure as President at the College of New Jersey. Witherspoon (1723–94), originally from Haddington and educated at Edinburgh University, arrived in New Jersey in 1768 and built the College of New Jersey into the leading university in the country, its curriculum based on the moral philosophy of Hutcheson and Reid. Witherspoon's own manual of moral philosophy was to be adopted widely and paved the way for the centrality of the ideas of Hutcheson, Reid and, later, Dugald Stewart in American colleges. Thomas Jefferson, who had met Dugald Stewart in Paris in 1788, wrote to congratulate him on his *Elements of the Philosophy of the Human Mind*, which had 'become the text book of most of our colleges and academies'.[3] By the mid-nineteenth century, Scottish common sense had developed its own American offshoots in the work of American thinkers such as Francis Wayland (1796–1865) and Noah Porter (1811–92). Similarly, in France, Reid's works became the official philosophy of the state in the post-Napoleonic period and helped shape French philosophy in the subsequent thirty years, making Reid the major figure in both of the linguistic communities of a country like Canada.

As A. B. McKillop documents in *A Disciplined Intelligence*, a history of intellectual life in Anglophone Canada, common-sense philosophy continued its dominance until the 1860s and 1870s. By then, however, its combination of religious belief with empirical science was coming under increasing pressure as a result of the 'age of the earth' controversies provoked by Charles Lyell's *The Principles of Geology* (1830–3) and the impact of Darwin's *On the Origin of Species by Means of Natural Selection* (1859). One of Darwin's major opponents was John William Dawson (1820–99), who had trained initially for the ministry of the Church of Scotland but established himself as Canada's leading geologist while also becoming the influential President of McGill College in Montreal from 1855 till 1893. Dawson's *The Origin of the World, According to Revelation and Science* (1877) argued for a parallelism between the discoveries of geology and the Biblical account of creation, with each of the major geological periods, as described by Charles Lyell, corresponding to the days of creation as outlined in 'Genesis'.[4] The 'geological order of animal life', Dawson suggested, 'agrees perfectly with that sketched by Moses, in which the lower types are completed at once, and the progress is wholly in the higher.'[5] And though the geological record is one of the death and extinction of species,

> Man is the capital of the column [of nature]; and if marred and defaced by moral evil, the symmetry of the whole is to be restored, not by rejecting

him altogether, like the extinct species of the ancient world, and replacing him by another, but by re-casting him in the image of his Divine Redeemer. Man, though recently introduced, is to exist eternally. He is, in one or another state of being, to be witness of all future changes on the earth.[6]

To aid him in the battle against Darwinism, in 1872 Dawson hired John Clark Murray, a Scot who had trained for ministry in the Free Church in Scotland and emigrated in 1862 to a post at Queen's College in Kingston, Ontario. As a student of Sir William Hamilton, whose edition of *The Works of Thomas Reid* (1846–63) was a sustained attempt to recuperate the relevance of Reid for the mid-nineteenth century, Dawson was no doubt confident in finding in Clark Murray a philosophical ally. Clark Murray, however, had decided doubts about Hamilton and, therefore, about the whole common-sense tradition. He rejected Reid's works on the basis that 'Reid's thinking never represents the speculative toil of a philosophic intellect, but merely the refined opinions of ordinary intelligence.'[7] Having demolished the tradition of Scottish philosophy, Clark Murray goes on to suggest that it can be rebuilt on different foundations – those provided by the 'idealism' of Edward Caird, who was appointed in 1866 to the same Chair in the University of Glasgow that had been held by Reid, before Caird then went on to be Master of Balliol College in Oxford in 1893. According to Clark Murray,

> Professor Caird's recent work on Kant is an evidence that the teaching which issues from the chair of Reid goes to a length which he could never have surmised, in protesting against the illusion which reduces human knowledge to a mere complexus of sensations.[8]

It was on Caird's recommendation that John Watson arrived in Canada, and he went on to develop the argument that Caird had deployed against the implied rejection of religion by Darwin and his principal defender, T. H. Huxley. Building on the philosophies of Kant and Hegel, Caird proposed that evolution applied not only to the natural world but to religion itself, and that the history of Western civilisation was the history of the evolution of our understanding of God as gradually revealing Himself to humanity as humanity's capacity for understanding itself evolved towards the capacity to apprehend God. Christianity is therefore a religion which

> reveals itself not only within but also without us, which is immanent in nature and in man, and which is working in him to still higher issues. But

this lesson, wrapped up at the dawn of Christianity in types and symbols borrowed from an earlier faith, and apprehended only by feeling, or at best by an imaginative intuition which had no means of explaining itself, is now becoming a reasoned conviction which can understand and criticise its own nature and evidence. The principle of Christianity has come to self-consciousness, and it is therefore capable of being held without that mixture of illusion which was inevitable in an earlier age. In the process of its own history, it has been working itself free of the alien elements which were mingled with it at first . . .[9]

The evolving spirituality of this Christianity provides the counterweight to the evolving materialism of evolutionary theory. It is not the struggle of the fittest for survival which is of contemporary significance but the struggle towards the fullest comprehension of the spiritual purposes of the universe, a comprehension which will also be the fulfilment of the original impulse of Christianity:

the present age, in spite of all the evils that afflict it, has gone beyond any previous age. For, on the one hand, the whole development of the organic and evolutionary idea of the world as interpreted by idealistic philosophy, and applied by criticism to the history of Christianity and of other religious systems, has for the first time furnished us with something like a rational proof of a creed which previously rested almost entirely upon the intuition of faith, and which, therefore, was generally mixed up with many elements of unreason. And, on the other hand, the humanitarian impulse of the present day – in so far as it has ceased to be a mere abstract cosmopolitan charity, or a religious zeal that ends with the spread of religion; in so far as it is guided by a deeper conviction that men must find salvation here as well as hereafter, and by a fuller understanding of all the physical and economical, all the intellectual and moral conditions of its attainment, – reproduces in a higher form the passionate impulse to seek and save the lost which Christianity brought into the world.[10]

For Caird, Kant and Hegel had pointed the road by which Christianity became a reasoned and not simply an intuited truth. A reasoned Christianity provided the foundation on which an ethical life could be based, and provided the foundation, too, of a reasonable – and, therefore, a caring – society, which could fulfil the 'impulse' of early Christianity. Scientific progress is not inimical to Christianity but leads to its justification. As John Watson put it: 'philosophy cannot accept any truth that is held in an immediate and uncritical way, but the actual result of its method is to give back to faith in a higher form the truth it contains'.[11] In Canada, Watson's idealism provided the nation with an imperial justification: it was not just a marginal left-over of North American history, likely to be incorporated economically if not politically into the United States, but an active contributor to the worldwide expansion of Christian civilisation made possible by the British Empire.[12] It was that combination of empire and idealism that Henry Jones, Professor of Moral Philosophy at Glasgow University and once a student of Edward Caird, presented to his audience in Sydney, Australia, in a series of lectures in 1908:

> But Idealism cures irreverence, especially the Idealism of Love, which Christianity is. It lifts the lowly, it asserts the rights of the weak, and breaks the power of the strong. From of old the prophets of this creed were revolutionaries. 'Those who have turned the world upside down are come hither also.' And their successors in the modern world are engaged in the same task of levelling upwards, 'pulling down the mighty from their seats, and exalting them of low degree'; dethroning the tyrannic state and the dogmatic church, and setting in their place a Sovereignty whose seat is in the heart of man, a Democracy which would be just, and a Religion which would be free – free to find God everywhere.[13]

The British Empire, as the vehicle of the spread of Christian civilisation, is also the vehicle of rational progress, and imperialism the means by which the world becomes both faithful and rational.

Caird's idealism has received even less attention from twentieth-century philosophers and historians of Scottish culture than Reid's 'common sense', which has at least continued to attract attention from North Americans interested in their country's cultural history. But in the last decades of the nineteenth century and the first of the twentieth, the worldwide spread of Caird's idealism probably represented the period in which Scottish philosophy achieved its greatest international impact – at least, that is, until the invention, in the 1960s, of the idea of the Scottish Enlightenment. Caird's version of 'idealism' became, in effect, the philosophy of the Anglophone Empire from Canada to New Zealand, and provided the foundations on which those countries would later build their own philosophical traditions. Thus John Watson not only played a key role in the formation of the United Church of Canada (formed in 1925 to bring together a variety of Protestant denominations) but has been credited by Christopher Humphrey with shaping the characteristic 'unity in diversity' emphasis that underpins much of twentieth-century Canada's social and political thought.[14] If, as John MacKenzie has argued,[15] there was a distinctive 'Scottish Empire' within the British

Empire, Caird's idealism, from the 1870s onwards, was its intellectual underpinning.

Caird attributes his own interest in German philosophy to the influence of Thomas Carlyle and Carlyle's proselytising for the virtues of German thinkers in the 1820s and 1830s, but as J. H. Burns has demonstrated, Scottish engagement with Kantianism goes back as far as the 1790s,[16] and some of the most influential Scottish thinkers of the early 1800s, from Thomas Brown and James Mackintosh to Sir William Hamilton, took seriously the importance of Kant's philosophy.[17] Equally, there were several early translations of Kant by Scots, but the most long-lasting was by J. M. D. Meiklejohn, whose version of the *Critique of Pure Reason* of 1856 was republished (in the Everyman Library series) in 1934,[18] and is still available in various formats today.[19] It was not only Kant who benefited from the interest of Scots: Hegel was first introduced into Britain by James Hutchison Stirling in his *The Secret of Hegel* (1865), a book for which Stirling prepared himself by many years of study in France and Germany after abandoning his medical practice. Caird himself followed his *Critical Account of the Philosophy of Kant* of 1877 with his study of *Hegel* in 1883, and Caird's Oxford friend William Wallace provided one of the most authoritative translations of Hegel's *Logic* (1873), as well as translating sections from the *Encyclopaedia* published under the title of *Hegel's Philosophy of Mind* (1894). Caird was both the outcome of Scottish engagement with German philosophy in the early nineteenth century and the driving force behind its prominence in the latter years of the century. The intertwining of Scottish and German philosophy is best summarised by Andrew Seth (also known as Andrew Seth Pringle-Pattison), in his *Scottish Philosophy: A Comparison of the Scottish and German Answers to Hume*, published in 1885, which attempts to identify in Scottish common-sense philosophy a similar, if apparently simpler, version of Kant's attempt to overcome Hume's sceptical metaphysic. Sophisticated as Kant's version may be, it is none the less itself a much simpler version of what was to be achieved by Hegel. For Seth, the key to Hegel's advance lies in 'the systematic recognition of the fact that thought is founded upon difference; whereas identity had hitherto been the god of the logician's idolatry',[20] and the importance of 'difference' is borne out by the discoveries of the evolutionary sciences:

> What is the biological explanation of life and the organism but a denial of dead identity? What is development but the same denial of static sameness, along with the assertion of identity in difference? But though the principle meets us everywhere, Hegel alone has been consistent in his metaphysical applications of it [. . .][21]

It is this that reveals the fundamental weakness of both Reid and Kant, for they are unable to take hold of a dynamic reality within the context of a systematic whole which explains the relations not only of part to part but of all the parts to the perspective from which they are discovered:

> Because the direct relation of all principles of explanation to the nature of the explaining self was not adequately grasped either by Kant or Reid, their enumerations of principles have unavoidably the appearance of being, as it were, in the air. The mutual connection of the principles is not displayed, and they do not lead up, as in Hegel they necessarily do, to the central principle from which they hold their own existence in fee.[22]

The Hegel who points the way forward for philosophy was also, however, the Hegel who saw the Prussian state as the highest embodiment of human ideals. In 1915, J. H. Muirhead noted, in his *German Philosophy in Relation to the War*, how closely identified Hegel had become with German militarism: 'It is on the ground of his exaltation of the State and his manifest leaning to the Prussian form of monarchy that Hegel has been accused of being the philosopher of the Prussian military tradition.'[23] While insisting that this did not in itself constitute a commitment to 'militarism', Muirhead none the less underlined the primary role of the state in Hegel's conception of human ideals:

> Hegel had lived through the enthusiasm of the French Revolution, and, like Burke, had come to realize the element of individualism and anarchy which it contained. He felt that the time had come to vindicate the reality of the State as the 'substance' of individual, family and national life. He was further convinced that justice could only be done to the unity of the State by a personal head as in modern constitutional monarchy.[24]

If this makes England sound like the ideal of Hegel's idea of the state, it was an idea given philosophical justification in the flourishing of Hegelianism in the nineteenth-century Anglophone world when such Hegelianism was being decisively rejected by philosophers in Germany itself. For Muirhead, the Germany with whom Britain is at war is the outcome 'of a violent reaction against all that German Philosophy properly stands for',[25] thus allowing British philosophers, despite the war, to continue to appeal to the Kantian and Hegelian traditions as what 'German Philosophy properly stands for'.

The tensions produced by the paradox of claiming the virtues of German philosophy while insisting on the need to overthrow German military ambitions was explored by another publication of 1915, a collection edited by W. P. Paterson (later Moderator of the Church of Scotland), entitled *German Culture: The Contribution of the Germans to Knowledge, Literature, Art, and Life*. Paterson's contributors set out to defend German culture against its own propagandists, who seek 'to create the conviction that nothing greater or fairer than German nationality has appeared in the whole history of humanity'.[26] In doing so, however, they also reveal that 'our case before the tribunal of history just is, that our civilisation stands for order, liberty, peace, justice, and humanity to an extent that a German world-empire would not be likely to do'.[27] For some, such as A. D. Lindsay, the outcome of the rise of German militarism is directly attributable to the earlier German philosophy:

> For all Hegel's realism there was in him much of that German love of the transcendent, that impatience with the limitations of time and place that thinks the understanding of the end to be attained the same as the attaining of it, and the ideal more real than the actual. Hegel is not to be tempted away from the actual by the ideal, but he sometimes insists, in spite of the most manifest facts, that the actual is itself already ideal.[28]

For Lindsay, 'Hegel's idealisation of the actual made him in practice a defender of the Prussian state and an opponent of the German Liberalism which was seeking to reform it'.[29] The consequence, in the end, is that 'There is no great difference between the state in Hegel's accounts of it and that modern German apotheosis of the state which is prepared in the name of the state to destroy all that makes the state worth having.'[30] For Paterson, however, the story of modern Germany is of a philosophical and theological decline that is precisely the reverse of the rise of neo-Kantianism and Hegelianism in the Anglophone world:

> It was a long descent from the moral rigour of Kant, and from the majestic sweep of Hegel's speculative philosophy, to the pessimism and cynicism of Schopenhauer, and still further to the level at which Haeckel was hailed as a philosopher and Nietzsche as a prophet. In the realm of Theology the Ritschlian School, the latest of capital importance, may be held in real respect and yet be judged to have been the most pedestrian of the succession which began with Schleiermacher.[31]

For John Watson, on the other hand, in his post-war book on *The State in Peace and War* – a book dedicated to Edward Caird – Hegel still represents the most advanced conception of the modern state:

> Hegel removes the last vestige of the false theory that the State is based upon contract, making its foundation to rest upon the true principle of the common will, as distinguished from the mere sum of individual wills. The State must indeed be powerful, but only because it is its function to maintain the external conditions essential to the best life. Thus Hegel really restores the fruitful conception of Aristotle, that the function of organised society is to secure the highest good of the citizen.[32]

Watson insists that, for Hegel, the state as a whole is 'the custodian of the conditions under which a given people manifests its ideal ends';[33] it is not an instrument of coercive force, but 'the highest expression of the reasonable will, the will which aims at the general good of the whole'.[34]

The evolutionary conception of philosophy as an ever closer approach to the understanding of God's presence in the world and in human history, which the Scottish idealists had inherited from Edward Caird, was put in serious doubt by the First World War. In his Gifford lectures before the war, John Watson had insisted that Kant and Hegel were the precursors of a new unity of faith and reason, one which discloses

> the central idea of religion, namely, that God is not a being who is complete in himself apart from the world, but one whose very nature is to manifest himself in the world and to come to self-consciousness in such manifestation.[35]

The First World War, to many, seemed like a very strange manifestation of such self-consciousness, and the optimism of the idealists rapidly came under attack from those who wanted a philosophy based not on the ideal or the absolute, but on the real and the factual. This challenge to idealism had begun before the war in the work of G. E. Moore, who, while living in Edinburgh, had read and approved the 'common sense' of Thomas Reid, and made a form of common sense central to his own philosophy, thus historically and intellectually undoing the foundations of 'Absolute Idealism'.[36] Moore was closely followed in the challenge to idealism by the various versions of Bertrand Russell's 'analytic philosophy'. In the same period, John Laird published a *Study in Realism* (1920), which set out to show the limitations of realism but actually ended up defending it as strongly as challenging it. Similarly, Norman Kemp Smith devoted much of his career to the translation and explication of Kant but his *Prolegomena to an Idealist Theory of Knowledge* (1924), as Alexander Broadie has underlined, defines an idealism that 'plainly implies a realist view of nature'.[37] Equally significant is the 'realism' promoted by John Anderson when he moved from Edinburgh to Sydney in 1927 and which became the foundation of what was adopted as a 'national' tradition in Australian philosophy.

Scottish philosophy in the inter-war period was thus caught between its (German) idealist heritage, around which it had built its worldwide reputation in the fifty years before 1914, and a resistance to idealism that had been magnified by the implication that idealism was a philosophy amenable to the militarism that had produced the war. For two of the Gifford lecturers in the years after the war the issue was more than a philosophical debate, since both W. R. Sorley and Andrew Seth Pringle-Pattison had lost sons in the war. Sorley's Gifford Lectures on *Moral Values and the Idea of God* (1918) is dedicated to his son, Charles Hamilton Sorley, probably the best of the Scottish war poets, who had died at the Western Front in 1915, and Sorley highlights the length of time it has taken to publish lectures delivered in Aberdeen in 1913 and 1914: 'In present circumstances it is perhaps unnecessary to apologise for the delay in its appearance.'[38] Sorley's theme has classic Kantian roots, trying to establish the objectivity of moral values and their relationship to a notion of human freedom which suggests – if not proves – a connection between the human and the divine: 'The question formulated at the outset of our enquiry was whether the facts of morality and ethical principles have any bearing and if so what bearing on the idea which we are justified in forming of ultimate reality.'[39] The conclusion, however, is haunted by the potential pointlessness of moral action, even in the context where there is some heavenly conclusion to human life: 'Morality, as we know it, consists in a life which never rests satisfied in the present but is always pressing onwards to fresh achievements. Experience does not fit a man for motionless ease, but for new endeavour.'[40] Given the restless striving involved in the effort to live a moral life, traditional conceptions of an afterlife of peaceful contemplation seem to be a diminution rather than a fulfilment of human experience:

> Must absorption in the one source of all life be the end, and must the true goal of life's fitful fever be the surrender of that separate individuality which has given its surpassing interest to the moral drama of the world?[41]

While trying to provide justification in seeing in morality humanity's special place in the universe, Sorley is unable to approach the issue with the confidence of his idealist predecessors. How, he asks, in such a scenario 'is the end better than the beginning?':

> For what purpose the infinite pain and effort of individuals, if their free consciousness must be relinquished, perhaps just when it has proved itself worthy of freedom? All that remains of their efforts could surely have been attained without their intervention. No time-process would have been needed to realise it, and the world would have been spared the evil and suffering of which it has been the scene. The one purpose which, so far as I can see, justifies the field of havoc through which the world passes to better things, is the creation of those values which only free minds can realise. And if free minds, when perfected, are to pass away, even for absorption in God, then that value is lost; and we must ask again the question, with less confidence in the answer, whether the values which the world's history offers are worth the price that has been paid for them.[42]

The confidence of idealism's belief that freedom releases human beings from the mere processes of material cause and effect is projected towards the afterlife to question whether any afterlife that does not repeat or re-enact the moral struggles of this life would be an adequate fulfilment of the moral justification of a mortal creature:

> Beautiful souls are always something more than beautiful; they have a moral energy which inactivity would not content. Surely there has been much irrelevant suffering in the making of such souls if, after the struggle has given them command of circumstances, all enterprise is shut off from them.[43]

It is hard not to see in such a discussion the ghost of the dead son haunting the speculation of the mourning father, or in the father the abandoned son of a once confident Scottish idealism:

> if free minds endure, it must surely be for a range of activity suited to the capacities and values which they have acquired in their mundane experience. And if, here or elsewhere, they attain that complete harmony between will and ideal in which moral perfection consists, they will surely be fitted thereby for nobler enterprise.[44]

In his Preface, Sorley notes that he has not tried to deal extensively with all the variants of his arguments in contemporary or recent philosophy because this had already been done by his predecessor as a Gifford lecturer, Pringle-Pattison, whose *The Idea of God in the Light of Recent Philosophy* (1915) had sought to reinforce the idealist position as it had developed in the late nineteenth century. Sorley's lectures take up and try to justify this version of idealism and Pringle-Pattison, in turn, in his Gifford lectures of 1922, tries to give philosophical substance to the notion of 'immortality' with which Sorley had struggled. For Pringle-Pattison, God is not beyond the world but within it, sharing through the role of the Son the sufferings which are necessary to the making of moral creatures:

> ... how (we may reply to Mill) can we conceive a moral being to be created at all except by allowing him to make himself in the stress of circumstance and temptation. And the same thing holds of the intellectual process: how but by the ceaseless effort and the conquest of difficulties can the thews of the mind be developed and strengthened. Mill's notion of outright creation – everything done by God 'in the first instance' – might give us a world of automata receiving their daily dole of pleasure, but it could give us neither the minds nor the characters we know.[45]

God's immanence means that the evolution of the world is also the evolution of God's relationship with the world, so that the 'ideal' of idealism is always a coming-to-be rather than the 'Absolute' which stands over against and separate from the world that we, as finite creatures, inhabit:

> And the existence of a finite world is not to be thought of as something that just happens to the Absolute, or develops itself within the Absolute only to be 'suppressed' again, 'merged' or 'absorbed'. On the contrary, the finite world is part of the inherent structure of reality. It is a process into which God pours his own life and receives it again with interest. And individuation is the method of the process, an individuation growing in distinctness and independence till it culminates in the self-conscious spirit of man, who, just because he has his own locus of existence, can enter into communion with his fellows and with his creative Source.[46]

Like Sorley, however, Pringle-Pattison struggles with the experience of the First World War and the death of his son Ronald. A telling passage uses the imagery of the front in order to underline the brutality of the world, if not redeemed by personal and moral virtues:

> Are we to attribute to the divine Friend and Lover of men a levity of attitude which we find offensively untrue of our ordinary human fidelities? Are we to liken Him to a military commander, who is content if

fresh drafts are forthcoming to fill his depleted battalions? To the military system, men are only so much human material, so many numerable units; but a chance encounter with one of the men in the flesh, one touch of human-heartedness, is sufficient to dissolve the abstraction which so regards them.[47]

Equally, like Sorley, Pringle-Pattison will have nothing to do with an immortality which confronts no challenges:

Those who think of heaven primarily as a place where all hardship shall cease, where no exertion shall be needed, but every harmless longing frustrated in the present life shall receive its fullest gratification, may well be preparing for themselves a disappointment. There are no signs that the universe is conducted on hedonistic principles, and just for that reason it appears to the hedonist 'a sorry scheme'. Desire in itself is irresponsible; seeing only its own object, it is blind to all the larger ends which are incompatible with its demands. So long, therefore, as it remains the desire of private satisfaction, no such desire can be regarded as secure of fulfilment.[48]

Human values – moral, aesthetic, political – are not the figments of subjectivity but are derived from a source which justifies them and is justified by them:

We did not make ourselves, and we do not weave our ideals out of nothing. They are all derived; they point to their source in a real Perfection, in which is united all that, and more than, it hath entered into the heart of man to conceive.[49]

In such a perspective, the accumulated deaths of the First World War are testimony not to the brutality of our existence in time, but to the necessity of death to the highest achievements of the human spirit:

For we may say without exaggeration that it is man's meditation upon death that has made him, and makes him, the human creature he is. His philosophy, his religion, his greatest poetry, all have their roots in the fact of death and in his refusal to accept it as final. The central and beneficent function of death in human experience has been finely expressed by Hawthorne: 'What a blessing to mortals,' he wrote, 'what a kindness of Providence, that life is made so uncertain, that Death is thrown in among the possibilities of our being. For without it, how would it be possible to be heroic, how we should plod along in commonplace for ever! . . . God gave the whole world to man, and if he is left alone with it, it will make a clod of him at last; but to remedy that, God gave man a grave, and it redeems all, and makes an immortal spirit of him in the end.[50]

The choice of quotation is a means of transforming not only the deaths in the war but the death which is the necessary medium of materialist evolution into the means by which humanity's spiritual superiority over death can be asserted.

In Sorley, in Seth and in others like A. A. Bowman, Scottish idealism survived the First World War but it was an idealism resolutely maintaining itself in a world which, whether in Russell's 'logical atomism' or the propositional logic of Russell's student, Ludwig Wittgenstein, or the 'logical positivism' of A. J. Ayer, had rejected the basis of idealist metaphysics. None the less, the German philosophical tradition continued to attract the attention of Scottish scholars. Norman Kemp Smith's translation of *Immanuel Kant's Critique of Pure Reason* (1929; rev. edn 1933) remained the standard version for Anglophone readers until the 1990s, and the German tradition remained the focus of much historical analysis by scholars such as H. J. Paton, who published his two-volume study of *Kant's Metaphysic of Experience* in 1936, to be followed a decade later by *The Categorical Imperative: A Study in Kant's Moral Philosophy* (1947). Idealism, according to John Passmore in his *A Hundred Years of Philosophy*, remained central to philosophy at Scottish universities through the first half of the twentieth century,[51] and, indeed, was still being taught down to the 1960s and 1970s by W. H. Walsh at Edinburgh University.

If few of these writers developed distinctive positions of their own, they kept open a line of communication with what became known as 'Continental Philosophy', a line that had rapidly closed in England under the influence of 'ordinary language philosophy'. Thus John Macmurray, himself a frontline soldier who was wounded in the war, developed the philosophy which climaxed in his Gifford lectures on *The Form of the Personal* (1952–4),[52] promoting positions which he had tested through much lecturing on the Kantian tradition.[53] Equally, John Laird's *Recent Philosophy* of 1936 is an encyclopaedic tour of philosophy in France, Italy and Germany, as well as Britain, and contains chapters on both Husserl's phenomenology and 'the new scholasticism' of Émile Gilson and Jacques Maritain. This continued engagement with philosophy in Europe was to result in John Macquarrie and Edward Robinson's translation of Martin Heidegger's *Being and Time* in 1962 and Macquarrie's own book on *Existentialism* in 1972, in which John Macmurray plays a leading role because he 'has many affinities with the existentialists'.⁵⁴ If the Scottish idealism that lingered uncertainly after the First World was seen as marginal to modern developments in British philosophy, it was also the foundation on which Scottish philosophers developed an ongoing involvement with the German-language philosophy that would be central to developments in European philosophy after the Second World War. Equally, Scottish theologians trained in the idealist tradition, such as T. F. Torrance, would provide the route by which the work of major theologians like Karl Barth entered the Anglophone world. The First World War might have threatened the death of Scottish philosophy's commitment to a Scoto-German tradition, but Scottish philosophers and theologians continued to form a bridge to German culture. They thereby not only pushed out the boundaries of their disciplines in the Anglophone world but also appealed, in many cases, to a wide general public – as, for instance, in John Macmurray's enormously popular broadcasts for the BBC in the early 1930s.⁵⁵

The continuing influence of the idealists can also be traced in some of the most prominent literary productions by Scottish writers in the 1920s. The centrepiece of the Scottish Renaissance movement of that decade was *A Drunk Man Looks at the Thistle* by Hugh MacDiarmid (C. M. Grieve), which precisely emulates the transformation of material evolution into an evolution of the spiritual that had been the burden of Caird's philosophy. Thus in the concluding sequence of the poem the Drunk Man confronts the displacement of humanity as central to the world's purposes:

> . . . Jesus and a nameless ape
> Collide and share the selfsame shape
> That nocht terrestrial can escape.⁵⁶

But this diminution of human significance is, like the idealists' transformation of material evolution into a spiritual evolution, only the prologue to the realisation that the nature of the universe and the nature of humanity's perception of it are one and the same:

> Oor universe is like an e'e
> Turned in, man's benmaist hert to see,
> And swamped in subjectivity.⁵⁷

If MacDiarmid, by the 1930s, was to adopt a Marxist materialism, his understanding of the mind's relationship to the world it inhabits was still profoundly shaped by the inheritance of Scottish idealism, in both its metaphysics and its social mission: 'In becoming one with itself my spirit is one with the world.'⁵⁸

Notes

1. Robert Mark Wenley, 'Edward Caird', *The Harvard Theological Review*, vol. 2, no. 2 (April 1909), pp. 115–38, p. 122. Available at <http://www.jstor.org/stable/1507019> (last accessed 3 May 2016).
2. J. R. McCluskey, *The Works of James Wilson*, vol. I (Cambridge, MA: Harvard University Press, 1967), p. 213.
3. Institute for the Study of Scottish Philosophy, 'Scottish Philosophy in North America'. Available at <http://www.scottishphilosophy.org/history/abroad/north-america/> (last accessed 1 June 2020).
4. J. W. Dawson, *The Origin of the World, According to Revelation and Science* (Montreal: Dawson Brothers, 1877), p. 341.
5. Ibid. p. 347.
6. Ibid. p. 358.
7. J. Clark Murray, 'The Scottish Philosophy', *Macmillan's Magazine*, xxxix (Dec 1876), 121.
8. *Macmillan's Magazine*, xxxix (December 1876), pp. 125–6.
9. Edward Caird, *The Evolution of Religion*, vol. II (Glasgow: James MacLehose and Sons, 1893), p. 316.
10. Ibid. p. 321.
11. John Watson, *The Interpretation of Religious Experience*, vol. I (Glasgow: James Maclehose and Sons, 1912), p. 360.
12. Robert C. Sibley, *Northern Spirits: John Watson, George Grant and Charles Taylor – Appropriations of Hegelian Political Thought* (Montreal and Kingston: McGill-Queen's University Press, 2008), pp. 43–4.
13. Henry Jones, *Idealism as a Practical Creed* (Glasgow: MacLehose, 1909), p. 28.
14. Christopher Humphrey, 'John Watson: The Philosopher of Canadian Identity', Historical Papers 1993: Canadian Society of Church History. Available at <churchhistcan.files.wordpress.com/2013/06/1993-7-humphrey-article.pdf> (last accessed 23 January 2018).
15. The beginning of the study of Scottish diasporas and their relationship to empire can probably be traced to MacKenzie's inaugural lecture at the University of Lancaster, later published as 'Essay and Reflection: On Scotland and the Empire', *The International History Review* (Simon Fraser University), vol. XV, no. 4 (November 1993), pp. 714–39.
16. J. H. Burns, 'The Scottish Kantians', *Journal of Scottish Philosophy*, vol. 7, no. 2 (2009), pp. 115–31.
17. Ibid. pp. 118–19.
18. Ibid. p. 124.
19. It is advertised on Amazon in hardcover, paperback and Kindle editions. Available at <https://www.amazon.co.uk/dp/B07H4DJH93/ref=dp-kindle-redirect?_encoding=UTF8&btkr=1> (last accessed 9 February 2019).
20. Andrew Seth, *Scottish Philosophy: A Comparison of the Scottish and German Answers to Hume* (Edinburgh: William Blackwood and Sons, [1885] 1899), p. 200.

21. Ibid.
22. Ibid. p. 201.
23. J. H. Muirhead, *German Philosophy in Relation to the War* (London: John Murray, 1915), p. 35.
24. Ibid.
25. Ibid. p. 93.
26. W. P. Paterson (ed.), *German Culture: The Contribution of the Germans to Knowledge, Literature, Art, and Life* (Edinburgh: T. C. and E. C. Jack, 1915), p. v.
27. Ibid. p. vii.
28. A. D. Lindsay, 'Philosophy', in Paterson (ed.), *German Culture*, p. 58.
29. Ibid. p. 59.
30. Ibid.
31. W. D. Paterson, 'Religion', in Paterson (ed.), *German Culture*, p. 382.
32. John Watson, *The State in Peace and War* (Glasgow: James MacLehose and Sons, 1919), p. 192.
33. Ibid. p. 132.
34. Ibid. p. 129.
35. Watson, *The Interpretation of Religious Experience*, vol. I, p. 343.
36. See Thomas Baldwin, 'Cambridge Philosophers V: G. E. Moore', *Philosophy*, vol. 71, no. 276 (April 1996), pp. 275–85, p. 284. For the on-going centrality of common sense to Moore's work, see p. 279.
37. Alexander Broadie, *A History of Scottish Philosophy* (Edinburgh: Edinburgh University Press, 2009), p. 327.
38. W. R. Sorley, *Moral Values and the Idea of God* (Cambridge: Cambridge University Press, 1918), p. xi.
39. Ibid. p. 505.
40. Ibid. p. 524.
41. Ibid.
42. Ibid. p. 525.
43. Ibid.
44. Ibid. p. 526.
45. A. Seth Pringle-Pattison, *The Idea of God in the Light of Recent Philosophy*, 2nd edn (London: Oxford University Press, [1915] 1920), p. 405.
46. A. Seth Pringle-Pattison, *The Idea of Immortality* (Oxford: Clarendon Press, 1922), p. 157.
47. Ibid. p. 191.
48. Ibid. p. 192.
49. Ibid. p. 194.
50. Ibid. p. 195.
51. John Passmore, *A Hundred Years of Philosophy* (London: Duckworth, 1957), p. 313.
52. These were published as *The Self as Agent* (London: Faber, 1957) and *Persons in Relation* (London: Faber, 1961).

53. See, for instance, G28.29 (E Gen 2162/3/32) 'Balliol notes: Kant and the Anti-Kantians', now housed in the Macmurray archive at Edinburgh University.
54. John Macquarrie, *Existentialism: An Introduction, Guide and Assessment* (London: Penguin, [1972] 1973), p. 100.
55. 'Few would have expected that at the height of a beguiling summer [1930] and at the unlikely hour of eight of the evening twelve broadcast talks on Philosophy would have produced a miniature renaissance among thousands of English listeners'; Charles Siepmann, Head of the Talks Department at the BBC, qtd in John E. Costello, *John Macmurray: A Biography* (Edinburgh: Floris, 2002), p. 180.
56. Michael Grieve and W. R. Aitken (eds), *Hugh MacDiarmid: Complete Poems 1920–1976*, vol. I (London: Martin Brien & O'Keefe, 1978), p. 160.
57. Ibid. p. 163.
58. Ibid. 'In the Slums of Glasgow', p. 563.

Part II

Individual Authors

Chapter 8

What Next?: Nan Shepherd and the First World War
Alison Lumsden

In the past few years Nan Shepherd has gained considerable critical attention for her meditation on hillwalking in the Cairngorms, *The Living Mountain* (1977). While this is to be welcomed, there has been less recent attention to her fiction and none at all to the fact that she attended the University of Aberdeen during the First World War and that experiences of that war are dealt with in her work. Nowhere is she described as a 'war author' but the war does feature, albeit obliquely, in *The Quarry Wood* (1928) and this essay will examine these traces. It will also explore her more overt engagement with the war in her second novel *The Weatherhouse* (1930) and the ways in which it deals with the broader question of how society may be rebuilt in the aftermath of war, a question that was prevalent in the inter-war period and addressed by, among others, her friend John Macmurray. Evidence of the Second World War can also be found in *The Living Mountain*, where the landscape is littered with the debris of crashed aircraft, thus demonstrating that the two wars in some ways punctuate the beginning and end of Shepherd's writing career.

Shepherd attended the University of Aberdeen from 1912 to 1915, graduating in 1915 with an MA. Her last year at university, consequently, coincided with the start of the war. It is clear that the outbreak of war had an early and profound effect on the student community at Aberdeen. While there was initially some resistance to the war among the student body (there was a pacifist society), for many male students the war put an immediate end to, or at least brought about a hiatus in, their studies. Many of the male students were in the Aberdeen University Corps and were at a training camp in Tain when the war broke out. They were mobilised immediately and sent to a training camp in Bedford, and then, in February 1915, many were sent to France. As R. D. Anderson recounts, these Aberdeen students stuck together and the university magazine, *Alma Mater* (which Shepherd edited for a period after she graduated), was frequently read at the front and reports from the front were included in it, thus maintaining an intimate connection with the University of Aberdeen.[1] It is hardly surprising, therefore, that throughout the war years the *Aberdeen University Review (AUR)* (which Shepherd eventually was also to edit) gave increasingly lengthy accounts of its students, staff and alumni who were at war, those who had been injured or killed in action, and others who were contributing to the war effort in various ways.

Indeed, as early as February 1915, *AUR* is reporting that 363 students or recent graduates are in service or under training,[2] and that 'of the 271 students commissioned or enlisted, a number have been granted leave to complete their studies at the University'.[3] Staff were also affected. A Mr G. A. T. Davies, who was second assistant to the Professor of Humanity and a lecturer in Roman History, was conducting research in Transylvania at the outset of war and was detained as a prisoner of war in Vienna;[4] he was still a prisoner in 1917. What was to become a fixed feature of *AUR* during the war period, a series of articles called 'The University and the War', sums up the situation in 1915, the year of Shepherd's graduation:

> The war in Europe has seriously affected the University and its work in several ways, both directly and indirectly. Large numbers of graduates and undergraduates, it is highly pleased to record have patriotically and cheerfully devoted themselves to the service of the country in the present national emergency. Hospital work, in particular, is being extensively discharged by many of our medical professors, lecturers and assistants ... Over a hundred graduates came forward applying for commissions in the Special Reserve of Officers ... Besides these, a considerable number of medical students of the third year and upwards volunteered for service as dressers at the various military hospitals in France and in this country. Seventy-nine students are enrolled for the course of instruction for cadets of the medical units of the Officers' Training Corps. At an early stage of the movement which has produced these excellent results, it was intimated that, as regards those students whose courses at the University are not yet completed the Senatus will do everything in its power to secure that their academic interests shall not be prejudiced by their service to the nation in the present crisis.[5]

As one might expect, as the war goes on, the tone of these articles becomes less celebratory. By June 1916, 64 of the 100 staff at the university were working for the war in some capacity and significant losses began to be recorded; a war obituary section supplements the roll call of those involved in the war effort.[6] As Anderson reports, 50 of the 100 students who had been mobilised from their training camp at Tain were dead within a year, and many of these had fallen at the Battle of Loos on 25 September 1915 when a unit from the 4th Gordons, which included the university company and a unit from Aberdeen Grammar School, was all but wiped out.[7]

Throughout the war years, poetry that both celebrates the war effort and gives voice to its cost to the north-east of Scotland also appears in the *Review*, including that by Shepherd's friend, Charles Murray. Murray's 'The Thraws of Fate', 'Fae France' and 'The Wife on the War' appear, along with W. B. Morren's response to 'Fae France' and 'Fae the Glen'. The February 1916 edition includes Mary Symon's poignant 'The Glen's Muster Roll'. In this poem Symon imagines the thoughts of a north-east teacher who has educated the boys from his local village but who, seeing them returning from war maimed and scarred, reflects:

> My Loons, my Loons! Yon winnock gets the settin' sun the same,
> Here's sklates and skailies, ilka dask a' futtled wi' a name.
> An' as I sit a vision comes: Ye're troopin in aince mair,
> Ye're back fae Aisne an' Marne an' Meuse, Ypres an' Festubert;
> Ye're back on weary bleedin' feet – you, you that danced an' ran –
> For every lauchin' loon I kent I see a hell-scarred man.
> Not mine but yours to question now! You lift unhappy eyes
> Maun answer wi' the bairn words ye said to me lansyne:
> 'I dinna ken, I dinna ken.' Fa does, oh, Loons o' Mine?[8]

Interestingly, the war also begins to have financial implications for the university, for not only are students leaving to join the war effort, but the war is also stopping them from even enrolling: 'there is no doubt that part at least of the reduction in the numbers of both men and women students has been due to their withdrawal to take the places in domestic and agricultural service of those who have enlisted', reports Principal George Adam Smith in June 1916.[9] A graduation address of June 1917 records that at least 141 alumni and students have died in the war[10] and by 1919 the university is discussing how best to commemorate the 301 students and former students who have fallen, with the war memorial in King's College Chapel eventually being decided upon as the most fitting tribute.[11]

Women do not go unmentioned in these articles. An Aberdeen University Women's First Aid Corps, consisting mostly of female graduates, is called into service as early as 1915 and some of the early female graduates offered their services to take the place of men who had left for war service.[12] For example, a Mrs F. W. Hasluck, who had graduated in 1907 with a first in Classics, offered to take the place of any Classical master or lecturer for the duration of the war to allow him to enlist; she offered to work free of charge, with the salary continuing to go to the lecturer's family. In February 1916, it is reported that a Miss Lilias Simpson is the first lady student to leave the university for national service. She had been attending classes on the making of munitions and was recruited by Messrs Mackinnon of Spring Gardens to work in their factory.[13] By March 1916, Aberdeen, along with the other universities, drew up a register 'containing classified information about educated women capable of filling responsible posts in the professional, commercial and industrial worlds vacated by men serving with His Majesty's Forces',[14] and from there on, the war roll of honour contains information about female graduates who are taking up these positions, many as teachers but also as medics, translators, social workers and forestry workers. Several Aberdeen female graduates received honours, including Sophia Mackworth Connal (MA 1907) who was given an MBE for work for the Red Cross in connection with the welfare of overseas troops in Nigeria.

During the war years, the demographic of the students also shifted significantly; in 1913–14 there were 732 men and 337 women, but by 1916–17 there were 236 men and 334 women. In an article in the *AUR* for 1942, entitled 'Women in the University Fifty Years: 1892–1942', Shepherd herself reports that 'In the war years the women kept the academic traditions alight,' noting too that the end of the war also brought a significant shift, for 'as the war-returned men poured into the Universities, so did the women'.[15] There were, in fact, 496 matriculated women by 1919, although it is notable that the many new academic posts that were filled immediately after the war were occupied by men.

This is the context against which *The Quarry Wood* is set. In her biography of Shepherd Charlotte Peacock sums this up:

> In 1915 Nan graduated MA. The ceremony, held at noon on Saturday 10th July, was one of the quietest ever witnessed beneath the vaulted roof of Mitchell Hall at Marischal College. Many of the undergraduates were in khaki. Service uniform was worn, too, by members of the university staff and glimpsed here and there among the audience filling the hall and galleries to overflowing, Dankester's mace was draped in crepe.

Britain was now in its twelfth month of war and in Principal George Adam Smith's address, which was interrupted continuously by bursts of applause, he talked with pride of Aberdeen's contribution to the war effort. The university's response to the war's call for recruits had been immediate, increasing steadily from week to week. Already the conflict had taken its toll; much of it on the 4th Gordons fighting in Flanders. Never in the university's history had there been such a drop in the numbers of matriculating students. The names of the fallen were read out; among them were more than twenty of Nan's Arts Class of 1912. After prayers for the university's 'martyrs in a sacred cause' the degrees were conferred.[16]

It seems, then, as if the war must have been central to Shepherd's experiences as a student at Aberdeen and immediately afterwards. So, how, if at all, does Shepherd present this situation in her fiction? Surprisingly, at first glance we can find very little evidence of the war in Shepherd's first semi-autobiographical novel set at King's, *The Quarry Wood*. Published in 1928, *The Quarry Wood* tells the story of Martha Ironside, who comes to study at the University of Aberdeen in the early years of the twentieth century. While the precise dates of Martha's time at university are never made clear, one can surmise from some of the internal references that it maps on to Shepherd's own experience. Nevertheless, the war is barely mentioned, apart from in one scene regarding Martha's suitor, Roy Rory Foubister. Martha has a brief flirtation with Roy but refuses to leave with him for South Africa. On the eve of his going the narrator tells us:

> 'We're done with each other,' [Martha] thought. 'We're strangers. He's come to see his father's old friend and I'm just her grand-niece.'
> Roy too was thinking, 'We're done with each other.' They parted with relief and supposed they would not meet again.

But the narrator then adds:

> In this they were wrong. He was back in Europe not so very long afterwards, fighting in France; and on his first leave came straight to Martha. Aunt Josephine was dead by then and Martha still teaching in Peterkirk. He wanted to marry her then and there, but she gave him a steady and smiling refusal.[17]

This is really the only reference to the war in *The Quarry Wood* and this apparent lack, in a novel where we might expect to see these experiences of the war described, is perhaps surprising. However, there may be good reasons for this: the world of the novel is predominantly female, and it explores the balance, and the synergies, between the intellectual life and the domestic, ultimately privileging, or at least celebrating, the local above the national or the international. It is notable that Roy's leave from fighting in France is balanced in the passage quoted above by the information that Aunt Josephine is dead and Martha is teaching at Peterkirk rather than by a further elaboration on world affairs; what is local, or even familial, this seems to imply, is as of much significance as what is international or global. As Catriona Macdonald has argued, it is only very recently that the idea of considering the Great War from a local perspective has emerged,[18] a position emphasised (although ultimately ironically) in Lewis Grassic Gibbon's *Sunset Song*:

> One night, the mid days of August as they sat at meat, the door burst open and in strode Chae Strachan, a paper in his hand, and was fell excited, Chris listened and didn't, a war was on, and Britain was to war with Germany. But Chris didn't care and Ewan didn't care either, he was thinking of his coles that the weather might ruin; so Chae took himself off with his paper again, and after that, though she minded it sometimes, Chris paid no heed to the war, there were aye daft devils fighting about something or other, as Ewan had said; and God! they could fight till they were black and blue for all that he cared if only the ley field would come on a bit faster, it was near fit for cutting but the straw so short it fair broke your heart.[19]

Similarly, in an interview where she reflects on her time as a student, Flora Garry, another early female graduate of the University of Aberdeen, who went on to be a poet, considers her experience of being a student during the war:

> The war was only part of your life, it had to be only part of your life because you were young, you were looking forward and you made the best of things and the war didn't affect us so intimately as the next war did. I mean we had no raid, or nothing much to speak of.[20]

This is perhaps a reminder to us that the war was not as much at the centre of all experience as we might believe in retrospect.

Shepherd's own immediate experience seems, too, to have been in some ways detached from first-hand contact with the war, and her own family does not seem to have been immediately touched by it. As Charlotte Peacock outlines, Shepherd's father would have been too old to enlist, and her brother Frank graduated in 1915 with a BSc in Engineering from the University of Glasgow. As a consequence, rather than going to fight in France, Frank went to work at the Royal Arsenal in Woolwich. Peacock tells us that conditions in the arsenal were 'ghastly' and that fatalities among the staff were common; from March 1916 there were at least two fatalities a week.[21] Tuberculosis and asbestosis were the main causes of death. Inevitably, this took a toll on Frank Shepherd and, in spite of travelling to South Africa in 1917 in the hope of recovering his health, he died in May 1917 and was buried in Bloemfontein.[22] The death of Nan Shepherd's brother, then, may have been tangentially caused by the war but it was not directly caused by it, a very different experience from that of, for example, the fictional Chris Guthrie in *Sunset Song*.

In looking for depictions of the war in Shepherd's novel of King's College, we may be searching in the wrong place. Shepherd deals far more directly with the war in her second novel, *The Weatherhouse*, published in 1930. This is perhaps telling; while much of Shepherd's work may be based on her own life experience and is set very much in the local terrain with which she was familiar, it is also elusive. *The Quarry Wood* was cut from its original form partly so that the characters in it would be less identifiable, yet it remains a first novel and is clearly based on Shepherd's own formative experiences. *The Weatherhouse* is more distanced as a piece of fiction. While Peacock rightly suggests that the character David Grey is based on Shepherd's brother and that the community of women depicted in the novel may bear a resemblance to the household at Cults, the novel is less overtly biographical in nature and it is interesting that it is here, in this more mature work, that Shepherd chooses to address the topic of the war.

The Weatherhouse

The Weatherhouse is the story of generations of one family of women living together in the north-east in a family home known as the weatherhouse because of its peculiar shape and multiple windows.[23] One of these women, Kate Falconer, is involved in war work as a cook at a nearby convalescent hospital. It is, however, the arrival of Lindsay Lorimer and Garry Forbes in the neighbourhood which really brings the war to the story. Garry has been fighting in France and is home on sick leave; he is engaged to Lindsay, who comes to the weatherhouse because she too is experiencing a 'sickness of the temper'.[24] As her mother reflects: 'I suppose she keeps thinking, well, and if he doesn't come back. It's this war that does it.'[25] Here, then, we find Shepherd dealing more overtly with the experiences of war. However, perhaps in accordance with the concerns explored elsewhere in Shepherd's work, initially this is from a female perspective:

> 'It's time it were put a stop to,' said Miss Annie.
> 'Yes,' sighed Mrs Andrew. 'And let things be as they were'.
> 'But they won't be', said Ellen.[26]

However, Lindsay's fiancé, Garry Forbes, has fought in France and his arrival at the weatherhouse brings a more overt engagement with the war. Garry has witnessed atrocities, most notably spending 'a day and a night in a shell hole, where, up to the thighs in filthy water, he had tried to suck the poison from another man's festering arm. The other fellow died where he stood,' we are told, 'slithered through his fingers and doubled over in the filth, and Garry was violently sick.'[27] It is tempting to speculate that Garry's experiences are based on accounts that Shepherd had heard from her fellow students who had gone to the war, and certainly she would have spoken to her close friend, John Macmurray, about his experiences at the Somme and Arras. As a result of such horror, and clearly experiencing the effects of trauma, Garry believes that he has discovered a 'fourth dimension' to life, something which the simple women of the weatherhouse will not be able to comprehend:

> 'You're a dimension short,' [. . .] 'Or no. You have three dimensions right enough, but we've a fourth dimension over there. We've depth. It's not the same thing as height,' he added, looking up. 'It's down in --- hollowness and mud and foul water and bad smells and holes and more mud. Not common mud. It's dissolution --- a dimension that won't remain stable --- and you've got to multiply everything by it to get any result at all. You people who live in a three-dimensional world don't know. You can't know. You go on thinking this is the real thing, but we've discovered that we can get off every imaginable plane that the old realities yielded.'[28]

Garry's response to this is to suggest that the post-war world must be rebuilt in a more practical way: in a world that has been 'unmade' by war, Garry wishes to embrace tables, civil engineering and 'a definite engagement in the war against evil'.[29] This 'war against evil' also takes the form of his campaign against a character called Louie Morgan. Louie claims, Garry thinks erroneously, to have been engaged to his friend, David Gray, who, like Shepherd's own brother, marched triumphantly through school and college, and, entering Woolwich Arsenal in the war, became night manager of a new fuse factory. His work was his passion. Brilliant, inventive . . . the artist's sensibility, the lover's exaltation, went to his work; and broke him. He developed tuberculosis, and in three months' time was dead.[30]

Lindsay Lorimer places the dead David Gray 'In her shrine of heroes' but Garry is far more aggressive in his defence of his friend, and fails to understand Louie's more complex (if slightly awry) understanding of the world, whereby truth and lies may not be as black and white as he believes: 'Garry was at a loss. He felt as though a roof had blown away and he was looking in amazement at a hive of populous rooms where things were done that he had never imagined.'[31] Ultimately, however, Garry comes to abandon his campaign against Louie, recognising that his search for the absolute truth may be futile.

Elsewhere, considering *The Weatherhouse* in the context of women's writing and feminist theory, I have argued that in this novel Shepherd explores a tension between a patriarchal system of thought epitomised by Garry and his experiences, and female models for understanding society, encapsulated in the women of the weatherhouse, Garry's Aunt Bawbie, and the ways in which the Louie Morgan incident is played out.[32] That reading is definitely available. However, revisiting *The Weatherhouse* in the context of Scottish war writing also opens up other possibilities.

Certainly, the ways in which Shepherd describes Garry's experiences in the trenches and the longer-term effects these have on him illustrate that, in spite of ignoring these topics in *The Quarry Wood*, Shepherd was fully cognisant of the horrors which her fellow students had suffered in France and the ways in which these affected them; her portrayal of the character of David Gray, whose experiences reflect those of her brother, also illustrates her awareness that these apparently more tangential relationships with the war were just as devastating, and through Lindsay Lorimer and Louie Morgan Shepherd also depicts the perhaps less acknowledged suffering of women as a result of the conflict.

However, *The Weatherhouse* also offers more than a simple awareness of the trauma of war. It also explores how the world might begin to be rebuilt in the aftermath of such devastation. Catriona Macdonald astutely notes that it is only with hindsight that we can see that the inter-war period is only a lull in hostilities and that for those who had lived through the Great War much of the point of it was that it was to put an end to fighting.[33] However, it is clear that what was to happen after the war and the understanding that it had changed society profoundly was evident almost immediately. When questioned about the end of the war Flora Garry comments:

> What I do remember is the class was dismissed and by myself I walked to the Bridge of Don and walked along the beach with nobody. I didn't want anybody there at all because I had to come to terms with a few things. One of them was the end of the war and the other was having done well in this essay. And I just walked along the beach all by myself and thought now that's the war over, what's the world going to be like? Will there be big changes? How am I going to do in this University? Is it going to be better or what? And you'd a feeling of hopefulness and you were afraid, and you had no idea what the country would be like, whether it would be a land fit for heroes or not.[34]

Similar questions vex the pages of the *AUR* from the middle of the war onwards. An article in the June 1915 edition, by an unnamed Arts Graduate, explores the relationship between the universities, the intelligentsia and the war, asking what the role of higher education will be in a Europe where the intelligentsia seems to have failed its youth.[35] Another article, published in June 1917, discusses the topic of 'Our Schools and the Work that Lies Before Them', and asks again what kind of education will be required if the country is to be properly provided for, once the war is at an end; will the old university curriculum suffice or will new, perhaps more practical, skills be required?[36]

These questions also underpin the philosophies of Nan Shepherd's friend, John Macmurray. The Macmurray family moved to Aberdeen in 1899 and became family friends of the Shepherds. John Macmurray attended Aberdeen Grammar School and was a friend of Nan Shepherd's brother. Some argue that Nan was in love with him and that he is the model for Luke in *The Quarry Wood*; it is certainly the case that she had a close intellectual friendship with him.[37] A brilliant scholar, Macmurray joined the Royal Army Medical Corps in 1914 and later fought at the Battle of the Somme. While at home on leave in October 1916, he married Elizabeth Hyde Campbell, Nan Shepherd's closest friend, and he was wounded near Arras. After the war, Macmurray studied at Balliol and was later to hold the Chair of Moral Philosophy at Edinburgh University. It is clear that his experiences in France profoundly influenced his philosophy, and questions about the nature of society and how we relate to it, both collectively and individually, recur in his work. Macmurray delivered a series of lectures for the radio between 1930 and 1932, which were later published as *Freedom in the Modern World*. In these lectures he ponders what kind of society can be rebuilt in the wake of the Great War: 'The War, and particularly the peace we made after the War,' he suggests 'have revealed something of the emotional forces of our social life to us.'[38] In these broadcasts Macmurray outlines his distrust of Cartesian boundaries, stating '[t]he tradition of our civilization is heavily biased in favour of the intellect against the emotions'. As a result of this, he proposes, we 'think it is wise to trust our minds, and foolish to trust our feelings'.[39] The importance of the body, he argues, must be recognised, since 'unless the emotions and the intellect are in harmony, rational action will be paralysed'.[40] He suggests that the physical, and the needs of the body, must be brought to the fore for society to function, thus privileging the physical and voicing scepticism concerning a world constructed upon intellect alone. 'What next?' he asks. 'What is to happen to the European tradition now that the Great War has unmasked the pretence which enabled it to hold emotion in servitude during the romantic era? It is still too early to give any definite answer.'[41]

Macmurray's distrust of the intellect leads to a call to trust the emotional life of the body and to a realisation that 'Europe cannot go backward'; it must, he suggests, 'think out again, in terms of our contemporary life, the problem of reality and freedom'.[42] Shepherd's fiction does not always entirely condone Macmurray's conclusions but it is clearly exploring similar questions; in particular, it recognises that a new society will not be built solely on intellectual abstractions. By 1930, when *The Weatherhouse* was published, Shepherd had worked in the education system for nearly fifteen years and would have been familiar with questions of how to rebuild a world in the aftermath of war, and she explores such questions in the novel. The ideas of her friend John Macmurray form part of this exploration and they are reflected in the character of Garry Forbes and the ways in which he thinks the world must be rebuilt. Macmurray's rejection of the Cartesian boundary between body and mind is reflected in Garry's experience in the shell hole, the consequent dissolution of the (intellectually constructed) self that he experiences, and the 'fourth dimension' that he claims to have found as a result. Such sentiments are echoed in Macmurray's musings on what constitutes reality: 'It is not what is real but what we think is real, not reality but what we take for reality, that directly determines our behaviour and so controls the current of our lives,' he states. And questions of perception, reality and how we act on our understanding of the relationship between the two similarly pervade Shepherd's novel.[43]

However, as a teacher of teachers, Shepherd was also acutely aware of the more practical applications of such philosophical enquiries and she also explores how the world is to be reconstructed in the wake of the destruction that the war had caused. Macmurray's insistence on a need to acknowledge the physical manifests itself in a call for greater sexual honesty and freedom.[44] In *The Weatherhouse*, however, Shepherd's exploration of the role that the physical will take in any post-war recalibration of society is translated into a more pragmatic sense of urgency. 'He wants to *do* things . . . Things with his hands,' Lindsay's mother complains, referring both to her son and to the influence Garry has had upon him:

> '"Good heavens mother, we've *un*-made enough, surely, in these three and a half years. I want to make something now. *You* haven't seen the ruined villages. The world will get on very well without the law and the Church for a considerable time to come . . . but it's going to be jolly much in need of engineers and carpenters." Make chairs and tables, that seems to be his idea.'[45]

'Frank'll never go to the college now,' Lindsay's mother laments. 'He swears he won't go to the University and won't . . . All my family have been in the professions.'[46] The intellectual will no longer suffice on its own and a new world has to be made, this seems to imply.

In *The Weatherhouse*, consequently, Shepherd, like Macmurray, asks 'What next?' However, unlike Macmurray, she is more cautious about offering solutions. Many of the locals in the novel see Garry Forbes as no more than a fool, and we are never sure that his views are being condoned by the women of the weatherhouse itself or, indeed, by the novel as whole. The end of the book sees both Lindsay and Garry recovered, and happily married, but there is a fragility about their marriage which might suggest that Shepherd is not wholly confident in the world they – and, by extension, post-war society – have made: Lindsay is happy and has three bairns, and Garry is involved in politics but, as Miss Theresa ponders, 'nine years was not so very long a time' and 'she [Lindsay] may greet again for all her dancing'.[47] Sadly, Europe did 'greet again' all too soon, perhaps because of the failure of society to rebuild itself fully. Shepherd is aware that Garry's solutions may not be totally adequate, and indeed the novel offers no solution to how a post-war society is to be remade.

This is, in some ways, what underpins a later meditation by Shepherd on the aftermath of war, 'Descent from the Cross'. Published in 1943 in *The Scots Magazine* and only recently reprinted, 'Descent from the Cross' is a long short story about a veteran who returns from the Great War with the aim of writing a philosophical work that will capture something of the horror he has experienced. Like Garry, Tommy is profoundly changed by his experiences: 'He seemed to be out of the body, pain was gone: and with superhuman clarity he saw the truth of things.'[48] From that point onwards, 'nothing had really mattered but getting it into words'. However, in spite of Tommy's efforts, 'nothing coherent' emerges and his health is eventually broken by the struggle to articulate the truth that he believes he has perceived.[49] Juxtaposed with the healthy vigour of his wife (who is rebuilding the world in a more practical way through her work as a social worker), Tommy is presented as a man incapable of living, but also one, ultimately, content to recognise that the horrors he has experienced in war cannot be captured in any form of words.

Like her character in 'Descent from the Cross', Shepherd was clearly aware of the inadequacies of words to capture the horrors of the war she had lived through. As a consequence, it is perhaps hardly a surprise that, in spite of the clear effects of the war on the University of Aberdeen in the years when Shepherd was studying there, it barely features in her novel of King's College. However, she was also well aware of the dilemmas and challenges that the war had created for her generation and she did seek ways to address these in her fiction, although, ultimately, like Tommy, she recognises that no simple solution is satisfactory. Shepherd, to date, has been read in the context of women's writing, and more recently, emphasis has been on *The Living Mountain*, thus situating her as a proto-ecocritic offering a female perspective on our engagements with landscape. However, reading Shepherd's *The Weatherhouse* in the framework of Scottish war fiction and within the context of the effects of war upon the University of Aberdeen offers opportunities to see it afresh. In *The Weatherhouse*, Shepherd provides a depiction of the horrors of war, its effects upon families and, perhaps above all, a meditation on the kind of world that can be built in its aftermath.

Notes

1. See R. D. Anderson, *The Student Community at Aberdeen 1860–1939* (Aberdeen: Aberdeen University Press, 1988), p. 83.
2. *Aberdeen University Review*, vol. 2: 1914–15 (Aberdeen: Aberdeen University Press, 1915), p. 172.
3. *AUR*, 1915, 2.173.

4. *AUR*, 1915, 2.65.
5. *AUR*, 1915, 2.64.
6. *AUR*, 1915–16, 3.218.
7. Anderson, *The Student Community at Aberdeen 1860–1939*, p. 83.
8. *Aberdeen University Review*, vol. 3: 1915–16 (Aberdeen: Aberdeen University Press, 1916), 3.137.
9. *AUR*, 1915–16, 3.219.
10. *Aberdeen University Review*, vol. 4: 1916–17 (Aberdeen: Aberdeen University Press, 1917), 4.412.
11. *Aberdeen University Review*, vol. 7: 1919–20 (Aberdeen: Aberdeen University Press, 1919), 6.80.
12. *AUR*, 1914–15, 2.173.
13. *AUR*, 1915–16, 3.178.
14. *AUR*, 1915–16, 3.270.
15. Nan Shepherd, 'Women in the University Fifty Years: 1892–1942', in *Aberdeen University Review*, vol. 29: 1941–42, pp. 171–81, p. 179–80.
16. Charlotte Peacock, *Into the Mountain: A Life of Nan Shepherd* (Cambridge: Galileo Publishers, 2017), pp. 91–2.
17. Nan Shepherd, *The Quarry Wood* (Edinburgh: Canongate, [1928] 1996), p. 179.
18. Catriona M. M. Macdonald, 'Going Back to Yesterday: The Legacy of War', *History Scotland* (May/ June 2019), pp. 46–50.
19. Lewis Grassic Gibbon, *Sunset Song* (London: Penguin Books, [1932] 2007), p. 191.
20. Interview with Flora MacDonald Garry [nee; Campbell, (1900–2000), (M.A. 1922), 4 January 1986, University of Aberdeen Special Collections, MS 3620/1/ 41. Quoted with the permission of Special Collections, University of Aberdeen.
21. Peacock, *Into the Mountain*, p. 100.
22. Ibid. p. 102.
23. A weather house is also a toy used to predict the weather. It takes the form of a small house with figures of a man and woman standing in two porches; the man comes out of his porch in wet weather and the woman out of hers in dry. These were often found in houses in Scotland in the early twentieth century.
24. Nan Shepherd, *The Weatherhouse* (Edinburgh: Canongate, [1930] 1996), p. 11.
25. Ibid. p. 11.
26. Ibid. pp. 11–12.
27. Ibid. p. 53.
28. Ibid. p. 114.
29. Ibid. p. 66.
30. Ibid. p. 45.
31. Ibid. p. 106.

32. Alison Lumsden, '"Journey into Being": Nan Shepherd's *The Weatherhouse*', in Carol Anderson and Aileen Christianson (eds), *Scottish Women's Fiction, 1920s to 1960s: Journeys into Being* (East Linton: Tuckwell Press, 2000), pp. 59–71.
33. Macdonald, 'Going Back to Yesterday', pp. 46–50.
34. Interview with Flora MacDonald Garry.
35. 'The Universities – Intelligentsia and the War', *AUR*, 1914–15, 2.213–18.
36. Sir Henry Craik, 'Our Schools and the Work that Lies Before Them', *AUR*, 1916–17, 4.204–215.
37. See, for example, Peacock, *Into the Mountain*, pp. 115–119, where Peacock also draws similarities between Macmurray's experiences and those of Garry Forbes.
38. John Macmurray, *Freedom in the Modern World* (Atlantic Highlands, NJ: Humanities Press, [1932] 1992), p. 31.
39. Ibid. p. 22.
40. Ibid. p. 23.
41. Ibid. p. 57.
42. Ibid. p. 57.
43. Ibid. p. 77.
44. See Macmurray, *Freedom in the Modern World*, pp. 22–3.
45. Shepherd, *The Weatherhouse*, p. 12.
46. Ibid.
47. Ibid. pp. 195–6.
48. Nan Shepherd, 'Descent from the Cross', in *Wild Geese: A Collection of Nan Shepherd's Writing*, ed. Charlotte Peacock (Cambridge: Galileo, 2018), pp. 1–38, p. 7.
49. Shepherd, 'Descent from the Cross', pp. 7–8.

Chapter 9

Pagan Modernism: First World War and Spiritual Revival in Lewis Grassic Gibbon's *Sunset Song* and Neil M. Gunn's *Highland River*

Scott Lyall

Introduction

A significant scene in Lewis Grassic Gibbon's *Sunset Song* is Will Guthrie's return on leave from the war to visit his sister, Chris, at Kinraddie. Will escaped Kinraddie and the dour Calvinist morality of his father to emigrate to Argentina and marry his sweetheart, Mollie. While there, Will joined the French Foreign Legion. Chris asks Will if he and Mollie will one day return to Scotland, and Will replies: '*Havers, who'd want to come back to this country? It's dead or its dying–and a damned good job!*'[1] Chris is angry that her brother feels this way about their country, but her reflections on what Scotland means to her go no further geographically than Kinraddie. Instead, she thinks of the 'seeds that pushed up their shoots from a thousand earthy mouths', which confirm to her that 'Scotland lived, she could never die, the land would outlast them all, their wars and their Argentines'.[2] Scotland, to Chris, is the land itself, the natural world that sustains her emotionally and economically. Chris then asks Will if he will come with her the following day to pay their respects at their father's grave in Kinraddie churchyard. Will asks mockingly if she has become religious, but she replies seriously:

> *I don't believe they were ever religious, the Scots folk, Will – not really religious like Irish or French or all the rest in the history books. They've never BELIEVED. It's just been a place to collect and argue, the kirk, and criticise God.*[3]

For Chris, the Scots, especially post-Reformation Scots, in contrast to predominantly Catholic peoples such as the Irish and French, have never been genuinely Christian. She might be named after Christ, but if Christine has a religion at all, it lives in the land, not with the Christian God.

In putting forward this view of Scottish irreligiosity, Chris is acting as her author's mouthpiece. Gibbon favoured an interpretation of world history that regarded religion as an unnatural aberration of civilisation. In 'Religion' (1934), Gibbon puts the case that pre-historical humans were not religious:

> Primitives – the food-gatherers, the ancient folk of all the ancient world – knew no religion. Their few and scattered survivors in this and that tiny crinkle of our planet are as happily irreligious as our own remote ancestors. They are without gods or devils, worship or cities, sacrifices or kings, theologies or social classes. Man is naturally irreligious.[4]

Undaunted by the anthropological speculations in J. G. Frazer's *The Golden Bough* (1890) on the religiosity of primitive peoples, Gibbon argues that these were examples of 'savages' infected with the 'disease' of civilisation, not true primitives still uncontaminated by the spiritual and moral sicknesses of modernity.[5] In this, Gibbon is keeping faith with his understanding of diffusionism, an anthropological theory locating the source of human cultures as diffusing from one source in the Nile Delta. Believing 'the Golden Age . . . is inseparable from that historical reconstruction of the past known as Diffusion', the ruralist H. J. Massingham summarises the diffusionist position in *The Golden Age* (1927).[6] Civilisation grew organically only at its seminal point: Egypt. Elsewhere, it was 'a sudden and arbitrary imposition' on guileless primitives, among whom violence was unknown until being 'introduced by civilized human beings'.[7] Civilisation, thus, is a process of involution initiated by human settlement, contrasting with the freedom enjoyed by hunter-gatherers – regarded by Gibbon as ancestors of the pagan Picts – in a pre-civilisation golden age.

Gibbon claimed to be irreligious, but his novel sparks with spiritual elements that pre-date Christian civilisation. This is even more true of Neil M. Gunn's *Highland River*, which is a search for spiritual sustenance in a spiritually starved post-war world. Both novels were published in the 1930s, but retain a focus on the First World War: *Sunset Song* (1932) takes place mostly in the run-up to the war, and *Highland River* (1937) is set largely after but with sections that take us back to the main character Kenn Sutherland's boyhood before he served in the war, as well as depicting war scenes. War destroys a local culture in *Sunset Song*, and Gibbon's response is to suggest the need for a socialist society, especially in the next two novels of the *Scots Quair* trilogy, *Cloud Howe* (1933) and *Grey Granite* (1934). Kenn in *Highland River* goes back to 'the source': this in part means reacquaintance with his local culture, but it also means finding reconnection after the war with the natural world of his childhood, enjoyed by *Sunset Song*'s Chris in the mostly pre-war setting of Kinraddie. Associated with this integration with nature, these novels suggest a still possible route back to a golden age era of pre-Christian values that, their authors imply, can renew Scotland and the modern world. In each novel, the First World War is the terminal point of a disintegrating Christian civilisation.

Writing of the popularity of war novels in the late 1920s and early 1930s boom following the success of Erich Maria Remarque's *All Quiet on the Western Front*, Modris Eksteins claims that 'All the successful war books were written from the point of view of the individual, not the unit or the nation.'[8] Although they are focalised largely through individual characters, Chris Guthrie and Kenn Sutherland, *Sunset Song* and *Highland River* are not immediately war novels in the vein of Remarque's 1929 work. Rather, they are attempts to understand the civilisation, in the longest span of that term's meaning, that would lead to the war, and how to change or abolish that civilisation so war could never happen again. They are, at the same time, Scottish novels, not merely in terms of location, but also in their concern with the death of the local culture and its potential post-war revival. That revival is proposed in the form of a 'pagan modernism'.

The Modernist Context

Modernism is traditionally seen as a movement of secularisation stemming from multiple complex causal factors. These include Newtonian and Darwinian scientific developments; nineteenth-century philosophical doubt (Strauss's and Renan's demythologising biographies of Jesus; Nietzsche's madman pronouncing God's death); autochthonous challenges to Christian imperialism and the collapse of centralising, divine-right monarchies; the Bolshevik Revolution; and rising literacy rates, burgeoning popular culture and increasing democratisation.[9] The First World War plays an important but not determining role in this modernist secularisation thesis, which, despite catastrophic historical interruptions such as the war, represents history largely as a progressive straight line of Western development.

Modernist cultural forms, often resistant to the nightmare of history, reflect these influences and pressures in nuanced ways. Modernism is, among other things, an artistic endeavour to find spiritual enchantment in an exhausted world, described by Wassily Kandinsky, in *Über das Geistige in der Kunst* (1911), as 'The nightmare of materialism, which has turned the life of the universe into an evil, useless game'.[10] Recent criticism has characterised modernism in terms that are anything but straightforwardly secular. Roger Griffin has argued, for instance, that

> Modernism is *not* a generalized historical condition ... but a generalized revolt against even the intuition made possible by a secularizing modernization that we are spiritual orphans in a godless and ultimately meaningless universe. Its hallmark is the bid to find a new home, a new community, and a new source of transcendence.[11]

Griffin's point that modernism is not a securely secular moment but an attempt to create new forms of home, community and transcendence out of the ruins of the old is highly pertinent to *Sunset Song* and *Highland River*. These novels are part of the Scottish literary revival that emerged after the war, an engagement, broadly speaking, with modernist themes and forms from a Scottish perspective.[12] Hew Strachan comments of the First World War, 'Scots took up arms for Britain and the empire, but Scotland became more conscious of itself as it fought.'[13] This developing cultural and political consciousness found post-war expression in a Scottish revival with modernist resonances. This is especially true in the spiritual turn apparent in this period. Roland N. Stromberg links the irrationalism of modernism to a 'quest for community'; as Weberian rationalism destroyed links to organic folk cultures, myth and 'spiritual awakening' were employed by modernists to reclaim an integrated past.[14] Modernism upsets Christian cosmology, but often replaces it with other metaphysical meanings. Looking back beyond Christian civilisation in order to propose a rejuvenated post-war future, *Highland River* and *Sunset Song* suggest a pagan divinisation of land and locality.

Pagan Revival

While the mythic tendencies of modernism are more fully understood, the role played in the period by pagan sensibilities and ideas is less well charted. Yet this is important to understand to allow a clearer view of modernism's relationship to religion and its revolt against modernity. After all, modernism (or aspects of it) is not only a formal challenge to nineteenth-century realism, but a broader cultural rebellion against key features of modernity such as urbanisation and industrialisation. As such, the importance to paganism of a connection to nature – what Kathryn Rountree calls paganism's 'spiritual orientation to the natural world' – links it to our contemporary awareness of ecological issues, as well as to romanticism's revolt against the urbanised rationalisation of experience in the late eighteenth and early nineteenth centuries, a revolt continued by some modernists.[15]

The Victorian and Edwardian periods saw a pagan revival of sorts. Alternative spiritualities, such as theosophy, received inspiration from Helena Blavatsky's eclectic mix of esoteric spiritualism and traditional religious ideas, which influenced the mystical revival of the 1890s, galvanising the polytheistic MacGregor Mathers's Golden Dawn and W. B. Yeats's Irish Revival. Yeats combined pagan and Christian occultism to buttress his Order of the Celtic Mysteries (1896–1902) and this stimulated Scotland's Celtic Revival, described by Mark Williams as 'an anti-industrial aesthetic movement centred in Edinburgh but that looked to Ireland for an example'.[16] William Sharp, known to Yeats and others as his visionary alter ego Fiona Macleod, edited the *Pagan Review* for its sole edition in 1892; Williams pinpoints the creative denomination of Sharp/Macleod as 'pagan-Catholic', while Michael Shaw calls Sharp a neo-pagan.[17] The Scottish artist John Duncan provided images of Celtic-pagan gods for *The Evergreen*, the key journal of the Scottish Celtic Revival, edited by Sharp and Patrick Geddes.

These are principally Scottish and Irish manifestations of a wider cultural interest in paganism, one that was often connected to local landscapes and an affirmation of the natural. For instance, paganism plays a key role in Thomas Hardy novels such as *The Return of the Native* (1878) and *Tess of the D'Urbervilles* (1891), with the latter's ending, at the stone circle of Stonehenge, echoed in the importance of the standing stones to Gibbon's heroine in *Sunset Song*. Gibbon claimed the influence of Percy Shelley on his political ideas, but the way that he focuses on the rural peasantry and the landscape of his particular local area, the Mearns, and the manner in which the significance of nature is highlighted through pagan symbolism owe much to Hardy's imaginative creation of 'Wessex'.[18] Kenneth Grahame, Scottish author of the Pan-infused *The Wind in the Willows* (1908), a pastoral idealisation of rural southern England, published the non-fiction *Pagan Papers* in 1893, a period in which the decadent *Yellow Book* was damned as 'neo-pagan'.[19]

These developments influenced high modernism. Paganism remained important in early twentieth-century literature, informing, for example, D. H. Lawrence's Australian novel *Kangaroo* (1923), *Lady Chatterley's Lover* (1928) and his posthumous non-fiction, *Apocalypse* (1931), all of which reject various aspects of Christian civilisation and modernity. Raymond Williams picks up on the '"pagan" emphasis which is always latent in the imagery of the earth' in *Sunset Song*, comparing this to the opening of Lawrence's *The Rainbow* (1915).[20] But whereas Lawrence's response to the shift from country to city and the break-up of organic peasant life is, in *Kangaroo* and *The Plumed Serpent* (1926), a search for community in a fascist pseudo-primitivism, Gibbon remained radical through suggesting a pagan communalism in opposition to the disintegration provoked by war.

Ronald Hutton argues that the paganism of our own time comes from eighteenth-century German romanticism and its 'admiration for ancient Greece, nostalgia for a vanished past, and desire for an organic unity between people, culture, and nature'.[21] These three facets would remain important in the late nineteenth- and early twentieth-century modernist period, with the last feature, connection between land, culture and folk, being especially significant to small-nation revivals such as that in Ireland, which might be seen as straining against imperial control, and Scotland. These strands were also central to fascist movements of the 1920s and 1930s. The Italian philosopher Julius Evola called for a 'return to the Nordic pagan tradition' in rejection of modernity's basis in Judeo-Christian culture in *Imperialismo pagano* (1928), published in a German edition of 1933, in which he hails the fascist symbols 'of the Swastika, the Eagle, and the Axe'.[22] Evola, an ex-serviceman who impressed Mussolini and courted the Nazis, proposed 'pagan imperialism' – a return to the values of Roman imperiality – as a solution to the 'decline of the West'.[23] The politics of modern paganism could be potentially liberating, but also fearfully oppressive.

This brief summary of some of the diverse manifestations of pagan ideas in modern literature leads to three main points. Firstly, the writers who employed paganism were not solely or distinctly 'Celtic' but came from a range of cultures within and outside of Britain.[24] Secondly, the adaptation of pagan ideas and symbols did not necessarily imply the author's belief in paganism as a spiritual way of life but was often used as a means to oppose Christianity or aspects of modernity; in some cases, this might imply a reactionary or nostalgic worldview, in others a more libertarian or radical disposition. This point will be revisited when discussing what Gibbon and Gunn make politically of the pagan motifs in *Sunset Song* and *Highland River*. Thirdly, as has been noted, paganism was often connected to the countryside and the pastoral. This siting of ancient spiritualities in rural settings is an attempt to counter urbanisation, and yet is also a bid to bring the land itself alive through pagan magic. It is the countryside and countryfolk, inheritors of pagan values, that will save the nation from degeneration. While the term 'pagan modernism' fits the rural novels *Sunset Song* and *Highland River*, this is not to suggest that the paradigm describes the Scottish revival as a whole: for instance, Edwin Muir's mature poetry is essentially Christian, and there are many novels of urban experience, such as Catherine Carswell's *Open the Door!* (1920), to give only two examples of the revival's diversity.

The pagan revival declined somewhat after the First World War, but continued to favour natural settings.[25] Gunn and Gibbon used the land and pagan connection to the natural world and ancient folk to condemn the modern civilisation that produced the war. They did so not as an escape from modernity, as in the classic terms of pastoral,[26] but as a means to propose a new relation to a broken modern world. Post-war redemption is presented as possible through a return to a pre-Christian autochthonous spirituality connected to the land, not as *patrie*, but as a site of radical political and personal reawakening.

Numinous Landscapes

Owen Davies explains that the Latin root of pagan, *paganus*, relates to 'rustic' and 'of the countryside'.[27] Pagan has often been translated into English as 'peasant', and also has connotations of local and rooted non-Christian 'country folk', in opposition to Hellene and Roman cosmopolites.[28] *Sunset Song* and *Highland River* are regional novels concerned with the folk. 'The folk' refers to the indigenous crofters or fishers of the small rural communities of each novel, and to their primitive pagan ancestors; the term implies a down-to-earth people of communal principles who live close to the land.

Later, pagan became a synonym for anti-clericalism, as well as anti-Catholicism. Paganism, as Hutton comments, is most often understood as referring 'to the pre-Christian religions of Europe and the Near East' and is 'defined by and against the Christian faith'.[29] There is, at best, ambivalence towards Christianity in *Highland River*. The narrator observes that Kenn's parents did not take communion because they felt themselves 'unworthy', yet Kenn's mother possessed a 'humility' comparable to Christ's.[30] Kenn complains that in school they had been taught nothing of pre-Christian history, even though Druidic sacrifices may have taken place locally. *Sunset Song* is fiercely anti-Christian. Ministers are corrupt and licentious, and Calvinist sex repression has soured John Guthrie's character. The schoolgirl Chris, bored by Sir Thomas Browne's seventeenth-century Christian confessional *Religio Medici*, lent to her by the minister, finds greater fun in washing bedsheets with her mother. Jean Guthrie's joyful exclamation on seeing her daughter in her underwear – '*God, you've stripped!*' – contains no hint of blasphemy, in contrast to her father John Guthrie's embarrassment and stifled lust, which shames Chris's naturalness.[31] Both novels see the First World War, which Gunn calls 'the great Poison War', as the violent culmination of the Christian era.[32]

Two further pagan characteristics are 'deification of nature' and 'veneration of ancestors'.[33] Nature and closeness to a natural state are important in these novels and are signified in their titles: 'sunset', 'river'. This often combines with feelings of connection to primitive folk. On first arriving at Blawearie farm, Chris imagines a ghostly prehistoric figure who cries, '*The ships of Pytheas!*', as if in warning that the Greek navigator Pytheas, first historian of Britain in *On the Ocean* (BCE 320), represents a threat to the land and an ancient way of local life – a threat re-emerging with the war.[34] Finding solace in the land, Chris retreats to the standing stones, but the pagan stones illicit a 'shiver' from her Christian father, who says they were 'raised' by 'skin-clad savages'.[35] Chae Strachan, back on leave from the war, drunkenly envisions an ancient warrior, one of the Caledonians led by Calgacus who fought the Roman invasion of Scotland, at the standing stones. This is Chae's intimation of his own death in the war, but it is also a reminder that civilisations and their wars come and go, and attests to the connection drawn by Gibbon between the people of Kinraddie and ancient Scots.

Chae's name will later be inscribed on one of the stones on its transformation into a war memorial. Randall Stevenson describes the standing stone memorial as being 'as straightforward and austere as a casualty list'.[36] Written into the stone are the local war dead and the ritual history of a prehistorical civilisation, one that, throughout his *œuvre*, the diffusionist Gibbon idealises as pacific. As he claims in 'The Antique Scene' (1934), prior to the Bronze Age, 'Archaic civilisation in Scotland, as elsewhere, was one singularly peaceful and undisturbed. Organised warfare had yet to dawn on the Western

World.'[37] The ancient pagan folk society is a judgement upon the violent civilisation of modernity. The dignity of the war memorial cast on pagan stone in *Sunset Song* is in contrast to the war memorial in the town of Segget in *Cloud Howe*: a Christian 'angel set on a block of stone, decent and sonsy in its stone night-gown', derided by Chris as 'this quean like a constipated calf!'.[38] Chris's minister husband Robert Colquohoun believes that *'Folk'll think it a joke when we've altered things'*, alluding to his vision of a fairer society.[39] Yet Robert's evaluation of the stone angel and the society it epitomises sits somewhat oddly in the mouth of a Church of Scotland minister. Segget's memorial is not only too gaudily ornate, it is also too religious and too Christian. It stands as an idealisation or a kind of ideological sublimation of the brutality, filth and futility of war. As such, it does not invest the war dead with respect. The supernatural angel will not re-enchant the post-war world. Stone is central to the narrative design of *Grey Granite*; the materiality of stone indicates a materialist age requiring a materialist solution to problems such as the Depression. That solution is Chris's son's communism; significantly, Ewan, future communist, who as a boy is interested in Druid flints, the weapons of prehistory, is born during wartime. The aim and meaning of Ewan's communism is to make Christian civilisation a species of prehistory. The contrast between the two stone memorials in *Sunset Song* and *Cloud Howe* – one ancient, from a prehistorical culture that we do not fully understand, but possessed of mysterious numinous qualities, the other modern and entirely lacking in spiritual value, despite being overabundantly laden with Christian meaning – symbolises the degeneration of civilisation from the peaceable pagan period to the war-torn twentieth century.

The standing stones provide Chris with a perspective on history and time in which Christianity and war are merely passing clouds; they also provide her with a place of personal contemplation that seems to be outside of time. The land reminds her that everything is temporal. Afforded the opportunity on the death of her father of going to university to become a teacher, Chris decides to stay in Kinraddie because she feels a deep emotional attachment and visceral connection to the land.

> The wet fields squelched below her feet, oozing up their smell of red clay from under the sodden grasses, and up in the hills she saw the trail of the mist, great sailing shapes of it, going south on the wind into Forfar, past Laurencekirk they would sail, down the wide Howe with its sheltered glens and its late, drenched harvests, past Brechin smoking

against its hill, with its ancient tower that the Pictish folk had reared, out of the Mearns, sailing and passing, sailing and passing, she minded Greek words of forgotten lessons, Παντα ρει, *Nothing endures*. And then a queer thought came to her there in the drookèd fields, that nothing endured at all, nothing but the land she passed across, tossed and turned and perpetually changed below the hands of the crofter folk since the oldest of them had set the Standing Stones by the loch of Blawearie and climbed there on their holy days and saw their terraced crops ride brave in the wind and sun. Sea and sky and the folk who wrote and fought and were learnéd, teaching and saying and praying, they lasted but as a breath, a mist of fog in the hills, but the land was forever, it moved and changed below you, but was forever, you were close to it and it to you, not at a bleak remove it held you and hurted you. And she had thought to leave it all![40]

From the soaked earth beneath her feet, we move with the mist over a local area from Laurencekirk to Forfar, before going back in time to Chris's Pict ancestors. The standing stones and 'holy days' create a spiritual quality, undercut by the thought that even the sacred is mutable. Chris has misremembered her Greek: $πάντα\ ῥεῖ$, from Heraclitus, means 'everything flows' and Gibbon's prose exemplifies this philosophy, moving over space and time in modernist vein, and mixing third-person pronouns 'she' and 'her', referring solely to Chris, and second person 'you', which may in the singular refer to Chris, but in the plural could also include the reader, the folk of Kinraddie and the ancient Picts. Chris's being dwells in the land, and *Sunset Song* presents an eco-critique of the mass destruction wrought by the war and the war mentality of a materialist civilisation. But we now know that Chris is wrong. Even the land will not endure.

Highland River's Kenn, called by Gunn's biographers an 'ascetic pagan', finds freedom from school in land, sky and river; when hunting salmon, he is in opposition to civilisation and its gatekeepers.[41] Joining up at seventeen, he is blinded by gas at the Somme and, like Ewan in *Sunset Song*, he runs away from the frontline. Kenn is invalided to Leicester, an industrial English city embodying Kenn's experience of the imperial disciple of school and the teaching of a foreign history. Kenn loses his sight in war in order to regain a primal and local, Celtic-pagan vision in peace. *Highland River* is a novel of sensing and being – as in Nan Shepherd's *The Living Mountain* (1977), these two qualities are bound together. Gunn's novel is replete with an acute sensory awareness of nature, one possessed of spiritual meaning. As Douglas Gifford puts it, 'Gunn believes that the land *is* spiritual, animate and filled with living qualities.'[42] Sunlit trees are described as dancing 'the ballet of green fire'.[43] Birds especially are associated with the joyfulness of free existence.

> It was quiet and grey and alert here. *Spink!* said a chaffinch above them. *Spink! Spink!* He had never heard the note so detached and clear. In the sheltered strong sunlight, it was like a sound in another world, or, rather, the world just beyond the known one. The note was not clear, was sibilant a little, like the cry of a peewit, yet it was round and bright with happiness, and hopped from branch to branch like a coloured bubble.[44]

However, in another passage, the curlew's cry reminds Kenn of the lamentation of those cleared from Strathnaver in the nineteenth century: 'The spirits of his people, the disinherited, the nameless, the folk'.[45] Likewise, the smell of heath fire evokes for Kenn 'something definitely primordial', such as 'tribes hunting and trekking through lands beyond the horizons of history'.[46] Nature is related to folk history – Kenn's own folk of the recent Highland past and the pagan folk of prehistory. If *Highland River* is ostensibly about Kenn's search for the source of the river and his boyhood rite of passage in catching salmon, it is more intensely concerned with recapturing an ancestral alertness to the numinosity of the natural locality: 'The mind that secretly quickened before a broch, before a little path going up through a birch wood, to presences not looked at over the shoulder, possessed a magic that it seems more than a pity to have lost.'[47] Kenn understands that the 'adventures of boyhood were adventures towards the source' of himself and his local culture.[48] Just as the natural magic of boyhood and the magic of nature is needed to revive the man, so pagan magic is needed to revive modernity. To bring such enchantment back into the post-war world would be to 'recapture not merely the old primordial goodness of life but its moments of absolute ecstasy'.[49]

In searching for 'the hazel nuts of knowledge and the salmon of wisdom', Kenn's story becomes a modern version of the Celtic Fenian Cycle in which Fionn gained all the world's knowledge by eating the salmon.[50] Gunn wrote that he would 'like to create a philosophy (appalling word) of sorts' with *Highland River*, and critics have been led by Gunn's *The Atom of Delight* (1956) to find Zen in his works.[51] Kenn, Scots ('ken') for 'to know', might be derived from the Buddhist *kenshō*, meaning enlightenment or awakening, positioning Kenn as a seer and *Highland River* as a Scottish *satori*. However, 'the truth of life to Kenn was that at its core there was a wise pagan laughter', which he relates to the Celtic myth of the serpent that swallows its tail, symbolising wisdom and eternity, also utilised by Hugh MacDiarmid in the long poem *To Circumjack Cencrastus* (1930).[52] In the disenchantment following the First World War, the 'Northern paganism' of Gunn's work, also found in Gibbon's depiction of the land and history, locates in the pagan past a golden age with modern political implications for social, national and spiritual revival.[53]

From the First World War to the Golden Age

Trevor Royle calls *Sunset Song* 'Perhaps the greatest literary evocation of Scotland's wartime experience'.[54] Yet in Gibbon's novel the war happens mainly off-page, with no direct depiction of soldiering. The closest the reader gets to the frontline is Chae telling Chris of her husband Ewan's desertion and shooting in France. Ewan deserts in a futile attempt to win back Chris and make up for his brutish behaviour towards her when at home on leave. Whereas in the 'mud and blood and flesh' of the trenches, the narrator of Roderick Watson Kerr's 'From the Line' encounters 'nothing fresh / Like grass, or trees, or flowers', Ewan is awakened to his true self by the wind bringing a smell of the earth that reminds him of his farm at Blawearie.[55] In recounting his feelings to Chae, Ewan, who 'had fair the land in his bones', reminisces about his plough horses and the plaintive sound of the peewits.[56] Wind, earth, horses, birds: Ewan's memories of his native land are bound to nature. That land is not Britain, Scotland or even the Mearns, it is his farmland of Blawearie. Chris makes this point on receiving the telegram informing her of Ewan's death:

> what matter to him their War and their fighting, their King and their country? Kinraddie was his land, Blawearie his, he was never dead for those things of no concern, he'd the crops to put in and the loch to drain and her to come back to.[57]

To Chris, the war is 'the madness beyond the hills' of Kinraddie.[58] John Lewis-Stempel maintains that men enlisted not just for country but for countryside, to protect their distinct locality: 'war service was exile from a landscape that was part of their being, from which they were *uprooted* by service'.[59] Motivation for enlistment varied greatly by occupation and community, with lower recruitment figures among agricultural than urban workers.[60] None the less, relative to population and size, Scottish rural communities paid a high price in the First World War.[61]

Gibbon's real concern in *Sunset Song* is the war's devastating effect on the village of Kinraddie. Driven by anti-German newspaper propaganda, the war fuels suspicion and division in Kinraddie. Long Rob is taken by some to be pro-German because he does not immediately enlist, and he is even confronted by the minister over his stance. Rob, individualist and atheist, who 'would say what Scotland wanted was a return of the Druids', puts the minister in his place.[62] But the Christian God is now doubted by others, too. Mistress Mutch asks the on-leave Chae if, since his war experience, he still believes in God, leaving Chae shocked to hear such doubts expressed by a woman, while questioning his own beliefs. It is Chae who is the first to realise the long-term damage that will be done to farming in the area with the cutting down of the woods for timber for the war effort; this 'would lay the whole Knapp open to the north-east now, and was fair the end of a living there'.[63] But it is not just the Strachans' farm at Pessie's Knapp that is compromised by the loss of the wood's shelter; the whole of Kinraddie is deforested, irreparably damaging the ecosystem of the environment for those who had farmed there for generations. Even a relative newcomer such as Chris, who arrived in Kinraddie as a girl in 1911, thinks that the foresters had 'left a country that looked as though it had been shelled by a German army'.[64] The war transformed the home front in various ways, but in a novel that sings the praises of the enduring land, Gibbon's depiction of the destruction of the land as a viable crofting community is especially poignant.

When the townsfolk gather to mourn the deaths of Chae, Rob, Ewan and James Leslie (the first from Kinraddie to enlist is given Gibbon's birth forenames) at the standing stones, the minister's peroration mourns not only their deaths but the demise of *'the Last of the Peasants, the last of the Old Scots folk'*, whose spirit is connected to that of the pagan Druids who erected the sacred stones; significantly, the piper plays 'The Flowers of the Forest', sung by Chris on her wedding day, a song linking the war dead to the Scots killed at the Battle of Flodden (1513), and signifying the more recent war's destruction of the natural environment.[65] The Reverend Colquohoun's speech castigates war profiteering and the heartless materialism of the new age, which, he claims, the war dead would have opposed: *'They died for a world that is past, these men, but they did not die for this that we seem to inherit.'*[66] This, for some disgruntled townsfolk, is 'sheer politics', but it is politics clothed in the language of spiritual revival: *'Beyond it and us there shines a greater hope and a newer world, undreamt when these four died.'*[67] The rising morning star of Revelation 2: 28, on which the minister's reading is based, suggests the red star of communism, symbol of the desire for a future society fairer than that of the pre-war world on which the sun is setting. Robert Colquohoun is the son of a cleric who had been beaten to the ministership of Kinraddie by the Reverend Gibbon; Colquohoun senior was a preacher of the return of the golden age with little time for royalty, beliefs manifested in the Christian socialism of his son. The war section of *Sunset Song* takes place entirely in the chapter 'Harvest'. Britain entered the war in August 1914: harvest season. For Gibbon, a corrupt civilisation will reap what it sows in the bitter harvest of war. But despite the war's enormous death toll, the cycles of the land and the seasons manifested in the rhythms of the farming year – 'Ploughing', 'Drilling', 'Seed-Time' and 'Harvest' are the novel's chapter titles – promise rebirth. The circular time patterning of each chapter reflects both the non-linear nature of time in primitive societies and the pagan stone circle, amidst which lies a memorial to the war dead.[68]

The pagan circle of the Druids has magical connotations that are symbolically allied in *Sunset Song* with a political engagement to transform post-war modernity by connecting the folk past to the present. This too is a concern of *Highland River*, in which there is a measure of thematic and formal circularity in Kenn's quest to find the source of the river and himself. Kurt Wittig, who describes Gunn's prose as 'full of pagan animism', plots the course of the river against Kenn's quest:

> First, he makes the lower part of the river, the realm of man, his own; then he conquers the middle part, the strath with its darkness and ancestral memories. And finally, after the war and a career as a scientist, Kenn finds the way from the habitation of man by the sea to the source in the moor, where he discovers what man has lost. And he also finds his own soul.[69]

Kenn comes full circle in his pursuit of the source, relying on his childhood self, 'little Kenn', as 'his guide' to the landscape, and as his way back to the receptive childlike delight in the natural world through which the adult war survivor finds himself again.[70] In searching for the river's source, Kenn also finds 'the source of his forebears back beyond the dawn of history', including Gaels, Picts and Norse influences.[71] Kenn is a brilliant student, but he does not know the history of his native place due to a schooling that has taught only English geography and industrial history. This is brought home to him during the war, brief scenes from which are caught in flashbacks.

Kenn meets his brother, Angus – an emigrant, like Will in *Sunset Song* – near Mametz Wood on the Somme, where Angus is posted with the Canadian Infantry. It is Angus's Canadian friend, Gus Mackay – 'a Mackay out of the Mackay country – Strathnaver' – who explains to Angus and Kenn the meaning of the Province of the Cat, which 'was the Province of Caithness and Sutherland, and at one time it was the roof of Scotland'.[72] As Kenn and Angus are Sutherlands, their ignorance of their local history also constitutes an ignorance of their own genealogy with negative implications for their understanding of their selves. While Kenn admits to Gus that he and his brother do not have a command of history, they do know the local terrain – 'we know a lot about the ground itself' – and he offers to take Gus on a poaching trip for salmon to Achglas and their river.[73] This sparks in Kenn a memory of curlews and peewits flying over the field at Achglas, to which Gus responds: '"The curlew and the peewit! The words used to make my grandmother homesick. Hear that, Angus? The cry of the curlew and the peewit. Incantation of the old Druids!"'[74] This incantation of the pagan past does nothing to rouse Angus from his morbid condition, most likely shell-shock.[75] Like Ewan in *Sunset Song*, Angus is lost to the war before he is killed by it, changed psychologically and emotionally from the lively brother Kenn had known to a fearful and silent man with little care for memories of home. For Angus in the trenches of France, 'there was no reality in the river. There was no reality outside the world in which he was.'[76] Angus, lost to himself, has also lost touch with his own past and the folk past, embodied by the river. The magical prospects of childhood in the numinous landscape of home have been destroyed by his experience of war.

In spite of his own war experiences, Kenn believes in a golden age. The smell of heath fire and primrose and the reality of the river allow Kenn to experience, to know intuitively that there was, a golden age. If Proust's madeleine sparks an involuntary memory of a lived experience (childhood at Combray), Kenn's acute sensory perception of the countryside elicits that of which he could have had no experience: an almost certainly mythical period of prehistory. Kenn traces a direct line from the golden age to the war:

> What a subject for a cinema film – from the time when the hunters of the golden age first 'settled down' and started the creation of gods and demons, priest-craft and sacrifice, kings and slaves, right up to the perfect culmination and co-ordination of these elements in the Great War![77]

This passage could be from any number of modernist works by J. Leslie Mitchell (Gibbon's birth name), whose novels frequently contain a hero who explains human society from a diffusionist perspective. Gunn organised many of his novels around the search for or loss of a golden age, expressly in relation to Highland community. While the novelists shared a belief in the golden age, this came from different political and philosophical roots: Gibbon's stimulus lay in diffusionism and a belief in radical freedom, whereas Gunn found an influence in the work of Irish nationalist Patrick Pearse. Under the pseudonym Dane McNeil, a name conflating Norse and Gaelic influences, Gunn wrote articles on Pearse for the *Scots Independent* in 1929–30, excited by the 'delight' and 'native joyousness' Pearse found in the Gael;[78] although Pearse had to 'go back through the centuries to find its golden age', such a tradition, for Gunn, is 'not merely worth writing about, but living for and dying for'.[79] Violence and the sacred combined in Pearse's synthesis of the pagan Cúchulainn myth with Christian Catholicism to inspire the 1916 Easter Rising. Gunn's *Sun Circle* (1933), with its Druid Master and battle between paganism and Christianity, echoes Pearse's play *The Master* (first performed in 1915). There is in Gunn, as Hart and Pick point out, a 'vision of childhood as an archaic link with a golden age' that the Scot drew from Pearse.[80]

The First World War, apotheosis of the nightmare of civilisation and loss of childlike innocence, is confirmation for Kenn that 'Our river took a wrong turning somewhere!'[81] Modern civilisation remains 'a far cry to the golden age, to the blue smoke of the heath fire and the scent of the primrose', but Kenn believes that as a scientist he can 'make war impossible'.[82] Scientists will work for, and in harmony with, the communal values of the folk to create a better world. Kenn's intuited connection to a pagan past is united to a modernist awareness. Massingham identifies several Ages of Gold: prehistoric, primitive and civilisation's imaginative portrayals, which have variously represented the golden age as 'a mould of ideas, a dynamic urge to the reconstruction of the social fabric and an inspiration to the heart of man' – an apt digest of Gibbon's and Gunn's positions.[83] If *Highland River* and *Sunset Song* suggest that the catastrophe of the First World War can be traced to the death of the ancient golden age, they also imply that its ancestral memory, alive still in the survival of the pagan folk, makes possible a golden age of the post-war future. Still imaginable when Gibbon's novel was published towards the end of the war books boom, this prospect became increasingly improbable once Hitler came to power and the world rumbled towards another war.

Notes

1. Lewis Grassic Gibbon, *Sunset Song*, in *A Scots Quair*, ed. Tom Crawford (Edinburgh: Canongate, 1995), p. 216. Dialogue in Gibbon's novel is always emphasised in the original.
2. Ibid. pp. 216–17.
3. Ibid. p. 217.
4. Lewis Grassic Gibbon, 'Religion', in Lewis Grassic Gibbon and Hugh MacDiarmid, *Scottish Scene, or The Intelligent Man's Guide to Albyn* (London: Hutchinson, 1934), p. 258.
5. Ibid. p. 259.
6. H. J. Massingham, *The Golden Age: The Story of Human Nature* (London: Gerald Howe, 1927), p. 34.
7. Ibid. pp. 35, 34.
8. Modris Eksteins, *Rites of Spring: The Great War and the Birth of the Modern Age* (New York: Mariner Books, [1989] 2000), p. 290.
9. See Stephen Kern, *Modernism After the Death of God: Christianity, Fragmentation, and Unification* (New York and London: Routledge, 2017), pp. 2–3. David Friedrich Strauss, *The Life of Jesus, Critically Examined* (1835); Ernest Renan, *Life of Jesus* (1863). For 'God is dead', see Friedrich Nietzsche, *The Gay Science*, trans. by Walter Kaufmann (New York: Vintage, [1882] 1974), p. 181.
10. Wassily Kandinsky, *Concerning the Spiritual in Art*, trans. by M. T. H. Sadler, (New York: Dover, 1977), p. 2.
11. Roger Griffin, 'Series Editor's Preface', in Erik Tonning, *Modernism and Christianity* (Basingstoke: Palgrave Macmillan, 2014), p. xiii.
12. See Margery Palmer McCulloch, *Scottish Modernism and its Contexts 1918–1959: Literature, National Identity and Cultural Exchange* (Edinburgh: Edinburgh University Press, 2009).
13. Hew Strachan, 'Foreword', in *Beneath Troubled Skies: Poems of Scotland at War, 1914–1918*, ed. Lizzie MacGregor (Edinburgh: Polygon, 2015), p. xii.
14. Ronald N. Stromberg, *Redemption by War: The Intellectuals and 1914* (Lawrence, KS: Regents Press of Kansas, 1982), pp. 10, 40. For modernist irrationalism, see also Alex Owen, *The Place of Enchantment: British Occultism and the Culture of the Modern* (Chicago and London: University of Chicago Press, 2004).
15. Kathryn Rountree, 'Neo-Paganism, Animism, and Kinship with Nature', *Journal of Contemporary Religion*, vol. 27, no. 2 (2012): pp. 305–20, p. 306.
16. Mark Williams, *Ireland's Immortals: A History of the Gods of Irish Myth* (Princeton and Oxford: Princeton University Press, 2016), p. 361.
17. Ibid. p. 374; Michael Shaw, 'William Sharp's Neo-Paganism: Queer Identity and the National Family', in Duc Dau and Shale Preston (eds),

Queer Victorian Families: Curious Relations in Literature (New York: Routledge, 2015), pp. 77–96.
18. For Shelley's importance to Gibbon, see Ryan D. Shirey, 'Gibbon, Shelley and Romantic Revolutionary Renewal', in *The International Companion to Lewis Grassic Gibbon*, ed. Scott Lyall (Glasgow: Association for Scottish Literary Studies, 2015), pp. 89–104. Ronald Hutton points to the archaeological richness of Wessex in Neolithic monuments in *Pagan Britain* (New Haven, CT, and London: Yale University Press, [2013] 2014), pp. 106–21.
19. Ronald Hutton, *The Triumph of the Moon: A History of Modern Pagan Witchcraft* (Oxford: Oxford University Press, 1999), p. 29.
20. Raymond Williams, *The Country and the City* (London: Vintage, [1973] 2016), p. 389.
21. Hutton, *The Triumph of the Moon*, p. 21.
22. Julius Evola, *Pagan Imperialism*, trans. by Cologero Salvo (n.p.: Gornahoor Press, 2017), p. 26.
23. Evola translated Oswald Spengler's *Decline of the West* into Italian. For Evola and fascism, see Mark Sedgwick, *Against the Modern World: Traditionalism and the Secret Intellectual History of the Twentieth Century* (Oxford: Oxford University Press, 2004), pp. 98–109.
24. Our continuing ideas of Celticity derive largely from the nineteenth-century nationalist configuration of race, language and culture defining the *ethnie* and cannot with confidence be ascribed to British prehistory; see Hutton, *Pagan Britain*, pp. 166–71.
25. See Hutton, *The Triumph of the Moon*, p. 30.
26. 'Pastoral is essentially a discourse of retreat which may . . . either simply *escape* from the complexities of the city, the court, the present, "our manners", or *explore* them'; Terry Gifford, *Pastoral* (London and New York: Routledge, 1999), p. 46.
27. Owen Davies, *Paganism: A Very Short Introduction* (Oxford: Oxford University Press, 2011), p. 2.
28. Ibid.
29. Hutton, *Pagan Britain*, p. viii.
30. Neil M. Gunn, *Highland River* (Edinburgh: Canongate, [1937] 1991), p. 93.
31. Grassic Gibbon, *Sunset Song*, p. 59.
32. Gunn, *Highland River*, p. 120.
33. Davies, *Paganism*, p. 13.
34. Grassic Gibbon, *Sunset Song*, p. 39. For Pytheas, see Barry Cunliffe, *The Extraordinary Voyage of Pytheas the Greek* (London: Allen Lane, The Penguin Press, 2001).
35. Grassic Gibbon, *Sunset Song*, p. 41.
36. Randall Stevenson, *Literature and the Great War 1914–1918* (Oxford: Oxford University Press, 2013), p. 190.

37. Grassic Gibbon, 'The Antique Scene', in *Scottish Scene*, p. 19. Repudiation of this view of a peaceable prehistory can be found in Hutton, *Pagan Britain*, pp. 77–80.
38. Lewis Grassic Gibbon, *Cloud Howe*, in *A Scots Quair*, ed. Tom Crawford (Edinburgh: Canongate, 1995), pp. 44, 45.
39. Ibid. p. 43.
40. Grassic Gibbon, *Sunset Song*, p. 119.
41. Francis Russell Hart and J. B. Pick, *Neil M. Gunn: A Highland Life* (London: John Murray, 1981), p. 22.
42. Douglas Gifford, *Neil M. Gunn and Lewis Grassic Gibbon* (Edinburgh: Oliver and Boyd, 1983), p. 13.
43. Gunn, *Highland River*, p. 164.
44. Ibid. p. 130.
45. Ibid. p. 206.
46. Ibid. pp. 109–10.
47. Ibid. p. 54.
48. Ibid. p. 55.
49. Ibid. p. 54. For the Druids as magicians, see Hutton, *Pagan Britain*, p. 175.
50. Gunn, *Highland River*, p. 139.
51. Neil M. Gunn, letter to Frank Morley, quoted in Hart and Pick, *Neil M. Gunn*, p. 138. For Gunn and Zen, see, for instance, John Burns, *A Celebration of the Light: Zen in the Novels of Neil Gunn* (Edinburgh: Canongate, 1988).
52. Gunn, *Highland River*, p. 218.
53. 'Northern paganism' is Frank Kendon's phrase, quoted in Hart and Pick, *Neil M. Gunn*, p. 102.
54. Trevor Royle, *The Flowers of the Forest: Scotland and the First World War* (Edinburgh: Birlinn, 2006), p. 297.
55. Roderick Watson Kerr, 'From the Line', *Beneath Troubled Skies*, p. 109.
56. Grassic Gibbon, *Sunset Song*, p. 22.
57. Ibid. p. 235.
58. Ibid. p. 232.
59. John Lewis-Stempel, *Where Poppies Blow: The British Soldier, Nature, The Great War* (London: Weidenfeld and Nicolson, [2016] 2017), p. 6.
60. See Ewen A. Cameron, *Impaled Upon a Thistle: Scotland Since 1880* (Edinburgh: Edinburgh University Press, 2010), pp. 110–11.
61. See Strachan, 'Foreword', p. xi.
62. Grassic Gibbon, *Sunset Song*, p. 31.
63. Ibid. p. 202.
64. Ibid. p. 214.
65. Ibid. p. 256.
66. Ibid. p. 256.
67. Ibid. pp. 257, 256.

68. For the cyclical nature of time in primitive societies, see Julius Evola, *Revolt Against the Modern World*, trans. by Guido Stucco (Rochester, VT: Inner Traditions International, [1934] 1995), pp. 144–5.
69. Kurt Wittig, *The Scottish Tradition in Literature* (Edinburgh: Oliver and Boyd, 1958), pp. 335, 339.
70. Gunn, *Highland River*, p. 114.
71. Ibid. p. 52.
72. Ibid. p. 155.
73. Ibid. p. 156.
74. Ibid. p. 156.
75. See Margery Palmer McCulloch, *The Novels of Neil M. Gunn: A Critical Study* (Edinburgh: Scottish Academic Press, 1987), p. 80.
76. Gunn, *Highland River*, p. 157.
77. Ibid. p. 113.
78. Dane McNeil [Neil M. Gunn], 'Padraic Pearse: I. The Man Called Pearse', *The Scots Independent*, vol. 4, no. 1 (November 1929), pp. 9–10, p. 9.
79. Dane McNeil, 'Padraic Pearse: II. Poems, Plays, Stories', *The Scots Independent*, vol. 4, no. 2 (December 1929), p. 21.
80. Hart and Pick, *Neil M. Gunn*, p. 96. Pearse frequently uses boyhood as inspiration for Irish national revival, such as in the story 'Íosagán'; see Elaine Sisson, *Pearse's Patriots: St Enda's and the Cult of Boyhood* (Cork: Cork University Press, 2004).
81. Gunn, *Highland River*, p. 114.
82. Ibid. pp. 114, 216.
83. Massingham, *The Golden Age*, p. vii.

Chapter 10

A Bounded Heaven: George A. C. Mackinlay and Great War Pastoral
Randall Stevenson

To describe George A. C. Mackinlay as a little-known Scottish poet would be an understatement. One of his comrades in the Great War recalled continuing to enjoy Mackinlay's poetry in the early 1970s, more than fifty years after his death. In the half-century or so thereafter, Mackinlay might be assumed to have had few remaining readers, at any rate until one of his poems was included in the anthology *Beneath Troubled Skies: Poems of Scotland at War, 1914–1918* (2015). Details of his life are similarly sparse. He was born in Glasgow, in Partick, in October 1890, later moving with his parents to Bank Street, in Kelvinbridge, and attending Hillhead High School, where he was an enthusiastic rugby player and a founding editor of the school magazine. He went on to Glasgow University, graduating with an honours MA in English Literature, Language and History in 1912, and then to a teacher-training course. After working for a year or so as an English teacher at Perth Academy, he joined the 5th Scottish Rifles (The Cameronians) in 1914, and was killed in action near Ypres on 15 August 1917, during the Passchendaele campaign. As his name appears on the Ypres (Menin Gate) Memorial, but he has no marked grave, his remains were probably never found.

Between 1911 and 1915, Mackinlay published eight poems in the *Glasgow Herald*, accredited to 'G. A. C. M.'. In the year after his death, these and others written since 1908 – around fifty in all – were collected and published by his friends as *Poems: By George A.C. Mackinlay*. As its editor – identified only as 'A.H.' – explains in a Preface, the collection was intended as a 'real memorial' and 'a tribute to his memory'.[1] This intention and the volume itself are typical of attempts at memorialisation – seldom very successful – made by bereaved families and social circles during or just after the Great War.

Arthur Graeme West wrote scathingly, in one of his poems, about the quality of work such collections offered – though, ironically, his own reputation as a Great War writer survives largely through a selection of his poetry and journals published in just this way. Charles Hamilton Sorley's *Marlborough and other Poems* – discussed later in this chapter – likewise retained a readership well beyond the poet's immediate friends and family. Published in 1916, the year after his death, it quickly became a critical success. Sorley's extraordinary imagination has ensured that his writing is still admired and anthologised more than a century later, making him probably the best known of Scottish Great War poets.

Mackinlay is a less extraordinary poet than Sorley, but his work deserves still to be read for some engaging qualities, and for a typicality which extends well beyond the original memorialising function of *Poems*. The poems themselves typify literary modes dominant before and to an extent during the Great War, also indicating ways in which these were challenged by the conflict, and suggesting some particular implications for Scottish writers. Mackinlay's poetry is, above all, exemplary of the Georgian idiom well established in pre-war verse in English, and still in evidence after 1918. Five anthologies entitled *Georgian Poetry* appeared between 1912 and 1922, enjoying strong sales at the time. Originally intended to support the work of new and innovative writers, the anthologies did for a time offer newly authentic treatments of ordinary speech and daily life. Later volumes included some of the first published work of combatant poets such as Edmund Blunden, Isaac Rosenberg, Siegfried Sassoon and Robert Graves, along with poetry by W. W. Gibson, one of the first authors on the home front to move beyond conventionally patriotic, unrealistic views of the war. Yet throughout the series, especially in its later stages, the anthologies more and more often favoured the innocuous rural settings that W. H. Davies defines in 'A Great Time' – ones 'beyond the town, where wild flowers grow' – often described in aureate language and conventional, prettily pastoral terms.[2]

Georgian poetry has regularly been considered, in consequence, as simply an extension of the 'doughy mess of third-hand Keats, Wordsworth ... fourth-hand Elizabethan sonority' which Ezra Pound discerned in English verse between 1890 and 1910 – urgently in need of his perennial injunction to 'make it new'.[3] Even new or younger poets included in the Georgian anthologies found it hard to avoid traditions of pastoral and nature writing extending from romantics such as Keats and Wordsworth, or earlier. Blunden, for example, recalled that when he began writing poetry around the war years – as 'a picturesque interpreter of the English countryside' – it was in inevitable awareness of 'so rich a literature ... already in that field'.[4] Edward Thomas likewise began writing poetry during the Great War, and though his work usually offers harsher and more authentic views of the countryside than the Georgians', it, too, can occasionally seem flower-strewn and aureate. 'October', for example, names seven flowers and squeezes seven other plants into its twenty-one lines. Encountering this kind of writing, or much of the material in the Georgian anthologies, any newcomer to English literature early in the twentieth century might have wondered whether poetry had somehow become a branch of botany or biology.

A newcomer himself to poetry in the first decade of the century, Mackinlay naturally adopted conventions so widely established in literature at the time, and probably featuring strongly within the educational system he encountered at school and university in Glasgow. When *The Scotsman* reviewed his recently published *Poems* on 24 November 1919 – mentioning the 'refined and elevated pleasure' his work might offer to 'any serious lover of poetry' – its brief notice appeared immediately above a review of the fourth volume of *Georgian Poetry*. The proximity of the two reviews is entirely appropriate, as the reviewer's further praise for Mackinlay's writing confirms – for the 'fresh bloom of its musings ... over the beauty of flowers and fair women'.[5] As that page of *The Scotsman* suggests, the 'Young leaves! Green leaves!' of Mackinlay's *Poems* could scarcely be more closely intertwined with the innocuous interests predominant in the Georgian anthologies – in skies, seasons, trees and the beauty of nature generally.[6] What 'wild flowers ... whisper' is what Mackinlay most wants to hear, both for what is communicated about nature itself, though also how this relates to his own experience.[7] Like many of the Georgians, or the romantic poets whom they followed, Mackinlay seeks in the physical world sympathetic relations with the self, valuing nature's power of 'fusing/. . . /With each longing, with each mood' – whether of forlorn love or wondering religious faith.[8]

His depictions of nature are sometimes also mediated, and enhanced, by a distinctive wit and self-consciousness that his poetry brings to them. 'The Spring Poet to his Love', for example, suggests that the fascinations *The Scotsman* identified with 'fair women' and with 'the beauty of flowers' may not always be wholly compatible. Published in *The Glasgow Herald* in April 1911, the poem apologises for a 'sad neglect / Of love and all that does pertain thereto', unfortunately made unavoidable by the extensive obligations, in spring, enforced upon an admirer of nature.⁹ 'How much I've had to do,' the poet complains, explaining to 'his love' that:

> The brightening sky, the gentle showers of Spring,
>   The snowdrops and the buds upon the trees,
> And all the little birds that hop and sing –
>   I've had to sing of these.
>
> And now I fear I must to work again;
>   But p'raps between the tulip and the rose,
> I'll find a little time for love, till when
>   Farewell – except in prose.

Mackinlay is similarly self-aware in other poems – even ironic – about his unwavering allegiance to the natural world, acknowledging that maintaining it 'in the city's heart' requires some carefully selective treatment of the 'long defiles of city street'.¹⁰ In order to find 'gardens with flowers and trees and easy lawns', he explains in 'Going Home', a route back from work must be carefully chosen to avoid 'streets and shops and homeward hurrying folk'.¹¹ Perhaps it was fortunate that Mackinlay's youth was spent around Kelvinbridge, an unusually leafy part of Glasgow, close to Kelvingrove Park and the Botanic Gardens. Yet pastoral poetry has often thrived on the distanced, idealising views of the countryside favoured by city dwellers – ready, like W. B. Yeats in 'The Lake Isle of Innisfree', to stand 'on the roadway, or on the pavements grey' but still hear 'lake water lapping . . . / . . . / . . . in the deep heart's core'.¹² What seems more surprising is how seldom Mackinlay acknowledges the character and location of landscapes he describes beyond the city.

In much of his poetry, it is hard to recognise these as Scottish. There are a few hints. In a poem beginning 'Raining! What matters it? Is it not June?', Mackinlay seems determined to celebrate the early summer in defiance of what is evidently a typically unpromising spell of Scottish summer weather.¹³ Following 'the slow-won victory over winter's pain' which this poem describes, the next in the collection continues to deploy a dogged Caledonian preparedness – while still supposedly celebrating summer – not to 'grudge that raindrops gladly stray / Down from a pure cold greyness of the skies'.¹⁴ In 'Brodick to Corrie', too, references to 'hills' eternity' and to 'might of mountain, pride of pine' do suggest a Scottish landscape – even independently of the title – and descriptions of gales, snow-capped peaks and 'pine trees spread, full grim and bare' work to similar effect in 'Early Spring'.¹⁵

For the most part, though, Mackinlay avoids 'might of mountain' and turbulent wind and weather. Preferences for prettiness and tranquillity in his vision of birds, flowers and trees confirm an allegiance to Georgian idioms, whose 'third-hand' derivation from the romantics had eliminated much of the wildness in nature which originally inspired Wordsworth and his contemporaries. This placid vision was also owed to the domicile of most of the authors concerned. English almost to a man (few women were included in the Georgian anthologies, and only a rare Irishman or colonial writer), many lived in or described the relatively tranquil landscapes of the southern counties. Questions inevitably arise – conveniently focused by Mackinlay's poetry – about the extent of influence, throughout British writing early in the century, of a Georgian idiom mostly quite limited and specific in the landscapes that inspired it, and not necessarily ideally adopted by writers working elsewhere.

These questions obviously have particular and (literally) far-reaching implications for Scottish literature, assessed by commentators such as MacDonald Daly as still, at the time of the Great War, 'so dependent on English literary models and English literary temperament'.[16] Since the questions concerned require analysis of issues as fundamental as the relation of imagination to the external world, and the ways in which a national literature is shaped by topography, climate, geology and agriculture, a thorough response lies beyond the scope of this chapter. The divergent demands that different landscapes make on poetic imagination may nevertheless be concisely highlighted. Rewriting the first lines of Edward Thomas's celebrated pastoral lyric 'Adlestrop' (1917) – 'Yes. I remember Adlestrop – / The name' – as 'Yes. I remember Achnasheen – / The name', for example, would obviously be acceptable metrically but challenging imaginatively. Apart from memorable nomenclature, and a railway station, the two locations share few features in common. Like much Georgian poetry, 'Adlestrop' belongs in the landscape of England's tranquil southern shires, among 'meadowsweet and haycocks dry', birdsong resounding for miles around, and a summer 'afternoon / of heat' enjoyed beneath unthreatening 'high cloudlets in the sky'.[17] Achnasheen, by contrast – a remote station on the line from Inverness to Kyle of Lochalsh – is seldom dry, warm or sunny for very long, even in summer. Rocky, wet and empty, the surrounding moorland is often swathed in low cloud, or mist thick enough to obscure mountains bleakly straddling the horizon. Scottish landscapes of this kind obviously offer their own promise to the imagination, but in terms very different from Georgian poetry's engagement with a domesticated countryside, easily and consolingly connected with the moods and needs of the individual. Uninhabited moorland and granite mountains north of the border are likelier to suggest, instead, an altogether indifferent external world – one whose remorseless topography and meteorology may seem altogether independent of human needs and volition, even contrary to them.

W. H. Auden's 'In Praise of Limestone' (1948) reflects comparably on diverse topographies and geologies, within and beyond Britain. Auden finds the limestone landscape of southern England a likeable 'region / Of short distances and definite places', pleasantly characterised by 'rounded slopes / With their surface fragrance of thyme'. 'The granite wastes', on the other hand, he considers to have little to say to humanity beyond '"how accidental / Your kindest kiss, how permanent is death"'.[18] Published shortly after the Second World War, 'In Praise of Limestone' might have implications for Scottish writing, during and after the Great War, less thoroughly negative than those comments offered by 'the granite wastes' immediately suggest. A landscape so consonant or co-extensive with the permanence of death might, after all, have some obvious potential for elegy. The powerful elegiac effects that Lewis Grassic Gibbon generates in *Sunset Song* (1932), for example, are owed partly to the austerity of the memorial his closing pages describe – the names of Kinraddie's dead carved unadorned, with the stark straightforwardness of a casualty list, on to the ancient standing stones above the village. The location of these stones greatly adds to this conclusion's effect. Brooding on the edge of empty moorland, they open on to spatial distances as immense as the reaches of past time that they have come to represent in the novel, conveying the names of the dead and the losses of recent history towards eternity and infinitude.

Landscapes of eternity and infinitude may also, as Auden describes, simply render irrelevant all human activity – a possibility explored in Virginia Woolf's *To the Lighthouse* (1927). As critics have often remarked, the novel's setting on Skye is never entirely plausible – the Ramsay family's enjoyment of 'airy sunny' evenings, in the garden of their holiday retreat, scarcely seeming consistent with the kind of Scottish summer weather Mackinlay describes. Some appropriateness in Woolf's use of Skye – a stark, bare landscape containing some of the oldest rocks in the world – nevertheless becomes apparent in the novel's short, sharp, second section, 'Time Passes'. Nature and its perennial cycles – remorseless winds, shifting seasons of sun or rain, the endless surge of the tides – threaten in this section simply to overwhelm human agency. This threat is exacerbated by the effects of the

Great War. Anyone walking on the beach at this time, Woolf suggests, might find soiled, staining traces of naval action disturbingly at odds with 'the usual tokens of divine bounty' that nature is often supposed to provide. Longstanding assumptions that 'beauty outside mirrored beauty within', or might 'reflect the compass of the soul', are consequently difficult to maintain. Visions of the kind Mackinlay expresses, of nature 'fusing . . . with each longing, with each mood' ceased to be viable during the war years, *To the Lighthouse* suggests. 'Did Nature supplement what man advanced?', Woolf asks, 'did she complete what he began?', answering only that 'with equal complacence she saw his misery, condoned his meanness, and acquiesced in his torture'.[19]

This answer raises further questions: not only about the fate of pastoral imagination during the Great War, but even about the love of nature generally at the time. These issues are vigorously, though tendentiously, re-examined in *Where Poppies Blow: The British Soldier, Nature, the Great War* (2017). John Lewis-Stempel's study persuasively demonstrates how thoroughly British soldiers often engaged with the natural world – sometimes relying on unusual evidence, such as his list of thirty different animal species (not even counting eighteen breeds of dog) which were adopted as regimental mascots at the time. Soldiers' own accounts of the war in any case provide much further testimony of their appreciation of the natural world. George Ramage, for example, a well-educated Scottish Lance Corporal – a teacher, like George Mackinlay – almost rivals Edward Thomas's 'October', listing by name, in his (unpublished) journal, a dozen species of wild flower blooming near the front in May 1915. Like many servicemen when first posted to France, Ramage relished the novel experience of an outdoor life, regularly describing the loveliness of landscape and sky, even near the trenches – such as the way a 'gorgeous, golden, immense, egg shaped moon rose behind a thin line of gaunt trees'. His journal also records sensitive appreciation of nature surviving even under the rough conditions of army life in France, mentioning 'a nest which contains a very tame & spry bird with four chicks – prominent on the bush is the notice "Be careful, birds nest" – soldiers watch it feed its young'.[20]

As Lewis-Stempel emphasises, many poets similarly continued to view nature closely and affectionately after enlisting in the army, extending popular Georgian idioms into the years of the Great War. No poet – early in the war or for many years afterwards – achieved a greater popular impact than Rupert Brooke, who had been instrumental in initially organising publication of the Georgian anthologies. His celebrated 'Sonnets' of 1914 extend the affirmative vision of nature that the anthologies favoured, Brooke describing himself in 'Safety' as 'armed against all death's endeavour', by

> all things undying,
> The winds, and morning. . . .
> The deep night, and birds singing, and clouds flying.[21]

Similar consolations offered by the natural world figure in the work of other poets much admired at the time – such as Julian Grenfell, whose 'Into Battle' expansively envisages that

> The fighting man shall from the sun
> Take warmth, and life from glowing earth.[22]

Though less euphoric, Edmund Blunden and Ivor Gurney also find strong consolations in nature, using landscapes remembered from English country life, or ones closer to the trenches, to 'help the mind' – as Gurney puts it – 'to escape . . . its vain / Own circling greyness and stain' during wartime service.[23] Nature plays a significant role, too, in the work of the other most distinguished of Great War poets – Wilfred Owen, Siegfried Sassoon, Isaac Rosenberg and Charles Hamilton Sorley.

Yet the most significant aspect of this role – including in the poetry of Blunden and Gurney – was that the consolations nature offered proved much less than consistently reliable, often vanishing altogether, much as Woolf suggests. The limitation in Lewis-Stempel's naïvely patriotic study is that it identifies affirmative engagements with nature, among poets and servicemen, without acknowledging how often and how thoroughly these were eroded – along with many other bright ideals – by the experience of life and death at the front. Some of this disillusion was simply practical in origin. Even before encountering violent action, new soldiers were likely to find outdoor life at least as full of privation as pleasure. That wartime comrade of George Mackinlay's who continued reading his poetry in the 1970s, R. L. Mackay, kept a diary of his experiences at the front with the Argyll and Sutherland Highlanders. This mentions scathingly that

> we have been living in a sort of rustic bower such as the poets sing about – until they have to live in one in a rainstorm. This quickly-fabricated one of ours let in everything, the birds of the air, the beasts of the field, and RAIN, in buckets.[24]

Such discomforts could obviously be experienced more extremely, as Wilfred Owen's poetry makes especially clear. In 'Exposure', Owen offers views of 'the winds, and morning' very different from Brooke's, describing the 'poignant misery of dawn' and of 'merciless iced east winds that knive us', and concluding that soldiers 'only know war lasts, rain soaks, and clouds sag stormy'.[25]

Owen's other poems often reach similarly bitter conclusions, sometimes working for a time within pastoral conventions, only to challenge or discard them later. In 'Spring Offensive', fighting men take warmth from the sun and 'life from glowing earth,' much as Grenfell recommends, appreciating that the feeling of 'summer oozed into their veins', along with prospects of

> the long grass swirled
> By the May breeze, murmurous with wasp and midge.

But the poem makes it steadily clearer that 'Offensive' in its title can be read more appropriately as an adjective than a noun. Owen's soldiers realise that earth and sky, described so beneficently in some of the poem's earlier lines, offer only a sunny seduction towards utter destruction. Dejectedly, they turn away from the sun, as if from 'a friend with whom their love is done'.[26]

Sunlight and the natural world appear still more duplicitous in Owen's 'Futility'. Though the sun 'wakes the seeds' and first stirred into life the whole 'cold star' of planet Earth, it has no power to revivify a frozen soldier's cooling, dying body – leaving the poem to question whether there was ever any purpose in nature or in the creation of life itself:

> Was it for this the clay grew tall?
> – O what made fatuous sunbeams toil
> To break earth's sleep at all? [27]

Poems such as 'Spring Offensive' and 'Futility' show Owen discarding his earlier allegiance to pastoral imagination – ready to envisage the sun 'blessing all the field and air with gold – which he recalls sceptically in 'A Palinode', written in 1915. Disparaging this previous

> mood
> When what we know as 'Nature' seemed to me
> So sympathetic, ample, sweet, and good,

'A Palinode' also anticipates further direct criticisms of the pastoral mode in Owen's later poetry.[28] 'Insensibility' warns that

The front line withers.
But they are troops who fade, not flowers,
For poets' tearful fooling.²⁹

In 'À Terre', Owen quotes from Shelley's pastoral elegy *Adonais* (1822), 'I shall be one with nature, herb, and stone' but interprets this wish 'to be one' with disturbing literalness. 'The dullest Tommy hugs that fancy now', 'À Terre' explains: '"pushing up daisies" is their creed'. The wounded soldier supposedly delivering Owen's dramatic monologue elaborates this 'creed', exhorting 'to grain, then, go my fat, to buds my sap'. Dissolution of his body into the earth, he reasons, may allow him to be 'turned to fronds', and to nourish 'plants that share / More peaceably the meadow and the shower'.³⁰

Another version of this 'creed', equally bereft of romantic idealism, had already appeared in the work of Charles Hamilton Sorley. In a letter late in 1914, Sorley remarked that 'the earth even more than Christ is the ultimate ideal of what man should strive to be'.³¹ Such striving hardly even seems necessary in his poetry, so surely is ultimate dissolution into the earth guaranteed. In 'All the hills and vales along', Sorley's soldiers are urged to rejoice and sing, not as a distraction from the imminence of death, but in celebration of its certainty – of their assured, fertile, absorption into the 'teeming earth', cheerfully ready to 'store / All the gladness that you pour'.³² Along with Owen's 'À Terre', and despite its jaunty tone, Sorley's 'All the hills and vales along' marks a wartime climacteric in pastoral imagination, sharing Woolf's recognition of the disappearance of 'divine bounty' from nature at the time. Each poet brings the idealising vision of nature down to earth, decisively and literally, calling a bluff inherent in much romantic imagination. Interfusions of self and nature in conventional pastoral are, always and inevitably, metaphoric. In pushing pastoral beyond its usual conventions, under the pressure of war, Owen and Sorley demonstrate that in any absolute unity with nature – literal rather than metaphoric – human beings are mere molecules and matter; dust and earth without identity or individuality; soil without soul.

These views epitomise fundamental desolations in wartime imagination, and indicate the origins of a general shift in the mood of twentieth-century poetry. The changes involved became inescapably apparent with the publication of T. S. Eliot's *The Waste Land* (1922), fulfilling more than any other contemporary poem Pound's longstanding determination to 'make it new'. Pound's own editorial interventions into Eliot's work were, of course, partly responsible, but *The Waste Land* also extends the kinds of change in rhetoric and outlook that the war poets had initiated. Eliot's strikingly counter-conventional description of April's cruelty, at the start of *The Waste Land*, firmly discards the conventions of Georgian poetry, extending instead anti-pastoral views of the kind Owen expresses in 'Spring Offensive' and 'Futility'. The sprouting, blooming corpse described later in the first section of *The Waste Land* can likewise be connected with the blossoming, teeming earth and its 'reaping' described in Sorley's 'All the hills and vales along', or with the preferences for 'pushing up daisies' expressed in Owen's 'À Terre'. For these combatant poets, and others at the time, experience of the Great War made the relative complacencies of Georgian poetry manifestly unsustainable, and the need to 'make it new' more and more obviously imperative.

Yet this appears clearly in Owen's poetry only towards the end of the war, whereas for Sorley it was evident almost from the beginning – 'All the hills and vales along' was probably written in 1914 or early 1915 – and even, in embryonic form, in the pre-war years. In 'Rain', written three years before his death in action in October 1915, Sorley is already expressing some scepticism of conventional pastoral – of a land 'of light and glory',

> a distant land, so fine,
> Where the bells for ever ring,
> And the suns for ever shine.

Sorley suggests that a 'happy land' for poetic imagination need not be distant, but can be found instead when 'the rain sweeps over all': from a vantage high in a bleak landscape, or amid 'moving mists and sweeping wind', or beneath 'skies of dirty white / And the drifting veil of rain'.[33] Such preferences for the 'bleak barren' prospects 'Rain' describes may have been partly personal – particular to Sorley's extraordinary, idiosyncratic imagination – but they may also reflect something of his Scottish background. Though 'Rain' refers to experiences at an English public school, it is difficult not to hear in it echoes of George Mackinlay's grimly resilient response to the 'pure cold greyness' of Scottish skies. Sorley's wartime poetry likewise resonates with Auden's assessment of granite or upland landscapes as those likeliest to suggest 'how permanent is death' – particularly when death is addressed directly, in the first of his 'Two Sonnets' of 1915. Sorley suggests of death that 'in every road on every side / We see your straight and steadfast signpost', adding that:

> I think it like that signpost in my land
> Hoary and tall, which pointed me to go

Upward, into the hills, on the right hand,
Where the mists swim and the winds shriek and blow,
A homeless land and friendless, but a land
I did not know and that I wished to know.³⁴

Proximity to such landscapes in his early years, or preferences for equally desolate ones during his schooldays, may have particularly prepared Sorley to confront war experience and the permanence of death independently of conventional Georgian pastoral consolations. Rupert Brooke provided probably the most celebrated version of these consolations in another of his 'Sonnets' of 1914, remarking

If I should die, think only this of me:
    That there's some corner of a foreign field
That is for ever England.³⁵

To this invitation to 'think only this' there could be no more decisive response than Sorley's warning to 'say only this'. 'Say not soft things as other men have said,' Sorley cautions in his sonnet 'When you see millions of the mouthless dead', but instead, in response to the dead, 'say only this, "They are dead"'.³⁶ No wonder Sorley's *Marlborough and Other Poems* was so influential among combatant poets seeking the 'bleak barren' tones required in response to the Great War. Robert Graves gave a copy to Siegfried Sassoon, who passed it on to Wilfred Owen. The writers concerned might have found their wartime voice more rapidly, and poetry might have renewed itself, generally, in ways Pound considered so urgent, had the bleak landscapes Sorley favours – rather than the more 'rounded slopes' of southern England – occupied a fuller role in literature earlier in the twentieth century. Poets in 1914 understandably 'did not know' how to confront death on a historically new and scarcely imaginable scale: as David Goldie has suggested, despite 'a sophisticated poetic education' – or perhaps because of it – many authors were 'ill-equipped to deal with even the simplest of war's arbitrary brutalities'.³⁷ Sorley's unconventional imagination offered a signpost towards territories these poets might have 'wished to know', or needed to know – directions which still have complex implications for relations between imagination and landscape, history and elegy, romantic and later pastoral – and between Scottish and English literature.

How fully does George Mackinlay's poetry illustrate the developments discussed above? How far was his Georgian idiom challenged or changed by experience of the Great War? Once again, his writing seems revealingly typical – demonstrating concisely, in a handful of poems, some of the broader transformations apparent in literary priorities at the time. Altered moods are suggested, generally, by a slight harshening of rhetoric in his wartime writing, and a more regular interest in 'fair women' rather than the flowers and leafy prospects so prevalent in his poetry before 1914. Landscapes of the kind surveyed in Georgian pastoral poetry are even criticised directly in one of the last poems he wrote, 'Down in Essex' – differing in vision from most of his earlier work, and also more complex in thought and syntax. Though 'daisies, violets, cowslips whisper low' about the peacefulness of a southern landscape of 'fair fields' and 'Maygreen woodland', Mackinlay finds its scenery flat and constraining, favouring instead what Auden would no doubt have defined as 'granite wastes'. 'Down in Essex' complains that:

> In this vain land there are no heights at all
> Whereto a man may lift his eyes for aid,
> Letting his soul drink wassail magical
> Where the cloud-shadows and the eagles dwell;
> No pine-clad hill, nor rocky craig arrayed
> In kingly forestry . . .[38]

'Down in Essex' shares in this way the exasperation – even with a landscape manifestly attractive in many of its aspects – expressed a few years earlier by another Scottish Great War poet, E. A. Mackintosh, in 'Mallaig Bay'. Some of Mackintosh's pre-war poetry, while he was a student in Oxford, shared with much of Mackinlay's early writing a preference for the kind of landscape he describes in 'Wanderer's Desire':

> Where fields are fresh and green,
> And hedges lie on either hand
> With a white road between.[39]

'Mallaig Bay', on the other hand, further emphasises the distinctions between Scottish and southern English pastoral imagination, and between landscapes sublime and merely attractive, when Mackintosh records being:

> sickened of the south and the kindness of the downs,
> And the weald that is a garden all the day.
> And I'm weary for the islands and the Scuir that always frowns,
> And the sun rising over Mallaig Bay.[40]

Even before rejecting 'fair fields' in 'Down in Essex' – in a poem dated a year earlier – Mackinlay was hinting at radical shifts of interest, possibly away from landscape and the natural world generally. 'May, 1915' begins conventionally, reflecting that the charms of nature, such as 'beechleaves filled with sunlight, / – As crystal filled with wine', will 'all come again and again / In a man's brief time'. Yet Mackinlay concludes with an uneasy question:

> It will all come again, but, ah!
>   Will it ever return to thee
> With a step well swung and a rifle slung
>   And camaraderie?

In one way, the poet may simply be anticipating his own death, like many writers during the Great War who measured their mortality against the eternity or perennial recurrences of the natural world. Yet 'May, 1915' might also suggest that, as the poet moves beyond his 'youthful prime', a new rhythm – that 'step well swung' – or the camaraderie of army life may lead to lost or less exclusive interests in nature and the swing of the seasons.[41]

A changed view of nature appears more decisively in 'Route March Roundelay: A Horse', quoted here in full:

> Knee-deep in grasses, fetlock deep in dew,
> Heart-deep in clover, full and cool and wet.
> He, the Beast of Burden, watched us tramp it through
> 'Twixt the twining hedge-rows that bounded off his Heaven,
> Layer deep in dust, blasphemy deep in sweat,
> Full pack, and blanket, and a hundred of 'Mark Seven.'[42]

The horse inhabits a domain of alluring pastoral verdure, fulsomely described, but it is a Heaven now 'bounded off'. Inaccessible to the poet, it has little scope to provide the kind of 'quiet benison' Mackinlay still records receiving from nature in some earlier wartime poems – such as 'In a Meadow', published in *The Glasgow Herald* in August 1915.[43] Instead, consolatory pastoral vision has been partly reversed. It is not only the poet who observes nature, but nature, in the form of the horse, that looks back at the poet, and in ways highlighting *his* soldierly role as a substitute 'Beast of Burden', encumbered by dust, sweat, ammunition ('Mark Seven') and military accoutrements.

Similar distancing or scepticism regarding pastoral idioms shape 'Sentry-Go', tellingly subtitled 'Lines written in Springfield Goods Station, Falkirk'. The poem begins with almost parodically effusive descriptions of

> The sweet o' the morn and the sweet o' the year;
> Fresh, young airs and a wondering light,

of a blackbird's 'infinite song', and of

> The winsome, farewell glance of the last lone star
> Where the gates of Heaven wait ajar.

Yet although these gates seem 'ajar', they offer only another 'bounded off . . . Heaven', or none. The poem concludes by describing

>   all the Heaven my sense doth know:
> – Three lemonade boxes in a row;
> And the muddled dream I left an hour ago.[44]

Juxtaposing – even equating – lemonade boxes and 'muddled dream' with the once-promising 'Heaven' of the natural world, 'Sentry-Go' provides an envoi or epitaph for the lone stars and fresh young airs which so often graced poetry in 1914. Alongside 'Route March Roundelay', 'May, 1915' and material earlier in the volume, it might make *Poems: By George A.C. Mackinlay* an ideal introduction both to the Georgian idiom dominant at the start of the Great War and to the conditions and causes of its subsequent demise.

Unfortunately for this possibility, just as the evidence it is based on is conveniently concise, it is also inescapably slender. Only around a dozen poems written after July 1914 appear in the collection, and of these, few, apart from those described, mention the war or its effects. Mackinlay's relative paucity of output at the time might, of course, be indicative itself of difficulties, confirmed by 'Sentry-Go', of adjusting poetic conventions, or even poetry more generally, to the harsh conditions of wartime. Another possibility is suggested by the collection's editor, whose Preface explains that 'an attempt has been made to include every poem which may help to recall [Mackinlay] to his friends. On this principle alone the selection has been based.'[45] Might there have been other poems, perhaps less light-hearted or more 'blasphemy deep' than 'Sentry-Go' or 'Route March Roundelay' – or even radically different from Mackinlay's earlier writing – which the editor omitted because they would *not* readily have recalled him to his friends? This raises the tantalising possibility that somewhere in a neglected drawer or bookcase in Glasgow there might still be a sheaf of unpublished Mackinlay poems, awaiting rediscovery. Perhaps someone's memory might be jogged, following publication in *The Guardian* in October 2018 of Andrew Motion's centennial poem for the Commonwealth War Graves Commission and National Poetry Day, 'Armistice'. This memorialised another pupil from Mackinlay's former school: 'Private Roy Douglas Harvey who was killed / a reserved and thoughtful schoolboy from Hillhead'.[46]

Without the rediscovery of unpublished material, Mackinlay will remain partly a poet of 'what ifs'. What if he had been drawn earlier to poetry outwith the Georgian idiom and more appropriate to cloud-shadows and rocky craigs in Scotland? What if, instead of using Scots in only one poem, he had employed the dialectal immediacy of wartime writers such as John Buchan, Joseph Lee, Neil Munro, Violet Jacob or the Doric poets Charles Murray and Mary Symon? 'It's soon', no' sense, that faddoms the herts o' men,' Hugh MacDiarmid later remarked in 'Gairmscoile', and the 'rauch auld Scots' he recommends adds a strong sense of locale, and of heart-fathoming immediacy, to poems such as Symon's 'The Glen's Muster Role', one of the most poignant Great War elegies.[47] Dialect employed by the other poets mentioned likewise connects voice, person and place intimately enough to suggest sorrow sighing over the landscape itself, as well as through the breath of its bereaved inhabitants – the pervasive 'Sough o' War' Charles Murray took as the title of his 1917 collection of war poetry. In poems such as 'The Field by the Lirk o' the Hill', describing 'the lang cauld licht / O' the spring months' – another 'Spring Offensive' – Violet Jacob's dialect similarly accentuates a desolate Scottish landscape and climate especially apt, as discussed above, for representing contemporary panoramas of death and loss.[48]

Mackinlay might have gone on to explore some or all of these possibilities, had he survived – another, final, 'what if' – beyond his 'youthful prime', enjoying the chance for another 'step well swung', or several, towards fuller poetic maturity. How far, and in what directions, might this have taken him beyond the 'Young leaves! Green leaves!' that evidently enthralled him, even on long 'defiles of city street' – Great George Street, or Cecil Street, probably, on his daily walks to school and university? Unanswerable, such questions highlight a final aspect of George A. C. Mackinlay's typicality – of a life vanished, like hundreds of thousands of others, without further fulfilment; without extension into later years of the lively imagination his poetry demonstrates. The evidence that this writing offers, regarding the Great War's effects on Scottish life and literature, may be all the more telling because it is so slender, allowing no final certitude or closure, but instead a raw reminder of loss – of how much the Great War left forever unresolved and incomplete.

Notes

For help and advice with this chapter, I'm grateful to David Goldie, Pam King, David Rennie and Roger Savage. I would also like to thank William

Christie and the Humanities Research Centre in the Australian National University, Canberra, for a Research Fellowship which offered invaluable time and resources for completing the work involved.
1. George A. C. Mackinlay, *Poems: By George A.C. Mackinlay* (Glasgow: Lyon, 1919), p. 3.
2. Edward Marsh, ed., *Georgian Poetry: 1913–1915* (London: The Poetry Bookshop, 1918), p. 69.
3. Ezra Pound, 'Hell', *Literary Essays of Ezra Pound*, ed. T. S. Eliot (London: Faber & Faber, [1954] 1960), p. 205.
4. Edmund Blunden, *The Poems of Edmund Blunden* (London: Cobden-Sanderson, 1930), p. vii.
5. *The Scotsman* (24 November 1919), p. 2.
6. Mackinlay, *Poems*, p. 29.
7. Ibid. p. 16.
8. Ibid. p. 42.
9. Ibid. p. 18.
10. Ibid. pp. 16, 27.
11. Ibid. p. 20.
12. W. B. Yeats, *The Collected Poems of W.B. Yeats* (London: Macmillan, 1971), p. 44.
13. Mackinlay, *Poems*, p. 24.
14. Ibid. p. 25.
15. Ibid. pp. 42, 45.
16. MacDonald Daly, 'Scottish Poetry and the Great War', *Scottish Literary Journal*, vol. 21, no. 2 (November 1994), p. 81.
17. Edward Thomas, *The Annotated Collected Poems*, ed. Edna Longley (Northumberland: Bloodaxe, 2008), p. 51.
18. W. H. Auden, *Collected Shorter Poems* (London: Faber, 1971), pp. 239–40.
19. Virginia Woolf, *To the Lighthouse* (Harmondsworth: Penguin, [1927] 1973), pp. 211, 152, 146, 153.
20. George Ramage, *The Rather Tame War Experiences in Flanders 1915 of Lance Corporal George Ramage, 1st Battalion Gordon Highlanders*. National Library of Scotland MS944-7, I: 82; III: 41–2.
21. Rupert Brooke, *The Complete Poems* (London: Sidgwick and Jackson, [1933] 1945), p. 147.
22. Dominic Hibberd and John Onions, eds, *The Winter of the World: Poems of the First World War* (London: Constable, 2008), pp. 52–3.
23. Ivor Gurney, 'First March', in *The Complete Poems of Ivor Gurney*, ed. P. J. Kavanagh (Oxford: Oxford University Press, 1982), p. 75.
24. R. L. Mackay, *The War Diary of Lieut. R.L. Mackay, 11th and later 1st/8th Battalions, Argyll and Sutherland Highlanders, September 1916 to January 1919*. National Library of Scotland Acc.12350/18, 14.
25. Wilfred Owen, *Wilfred Owen: The Complete Poems and Fragments*, ed. Jon Stallworthy. (London: Chatto and Windus, Hogarth Press and Oxford University Press, 1983), I, 185.

26. Ibid. I, 192.
27. Ibid. I, 158.
28. Ibid. I, 77.
29. Ibid. I, 145.
30. Ibid. I, 178–9.
31. Charles Hamilton Sorley, *The Collected Letters of Charles Hamilton Sorley*, ed. Jean Moorcroft Wilson (London: Woolf, 1990), p. 200.
32. Charles Hamilton Sorley, *Marlborough and other Poems* (Cambridge: Cambridge University Press, 1916), p. 57.
33. Ibid. pp. 90–2.
34. Ibid. p. 67.
35. Brooke, *The Complete Poems*, p. 150.
36. Sorley, *Marlborough and other Poems*, p. 91.
37. David Goldie, 'Archipelagic Poetry of the First World War', in Santanu Das (ed.), *The Cambridge Companion to Poetry of the First World War* (Cambridge: Cambridge University Press, 2013), pp. 159–72, p. 165.
38. Mackinlay, *Poems*, p. 58.
39. E. A. Mackintosh, 'Wanderer's Desire', in *A Highland Regiment* (London: John Lane, 1917), p. 64.
40. Mackintosh, *A Highland Regiment*, p. 59.
41. Mackinlay, *Poems*, p. 54.
42. Ibid. p. 57.
43. Ibid. p. 48. *The Glasgow Herald* (5 August 1914), p. 6. Perhaps deliberately, Mackinlay's poem is placed immediately below an article, 'British Graves in France', which celebrates 'the music of birds and the dominating splendour of the forest' around a war cemetery, concluding 'let us be thankful to Nature'.
44. Mackinlay, *Poems*, p. 53.
45. Ibid. p. 3.
46. Andrew Motion, 'Armistice', *The Guardian*, 4 October 2018. Available at <https://www.theguardian.com/books/2018/oct/04/andrew-motion-poet-laureate-publishes-new-war-poem> (last accessed 13 November 2018).
47. Hugh MacDiarmid, 'Gairmscoile', in *The Complete Poems: 1920–1976*, ed. Michael Grieve and W. R. Aitken (Manchester: Carcanet, 1993), I, 74.
48. Violet Jacob, 'The Field by the Lirk o' the Hill', in *Beneath Troubled Skies: Poems of Scotland at War, 1914–1918*, ed. Lizzie MacGregor (Edinburgh: Scottish Poetry Library and Polygon, 2015), p. 77.

Chapter 11

Pastoral as Propaganda in John Buchan's Wartime Writing
Fiona Houston

While modern popular imagination of the First World War conjures trenches and Belgian mud – through the verses of soldier poets and novels such as Erich Maria Remarque's *All Quiet on the Western Front* (1929) and Robert Graves's *Goodbye to All That* (1929) – during the war and in the years that followed, it was literature that reflected on a rural idyll of home that was favoured by British civilians. In her recent biography of her grandfather, Ursula Buchan observes that between 1920 and 1929, around 30,000 copies of Rupert Brooke's collected works were sold – with their heavy focus on the natural world – compared to only 1,430 copies of Wilfred Owen's first collection.[1] Much of the contemporaneously popular literature was not entrenched in the European mire, but instead offered escape through patriotic prose and nostalgic reminiscences of home. Home is achingly absent from the pockmarked landscape of war, yet evocative literature can arouse sentimental reflection on one's country. Not only this, but appropriation of rural beauty is a powerful motivator in influencing men to fight. Kate McLoughlin talks of how 'descriptions and visual images of the English countryside' act as 'motivating propaganda [. . .], appealing to individuals' sense of attachment towards land [. . .] to induce them to defend the nation'.[2] Richard Hannay, the hero of John Buchan's 'shocker', *The Thirty-Nine Steps* (1915), acknowledges, 'if you're going to be killed you invent some kind of flag and country to fight for'.[3] Buchan's writing during the war did just that: his pastoral reflection of Scotland and England unites the two nations into one state which its civilians would be proud to defend.

Buchan's relationship with the landscape, and Britain itself, is complex. David Goldie argues that Buchan is the 'archetypal Imperial North Briton' – one who 'arrives at a defining Scottishness by way of a wider British formation'.⁴ On the other hand, Macdonald Daly points, in some of Buchan's war poetry, to the both stark and consoling potential of the Scottish landscape.⁵ Daly explores the political possibilities of invoking the Scottish countryside while simultaneously supporting a British war effort. There is a duality in Buchan's relationship with the British countryside and Kate Macdonald describes Buchan as having an 'inescapably dual identity'.⁶ Born in Perth, Scotland, in 1857, Buchan attended Glasgow University at age seventeen before transferring to Brasenose College, Oxford, in 1895 – both Scotland and England, therefore, were influential in his education and formative years. When war broke out in August 1914, despite being young enough to enlist, Buchan suffered from perpetual duodenal ulcers which prevented him from joining the army. In June 1916, however, he did travel to the Western Front as part of the British Army's General Head Quarters Intelligence Section, and he wrote articles for *The Times* newspaper throughout 1915 based on what he witnessed in France and Belgium. He received a field commission to Second Lieutenant in the Intelligence Corps, and in 1917 was named Director of Information under the direction of Lord Beaverbrook. This chapter argues that Buchan's celebration of British landscape through his newspaper articles and Hannay novels not only indicates his identification with both Scottish and English nationality, but encourages men to fight as a form of propaganda. While much of Buchan's wartime literary output was derogatory and antagonist towards the Germans, this study chooses instead to focus on Buchan's work which carries a message of integration.⁷ It is a propaganda that relies on patriotism and sentimental reflection on home, rather than alienation and slander of the enemy. While many scholars previously have addressed Scottish identity and pastoral as a tool of propaganda, this study explores Buchan's adoption of typical symbols of pastoral – shepherds and birds, neighbourly invitation, the sanctuary of the humble cottage – alongside traditional Scottish literary technique – such as oral folk tales and song – to create an identity that is simultaneously proudly Scottish and proudly British.

Buchan and Scotland

The early twentieth century witnessed social and technological change, much of which was accelerated by the outbreak of the First World War. For the majority of Britain there was increasing uncertainty as traditional ways of life began to diminish; threat of civil war in Ireland continued to simmer and labour strikes spread across the nation. In times of such insecurity, the perpetuity of the land can offer comfort and reassurance. In his memoirs, *Memory Hold-the-Door* (1940), Buchan acknowledges that 'when the future is uncertain the mind turns naturally to the certainties of the past and finds comfort in what is beyond the peril of change'.[8] While the natural world can be threatened by the effects of conflict, as this chapter demonstrates, there is comfort to be gleaned from nature through its perceived endurance. Christoph Ehland confirms this, writing that Buchan's novel *Mr Standfast* (1919) portrays a 'coming to terms with a world in flux' and that the pastoral descriptions found in this novel betray a 'yearning for an unspoiled, pre-modern rural haven'.[9] This pastoral nostalgia is also developed through the shepherd trope.[10] Buchan demonstrates real love and respect for shepherds, in addition to a feeling of familiarity with them. In *Memory Hold-the-Door*, he recalls how he was admitted by shepherds 'into the secrets of a whole lost world of pastoral [. . .] I learned the soft, kindly, idiomatic Border speech [. . .] From that countryside an older world had not quite departed.'[11] There is here an echo of the loss of traditional ways of life, and it is through this sense of a lost world that war pastoral is so effective: nostalgia for a past life is reapplied to the nostalgia for a life in peacetime. The shepherds and crofters of Scotland belong to a past age and are lost at the same time as peace is lost.

During such a destabilising, fragmenting experience as total war, pastoral security is sought after to a greater extent. McLoughlin reflects on this relationship between war and the land, recognising how 'the ancient literary mode of pastoral is pressed into service' as a tool of public influence during wartime.[12] War pastoral relies on many of the traditional tropes of Georgic literature, and Paul Fussell, in his exploration of First World War literature, remarks how, 'in addition to shepherds and sheep, pastoral requires birds and birdsong'. He states that:

> one of the remarkable intersections between life and literature during the war occurred when it was found that Flanders and Picardy abounded in the two species long the property of symbolic literary pastoral – larks and nightingales. The one now became associated with stand-to at dawn, the other with stand-to at evening.[13]

The war appropriated this literary tradition, assigning new meaning to longstanding metaphor. Art and literature were still present, and moreover still relevant, at the front, in spite of its melancholy aspect and the surroundings' apparent lack of artistic inspiration.

For Buchan, birds are integral to his depictions of rural Scotland. In *The Thirty-Nine Steps*, he observes that 'nesting curlews and plovers were crying everywhere, and the links of green pasture were dotted with young lambs'.[14] Ovine and avian flocks unite to create a pastoral paradise. The narrative of this novel remains firmly set on British soil, yet the larks which Fussell claims were so poignant on the Western Front are of equal importance to Buchan in his portrayals of home. He describes 'shining blue weather, with a constantly changing prospect of brown hills and far green meadows, and a continual sound of larks and curlews and falling streams'.[15] The contrast of the constant 'changing' is mirrored in the enduring call of the lark against the transience of the stream. This poeticism is propagandist, as Buchan uses romantic description to induce pride and patriotism. The vivid blues and greens of home are in stark contrast to the colourless wilderness of no-man's-land, where any playful music of running water is surely drowned by the shriek of battle or replaced by the stagnant pools of shell holes. How hard it must be, when entrenched in mud and clay, to remember the beauty of home and what you are fighting to defend. How powerful, then, are Buchan's agrarian illustrations as a reminder and motivator to continue fighting.

Certainly, rural Scotland is an enduring and important motif throughout the Hannay novels; the land is celebrated for its beauty and raised as a symbol for which to fight in contrast to the bleakness of the war zone. For Hannay, the 'high heathery mountains' of the border lands offer him 'sanctuary'.[16] He rejoices in the countryside where the hills are 'cut amethysts'.[17] In a way that echoes Brooke's patriotic verse, Buchan's bejewelled countryside is at once both beautiful and precious – it is worth fighting for. Buchan's is effective propaganda, influencing both those who are at the front – reminding them of the beautiful land for which they fight – and those at home who develop a sense of duty to protect this stunning landscape. Even in the midst of enemy Europe, the allure of the Scottish countryside is not forgotten. In *Mr Standfast*, while crossing the Col of the Swallows in a desperate race across Austria, Hannay refers to the desolate valley using the Scottish term 'glen'.[18] In using this word, Buchan renders the unfamiliar and disturbing somewhat comforting and intimate; Hannay is soothed by the familiarities of the Scots language while in the alien landscape.

The same is seen in Buchan's short story 'The King of Ypres' (1915), where the private, Peter Galbraith, makes constant reference to his home in Motherwell. The tale is based on a legend that circulated on the Western Front and tells the story of a private, Galbraith, who falls asleep in a cellar while stationed in Ypres.[19] In the night, the troops are withdrawn, leaving the town undefended and Galbraith in his cellar, unaware. Left alone in Ypres, Galbraith takes it upon himself to maintain law and order in the town, earning himself the title 'le Roi d'Ypres'. In Buchan's fictional retelling of the legend, everything from the sound of dropping shells to the rowdiness of Galbraith's battalion reminds the private of his Scottish home town, which is elicited three times in the first two paragraphs alone.[20] Buchan's writing was popular amongst the men in the trenches, and these moments are the literary articulation of the comfort that is missed, serving as a reminder to the absent Tommy that home lies waiting.

This familiarity of the Scottish countryside also has a more sinister effect. Buchan's 'Inter Arma' collection of poems (1916–17) is written in the Lowlands Scots dialect and told from the first-person perspective of a soldier. In the poem 'On Leave', a soldier walks in his native land while home from the front but is unable to escape the influence of the war. He sees hills in the distance, but equates them to battlefield graves:

> But I kenned they werna hills,
> But the same as mounds ye see
> Doun by the back o' the line
> Whaur they bury oor lads that dee.
> They were juist the same as at Loos . . . (lines 33–7)[21]

The beauty of the rural world is corrupted here through association with the battlefield in an inversion of Hannay's and Galbraith's experiences, discussed above. Even the perceived security provided by the natural world cannot, ultimately, defeat the destruction caused by warfare. Traditionally, the pastoral mode was used to express loss and longing, and the barbarity of man destroying man on foreign shores contrasts sharply with Georgian harmony. John Burnett and Kate Mackay argue that Buchan, too, felt this longing for former times; he was 'aware of the fading away of traditional forms of farming, and the kind of life that went with them'.[22] From the outbreak of the conflict he sensed that 'an old regime was passing away [. . .] the point of contact of a world vanishing and a world arriving'.[23] It was an age of transition, where the days of the past had not wholly disappeared; nor had the new era yet arrived.

This melancholy does not last, however. It is not long before the beauty of nature reasserts itself. The soldier is able to make his peace with God (line 28), forgetting the 'stink o' gas' and the colour 'o' bluid' (lines 21–2), thanks to the beauty of the sun setting in the 'Wast' [west] (line 27) and the Scottish 'heather and thymy sod' (line 26).[24] He knows the war is still taking place, but his immersion in the Scottish countryside and the smell of the summer evening force away the smell of the gas (lines 46–7).[25] Nature, after all, overcomes. Moreover, adopting Scots allows Buchan to identify more closely with the individual soldier at the same time as demonstrating the fondness he holds for the country of his birth. In *Memory Hold-the-Door*, he recalls how it was only after having moved to England that he truly was able to 'discover Scotland'.[26] As a 'temporary exile' he was able to acquire 'all the characteristics of the Scot abroad' and 'cultivated a sentiment for all things Scottish'.[27] The beauty of Scotland is the remedy to the suffering of the war zone, and is felt all the more keenly when experienced after an absence.

Buchan's 'Home Thoughts from Abroad', also from the 'Inter Arma' collection, depicts the excitement of a soldier returning home to Scotland from the war. The soldier looks forward to making a 'pet' of himself and pictures the life of fishing and contentment he and his friend Davie will enjoy once they leave the fighting:

> Davie will lauch like a wean [child] at a fair
> And nip my airm to mak certain shüre
> That we're back frae yon place o' duel and dreid. (lines 45–7)[28]

The two men will be like children at a fair, pinching themselves to make sure they are truly home, their joyful laughter ('lauch') contrasting greatly with the fighting and dread ('duel and dreid') of the front. However, Buchan cuts off the last line of the stanza and the final lines of the poem are italicised and justified to the right. The tone shifts dramatically: '*But Davie's deid!*' (line 49). Buried near Beaumont, Davie will not return home, leaving half of his friend's heart '*in the mools* [earth] *aside him*' (lines 51–2). The happy dream that has been kept alive by the soldier at the front will only be half realised – his friend is dead. Home will not be the same again, and while the soldier might leave the front, physically, mentally and emotionally there will always be part of him that was left behind. Daly observes that, statistically, more Scots voluntarily enlisted in the British Army than any other British nation.[29] Buchan's poem celebrates the sacrifice made by Scotland's men: they become part of a new allied identity as their bodies now form part of the foreign land in which they fought. Scottish pride has transcended national boundaries.

Buchan's Hannay novels celebrate Scotland, relying on emotive pastoral tropes and emulation of the Scottish national culture; his is a propaganda founded on glorification of a native landscape, its inhabitants and its culture. The Scots language is used to facilitate Hannay's many disguises. In *Mr Standfast*, he adopts the Lowlands Scots vernacular as he pursues foreign spies from the streets of Glasgow to the Cuillin mountains of Skye. When questioned and at risk of capture, he changes guise: 'no Lowlands Scots for me now. My tone was that of an adjutant of a Guard's battalion.'[30] The Scottish tongue is his camouflage and he switches, chameleon-like, between dialects. Similarly, in *Greenmantle* (1916), Sandy Arbuthnot, one of Hannay's accomplices, finds himself under cover on an enemy boat which is attacked by a British submarine. As Sandy and the rest of the shipwrecked survivors float away, he is recognised by an old friend, Tommy Elliot, on the attacking vessel. Sandy shouts:

> in the broadest of Scots, which no man in the submarine or in our boat could have understood a word of. 'Maister Tommy,' [. . .] 'what for was ye skail a dacent tinkler lad intil a cauld seas? I'll gie ye your kail through the reek for this ply the next time I forgaither wi' ye on the tap o' Caerdon.'[31]

The Scots tongue transforms to a code, uniting the two allies in the midst of the enemy. The reference to the Caerdon hill and the evocation of the Scottish rural landscape call upon the friends' shared memories of Scotland – a recalled place becoming a talismanic password. Explanation between the two men is not necessary, as all is communicated through their shared memories, and Josephine Dougal reflects that collective meaning inferred through place can supplant 'sequential narrative'.[32] She further argues that '[H]ome, like nation, is symbolically constructed through the deep personal meanings that attach to it'.[33] Likewise, Benedict Anderson writes that 'the nation is always conceived as a deep, horizontal comradeship', and that it is this 'fraternity that makes it possible [. . .] for so many millions of people [. . .] willingly to die for such limited imaginings'.[34] The frequent nostalgia of peaceful countryside in the Hannay novels serves as a reminder of home and their motivation to enlist to those who are fighting in Belgium and France. Buchan creates an atmosphere of shared nationhood and inspires men to defend it.

It is not merely through these rural descriptions, however, that a sense of the pastoral can be evoked. The cottage as a place of refuge is relied upon by Hannay throughout his adventures, and he often depends upon the kindness of peasants and shepherds to shelter him. Kimberly Huth discusses the importance of invitation to the pastoral mode, and its representation through the 'homely cottage'.³⁵ In *The Thirty-Nine Steps* it is the cottage of a Borders shepherd, and in *Mr Standfast* Hannay is invited to stay in the cottages of fishermen and various peasants. However, it is in *Greenmantle* that the invitation of humble sanctuary is most poignant. It is a German peasant – the impoverished wife of a woodcutter, whose husband is fighting on the Eastern Front – who shares what little she has and saves Hannay in his hour of need. The kindness of the Borders folk is echoed and reapplied in the heartland of the enemy. Huth argues that:

> Pastoral is not simply a literary form of place or of ethos but more accurately a mode through which the values of that place and the aspects of that ethos are communicated from one individual to another. This understanding of the pastoral extends it beyond any boundaries of location and makes it available to anyone willing to issue an invitation.³⁶

The values of the Scottish herdsmen break past geographical boundaries, and the pastoral paradigm crosses nations. In a text which is propagandist in its jingoistic portrayal of the Allied forces, it is incongruous to see such a portrayal of the foe. Buchan shows how every German is not evil, but moreover how pastoral kindness unites all humanity, regardless of nationality. Macdonald confirms this interpretation, arguing that *Greenmantle* 'has a strong message of tolerance' and that Buchan 'took the trouble to portray German and Turkish civilians, both enemy nations to the British, as sympathetic individuals and recognizable neighbours'.³⁷ Buchan's writing is not wholly biased – not ignorant of the humanity of those living in enemy nations. Of course, this positive portrayal also serves a political purpose, however, by showing that the whole German nation is not behind the war effort in the way the British are. It is a subtle form of propaganda.

In much the same way, the poem 'Sweet Argos' from 'Inter Arma' is subtle in its manipulation of the reader to encourage participation in the war. Written as a letter from one soldier, 'Jock in billets', to his friend, 'Sandy in the trenches', the verse is initially used to portray the suffering undergone during the conflict. Jock describes the 'wet drips' which leak into his dugout: 'There's comfort naether oot nor in' (lines 13 and 15).³⁸ War is 'hell' and enough to make the very devil sick (lines 106 and 108).³⁹ The unending monotony of stalemate in the trenches takes its toll:

> For sax [six] weeks hunkerin' in a hole
> We'd kenned the worst a man can thole [tolerate] –
> Nae skirlin' dash frae goal to goal. (lines 31–6)⁴⁰

While Buchan acknowledges Jock's suffering, the regularity of the metre mitigates the description here. The rhythm is steady and regular, wholly divorced from the chaos described. Buchan counteracts the unsavoury tone at the start of the poem by encouraging men to fight, despite the hardships at the front. Jock realises that the reason the men fight is 'luve, my man, nae less nae mair –' (line 109).[41] It is love for:

> auld freends at Kirk and fair,
> Auld-farrant sangs [old-fashioned songs] that memories bear
> [. . .]
> Some wee cot-hoose far up the muir [moor]
> Or doun the glen. (lines 110–14)[42]

It is the love of home and country that encourages men to fight, and Buchan calls upon this imagery, manipulating the patriotism felt by the Scottish soldier.

Buchan appropriates the Sottish landscape, yet in 'Sweet Argos' he shows how the same patriotic sentiment is experienced by the German:

> Gairmans are nae doot [doubt] the same:
> The lad ye've stickin' in the wame [belly]
> Fechts [fights] no for deevilment or fame,
> But jurist for pride
> In his bit [small] decent canty [contented] hame
> By some burnside [riverside]. (lines 115–20)[43]

No longer an enemy 'other', Buchan concedes the similarities between the two armies – British and German alike are fighting for the pride of their countries. More than this, the German home is 'decent'. It is a very different sentiment to that expressed by Buchan in an article for *The Times*, 'Thrust for Lorgies' (19 May 1915), where he describes the Germans as an 'unclean' race.[44] While alluding to the very real trials that took place in the trenches, the poem still encourages men to continue fighting, and moreover makes it a worthy war against a worthy and valiant enemy. Buchan elevates it from a doleful stalemate into a heroic fight.

While Buchan's evocation of patriotic amour does elevate the war, it is important to remember that in his sentimental descriptions of Scotland, Buchan omits the reality of much of the country. These representations of a British rural idyll are problematic: not every citizen was fortunate enough to live in a rural paradise. What about those who live in rural poverty? Or should those who live in cities have less desire to protect their homes? In *Mr Standfast*, Buchan alludes to this difference of experience among the population of Scotland. In contrast to the idyllic rural of the Borders, Glasgow is described as having 'many chimneys' and a 'pale yellow sky against which two factory stalks stood out sharply'.[45] The pigments are diluted and there is suggestion of a sulphurous haze.[46] There is contrast between the urban and the rural. Buchan appropriates this sentimental, rural idealism and ignores the urban experience of many citizens.

Buchan and England

As discussed above, Buchan's identity was forged on both sides of the border between Scotland and England. Yet while Buchan may embrace his dual identity, relations between Scotch and Englander were not historically amicable. In times of warfare, it is important to unite, forgetting old animosity and redirecting hostility towards the new enemy. Buchan's propaganda during the war celebrates the English countryside at the same time as uniting Scotland and England against enemy Germany. Jacques Ellul, in his analysis of propaganda, differentiates between a 'propaganda of aggression' and a 'propaganda of integration'. According to Ellul, integration propaganda 'aims at stabilizing the social body, at unifying and reinforcing it'.[47] It is this unification that Buchan attempts as his love of the landscape reaches across the border.

In much the same way as the Hannay novels celebrate rural Scotland, England, too, is glorified for its rural beauty. In *Mr Standfast*, Hannay is transported by the beauty of the landscape surrounding Fosse Manor in the Cotswolds:

> I could see the stream slipping among its water-meadows and could hear the plash of the weir. A tiny village settled in the crook of the hill, and its church tower sounded seven with a curiously sweet chime. Otherwise there was no noise but the twitter of small birds and the night wind in the tops of the beeches. In that moment I had a kind of revelation. I had a vision of what I had been fighting for, what we all were fighting for. It was peace, deep and holy and ancient [. . .] It was more; for in that hour England first took hold of me.[48]

The passage echoes the sentimentality of 'On Leave' and 'Sweet Argos' as Buchan evokes the natural world as a reason to continue fighting. It is the ancient peace of nature that once again provides a sense of security. Yet here there is also representation of religious love entwined with that of the rural. Buchan's use of the word 'revelation' has Biblical allusions, and the chiming of the church bell mingles with the songs of the birds and the splashing of the stream. The power of religious imagery is a reliable technique in the creation of propaganda. Harold Lasswell argues that since the 'flaming vocabulary of religion still has the power to move the hearts of many men, it is a poor propagandist who neglects the spiritual and ecclesiastical interpretation', and Edward Bernays discusses the power of the church in moulding public opinion: the 'preacher upholds the ideals of society. He leads his flock whither they indicate a willingness to be led.'[49] Buchan's propaganda, then, is difficult to resist as it calls upon both powerful pastoral tropes and the emotive power of religion.

The link between religion and propaganda is understandable, as propaganda taps into deeply held shared values and a desire for belonging and comfort. Nietzsche's belief is that religion 'quietens the heart of the individual in times of loss, deprivation, fear, distrust' and that governments could appropriate this as, 'even in the case of universal, unavoidable [. . .] evils (famines, financial crises, war), indeed, religion guarantees a calm, patient, trusting disposition among the masses'.[50] Buchan uses religion to manufacture an impression of calm during time of war. To appropriate religion was to appropriate a ready-made understanding of community and security created by the church.

It is not only religion that fosters this perception of community. Buchan creates a sense of unity in Britain through the use of song. Paul Alpers observes that song announces the idea of 'coming together. Pastoral convenings are characteristically occasions for songs.'[51] Music is a unifying force, and Matthew Gelbart, in his article on Scottish national music, speaks of the 'implied narrative' of music, in addition to the power that music has of 'rallying people around a common identity'.[52] Songs are used throughout the Hannay novels as a form of recognition or password between characters. In the episode discussed above between Sandy Arbuthnot and Tommy Elliot, Elliot's attention is first caught by Sandy playing 'Flowers of the Forest' – an old Scottish tune – and it is this which alerts Elliot that an ally is near. In *The Thirty-Nine Steps*, after having returned to London from Scotland, and still uncertain of his own safety, Hannay whistles the Scottish tune 'Annie Laurie'; a fisherman then appears, and he too whistles the same song. It is then that the men recognise in each other an ally. It is noteworthy that it is through the music of Scotland, and the sentiments this kindles, that Buchan presents these shared meanings. While in danger, Hannay is comforted by the recollection of security he experienced in the hills of Lowland Scotland and recaptures that in England through song. Gelbart acknowledges the 'advantages of music over words in crossing cultural and geographical boundaries'.[53] The border between the two nations is removed and the two cultures are united.

In *Mr Standfast*, it is an English tune, 'Cherry Ripe', whistled by both Hannay and his lover, Mary Lamington, which acts as a sign to each other that they are safe and in each other's company. 'Cherry Ripe' was a popular tune during the First World War, based on a poem of the same name by Robert Herrick, the lines of which allude to a country which is distant:

> There
> Where my Julia's lips do smile
> There's the land. (lines 4–6)[54]

The repetition of 'there' alludes to a land that is absent – a land that is missed – and is therefore poignant in the context of entrenched soldiers miles from their homes in France; it evokes home while in the midst of danger on foreign soil. It is a tune that, for Hannay, has 'all the lingering magic of an elder England and of this hallowed countryside'.[55] Dougal remarks how the 'meaning that a place has is perhaps especially compelling for those whose connections to that place have been disrupted', and notes the chasm felt between 'homeland and hereland'.[56] Buchan recognises the pain felt by the soldiers at being absent from home, recognising it and providing comfort through his literature. His characters suffer the same homesick pangs as the fighting man and desire the same familiarity of homely reminiscence.

Collective understanding through music is reminiscent of Sir Walter Scott's novel, *Redgauntlet* (1824). Buchan greatly admired Scott, and Greenmantle is a principal character in Scott's book. It is a historical novel that describes a fictional third Jacobite Rebellion. The hero, Darsie Latimer, is held captive and hears the sound of fiddle music drifting through to him from the minstrel Wandering Willie. Latimer infers meaning from this tune, and hopes that:

> desired communication might be attained; since it is well known that, in Scotland, where there is so much national music, the words and airs of which are generally known, there is a kind of free-masonry amongst performers, by which they can, by the mere choice of a tune, express a great deal to the hearers.[57]

This echoes Dougal's observation of the irrelevance of a sequential narrative when there is a shared knowledge of place. Similarly, there is, as Gelbart describes it, an 'implied' narrative of a national music.

These tunes unite Scotland and England – both nations seek the same comfort and receive it through the familiarity of song. Gelbart remarks how identification through Scottish culture was traditionally employed to unite Scotland as a nation in the 'face of English dominance'.[58] Buchan's use of these English and Scottish songs in turn unites Britain against a German dominance in another subtle form of propaganda. Indeed, this perception of a unified Britain was vital to counteract the dissent from the Scots towards the English based on historical animosity. Tommy Elliot's 'Flowers of the Forest' was written about the Scottish defeat by the English at Flodden and is a song which is full of resentment towards the English. It was a resentment of which Buchan was aware and, in his memoirs, he recalls how, '[A]gainst our little land [Scotland] there had always stood England, vast, menacing and cruel'.[59] It was important for Buchan to work against these deep-set prejudices and to counteract these divisions by creating unity. It was a divided kingdom that was to unite against the 'Hun', fabricating a new 'Other' and forgetting old animosity. He celebrates Scotland and England alike and diminishes the differences between the nations, making instead one unified state. In his article for *The Times*, 'The Battlefield of Loos' (6 October 1915), for instance, Buchan notices Battalions returning from the trenches, with 'Khaki and tartan alike white with chalk mud from the rain of yesterday'.[60] There is no way of identifying the national differences in dress; the experiences at the front have rendered Scot and Englander the same – a new, military, world has been created.

Buchan and the Front

On the battlefield, however, these pastoral reveries appear out of place and inappropriate where the landscape is bleak and desolate. In an article for *The Times* on 17 May 1915, Buchan describes the war zone as a 'black landscape with stagnant water in every bottom and draggled worlds of larch and waterlogged meadows'.[61] War has literally flooded the landscape; the water here is not the clear, flowing streams from the pastoral of Buchan's fiction, but rather the motionless, putrid pools of no-man's-land – the stagnation of the water mirroring the stagnation of the armies entrenched in their war of attrition. The pastoral idyll is non-existent; the vivid hues of Hannay's Scottish paradise are absent, replaced with dullness and a lack of colour. The earth only exists – it does not thrive.

In another article, 'Ypres Today' (22 May 1915), Buchan inverts the traditional romantic idea of pastoral, and the imagery of birds – used so sentimentally in his descriptions from *The Thirty-Nine Steps* – no longer embodies a symbolic comfort. He describes the ruined town of Ypres and observes that jackdaws were 'cawing from the ruins and a painstaking starling [was] rebuilding its nest in a broken pinnacle'. He then observes an old cow, 'a miserable object, [. . .] poking her head in the *debris* and sniffing curiously at the dead body of a horse'.[62] Here, the natural world struggles to reassert its stronghold in the broken aftermath of human destruction; the traditional pastoral bovine herd animals are 'miserable' and the gruesome image of the dead horse provokes revulsion. Buchan proceeds to describe an abandoned house, wherein there are 'glimpses of greenery'. He initially lulls the reader into a false sense of security as he describes the 'carefully-tended garden' and the 'spring flowers. A little fountain still splashes in a stone basin.' However, the narrative shifts, and we learn that:

> at one corner an incendiary shell has fallen on the house, and in the heap of charred *débris* there are human remains. Most of the dead have been removed, but there are still bodies in out-of-the-way corners. Over all hangs a sickening smell of decay, against which the lilacs and hawthorns are powerless. That garden is no place to tarry in.[63]

Here, nature is not able to conquer the devastation of human war; the flowers are powerless against destruction. The pastoral world has been destroyed by the warring hands of man.

Yet Buchan's article, although briefly acknowledging this grim picture of the consequences of conflict, soon reverts to pastoral reverie and celebration of the land he oversees. He exclaims that the battlefield is as 'green as Oxfordshire', that:

> white clouds drift in a clear sky, as in some Flemish painting. Here, on the hill-side, broom and lilac and wild hyacinths are everywhere. Cattle graze in fields round the little red homesteads below.[64]

Buchan calls the pastoral into service with the evocation of flocks, and once again applies the familiar to the unfamiliar with his allusion to Oxfordshire. The sky is 'clear', clear from clouds and clear from trouble; if this was pathetic fallacy, then the picture that Buchan paints is one of cheerful jocundity. He is even able to take note of the flowers, suggesting a sense of leisure. Buchan does admit that what he sees is merely an 'illusion', as truly 'Ypres is doomed beyond hope', yet this is too small a statement in contrast to his hyperbolic, light-hearted pastoral prose.[65]

This is a vastly different picture from what Philip Gibbs – Buchan's fellow war correspondent – describes in his post-war work *Now It Can Be Told* (1920). Like Buchan, Gibbs travelled to the Western Front to report on the war, and the book is his attempt to voice the truth he felt he had been forced to repress during the conflict. In it, Gibbs recalls the 'odor of human filth' and a 'tide of wounded; wounded everywhere, maimed men at every junction'.[66] Of course, due to DORA legislation Buchan could not have published such graphic details in 1915 as Gibbs was able to in 1920. The Defence of the Realm Act was passed in August 1914 and included regulations controlling the press. Nothing was to be published that could be useful to the enemy. Printing information on 'movement of troops, ships and aircraft, or location or description of war material' was prohibited, as well as anything that could be seen as damaging to British morale.[67] The very title of Gibbs's account demonstrates that it is only 'now' the war is over that he is able to disclose the truth. Hazel Hutchison observes that, during the war, it was mostly only in American magazines that this graphic detail and description were more common.[68] Buchan, writing for British publications and British publishing firms, would have been restricted during wartime in ways that his transatlantic peers would not.

Nevertheless, his articles for *The Times* can make for difficult reading, as the cheerful tone is in danger of belittling the experiences of the fighting man. He recalls meeting 'weary and dusty men returning from the trenches after a heavy fight', but then, 'two days later you find the same men washed and shaved and good humoured, taking their ease among the lush Flemish meadows'.[69] Little attention is given to the 'heavy fight', and instead the reader is once again drawn into a pastoral description of verdant fields; Flanders is rendered practically a rural paradise. Yet perhaps this is simply another attempt on Buchan's part to apply homely, familiar scenes to the alien landscape before him. Certainly, in his article 'On a Flemish Hill' (17 May 1915), he observes that the ground 'from a distance looks like well-arranged covers on an English estate', and in 'The Allies Advance' (29 September 1915), he remarks how a 'Scots mist settled' on the foreign battlefield.[70] Buchan applies the characteristics of home to the foreign land, helping the soldier find comfort. This is not a rare phenomenon in war literature, and Randall Stevenson states that 'many war poets shared this readiness to find redeeming, restorative features not only in remembered landscapes but even in close proximity to the battlefields'.[71]

In 'Ypres Today', Buchan describes the countryside surrounding Ypres, 'where every yard has been fought over'; attention is drawn to the familiarity of the landscape as Buchan observes that 'in appearance the country is very like rural England – red-roofed farms and cottages, little straggling villages, and masses of lilac, may and laburnum everywhere'.[72] This reads rather more like a travel brochure for a holiday town in England than as a report of fierce fighting on foreign soil. Buchan remarks how 'civil life goes on up to the very edge of the fire zone. In the hamlets, girls sit outside their doors, busy lace-making; the country people are at work in the fields, and children are playing round the cottages'.[73] One would not know that a war was taking place. This could be read in two contrasting ways: either Buchan belittles the suffering undergone by civilians forced to live in the proximity of war, or he celebrates their courage in persevering with normal life in spite of the disruption of conflict. Furthermore, as the DORA legislation meant that it was an offence to publish anything 'damaging to morale', Buchan can do no more than hint at what might be lying over the hill in the war zone. While he does rely on rural imagery frequently throughout his articles, this can be read more as an attempt to portray the contrast between war and the natural world than as a method of ignoring the tragedy of battle.

Twenty-first-century readers cannot be sure about Buchan's intentions, but censorship regulations make it doubly complicated for modern-day readers to unpick the rights and wrongs of what writers were doing during the war. It would have been interesting to have been able to observe whether, as the war progressed into its third and fourth years, Buchan's pastoral optimism continued. These articles were written, after all, in 1915, when some of the initial excitement for the war still prevailed and when much of the undamaged rural scenery he describes still remained. He does not so much misrepresent as focus on part of what is there and edit out the damage. Unfortunately, though, it is not possible to observe any change in the tone of his articles as the war progressed: Buchan's last article for *The Times* was published in October of that year.

Buchan neglects to acknowledge in full the devastation wreaked upon the countryside by the war. He appropriates a sanitised image of the rural world, manipulating it as a tool of public influence. This pastoral reverie is projected on to the war zone where Buchan is in danger of omitting the truth of battle. Yet the frequent nostalgia for peaceful countryside in the Hannay novels serves as a comfort to those who are fighting on foreign soil, reminding them of a beauty made difficult to recall in the face of monstrosity. He creates a propaganda which draws upon the love of one's country as his texts promote the idea of nation, and identity in it. Buchan's pastoral descriptions allow the British population to discover and nurture an identity that is British, rather than distinctly Scottish or English. This identity fuels national pride and resentment towards an enemy nation threatening to destroy the native landscape and the shared identity.

Notes

1. Ursula Buchan, *A Life of John Buchan: Beyond the Thirty-Nine Steps* (London: Bloomsbury Publishing, 2019), p. 171.
2. Kate McLoughlin, *Authoring War: The Literary Representation of War from the Iliad to Iraq* (Cambridge: Cambridge University Press, 2011), p. 87.
3. John Buchan, *The Thirty-Nine Steps* (Ware: Wordsworth Editions Limited, [1915] 1996), p. 29.
4. David Goldie, 'The British Invention of Scottish Culture: World War One and Before', *Review of Scottish Culture*, vol. 18 (2006).
5. Macdonald Daly, 'Scottish Poetry and the Great War', *Scottish Literary Journal*, vol. 21, no. 2 (1 November 1994).
6. Kate Macdonald, *John Buchan: A Companion to the Mystery Fiction* (Jefferson, NC: McFarland, 2009), p. 49.
7. See, for example, Volume XXII of Buchan's *Nelson's History of the War* (1919), where the Allies are lauded as superior compared to the German 'menace', or *Greenmantle* for Hannay's unsavoury description of Colonel Stumm – the 'incarnation of all that makes Germany detested'. John Buchan, *Nelson's History of the War*, vol. XXII (London, Edinburgh and New York: Thomas Nelson and Sons, 1919), p. 69; *Greenmantle* (London: Penguin Books, [1916] 1956), p. 65.
8. John Buchan, *Memory Hold-the-Door* (London: Hodder and Stoughton, [1940] 1942), p. 182.
9. Cristoph Ehland, 'The Spy-Scattered Landscapes of Modernity in John Buchan's *Mr Standfast*', in *John Buchan and the Idea of Modernity* (London: Pickering & Chatto, 2013), pp. 111–124, pp. 121–2.
10. Paul Fussell, *The Great War and Modern Memory* (Oxford and New York: Oxford University Press, [1975] 2000), p. 241.
11. Buchan, *Memory Hold-the-Door*, p. 24.
12. McLoughlin, *Authoring War*, p. 84.
13. Fussell, *The Great War and Modern Memory*, p. 241.
14. Buchan, *The Thirty-Nine Steps*, p. 44.
15. Ibid. p. 89.
16. Ibid. p. 63.

17. Ibid. p. 43.
18. John Buchan, *Mr Standfast* (Oxford : Oxford University Press, [1919] 1993), p. 251.
19. Buchan alludes to the legend in his article for *The Times*, 'Ypres Today' (22 May 1915), and subsequently fictionalises it.
20. John Buchan, 'The King of Ypres', in *John Buchan: The Complete Short Stories Volume Three*, ed. Andrew by Lownie (London: Thistle, 1997), p. 34.
21. John Buchan, 'On Leave', in *Poems Scots and English* (London, Edinburgh and New York: Thomas Nelson and Sons, 1917), p. 144.
22. John Burnett and Kate Mackay, *John Buchan and the Thirty-Nine Steps: An Exploration* (Edinburgh: NMS Enterprises, 2014), p. 45.
23. Buchan, *Memory Hold-the-Door*, p. 166.
24. Buchan, 'On Leave', p. 145.
25. Ibid. p. 146.
26. Buchan, *Memory Hold-the-Door*, p. 81.
27. Ibid.
28. John Buchan, 'Home Thoughts from Abroad', in *Poems Scots and English*, pp. 62–4.
29. Daly, 'Scottish Poetry and the Great War', p. 80.
30. Buchan, *Mr Standfast*, p. 84.
31. Buchan, *Greenmantle*, p. 143.
32. Josephine Dougal, 'Popular Scottish Song Traditions at Home (and Away)', *Folklore*, vol. 122, no. 3 (December 2011), p. 287.
33. Ibid. p. 287.
34. Benedict Anderson, *Imagined Communities: Reflections on the Origin and Spread of Nationalism*, revised edn (London and New York: Verso, [1983] 2006), p. 7.
35. Kimberly Huth, 'Come Live with Me and Feed My Sheep: Invitations, Ownership, and Belonging in Early Modern Pastoral Literature', *Studies in Philology*, vol. 108 (2011), pp. 44–69, p. 44.
36. Ibid. p. 67.
37. Macdonald, *John Buchan*, p. 86.
38. John Buchan, 'Sweet Argos', in *Poems Scots and English*, p. 48.
39. Ibid. p. 52.
40. Ibid. p. 49.
41. Ibid. p. 52.
42. Ibid.
43. Ibid. p. 53.
44. John Buchan, 'Thrust for Lorgies', *The Times* (19 May 1915), p. 8.
45. Buchan, *Mr Standfast*, p. 52.
46. Ibid.
47. Jacques Ellul, *Propaganda: The Formation of Men's Attitudes*, trans. by Konrad Kellen and Jean Lerner (New York and Toronto: Vintage Books, 1973), p. 75.

48. Buchan, *Mr Standfast*, pp. 14–15.
49. Harold D. Lasswell, *Propaganda Technique in the World War* (London and New York: Kegan Paul, Trench Trubner, 1927), p. 71; Edward Bernays, *Crystallizing Public Opinion* (Milton Keynes: Lightning Source UK, 2019), p. 36.
50. Friedrich Nietzsche, *Human, All Too Human: A Book for Free Spirits* (Cambridge: Cambridge University Press, [1878] 1996), p. 170.
51. Paul Alpers, *What Is Pastoral?* (London: University of Chicago Press, 1997), p. 81.
52. Matthew Gelbart, 'Allan Ramsay, the Idea of "Scottish Music" and the Beginnings of "National Music" in Europe', *Eighteenth-Century Music*, vol. 9, no. 1 (2012), pp. 81–108, p. 83.
53. Ibid. p. 100.
54. Robert Herrick, 'Cherry-Ripe', in *The Oxford Book of English Verse 1250–1900*, ed. Arthur Thomas Quiller-Couch (Oxford: Clarendon Press, 1919. Available at <http://www.bartleby.com/101/256.html> (last accessed 27 November 2018).
55. Buchan, *Mr Standfast*, p. 20.
56. Dougal, 'Popular Scottish Song Traditions at Home (and Away)', p. 286.
57. Sir Walter Scott, *Redgauntlet* (Oxford: Oxford University Press, [1824] 2011), p. 220.
58. Gelbart, 'Allan Ramsay, the Idea of "Scottish Music" and the Beginnings of "National Music" in Europe', p. 92.
59. Buchan, *Memory Hold-the-Door*, p. 46.
60. John Buchan, 'The Battlefield of Loos', *The Times* (6 October 1915), p. 8.
61. John Buchan, 'On a Flemish Hill', *The Times* (17 May 1915), p. 9.
62. Buchan, 'Ypres Today', p. 9.
63. Ibid.
64. Ibid.
65. Buchan, 'On A Flemish Hill', p. 9.
66. Philip Gibbs, *Now It Can Be Told* (New York: Garden City Publishing, 1920), p. 7.
67. Cate Haste, *Keep the Home Fires Burning: Propaganda in the First World War* (London: Penguin Books, 1977), p. 30.
68. Hutchison cites Alexander Powell's article 'On the British Line' as an example of this explicit description, acknowledging Powell's 'unflinching account of shell fire, gas attacks, shrapnel wounds, and the conditions at an evacuation hospital at Bailleul'. Hazel Hutchison, *The War That Used Up Words: American Writers and the First World War* (New Haven, CT, and London: Yale University Press, 2015), p. 86.
69. John Buchan, 'The Battle of Festubert', *The Times* (29 May 1915), p. 6.
70. Buchan, 'On a Flemish Hill', p. 9; 'The Allies Advance', *The Times* (29 September 1915), p. 9.

71. Randall Stevenson, *Literature and the Great War 1914–1918* (Oxford: Oxford University Press, 2013), p. 139.
72. Buchan, 'Ypres Today', p. 9.
73. Ibid.

Chapter 12

Charles Murray and *A Sough o' War*
Robert Crawford

Charles Murray was the only poet whose work I ever heard my father quote. While this says something about my father (who was born in 1914, who spent his 1920s teenage years in the manse beside the Alford kirkyard where Charles Murray would later be buried, and who left school at fourteen), it also says something about Charles Murray, and particularly about the way this poet's work was treasured by the local Aberdeenshire community. I was reminded of that when I read Charlotte Peacock's 2017 biography of Nan Shepherd, which begins with the nervous young writer Jessie Kesson meeting Shepherd for the first time, on a train in 1941. Having just heard an announcement on the wireless, Kesson blurts out the words, 'Hamewith's dead'.[1] 'Hamewith' was what my father and many, many other Aberdeenshire folk called Murray, the name taken from the title of his most famous poem and his best-known collection of verse.

What my dad loved about Hamewith's poetry was its sense of the language native to rural Aberdeenshire, and the lines he quoted (lines he had learned at school and that spoke to his own experience looking after creatures on the glebe of the manse) formed the opening of the poem that begins Murray's 1921 collection, *In the Country Places*:

> It wasna his wyte he was beddit sae late
>   An' him wi' sae muckle to dee,
> He'd the rabbits to feed an' the fulpie to kame
>   An' the hens to hish into the ree . . .[2]

I can still hear my father reciting those lines, but, unlike me and most other Scots, he could do so in an authentic Aberdeenshire Doric accent. Charles Murray's work was treasured in Aberdeenshire for its sense of pastoral rootedness, but it was also prized across Scotland. My oldest copies of Murray's early collections – more pamphlets than books – come not from my dad but from a Greenock relative of my mother's, John Murray (no relation of Charles). They are stamped with the name of John Murray's father, Arthur, who was active in Burns Clubs in Paisley and Greenock. Charles Murray was invited to give the Immortal Memory at Greenock Burns Club in 1913. To mark the occasion, he wrote – and later published – a poem, 'The Immortal Memory'. Not among his best works, this one is particularly revealing because it anticipates Murray's war verse, because it shows his bardic eagerness, shared by many poets, to identify with Burns as what Hugh MacDiarmid would come to call a voice of Scotland, and because it also signals his awareness of imperial and geographical distance:

> AULD Scotia, since that Janwar' win'
> Rare hansel on your bard blew in –
> Tho' mony a wintry blast has frayed
> The fringes o' your tartan plaid –
> Your sons hae borne your banner far,
> Still first in peace, no last in war,
> Till noo in mony a distant land
> The march-stanes o' your kingdom stand.
> Yet aye the ranger's heart's the same,
> An' dunts in tune wi' oors at hame,
> Bound fast in spite o' land an' sea
> By 'Burns' Immortal Memory.'[3]

This poem's title, 'The Immortal Memory, Greenock Burns Club, 1913', suggests that it was written before the Great War, though its publication in Murray's post-war collection gives it a different resonance. Its mention of a banner carried both 'in peace' and 'in war' across 'mony a distant land' is also a reminder that, long before the Great War, Murray had written to the War Office in 1899 from his father's house near Alford, volunteering to serve in the Second Boer War, which had broken out just twelve days earlier. Murray was a poet committed to imperial militarism, and one who, by the outbreak of the Second Boer War, had spent several years in 1890s South Africa. Soon, as part of his long-lasting South African career, he became a lieutenant in the Boer War-era Railway Pioneer Regiment from 1900 until 1902, part of what he called at the time 'the irregular forces of our great army'.[4]

Decades before World War I, then, Murray's sympathies were martial and imperial: as he wrote to his former schoolteacher, Anthony McCreadie, in Alford in 1900 just before returning to South Africa, 'I have felt all along I ought to be out doing something for the cause in which so many of my friends have given up their lives'.[5] He was also deeply conditioned by an awareness of what his 1913 Greenock Burns Club poem calls 'distant land'.[6] Most of Murray's poetry was published during the part of his life spent in South Africa. He may have returned home periodically to rural Aberdeenshire, and undoubtedly and repeatedly drew on memories of his Alford youth, but his Scots was bolstered by his participation in Scots clubs in South Africa. The Doric may have been his native language, and the distinctive density of his use of the Doric (one of the features which so endeared his work to readers such as my father) is striking; but his deep mining of the Doric was quickened by spending so much of his time far distant from its sources.

Murray's was at once an Alford Doric and a heightened Afro-Scots, the product of an intense sense of linguistic exile, as well as of longing to identify with his own distant heartland. As the epigraph to his collection *Hamewith* (first published in Aberdeen in 1900 but repeatedly republished in London) puts it,

Here on the Rand we freely grant
  We're blest wi' sunny weather;
Fae cauld an' snaw we're weel awa,
  But man, we miss the heather.

Just so that no one can miss the point, these lines are followed by the words '*JOHANNESBURG, S.A.*'[7] Andrew Lang was alert to what he called, in his Introduction to *Hamewith*, Murray's 'echoes of very rich Scots which reach us across the African continent', and Murray's intense Doric of distance still endeared him to Empire readers decades later.[8] Quoting Lang's words, an article entitled 'Charles Murray, The Scots Poet of Today' in the 1933 *Courier-Mail* in Brisbane, Queensland, Australia, remarks with fascination that 'It is rather paradoxical that the Chief Scottish poet of to-day should have written his verses in South Africa', then goes on to speculate what might have happened if Murray (Charles, that is, not Les) had settled in Australia – and links Murray's Scots to that of the Scots poem 'Bowmount Water', written 'in Australia' by Will H. Ogilvie – another example of what this Australian journalist calls 'the Scottish "animus revertendi"' [intention to return].[9]

What is striking is not just the global reach of Murray's reputation as late as the 1930s but how far different is his standing in the early twenty-first century, when few anthologists or critics include or even make reference to the one-time 'Scots Poet of To-day'. The 1933 Australian journalist calls attention to Murray's retaining 'the substance of the racial Doric uncontaminated'. Without mentioning

Hugh MacDiarmid, the journalist concludes that 'the Scottish poets of to-day are filling the old bottles with new wine. And it was Charles Murray who led the way.'[10] Coming from 1930s Queensland, where aboriginal Australians were viciously oppressed, an enthusiasm for 'racial Doric uncontaminated' may have been as tainted as some aspects of enthusiasm for the Doric among the Scots community in a South Africa where local native peoples and native languages were seen as racially inferior. If Charles Murray's Doric is Afro-Scots, then the way it does *not* include or even make reference to the black population of South Africa is very striking indeed. His Doric poems are written in a native language that may be constructed in part to withstand the natives of South Africa, an exclusive Scots tongue whose Doric purity is achieved as an *animus revertendi* that is both impressive and deserving of moral censure. From a post-colonial stance, Murray's Doric can be viewed as racialist and racist – a product of imperial South African white essentialism.

A Sough o' War

To see it *only* from that standpoint is reductive, though, and masks the impressiveness of Murray's most striking individual collection, *A Sough o' War* (1917). Perhaps only poets know how hard it can be to find the right title for a collection, and the words 'A Sough o' War' make a great title. 'Sough' is a word that Murray knows needs explanation for many readers, and he glosses it as having two meanings: 'rumour', as well as 'sound of wind'. The term 'sough' tends to go with breezes, and we do not associate soft sounds with war – especially not with the high-explosive shell-bursts of World War I: so the combination of the soft, sibilant, distinctively Scots 'sough' with the grave, heavier English (albeit Scots-pronounced) word 'war' is especially memorable. By 1917, war itself was much more than a rumour, even if rumours about what was going on at the front were omnipresent, which gives a further pang to Murray's use of the multivalent word 'sough'. Though his glossary does not point it out, 'sough' can also refer to 'song' or to a distinctive way of speaking. So *A Sough o' War* is also a distinctively Scots war song. The title fits the book to perfection.

The title poem, dated '1914' and set in the season of 'hairst', signals Murray's characteristic awareness of 'the land', presenting landscape and human as bonded in a way and in a language that hint at how his sensibility contextualises and underpins the later sensibilities of both Nan Shepherd and Lewis Grassic Gibbon. For all the explicit commitment that the title poem manifests, its opening image of 'scythes' – a traditional emblem of death – gives the work a sharp sadness:

> The corn was turnin', hairst was near,
>   But lang afore the scythes could start
> A sough o' war gaed through the land
>   An' stirred it to the benmaist heart.[11]

There is a fine ear at work here, not least in the near-rhymes between 'hairst' and 'heart' and between 'start' and 'stirred', which take the poem's acoustic body subtly and nourishingly beyond the foursquare end-rhymes of 'start' and 'heart'. Set beside the greatest individual Scottish war poems of World War I, Murray's war poems lack the cutting officer-class guilt of Ewart Allan Mackintosh's 'In Memoriam, Private D. Sutherland, Killed in Action in the German Trench, May 16, 1916, and the Others who Died', just as Murray's work lacks the frontline horror of Charles Hamilton Sorley's sonnet that begins with the most stunning first line of any Great War poem in any language, 'When you see millions of the mouthless dead'. Nevertheless, when taken as a whole, Murray's *A Sough o' War* collection is surely one of the best books of war poetry produced by a Scottish poet during the Great War.[12]

Just fifty-six small pages long (including its six-page Doric glossary), this diminutive, soft-covered volume, published in London in April of the same year as T. S. Eliot's *Prufrock and Other Observations*, and during the same period of paper shortage, looks as drab as Eliot's first, even shorter book. While, for some readers, Eliot's acoustically modern collection reads very strangely for a work published after three years of war, modern audiences find Murray's acoustically nostalgic pastoral volume awkward on account of its Scots language and because it does not fit certain more recent expectations of what war poetry should sound like. It is all the more striking for that, particularly after a century. Dedicated to his son, who was serving in France, and mainly written in South Africa, *A Sough o' War* mixes the perspectives of home front and battle front, youth and age, male and female, combatant and non-combatant: all this gives it imaginative reach. Moreover, the fact that its war poems are dated from 1914 until 1916 adds a sense of chronological reach and development too. Reading *A Sough o' War* gives a sense of intensely *Scottish*, rather than British or English, commitment. The book is dedicated 'TO A YOUNG SAPPER SOMEWHERE

IN FRANCE AND TO ALL IN WHATEVER AIRT UPHOLDING THE FAIR NAME AND HONOUR OF SCOTLAND'; its first poem addresses those who *'answer Scotland's cry'*; its second has the refrain, 'Auld Scotland counts for something still'; its third is entitled, 'Wha Bares a Blade for Scotland?'; its fourth invokes 'the auld Scots Hame'.[13] Words such as 'England', 'Britain' and 'British' feature nowhere in the book, so that (particularly, perhaps, for non-Scottish readers) it carries a distinctly Scottish nationalist ring, even though its author was a thoroughgoing British imperialist. Murray's sense of Scottish locality and Aberdeenshire language, intensified by his residence in Africa (where the poet, now in his fifties, was in uniform as a Lieutenant Colonel in the South African Defence Force), permeates the book, but does not mask a more nuanced sense of humanity.

This is a collection committed to the war effort, yet also aware of that effort's terrible cost. One of the most immediately affecting lyrics is 'When Will the War Be By?' Dated 1916, it is a plain, short, echoic yet relatively tight-lipped poem, and all the better for that.

> 'This year, neist year, sometime, never,'
> A lanely lass, bringing hame the kye,
> Pu's at a floo'er wi' a weary sigh,
> An' laich, laich, she is coontin' ever
> 'This year, neist year, sometime, never,
> When will the war be by?'[14]

The book does not confine its women's voices to one voice or to one tone. In 'The Wife on the War' we hear anger,

> 'Deil birst them,' quo she, 'I would pit them in jyle,
> Oonless they gie owre wi' the killin' o't'.[15]

This poem of 1915, centred on an argument between husband and wife, is one of a number of poems that do not just deal with European conflict but emerge, too, and tellingly, from local conflict and argument. Murray may be a supporter of the war effort, but he lets us hear and see the emotional strains. At once a pastoral and a battle-front poem, 'Fae France' effectively, plainly and disconcertingly applies farming talk to a gas attack:

> The reek at first was like ye've seen, fan at the fairmer's biddin',
> Some frosty mornin' wi' the graip, the baillie turns the midden.
> But it grew thick, an' doon the win' straucht for oor lines it bore,
> Till shortly we were pyoch'rin' sair an' fleyed that we would smore . . .[16]

The same poem, however, reveals class divisions in the trenches, and though ultimately it celebrates the overcoming of differences between judge and criminal as the two unite in the war effort, its power comes from a refusal to airbrush such differences away. It seems highly likely that Murray drew on his son's experiences in France for the battlefront moments in *A Sough o' War*, but he also drew on his own sense of the home front, sometimes for jolting comic effect, as when the '*nickum*' (mischievous boy) at 'Hame' writes to his brother Hairy (Harry) in 'some saft bog in France' asking him to

> Sen' something hame, to show them at the sooter's, –
> A weel-cloured German helmet or a heid.[17]

The most sustained, complex poetic tonality in *A Sough o' War* occurs in the book's finest poem, 'Dockens afore his Peers', which deals with an exemption tribunal – a hearing at which 'John Watt o' Dockenhill' tries to argue that his son and all his household should be exempted from military service.[18] Learning from Browning's dramatic monologues, Lietenant Colonel Murray allows Dockens to condemn himself out of his own mouth as he attempts to evade possibilities of conscription. This is the one poem of Murray's which Mick Imlah and I included in *The Penguin Book of Scottish Verse*, conscious that it is written in unusually dense Aberdonian Scots (which requires a lot of glossing for uninitiated readers) and that it is relatively long. Yet its length gives it a cumulative power, and its richly worded unveiling of hypocritical self-justification reveals a Murray who has learned better than almost any other admirer of Burns from the pioneering handling of unwitting self-condemnation in that great dramatic monologue, 'Holy Willie's Prayer'.

'Dockens afore his Peers'

'Dockens afore his Peers', the longest and most substantial poem in *A Sough o' War*, was written soon after the introduction of the Military Service Act in January 1916, which brought conscription for single men aged 18 to 40 years old, unless they were widowers with children or ministers of religion. Military Service Tribunals adjudicated cases where men argued for exemption from conscription – sometimes for the reason that their presence on the home front was necessary for the continuation of an essential business. So sensitive were these cases that in the years that succeeded the Great War, the British government asked local authorities to destroy the papers of Military Service Tribunals; as a result, the records for Aberdeenshire no longer exist. If, like 'Holy Willie's Prayer', Murray's poem depends on local gossip (as it may), the evidence is gone, and only 'Dockens afore his Peers' remains.

Murray's poem's early lines may seem innocent enough. The speaker nervously urges the members of the tribunal (whom he clearly knows well) not to take too long over his case because he has other errands to run in the community, such as delivering some eggs and speaking to the vet about a heifer's legs. Yet as 'Dockens afore his Peers' progresses, the speaker's self-interested ruthlessness becomes more and more apparent. Where 'Holy Willie's Prayer' makes readers laugh as well as censure, though, Murray's 1917 monologue is more likely to provoke a less humorous sense of revulsion as its wheedling wartime speaker, while according his wife some praise, slights his 'never weel' daughter, explaining that the kitchen maid does much of the work:

> She's big an' brosy, reid and roch, an' swippert as she's stoot,
> Gie her a kilt instead o' cotts, an' thon's the gran' recruit.

Dockens then proceeds to argue that all of the many men on the farm are vital for its successful operation, and should not be conscripted: some are half-witted, or too old, or too young. Eventually, he argues, though, that any of the people on the farm – wife, daughter, serving men – should be taken, rather than his own son Johnnie:

> Fat does he dee? Ye micht as weel spear fat I dee mysel',
> The things he hisna time to dee is easier to tell;
> He dells the yard, an' wi' the scythe cuts tansies on the brae,
> An' fan a ruck gangs throu' the mull, he's thrang at wispin' strae,
> He sits aside me at the mart, an' fan a feeder's sell't
> Tak's doon the wecht, an' leuks the beuk for fat it's worth fan fell't;
> He helps me to red up the dask, he tak's a han' at loo,
> An' sorts the shalt, an' yokes the gig, an' drives me fan I'm fou.

From all this, it emerges that Johnnie (who may be lazy) supports the farmer's hard and hard-drinking lifestyle, and that Dockens wants him exempted at least as much for his father's comfort as for the boy's own real usefulness. The poem makes manifest a self-interested hypocrisy that is all the more shocking because it does not try hard enough to conceal its selfish motivation.

Still, while to map 'Dockens afore his Peers' on to Burns's great portrayal of Holy Willie's hypocrisy makes considerable sense, it is not quite that aspect of Murray's poem which makes it remarkable. Instead, its peculiar force comes from its power to overawe the reader with Dockens's absolute dedication to land and language. The speaker may not be willing to have his folk fight for his country, but in his language and his obsessive commitment to the farm, he puts up a fight of his own which radiates a distinctive, disturbing but also impressive, invincibility.

The poem begins with an apparently throwaway remark, a conversation-starter: 'Nae sign o' thow yet.' This opener establishes a vernacular tone, but its focus on the weather, that aspect of life so significant to any farmer, indicates at the very start that from the poem's alcoholic beginning to its dram-drinking end, the speaker (who, not without swagger, also names himself in the first line) will be ruthlessly alert to anything that will benefit his farm. The word 'war' occurs in line two, but this is a poem where the farmer's weather takes precedence over the war.

One of the aspects of the poem that has so appealed to Doric readers and speakers over the decades is the intensified Scots, that 'Afro-Scots' made all the more impasto by its willed retention and artistic development by Murray in South Africa. For readers such as my father, there was not just the excitement of recognising Aberdeenshire words familiar in speech, though much less frequently found on the page; there was also the pleasure in registering the sheer literary density of Murray's Doric usage. Anyone who has to have recourse to the end-of-book glossary which Murray supplied with the first and subsequent editions of *A Sough o' War*, or even to the on-page glosses in *The Penguin Book of Scottish Verse*, is struck, surely, by the quantity of necessary translation. Murray's Doric here is an impressively impasto Scots.

> He slivvers, an' has sic a mant, an ae clog-fit as weel;
> He's barely sense to muck the byre, an' cairry in the scull,
> An' park the kye, an' cogue the caur, an' scutter wi' the bull.

Most readers need help with this, requiring to be told that 'slivvers' means 'drools'; that 'sic a mant' means 'such a stutter'; that 'ae clog-fit' is a club-foot; that a 'scull' is a basket; and that the third line quoted above translates into English (following the *Penguin Book of Scottish Verse* gloss) as 'And take the cattle to the field, feed the calves, and work awkwardly with the bull'. Even though these three lines may include Scots words that are still familiar to most Scottish readers (words such as 'byre', meaning 'cowshed'), no reader, whether from Aberdeenshire or far beyond, can fail to be struck by the virtuoso density of the Scots language here. The words are piled up, the texture thickened, and the mix enriched by kinds of repetition ('an' . . . an' . . . an'), alliteration ('barely . . . byre, cogue the caur'), and glances of internal rhyme ('barely . . . byre'), all of which add to the pronouncedly impasto effect of the vocabulary. On the whole, the verbal grain grows more dense as the poem progresses, even though the spoken acoustic remains strong. Murray does not leave the vernacular behind, but he does compact it to a point that impresses all readers, and causes problems for some; yet, this very problematic quality of the Doric for 'outside' readers is also a strength in the poem. Dockens is a man speaking out of a sense of tribal articulation: the more he talks of 'ploo', 'corn' and 'hens' (all words that readers are likely to understand), the more he stresses his indomitable identification with farming and land; even more so, when he speaks of having to 'park the kye, an' cogue the caur, an' scutter wi' the bull' he voices the dialect of a tribe apparently inseparable from its terrain.

Dockens is certainly aware of the world of 'trench' warfare, but his very mention of 'a trench awa' in fat-ye-ca't' signals that his impasto Scots will not really take in the foreign-ness of 'fat-ye-ca't' (presumably a Francophone place name). Dockens's stubborn, thrawn adherence to local language may be a sign of limitation, but in this poem it also goes with his unshakeably strong adhesion to his own rural ground. Enlisting he sees as something predominantly for urban folk and others who are not rooted on the farm:

> There's men aneuch in sooters' shops, an' chiels in mason's yards,
> An' counter-loupers, sklaters, vrichts, an' quarrymen, an cyaurds,
> To fill a regiment in a week, withoot gyaun vera far,
> Jist shove them in ahin' the pipes, an' tell them that it's War [. . .]

Dockenhill farm, though, is, for 'John Watt o' Dockenhill' the centre of the universe, and its survival, indeed, is essential to even the greatest metropolis: otherwise, 'faur [where] will London get the beef[?]'. Murray may portray his speaker towards the end of the poem as winning his argument, and exemption from military service, through corruption, but for many readers it is the strength of vocabulary and obsessive attachment to territory as much as (and even more than) the strength of corrupt practice that is most impressive. Murray may be writing a poem designed to show the cowardly trickery of a speaker who seeks to wriggle out of duties to King and Empire, but such is Murray's own intense delight in Doric and local fidelity that, perhaps despite his conscious intention, what he ends up producing is a testament to the undeflectable and almost maniacal adherence of Dockens to his own land and people.

The land is less 'Scotland' (mentioned once in the poem) than it is 'Dockenhill' (mentioned three times). Where Yeats in 'An Irish Airman Foresees his Death' emphasises, while using the national identifier 'Irish' in his title, that the military pilot's adherence is to specific locale more than to nation ('My country is Kiltartan Cross'), Murray in 'Dockens afore his Peers' has the resolutely non-military farmer–speaker enunciate a message that, for him too, locale seems to trump, though not necessarily deny, national affiliation.[19]

Naming is part of what creates this effect in Murray's poem: the farm name 'Dockenhill' becomes 'Dockens', and other folk in the poem (from 'Briggie' and 'Mains' early on to 'Larickleys' and 'Gutteryloan' at the inveigling end) are also called after their farms – further binding person to terrain. However, it is the Doric vocabulary more than anything else that enforces the inseparable bonding between the speaker and the territory with which he so tenaciously identifies. In the substantial poem, whose protagonist seems more stubbornly aware of the 'yafa wedder [awful weather]' and of how 'The ploos are roustin' i' the fur, an' a' the wark's ahin" than he seems *au fait* with details of the progress of the war, Murray has produced an impasto portrait of the sort of absolute bloody-mindedness and self-willed survival instinct necessary to stay on the land. John Watt (whom readers remember not by his given parental name but by the name he derives from his farm) becomes an unsettling but undeniably impressive north-eastern incarnation of the farmer as survivor. He speaks from and for the land.

This, surely, is why Nan Shepherd, in her very perceptive Introduction to the 1979 edition of *Hamewith: The Complete Poems of Charles Murray*, published for the Charles Murray Trust by Aberdeen University Press, calls 'the portrait of Dockens . . . a magnificent crag of a thing'. Shepherd also presents this poem, along with 'Fae France', as one of Murray's 'two poems of the First World War [which] come nearest of all to greatness'.[20] The poem's power comes not just through the way it indicts its own speaker, even as he secures exemption for the son who will inherit the farm, but also from its acoustically virtuosic articulation of an indomitable voice of the land. Arguably more forcefully than any of his lyric poems, including the poem 'Hamewith' (which gave Murray his pen name and which, in turn, became the name of so many dwelling-places), the poem 'Dockens afore his Peers' gives voice to what most impressed the soldier–poet Charles Murray about the farming community he came from.

Wider Connections

In the digital era, it is all too easy to assume connections where none may exist. Is it likely, for instance, that the title of Lewis Grassic Gibbon's most famous novel, *Sunset Song*, echoes the title of Elizabeth Akers's *The Sunset Song*, published in Boston over a quarter of a century earlier?[21] Probably not. However, digital scholarship may also lead us to rely too much on precise verbal links (easily searchable terms) rather than considering connections in literary culture which depend more on tone and stance. It seems extremely improbable that the young James Leslie Mitchell, a north-east Scottish teenager when *A Sough o' War* first appeared, grew up unaware of Murray's poetry, which was being published in the local newspapers as well as in book form; by the time Mitchell was about to publish his own first book, Murray's *Hamewith and Other Poems* (which collected the poems of *A Sough o' War* alongside the poet's other work) was being published in London by Constable. Certainly, we have clear evidence that Mitchell was aware of Murray's poetry when, as 'Lewis Grassic Gibbon', Mitchell co-authored with Hugh MacDiarmid the 1934 survey volume *Scottish Scene*; in the section called 'Literary Lights', 'Dr Charles Murray' has the dubious honour of being placed at the head of Scotland's 'innumerable versifiers' in a country that can boast 'hardly more than two poets'.[22]

Yet a glance at a rare example of Gibbon's own Scots-language versifying suggests a tonal debt to Dr Murray when Mitchell writes of the 'canty, couthy fouk' who are associated with being 'Hame in the hills o' Morven / An' the shielin' in the snaw'.[23] Unlike Nan Shepherd, whose stance and diction are shaped by her admiration for 'Hamewith', Gibbon, like MacDiarmid, wished to distance himself from 'Dr Murray'. Yet Gibbon's own commitment to the farming communities of north-east Scotland which had formed him and which gave him the language, setting and themes for his finest work is worth setting beside the poetry of Murray, and not least beside 'Dockens afore his Peers'. On the map featured on the front jacket of the first edition of *Scottish Scene*, the words 'But the Land is forever' are printed across the rural area around Aberdeen. Though not authored by Charles Murray, those words sum up one of the most impressive aspects of 'Dockens afore his Peers': that poem, like Gibbon's prose in *A Scots Quair*, skewers deviousness and sly malice, but it goes beyond that in its articulation of a sometimes frighteningly intense bond to locality. Murray offered later writers the most striking example of a rich Scots-tongued articulation of the war, but in 'Dockens afore his Peers' he showed, too, how it was possible to fuse awareness of war and wartime circumstances with the expression of an abiding, often harsh loyalty to the land. This is what Gibbon, too, would accomplish in his best prose.

As mentioned above, the poems of *A Sough o' War* are precisely dated in the original book. These dates are not reproduced in the 1979 *Complete Poems*, but they went on being printed after individual poems in the reprints of the 1920s and beyond. The dates are insistent reminders that these are war poems which may be written at a distance from the trenches but are composed, in terms of chronology, very much in the thick of the action. No poem is more precisely dated than that of Dockens, ascribed to 'March 1916'. This places it in a period when the earliest 'Military Service Tribunals' were being held (significantly, the poem carries the English explanatory subtitle 'Exemption Tribunal'), but before the major battles of Verdun and the Somme, which took place later in 1916. Given that Murray's book was first published in April 1917, its initial and subsequent readers would have been very aware of the seriousness of issues of exemption, and of their consequences. These dates give the work all the sharper 'bite' as war poetry; yet their removal from some modern editions may be helpful if it encourages readers to reflect on the poetry not just as war poetry but as work which might be capable of shaping wider literary currents, including the work of Shepherd, Gibbon and MacDiarmid.

MacDiarmid slighted Murray in his prose, yet had hoped at one time to present himself as a poet of the Great War. The Murray poem which most clearly influenced MacDiarmid does not come from *A Sough o' War* but is none the less a powerful war poem, written by the Alford poet when he looked back on the recent carnage from the vantage point of his 1920 collection *In the Country Places*. Murray's book title comes from the lines by Robert Louis Stevenson which he chooses for his volume's epigraph:

> In the highlands, in the country places,
> Where the old plain men have rosy faces,
> And the young fair maidens
> Quiet eyes.

But Murray's post-war war poem 'Gin I Was God' has an anger about it that sets it apart:

> Gin I was God, sittin' up there abeen,
> Weariet nae doot noo a' my darg was deen,
> Deaved wi' the harps an' hymns oonendin' ringin',

Tired o' the flockin' angels hairse wi' singin',
To some clood-edge I'd daunder furth an', feth,
Look ower an' watch hoo things were gyaun aneth.
Syne, gin I saw hoo men I'd made mysel'
Had startit in to pooshan, sheet an fell,
To reive an' rape, an' fairly mak' a hell
O' my braw birlin' Earth, – a hale week's wark –
I'd cast my coat again, rowe up my sark,
An', or they'd time to lench a second ark,
Tak' back my word an' sen' anither spate,
Droon oot the hale hypothec, dicht the sklate,
Own my mistak', an', aince I'd cleared the brod,
Start a' thing ower again, gin I was God.[24]

This is surely the poem that, more than any other, gives MacDiarmid the 'God's eye-view' technique which he develops as part of his cosmological imagination in poems including 'The Bonnie Broukit Bairn' and 'The Innumerable Christ', written not long after the publication of Murray's *In the Country Places*. For all that Murray may have given MacDiarmid that particular spur, however, his importance for the on-going current of Scots poetry lies in the density of his 'Afro-Scots' Doric, which, more intensely freighted with distinctively Scots vocabulary than the Scots poetry of Stevenson and other late nineteenth-century writers, prepared the way for MacDiarmid's love of impasto lexis and for 'synthetic Scots'.

Gibbon and MacDiarmid may have been justified in some of their withholding of praise from Murray's work: it lacks imaginative range and a sense of full engagement with modernity in its refusal to engage with the African and urban worlds in which Murray himself spent so much time; it is nostalgic; it lapses into sentimentalism. Yet at the same time its deliberate narrowing, and its hoarding of Doric locutions, allow it a deep purchase on local subject matter which gains a convincing resonance, a voice that carries. Murray's was at once a vernacular and a heightened art speech, one that may sound even more consciously heightened to most modern ears. Yet some of his best work was his war poetry, where he fused a sly vernacular bite ('O' my braw birlin' Earth – a hale week's wark –') with a feeling for form and rhyme, as well as with a love of compacting distinctively Scots words to thicken the weave of the verse ('Droon oot the hale hypothec, dicht the sklate') to produce a music that is characteristically his. This Doric music powers some of the finest and most distinctive poems written by Scottish poets during the Great War – and nowhere more so than in *A Sough o' War*.

Notes

1. Charlotte Peacock, *Into the Mountain: A Life of Nan Shepherd* (Cambridge: Galileo, 2017), p. 16.
2. Charles Murray, *In the Country Places* (London: Constable, 1921), p. 1.
3. Ibid. p. 25.
4. Charles Murray, letter to his wife, 3 December 1900, qtd in Alex R. Scott, *Ours the Harvest: A Life of Charles Murray* (Aberdeen: Charles Murray Memorial Fund, 2004), p. 67.
5. Quoted in ibid. p. 56.
6. *In the Country Places*, p. 25.
7. Charles Murray, *Hamewith*, with Introduction by Andrew Lang (London: Constable, 1921), p. vi.
8. Andrew Lang, Introduction to *Hamewith*, p. xiii.
9. Anon., 'Charles Murray, The Scots Poet of To-day', *Courier-Mail* (Brisbane, Queensland, Australia) (2 December 1933), Electric Scotland. Available at <https://www.electricscotland.com/poetry/charles_murray.htm> (last accessed 14 May 2020).
10. Lang, Introduction to *Hamewith*, p. xiii.
11. Charles Murray, *A Sough o' War* (London: Constable, 1917), p. 13.
12. For the full texts of these poems and discussion of them, see Robert Crawford, *Scotland's Books: The Penguin History of Scottish Literature* (London: Penguin, 2007), pp. 535–42.
13. Murray, *A Sough o' War*, pp. 5, 7, 9, 15, 18.
14. Ibid. p. 36.
15. Ibid. p. 21.
16. Ibid. p. 30.
17. Ibid. p. 49.
18. 'Dockens afore his Peers' is printed on pages 37–43 of *A Sough o' War*.
19. W. B. Yeats, *Collected Poems*, 2nd edn (London: Macmillan, 1950), p. 152.
20. Nan Shepherd, 'Charles Murray', in *Hamewith: The Complete Poems of Charles Murray* (Aberdeen: published for the Charles Murray Trust by Aberdeen University Press, 1979), p. xi.
21. Elizabeth Akers, *The Sunset-song and Other Verses* (Boston: Lee and Shepard, 1902). Though the title poem indicates that its author, like Grassic Gibbon, had an interest in Persia, the fact that the book seems to have enjoyed only a limited circulation and is not listed by COPAC as being held by any British libraries makes it very unlikely that the author of *Sunset Song* was aware of it.
22. Hugh MacDiarmid and Lewis Grassic Gibbon, *Scottish Scene, or The Intelligent Man's Guide to Albyn* (London: Jarrolds, 1934), p. 199.
23. 'Morven', in *Smeddum: A Lewis Grassic Gibbon Anthology*, ed. Valentina Bold (Edinburgh: Canongate Classics, 2001), p. 213.
24. Murray, *Hamewith*, p. 101.

Chapter 13

'But Change, Nothing Abides': *Sunset Song* and the Nature of Change
John Lucas

I.

Leslie Mitchell must have known he was on to something special when he conceived the idea of *A Scots Quair*. *Sunset Song*, the first novel of what from the outset the author planned as a trilogy, was, as his biographer, Ian S. Munro notes, written in a white heat of inspiration that often drove him to exceed the daily output of a thousand words to which he had committed himself. Munro also reports that the novel 'was composed . . . straight onto the typewriter, with practically no revision, and the original typescript shows only an occasional change of word'.[1] As for the overall title, *A Scots Quair*, it is a blend of modesty – that indefinite article – and ambition. Ambitious, but not uniquely so.

You can find other examples in the inter-war period of large fictional undertakings: to name three of the better-known instances, *The Forsyte Saga* (1922), *A Glastonbury Romance* (1932) and *A Chronicle of Ancient Sunlight* ((1951–69) (though this was published later, Williamson had been brooding over it for many years). Romance; chronicle; quair. All imply historical narratives which, depending on the manner of telling, can incorporate elements of folklore, the long perspectives of a shared past that feels remote and yet in some sense recoverable, if only through an effort of imagination – the effort made by the novelist. Munro notes that Mitchell was 'determined that his novel would be authentically and naturally Scottish. He had a retentive memory, and the places and folk of his childhood were fresh in his mind.'[2] And, as aids, the author drew on *Geography of the County of Kincardine* and a large-scale map of the district, which 'still retains three additions made in ink in the author's own hand, Kinraddie, Segget, and Dundon, the places of the three novels which make up the *Quair*'.³

For many looking back to pre-war days, the cataclysm of the 1914–18 war seemed to have brought about an absolute break between the pre- and post-war worlds:

> Never such innocence,
> Never before or since,
> As changed itself to past
> Without a word –.⁴

But, in fact, millions of words testified to the change: hence the second most quoted opening sentence of a novel after that of *Pride and Prejudice*, 'The past is a foreign country, they do things differently there.'⁵ L. P. Hartley's *The Go-Between*, published in 1953, is about Edwardian England. And certainly, the young gentlemen who people Hartley's novel are a world away from the teddy boys who, in 1953, were beginning to make their mark – often literally, by means of razor and bicycle-chain – on post-war society. There is still a widely shared belief that anyone living through the inter-war years accepted that the Great War marked the expulsion from paradise.

There were premonitions of this fall. As early as 1915, Henry James, in an essay called 'Within the Rim', wrote of how, at what he called 'the dark hour' – the declaration of war in August, 1914, he found himself summoning up all that made England a place of 'settled sea-confidence':

> the mere spread of the great trees, the mere gathers in the little bluey-white curtains of the cottage windows, the mere curl of the tinted smoke from the old chimneys ... the streaks of mortar between old bricks, not to speak of the call of child-voices muffled in the comforting air, became ... with a hundred other like touches, casually felt, extraordinary admonitions and symbols, close links of a tangible chain.⁶

And a year later, D. H. Lawrence wrote to Lady Cynthia Asquith to tell her that:

> When I drive across this country, with the autumn falling and rustling to pieces, I am so sad, for my country, for this great wave of civilisation, 2000 years, which is now collapsing, that it is hard to live. So much beauty and pathos of old things passing away ... many exhausted,

lovely yellow leaves, that drift over the lawn, and over the pond, like the soldiers, passing away, into winter and the darkness of winter ... For the winter stretches ahead, where all vision is lost and all memory dies out.[7]

James's essentially rural, pastoral vision of an England known through 'close links of a tangible chain' is, perhaps, excusable. I find it harder to sympathise with Lawrence mourning the great wave of civilisation which, after all, had done its damnedest to drown the many for whom lawn and pond belonged to a country in which they had no share, even though many soldiers were by then passing into the darkness of winter.

But not necessarily a winter where all vision is lost. What some saw as winter was for others a time of spring. Against Lawrence's words, we could, after all, set the address given by the Minister, Robert Colquhoun, when at the end of *Sunset Song* he unveils the memorial to the dead of Blawearie:

> these were the Last of the Peasants, the last of the Old Scots folk. A new generation comes up that will know them not, except as a memory in a song ... And the land changes ... a new spirit shall come to the land with the greater herd and the great machines.

Which words, the narrator tells us, left the folk standing 'dumb-founded, this was just sheer politics'.[8]

II.

Not the least remarkable achievement of the work is the invention of a narrative voice which can be now at a distance from the scene it records – a kind of voice in the clouds – and then able to scrutinise close up particular moments as they pass. The novel's Prelude reads, for all the world, like a fanciful history of Kinraddie, whose lands 'had been won by a Norman childe, Copatrick de Gondeshil, in the days of William the Lyon, when gryphons and suchlike beasts still roamed the Scots countryside and folk would waken in their beds to hear the children screaming'. If, as the *Oxford English Dictionary* says, a chronicle is 'a detailed and continuous record of events in order of time', we can probably agree that *Sunset Song* is a chronicle of sorts. It is, though, more difficult to accept the dictionary definition of a chronicle as providing a record which is 'without interpretation'.[9] No record, however detailed and continuous, can ever be complete; each omits whatever seems too insignificant to bother about. And as Socialist historians in particular have noted, chronicle histories have, until recently, excluded the mass of ordinary people and the events that shaped their lives. They did not count. Even more important than the interpretation of what counts and what does not, and therefore what can be excluded and what included, is the chronicler's attitude, the tone of voice, which extends all the way from reverence to condescension. As E. P. Thompson famously remarked, one of the functions of history from the bottom up is 'to rescue the poor stockinger . . . from the enormous condescension of posterity'.[10]

But one thing that chroniclers have in common is what, in narrative fiction, is sometimes called episodic intensification. Ten years may pass in a sentence; one day may require many pages. The chronicler of *Sunset Song*, like all chroniclers from *The Iliad* onward, requires both a panoptic vision and the ability to zoom in on moments that require intense scrutiny. To handle both with equal sophistication, as the author of *Sunset Song* does, is rare. To take one instance, the account of Chris's wedding celebrations is a triumph of attentive, intense celebratory writing, for which the only comparable instances I can think of in modern literature are the scene in *Far from the Madding Crowd* (1874) where Bathsheba and Gabriel work together through the lightning storm to save the newly made hayricks, and then Anna and Will's moonlight gathering of sheaves in *The Rainbow* (1915), which Lawrence, at some level, certainly derived from Hardy.

As for what I call the panoptic vision, there are the many moments where the novel's narrative voice withdraws to a distance, from where commentary can become by turns sardonic, sympathetic, wondering and caustic. This is the voice which, again and again, begins a sentence and, often, a paragraph with the word 'So'. 'So': that is how it happened, that is how events unfolded, that is how the history of a place reveals itself. 'So that was Kinraddie that black winter of nineteen-eleven'; 'So that was their coming to Blawearie'; 'So through the wood and right into the hands of the daftie she went'; 'So there father lay and had lain ever since'; 'So out they all went to the kitchen'; 'So they did as they'd planned, the afternoon flew, it was golden and green'; 'So Chae wandered his round of Kinraddie, a strange place and desolate with its crash of trees and its missing faces.'[11] So: this is how things turned out, this is the story, this is a Scots quair.

And this is a chronicle of a people living at a specific moment, one that is inevitably transient, as all moments are. As here, in the account of the immediate post-war Blawearie, where the memory of Long Rob's songs begins to fade: 'they were daft and old-fashioned, there were fine new ones in their places, right from America, folk said, and all about the queer blue babies that were born there, they were clever brutes, the Americans'.[12] Against the tragic events that affect individuals caught in a moment of time, there are the longer perspectives, the unravelling of time, of change. Another example: for Chae Strachan, the cutting down of the woods above his farm is calamitous, the end of his hopes for return to the place he left to go to fight. Home on leave, he meets one of the locals, Ellison, and Ellison says:

> *I'll bet you want back to the front line, eh?* And Chae said he'd be wrong in the betting, faith ay! *Did you ever hear tell of a body of a woman that wanted a new bairn put back in her womb?* And Ellison gowked and said *No*. And Chae said, *And neither have I, you gowk-eyed gomeril*, and left him at that; and it was hardly a kindly remark, you would say.
>
> But it seemed the same wherever he went in Kinraddie, except at the Mill and his father-in-law's: every soul made money and didn't care a damn though the War outlasted their lives; they didn't care though the land was shaved of its timber till the whole bit place would soon be a waste with the wind a-blow over heath and heather where once the corn came green.[13]

But by the end of the war Chae is dead, and with his death and, of course, the death of Long Rob, a kind of life goes, one that cannot be replaced. As Raymond Tallis says in his recent *Of Time and Lamentation*, 'the events that occupy 12 December 2016 [when Tallis was presumably writing that sentence] leave no time behind them when midnight strikes. The day is not there to be refilled.'[14] We may lament its passing but the chronicler cannot bring it again *except* as memory, and the only way to fill it is through the chronicling of the people who did fill it and whose language, argot, figures and rhythms of speech survive through the efforts of the chronicler, imperfect as these will be.[15]

Hence, the 'Note', with which Grassic Gibbon prefaces the trilogy:

> If the great Dutch language disappeared from literary usage and a Dutchman wrote in German a story of the Lekside peasants, one may hazard he would ask and receive a certain latitude and forbearance in his usage of German. He might import into his pages some score or so untranslatable words and idioms – untranslatable in their context and setting; he might mould in some fashion his German to the rhythms and cadence of the kindred speech that his peasants speak . . .
>
> The courtesy that the hypothetical Dutchman might receive from German a Scot may invoke from the great English tongue.[16]

III.

Ultimately, the voice, whether recording especial moments or reporting a sequence of events, is created by Lewis Grassic Gibbon. But this, as we know, is a pseudonym, one that Leslie Mitchell created specifically for his trilogy. Mitchell took the pseudonym from his grandmother's maiden name: Lilias Grassick Gibbon. This is the reversal of accustomed practice, one made familiar in the nineteenth century when women authors sheltered under male pseudonyms, or at least ones to which gender could not be confidently ascribed: George Eliot, Vernon Lee, Michael Field, Currer, Acton and Ellis Bell. Lewis Grassic Gibbon may not be for sure a woman's name, but intriguingly, when the novel was first published, some readers at least were unsure of the author's gender. A hostile review in the *Fife Herald* questioned whether 'the author, or authoress, is correct in the description of crofter girls' underwear'; and Donald Carswell wrote to praise the author for writing 'the best Scotch book since Galt', adding 'I don't know who you are, though I have several suspicions, all involving your sex.'[17]

Does it matter? Of course. 'But change, nothing abides,' Colquhoun says in his address, and *Sunset Song* does not merely endorse his remark, it is what the novel is about.[18] That is why it is significant that a woman should be at the novel's heart. Admittedly, this is not new. Many important nineteenth-century and early twentieth-century novels had women as their mediating voices or put them at the centre of events, and not only those written by women. There is, after all, Becky Sharp. There is Amy Dorrit, that weak figure with its strong purpose. There is Clara Hopgood, eponymous heroine of William Hale White's great, and greatly neglected, novel; there are Bathsheba Everdene and, perhaps, Sue Bridehead; there are the Schlegel sisters and, after them, Ursula and Gudrun Brangwen.

Most important, for the present discussion, is George Eliot's preoccupation with the role of women in society. It is Eliot who – above all others, perhaps – concerns herself about women as agents of change. And in this she has theory to sustain her. I do not want to go over yet again the well-documented history of Eliot's adherence to Positivistic ideas. We do, however, need to recall Comtean/Positivistic theory, which regarded progress through human history as inevitable – from the Theological epoch, through the Metaphysical to the Positivistic, at which humanity had now arrived. Comte required certain women, whom he called Saints of Humanity, to embody the Altruistic spirit on which change depended. It could not be managed without them.

Comte feminises the Great Man theory of history. Advancement into the fully Positivistic epoch depends on great women. To put it semi-parodically, Eliot's fiction explores ways in which the actions of women make possible a future in which, as is said at the end of *Middlemarch*, 'things are not so ill with you and me'.[19]

Though her fiction is unique in its measured, sympathetic assessment of how different individuals respond to crises in their lives, Eliot's melioristic vision is typical of nineteenth-century views of change. Change is progress. The future will surely be better, even if, at any one moment, change itself seems catastrophic to those who experience it: hence the requirement for a narrator who can both empathise with individual lives, as Eliot does, and see them in a larger, social context, as she also does. In some ways, her thinking about society anticipates that of Simone Weil, who, in *The Need for Roots*, argues that a healthy society is a repository of cultural values that symbolises respect for the past and aspiration for the future, and that it is important for each collectivity (her word for community, large as well as small) 'to preserve its roots in the past to the extent that it provides sustenance for a certain number of people'.[20]

But for all her imaginative identification with those of her characters whom she presents as gripped by the past, its superstitions, its ways of working, Eliot has a measure of impatience with its claims. Hardy's novels are more in sympathy with Weil's deep sense of the need for a rooted collectivity, and this is evident in the way he writes about women. Hardy is not, I think, a meliorist. Change is inevitable, but he is more ready than Eliot to count the cost. In *The Woodlanders*, for example, the young Grace Melbury is in love with Giles Winterbourne; but her father educates her to have greater expectations than to marry a yeoman and, as a result, she ends up in an unhappy marriage to Dr Fitzpiers. Grassic Gibbon's confrontation with the inevitability of change leans more to Hardy's measured embrace of the future. The fact of change is an ineluctable truth. But the cost can be terrible – catastrophic to those caught up in a particular moment of its enactment.

IV.

Education is one of the great engines of social change, for men and for women. Nan Shepherd's *The Quarry Wood* (1928) has at its centre a young woman who, unlike Chris Guthrie, does, in the words of Rory Watson, make the 'difficult journey towards intellectual and emotional maturity at a time when such space was seldom freely given to women'.[21] By contrast, Chris Guthrie chooses not to go to university, and it is inevitable that we speculate on whether Grassic Gibbon is responding to Shepherd in a masculinist way by implying that Chris's true place is hearth and home. That is where women belong. This is certainly what Angus Calder thinks. In his essay 'A Mania for Self-Reliance: Grassic Gibbon's *Scots Quair*', he argues that, by the end of the trilogy, Chris has reverted to 'present values [which] drag her into regression, stasis, and death'.[22]

It is possible. And certainly the title, *Sunset Song*, suggests that, from the first, Grassic Gibbon's novel is planned as an elegy for a way of life which the war has been instrumental in destroying. Ancient battles are evoked by the standing stone, which, at the opening of the novel, we are told was raised when the Picts beat the Danes, and which, at the end, carries the names of those killed in France – Charles Strachan, James Leslie, Robert Duncan, Ewan Tavendale. The stone acts as memorial to a way of life which, in his address, Colquhoun describes as gone beyond recall. '*The last of the peasants*', he tells his listeners,

> *those four that you knew, took that with them to the darkness and the quietness of the places where they sleep. And the land changes. Their parks and their steadings are a desolation where the sheep are pastured, we are told that great machines come soon to till the land, and the great herds come to feed on it, the crofter is gone, the man with the house and the steading of his own and the land closer to his heart than the flesh of his body.*[23]

Colquhoun's words, the narrator remarks, 'dumbfounded' his listeners. 'This was just sheer politics'.[24] Well, yes, and the politics are avowedly Socialist. But more than that. In 1932, their resonance would have had a special meaning, for this was the moment when Stalin began his war – scarcely too strong a word – to collectivise Soviet farms and dispossess the peasants of their homes and plots of land. And this was to be done in the interest of creating a new world. Below the four names on Kinraddie's standing stone we read 'REVELATION : II CH :28 VERSE'. What the verse says is 'And I will give him the morning star,' and the title of the preacher's address is 'FOR I WILL GIVE YOU THE MORNING STAR'.[25]

V.

At this point, I want to throw in another name, that of Hugh MacDiarmid, a great admirer of *A Scots Quair*. He was, though, no admirer of English accounts of the Great War. When the concluding volume of Siegfried Sassoon's memoirs, *Sherston's Progress*, was published in 1936, MacDiarmid wrote:

> Despite the undeniable honesty, the little literary gift,
> What is *Sherston's Progress* but an exposure
> Of the eternal Englishman
> Incapable of rising above himself,
> And traditional values winning
> Over an attempted Independence of mind.[26]

Immediately after the end of the war, Sassoon, who by 1917 had turned from patriotic soldier to vehement protester at the war's continuance, became a Socialist. But as the 1920s progressed, he began to regress into the squirarchical mode which makes his trilogy a lament for a lost way of life, what MacDiarmid calls 'traditional values'. By contrast, *Sunset Song* faces the inevitability of change with the hope implied by the famous phrase from Revelation, 'I will give him the morning star.'

And yet. Even Colquhoun's words imply something approaching an anguish of loss. The four men killed, 'the last of the peasants [. . .] took that with them'.[27] Took *what* with them, exactly? Peasant values, I suppose. Yet this seems an inadequate phrase, a kind of belittlement of individuality, especially in the figure of Long Rob. It comes as no surprise to find that, among the many letters written to the author in praise of *Sunset Song*, several identified Long Rob as their favourite character. One young woman went so far as to say that 'I often think it would be nice to marry someone like this', and added, 'I am not a frustrated spinster because I'm still nineteen.'[28]

I do not myself think it a weakness that the novel – perhaps the trilogy as a whole – should engage with, and perhaps be unable to resolve, the tension between what Wordsworth called 'forward looking thoughts' and the regret for a lost way of life.[29] In this irresolution can be found, I think, the 'roots' that Simone Weil spoke of as an essential to any true collective. And Grassic Gibbon's acknowledgement of this will explain the title the author gives to the final, post-war section of *Sunset Song*, EPILUDE: a term I take to be the novelist's coinage, what the Greeks call a hapex. The subtitle to EPILUDE repeats the one given to the novel's opening, 'The Unfurrowed Field'. That had referred to a time before the land was properly settled; this refers to a future where 'great machines' will replace man and horse.

The 1914–18 war was the first great machine war. 'The war machine' is, of course, an ambiguous phrase. It refers both to technology and to bureaucracy. In both inflexions, individual agency counts for little.

Heroism will not determine the fact, let alone the nature, of change. For Marx, belief in the crucial role of Saints of Humanity is simply hogwash. And by the early years of the twentieth century, Positivism had more or less died the death. As the events of 1914–18 made plain, social change was not engineered by heroic individuals but by 'hooded hordes'.[30] For T. S. Eliot, from whom that phrase, of course, comes, the war is catastrophe: the new age is a waste land.

Sunset Song does not endorse this reading of history, persuasive though it was for many, but in welcoming 'great machines to till the land' Colquhoun acknowledges the dwindling into death of heroic individualism. Long Rob, that man of lonely integrity and nay-saying wit, eventually becomes a soldier and dies in France; and the narrator reports that 'just notice of his death came through and syne a bit in the paper about him'. Yes, he died well: covering a retreat, for which he was awarded a medal. But, the narrator adds, 'Not that he got it, faith! He was dead, they came on his corpse long after, the British, but just as a mark of respect.'[31]

And Chris? As wife and mother, war at first means nothing to her:

> One night, the mid-days of August as they sat at meat, the door burst open and in strode Chae Strachan, a paper in his hand, and was fell excited, Chris listened and didn't, a war was on, Britain was to war with Germany. But Chris didn't care and Ewan didn't either, he was thinking of his coles the weather might ruin; so Chae took himself off with his paper again, and after that, though she minded it sometimes, Chris paid no heed to the war, there were aye daft devils fighting about something or the other, as Ewan had said [. . .][32]

But then war intrudes into her apparently safe, enclosed, essentially pastoral/peasant life. There is a sharp economy in the narrator's report of how the community becomes infected by war fever. At first sceptical, then outraged by the Reverend Gibbon's sermonising on the war as God's plague for the world's sins, then reassured by the Minister's discovery that, after all, the Kaiser was the Antichrist, the folk shift toward belief in the rightness of the war. Long Rob holds out:

> He said it was a lot of damned nonsense, those that wanted to fight, the M.P.s and bankers and editors and muckers, should all be locked up in a pleiter of a park and made to gut each other with graips [. . .][33]

His mill is stoned by men who accuse him of pro-Germanism, and Rob sends them packing. But, to repeat, *Sunset Song* calls time on romantic individualism. Rob goes to France and is killed.

This is Ewan's fate, too. Critics have objected that Grassic Gibbon does not make Ewan's change of mind convincing, and that the enlisted Ewan's brutal rape of his wife is frankly unbelievable. The author was having none of it. Replying to a woman reader who had complained about what she called the bad art of 'Ewan's sadistic behaviour to Chris', he said, 'Ewan and the war-change is the truth – factually if not artistically.'[34] By this he must mean that, however inadequate his depiction of Ewan's change from considerate husband to brutal rapist, what he calls 'the war-change' is a matter of observable fact. War did brutalise men, and women, too.

This is fair comment. We may be less convinced about the reason Ewan reportedly offers for the act of desertion, as a result of which he is court-martialled and executed. But then we are meant to be, I think. It is, after all, Chae who reveals to Chris that her husband was shot as a deserter. Until that moment, she believes Ewan to have been killed in the line of duty. But Chae tells her that he had managed to find where Ewan was being held prior to his execution, visited him, and heard from Ewan's own mouth that his friend had deserted

> in a blink of fine weather between the rains, because *I minded Blawearie, I seemed to waken up smelling that smell. And I couldn't believe it was me that stood in the trench, it was just daft to be there. So I turned and got out of it.*[35]

Well, maybe. And at least some of it is true, because Chae reports Ewan's regret at losing Chris's love through his own 'coarse daftness', a phrase which, wincingly inadequate though it may be as an admission of rape, is something Chae could not have known about.[36] But we do not know for sure that Chae is not making at least some of it up, softening the blow for Chris. The manner of so many deaths in war was, as they always will be, a matter of speculation, of heroising, or cleaning up the often brutal reality. It was only with the publication of Matthew Hollis's biography of Edward Thomas in 2011 that we learned that Thomas did not, as his widow always insisted, die when his heart was stopped by a nearby shell, his body left unblemished. His death was far messier. This is why it was an inexcusable error for Terence Davies, in his film of *Sunset Song*, to show Ewan in prison and to make him speak the words Chae reports to Chris because this sentimentalises and grossly falsifies the novel. And to say this brings me to a last consideration.

VI.

Chris, to repeat the obvious, is at the centre of events in the novel. Sometimes the narrator pays undue attention to her, or so Isobel Murray argues. Murray claims that the novel is not only 'drenched in sex' but emphasises 'the sexual desirability of Chris [which] is regularly seized on by her (male) creator and displayed to the male gaze'.[37] I have to say neither of these observations squares with my own, admittedly male, reading; I am, however, persuaded that Chris's sexual frankness – her gazing at her naked self in the mirror, for example – feels as if it belongs to the post-war world, a time when women were undoubtedly gaining a measure of sexual freedom that was one of the war's consequences. And I can also report that when I talked about the novel in the late 1960s with American students, the women in my class identified very closely with Chris. Her resistance to her father's incestuous desire represented a denial of patriarchal social structure, her delight in her naked body represented a feminist embrace of her own sexuality, her losing Ewan to war and the deaths of Chae and Rob represented the brutal masculinist energies that were then on display in Vietnam; all this could be taken into their own experiences. 'Where Have All the Flowers Gone', they sang, and, of course, 'We Shall Overcome'.

By the end of *Sunset Song* – the Epilude – Blawearie has been sold; many of the inhabitants of Kinraddie have moved, some made wealthy by the war, others disadvantaged; and Chris herself, as the chronicling voice remarks, has, according to scandalous rumour, taken up with the new Minister, Colquhoun, who announces their marriage banns at the same time as he reveals that the Kinraddie Memorial will be unveiled the following Sunday. The mourning for the dead, for the last of the peasants, is followed by the celebration of a new union. The sardonic – or, it may be better to say, disinterested, unillusioned, chronicling voice – here subsumes Chris Guthrie into a continuing history.

In his seminal work, *The Historical Novel*, Georg Lukács argues that what he calls 'typical characters' concentrate within themselves the salient aspects of a historical moment.[38] As a Marxist, Lukács is inevitably opposed to the idea that change depends on the interventions of great men – and, far more rarely, women. But nor can the agents for change be 'average' characters. As *Sunset Song* testifies, these are the ones who, at any one moment, are acted on by circumstances. At one second they oppose the war and at the next they stone Rob Duncan's mill. They are part of change but they are not agents *for* change. Leslie Mitchell could not have read Lukács's work because it was not published until 1937 (English edition 1962), but his own Marxist position is close to the Hungarian critic's in that *A Scots Quair* surely takes for granted that 'a truly historical vision sees the past as the necessary precondition of the present'.[39]

Readers of *The Historical Novel* know that Lukács finds most novels he examines wanting in some way or another. One of the few he greatly praises is *The Heart of Midlothian* (1818) which, given Scott's High Tory romanticism, seems odd, to say the least. But for Lukács, Jeannie Deans embodies a kind of energy of resistance to the status quo which is, in its modest way, transformative. I have no idea whether Mitchell had read Scott's novel, and anyway it isn't important. What counts is that Chris Guthrie's way of *being* asserts – indeed, embodies – a process which absorbs catastrophe into change. The novel ends with the unveiling of the memorial and, then, Chris listening to the piper playing 'Flowers of the Forest'; the chronicler reports that 'folk said that Chris Tavendale alone shed never a tear, she stood quiet, looking down on Blawearie's fields till the playing was over'.[40] From here she will move, in her new marriage, to fresh, city, circumstances. Epilude indeed.

Notes

1. Ian S. Munro, *Leslie Mitchell: Lewis Grassic Gibbon* (Edinburgh: Oliver & Boyd, 1966), p. 71.
2. Ibid. p. 71.
3. Ibid. p. 71.
4. Philip Larkin, 'MCMXIV', in *Collected Poems* (London: Faber & Faber, 2003), p. 99.
5. Leslie P. Hartley, *The Go-Between* (London: Penguin, [1953] 1961), p. 7.
6. Henry James, *Within the Rim and Other Essays* (London: Collins, 1915), p. 85.
7. D.H. Lawrence, *The Letters of D. H. Lawrence*, vol. 2, ed. G. J. Zytavak and J. T. Boulton (Cambridge: Cambridge University Press, 1981), pp. 431–2.
8. Lewis Grassic Gibbon, *Sunset Song* (Pan Books: London, 1973), p. 252.
9. 'Chronical', *Oxford English Dictionary*. Available at <www.oed.com> (last accessed 29 February 2020).
10. E. P. Thompson, *The Making of the English Working Class* (New York: Random House, [1963] 1964), p. 12.
11. Gibbon, *Sunset Song*, pp. 23, 39, 49, 104, 156, 171, 201.
12. Ibid. p. 242.

13. Ibid. p. 220.
14. Raymond Tallis, *Of Time and Lamentation: Reflections on Transience* (London: Agenda, 2017), p. 39.
15. A sweetly sad newspaper article in the *Daily Telegraph* of 11 September 2017 tells its readers that 'A century-old Scottish spruce that started life as a sapling in the muddy carnage of Passchendaele is in contention to be named Europe's finest tree. In 1917, Lt. David McCabe, of the 5th Battalion Canadian Light Infantry, rescued a handful of saplings on the battlefield and sent them home to his native Crieff in Perthshire in an ammunition box. The 32-year-old died later that year from wounds sustained in the battle of Vimy Ridge, but the life he preserved amid the slaughter successfully took root in Scottish soil' (p. 10). Sadly, of course, the trees cannot refill the day, to use Tallis's words, though I should note that not far from Nottingham, at a small village called Hickling, is a hillside lined by poplars. It is called Vimy Ridge.
16. Lewis Grassic Gibbon, *A Scots Quair* (London: Penguin, [1946] 1998), p. 14.
17. Munro, *Leslie Mitchell*, pp. 74–6.
18. Gibbon, *Sunset Song*, p. 252.
19. George Eliot, *Middlemarch* (London: Penguin, [1871–2] 1994), p. 838.
20. Simone Weil, *An Anthology* (London: Penguin, 1994), p. 39.
21. Rory Watson, 'Introduction', in Nan Shepherd, *The Grampian Quartet* (Edinburgh: Canongate, 1996), p. x.
22. Angus Calder, 'A Mania for Self-Reliance: Grassic Gibbon's *Scots Quair*', in D. Jefferson and G. Martin (eds), *The Uses of Fiction* (Milton Keynes: Open University, 1982), p. 112.
23. Gibbon, *Sunset Song*, p. 252.
24. Ibid. p. 253.
25. Ibid. p. 251.
26. Qtd in 'For Ever England: The Case of Siegfried Sassoon', in John Lucas's *Moderns and Contemporaries* (Sussex: Harvester Press, 1985), p. 134.
27. Gibbon, *Sunset Song*, p. 252.
28. Qtd in Munro, *Leslie Mitchell*, p. 94.
29. William Wordsworth, 'Michael', in *The Collected Poems of William Wordsworth* (Ware: Wordsworth Editions, 1994), pp. 131–7, p. 133.
30. T. S. Eliot, 'The Waste Land', in *T. S. Eliot: Collected Poems* (London: Faber & Faber, 2002), pp. 53–70, p. 67.
31. Gibbon, *Sunset Song*, pp. 241–2.
32. Ibid. p. 183.
33. Ibid. p. 191.
34. Qtd in Munro, *Leslie Mitchell*, p. 95.
35. Gibbon, *Sunset Song*, pp. 233–4.
36. Ibid. p. 234.
37. Isobel Murray, 'Gibbon's Chris: A Celebration with Some Reservations', in M. P. McCullock and S. M. Dunnigan (eds), *A Flame in the Mearns:*

Lewis Grassic Gibbon – A Centenary Celebration (Glasgow: Association for Scottish Literary Studies, 2003), pp. 54–63, p. 59.
38. For a succinct account of Lukács's position see Harry E. Shaw's 'The Historical Novel', in M. Coyle, Peter Garside, Malcolm Kelsall and John Peck (eds), *The Encyclopedia of Literature and Criticism* (London: Routledge, 1990), pp. 531–3.
39. Ibid. p. 534.
40. Gibbon, *Sunset Song*, p. 245.

Chapter 14

Ewart Alan Mackintosh in Memoriam: Leadership, Patriotism and Posthumous Commemoration
Neil McLennan

Ewart Alan Mackintosh fell in action on 21 November 1917 at Cambrai. Until recently, Mackintosh was a 'lesser-known' poet of the Great War. His writing was talked about during the conflict and emerged to prominence again after the Second World War, and again at the start of this century. Historians Colin Campbell and Rosalind Green brought Mackintosh to public attention in 2004 with their biography of the war poet.[1] This chapter will consider how Mackintosh's legacy has been shaped by post-war acts of commemoration and republication – leading to his current place as one of the most significant Scottish Great War writers. Mackintosh's work gives an insight into his thinking on leadership, nationalism and environment. His biographers unveiled much about the life of this English-born Scot, including the preoccupation with death as a theme in his poetry. However, an important question remained: 'how, precisely, did Ewart Alan Mackintosh die?'[2] Around one hundred years after his death, with oral history testimony and a review of extant evidence, a new analysis can be made of Mackintosh's final moments and how his death has been memorialised in post-war commemoration.

A Forgotten Poet

The English Review published Mackintosh's poem 'In No Man's Land' in 1916.[3] *A Highland Regiment* (1917) saw a collection of Mackintosh's poems published, half of them written in peace and the second part in war. All mentioned death. *War, The Liberator, and Other Pieces* (1918), a further collection of Mackintosh's poems, was published posthumously. Containing puissant war poetry – but also 'Parodies and Songs' – the volume received critical approbation. *Bookman* commented, 'Mr Mackintosh's poignant little volume must rank among the best "soldier verse" that the war has given us.'[4] John Lane Publishers went on to print, 'Mackintosh will rank highly in the brotherhood of soldier poets who have found themselves since the war began.'[5] Mackintosh did not, however, receive the high esteem given to Brooke, Owen, Graves or Sassoon during the post-war period.[6] Not every Great War poetry anthology included him. One exception was Brian Gardner's edited collection *Up the Line to Death: The War Poets 1914–1918* (1964), which included Mackintosh's 'In Memoriam'.

Over a century later, Mackintosh's works again sparked interest, especially in the lead-up to and during the World War I centennial commemorations. *Forever: The Official Album of the World War One Commemorations* (2014) featured actor Danny Dyer reading 'In Memoriam' with the Central Band of the Royal British Legion playing in the background.[7] On Remembrance Sunday in 2016, Welsh singer/songwriter Cerys Matthews was invited by the Western Front Association to read the same poem at the Cenotaph in London.[8] These acts suggest that Mackintosh had come of age within the commemorative Great War canon. Hew Strachan, in his Foreword to the anthology *Beneath Troubled Skies: Poems of Scotland at War, 1914–1918*, suggested, 'Sorley and Mackintosh can stand with the best of the English-language canon, and both died too soon'.[9] Sorley is the only Scots poet to feature on the 1985 Westminster Abbey memorial to sixteen Great War poets; Mackintosh being spoken about alongside Sorley and being read as part of the national commemorations demonstrates the esteem in which he is now held.

So, who was this poet? Born in Brighton in 1893, Ewart was the son of Scottish parents. His father hailed from Ross-shire. His mother's father was a friend of William Ewart Gladstone and it is supposed that this is the origin of Mackintosh's first name, although he used the name Alan. He excelled educationally and graduated in Classics from Oxford University, where he had also served in the Officer Training Corps. At the outbreak of war, Mackintosh immediately volunteered for service; however, he was rejected on account of his poor eyesight. Undaunted by this rejection, he reapplied and was accepted by the Seaforth Highlanders (the Ross-Shire Buffs). Mackintosh was commissioned as a Second Lieutenant in the 1/5 Battalion and gazetted on 31 December 1914. He saw action in

August 1915 on the Somme. His 1/5 Seaforth Highlanders formed part of the 51st (Highland) Division, which was the first British division to take over from the French there. Early in 1916, the Division moved to a network of trenches called 'the Labyrinth' near Roclincourt village, Arras. On 16 May 1916, he was involved in a trench raid near Arras, which saw him win the Military Cross. This experience had a profound effect on Mackintosh, who saw one of his charges very badly wounded. Despite Mackintosh's desire to leave no one behind, he could not drag the wounded man – Private Sutherland – back across no-man's-land and had to leave him on the parapet of a German trench. Later, Mackintosh would reflect in the poem 'In Memoriam' (subtitled 'Private D. Sutherland killed in action in the German trench, May 16, 1916, and the others who died') on the painful and emotive task of writing a letter to Sutherland's parents informing them of the worst possible news. Mackintosh's attachment to and care for his men were evident. Their well-being was uppermost in his mind, his leadership responsibility both clear and conducted with respect and rigour. Mackintosh himself was wounded at High Wood on the Somme in July/August 1916.[10] Robert Graves was also wounded in this area and Siegfried Sassoon, like Mackintosh, mentioned High Wood in his poems. Mackintosh was invalided home and spent some time recuperating, assisting with the training of potential officers at Cambridge University. His willingness to serve others was again evident in his work.

The Cambrai offensive in November 1917 saw Mackintosh himself back on the Western Front, this time attached to the 1/4 Seaforths. He had been transferred to them for only a matter of weeks when he saw action. During heavy fighting near Cantaing Mill, Mackintosh was killed by a shot to the head. His poetry has been likened to Rupert Brooke's. Like Brooke in 'The Soldier', Mackintosh seems to foretell his own death in the poem 'Cha Till MacCruimein' with the poignant ending 'MacCruimein comes no more'.[11] The poem is a sad and evocative piece – just as Mackintosh's death would have been to the men, who greatly respected the Second Lieutenant they affectionately called 'Tosh'.

From 'the pity of war' to Servant Leadership

During the war, the brutal realities of trench life and attrition warfare challenged the notion of a 'Great War for Civilisation'. The Battle of the Somme shook the British nation and changed perceptions. Since the war, the evaluative narrative has continued to fluctuate between 'anti-war' messaging and 'heroic victors' interpretations. Mackintosh slipped into complete obscurity after the war. He re-emerged in 1927, when his poetic lines were chosen to feature on the Scottish–American (Great War) Memorial in Edinburgh. However, largely, he and the war poets remained of mild passing interest – to specialists, if at all. Even the great champion of 'the pity of war', Wilfred Owen, only really emerged in scholarship studies in the 1960s and 1970s. This was after Cecil-Day Lewis's (1964) publication of Owen's poems. That publication occurred during the Vietnam War era – a period in which the anti-war messages of the Great War poets resonated with similarly terrifying world events. During an era in which the reputation of 'the Generals' took a barrage from historians – such as Alan Clark's *The Donkeys* (1961) and John Laffin's *Butchers and Bunglers of World War One* (1988) – supposedly 'anti-war' poets were in vogue. Nevertheless, Mackintosh was not specifically one of them; his resurrection would not come until later.

In between times, the tables turned again in this battle for perceptions of the past. This time the counter-attack came to the defence of 'the Generals'. Gary Sheffield's *Forgotten Victory* (2011) attempted to cast aside the perceptions of incompetent senior military leaders generated by Alan Clark, or by Joan Littlewood's *Oh What a Lovely War* (1965), and indeed by comic characters like General Melchett in *Blackadder Goes Forth* (1989). Melchett's sweeping up soldiers on his tabletop tactics map with a dustpan summed up the popular idea of top brass disdain. Sheffield, on the other hand, argued that General Haig learned the lessons of early mistakes and had actually orchestrated a tremendous victory. Despite his subsequently negative reputation, it is worth noting that Haig's funeral in 1928 was one of the largest the country had seen. In this ebb and flow of narratives, lines have been drawn between 'heroic victory' and 'the pity of war'. However, the reality is altogether more complex.

Mackintosh, hastily buried on the battlefield in 1917 at Orival Wood, re-emerged around the time of this revisionism, in the form of Campbell and Green's 2004 biography.[12] Mackintosh's poems navigate the complexity of war experience and the conflicting viewpoints it engendered in participants. Goldie and Watson note some of the shifts in the tone of Scottish war poets' work and the complex messages contained within. They state:

> And nor, after some early-war blustering about Scottish martial pride, is it much about national majesty, dominion or power. What we find instead is [. . .] much finer, more intimate gradations to measure and record the human cost of the war and the pity it engendered.[13]

In a 1917 letter Mackintosh wrote: 'I've had my taste of a show. It is not romantic. It is hell.'[14] Mackintosh's insight into both 'the pity of war' theme and also broader nationalism, and indeed antiquarian thinking, is revealing. He skirts the edge of nationalism but not with xenophobic euphoria, rather proud patriotism with humanity first. Even the 'ancient foe' of the poem 'The Undying Race' is little described. More focus is given to tales of old and the land fighters want to return to: 'One dream of home wherein we see / River and sea and hill'.[15]

In *Goodbye to All That* (1929) Robert Graves described a stereotypical Scottish soldier, although he differentiates between the Highland and Lowland types:

> The mess agreed dispassionately that the most dependable British troops were the midland county regiments [. . .] The Ulsterman, Lowland Scots, and Northern English ranked pretty high. The Catholic Irish and Highland Scots took unnecessary risks in trenches and had unnecessary casualties; and in battle, though they usually reached their objective, too often lost it in the counter attack; without officers they become useless.[16]

On the other side of no-man's-land, hardy perceptions of Scots were similar, to a certain extent. Ernst Junger (1920) recollected:

> The Scottish position was in a deepened ditch on the other side, it was some way below where we were, in those few seconds though, we were distracted from it; the vision of the Highlanders charging along the wire entanglement was all we had eyes for [. . .] He was an easy target.

Junger also notes high respect for the fallen Scots, notably with regional identification:

> We raced past stout figures, still warm, with strong knees under their short kilts, or we crawled past them. They were Highlanders and their way of fighting showed us that we were dealing with real men.[17]

Mackintosh's writing was not pro-war. However, it was certainly pro-Highland and pro-Scottish. Brigitte Van de Pas notes that there is vengeance in Mackintosh's 'Beaumont Hamel', although we do not see that specifically.[18] Whilst the poem 'Beaumont Hamel' ends on 'Scotland's warriors streaming, Forward evermore' we do not read whom they are fighting against nor feel any sense, far less hatred, of 'the enemy' or 'the other'. Riach notes that Mackintosh's earliest poems read like heroic glorifications of war but that he quickly recognised the horror and waste he was witnessing and began writing anguished parodies.[19] Even his early poems do not plumb to the depths of division and 'otherness'. A contemporary account felt that Mackintosh had got beyond the darkness of many poets of the period: 'his poems from the war, and even those written on the way to it, reveal him as a true poet, both born and made, with a style purged of all its former cleverness and insincerity'.[20]

Whilst there were no hard feelings towards German foes, darkness was to form part of Mackintosh's signature, with death his main character. However, Strachan does not feel this overpowered him:

> This ambivalence in Brooke is often overlooked and [. . .] is perhaps most coherently expressed in E.A. Mackintosh's 'War the Liberator'. Mackintosh's poem demands that the 'authoress' of 'Non-Combatants', to which it is a riposte, acknowledge the 'fragments of high Romance' in war. Mackintosh accepts death but refuses to become its slave.[21]

Indeed, Mackintosh asks, 'Why should you be afraid to die?'[22]

The war created many heroic leaders who also rallied against the 'pity of war'. Sassoon was notably a fearless leader in trench raids and also rebelled against government incompetence via letters to *The Times*; Owen wrote eloquently and yet was decorated for his valour. Mackintosh too was awarded a Military Cross and, like Sassoon, was honoured for both attacking and rescuing. Mackintosh's conspicuous gallantry saw him lead a raid on enemy trenches and also bring wounded men back under fire. However, his was not the heroic leadership of the 'Boy's Own Paper' of the era. His was a humbler reckoning. His poems were often written for others under his charge: for example, 'To a Dead Soldier' and his 'In Memoriam' poems to R. M. Stalker and David Sutherland. Mackintosh's *A Highland Regiment*, meanwhile, was dedicated 'To the Officers and Men of the 5th Seaforth Highlanders and especially to Major A.L. MacMillan who is and will be to me as to all the rest the Major for ever.' Even in acknowledgement, the respect comes from both Mackintosh and 'the rest.' The small Mackintosh archive held at the University of Texas, Austin, gives further evidence of Mackintosh wanting to put others before self and acknowledge the men. In letters to his publisher John Lane, founder of The Bodley Head, Mackintosh is keen to state 'I hope my dedication to the regiment is going in.'[23]

Mackintosh's leadership style is what, in modern terms, would be best described as 'servant leadership', a significant shift in early leadership theories and approaches where leadership focused on 'Great Men' with specific traits.[24] More nuanced leadership theories of today focus less on the leader and more on the practice of leadership,[25] something evident in Mackintosh's approach fifty years before the approach was theorised in leadership thinking. On being put forward for a heroism honour, Mackintosh wrote home: 'I believe I've been recommended for the Military Cross, but I'd rather have the boys' lives.'[26]

This model of servant leadership is exemplified in 'In Memoriam'. Here we reflect on the duty, challenge and pain of leadership – especially when men under your charge are lost in action: in this case, young Private David Sutherland. Beyond the initial loss remains the on-going duty to 'fifty sons'. This simultaneously causes anguish but also stimulates the will to go on. However, we might reflect on the pain of Priam and his 'fifty sons' in Homer's 'The Iliad'. Mackintosh does not reflect on the man who killed his sons, as Priam did. Mackintosh reveres the fallen. It is service rather than blind heroism that we see. Mackintosh also reflects on this in his 'case studies' notes on 'Studies in War Psychology'. He captures the story of a young soldier seeking revenge on German 'swines'. An experienced Major gives the soldier a clout on the head, calls him a 'young fool' and then takes him down to HQ.[27] Blind heroism serves no one. Service and loyalty to his men were strong features of Mackintosh's life. 'No man shall break the tryst they keep,' Mackintosh noted in his unusually upbeat poem titled 'Hope'.[28] One contemporary account described Mackintosh's care and leadership of his men as 'that of a chieftain'.[29] On another level, though, did Mackintosh feel loyalty to a greater calling?

Mackintosh's Environmental Patriotism

While Mackintosh may not have become death's slave, Europe had become enslaved to excesses of nationalism that chained nations into a complex set of alliances dragging the world into war. Mackintosh's biographers talk of World War I being the outcome of that fatal concoction of aggressive nationalism.[30] This may lead us to question the alternative possibility of passive nationalism. Mackintosh may be an example of it. Mackintosh can be seen as a patriot rather than a nationalist per se. He was pro-Scottish but also respectful of the environs, others, and both local and global complexities he was living through. Most of all, his subject was humans, and humans in their environment. A memoir to Mackintosh stated: 'There is strangely little, indeed, about the war in any of them [Mackintosh's poems], but much about the minds and hearts of those who wage it.'[31] We see examples of this humanity in his poems. 'In No Man's Land' shares the story of *not* killing a German. The speaker of the poem was aware of his enemy sitting in the next shell hole only because he can hear him coughing and sneezing, and cannot bring himself to kill 'you blighter', as he compassionately refers to the enemy so nearby. The poem warms the heart in a chilly scene and the even colder era of attrition warfare. Written in 1915 from Hammerhead Wood near Thiepval on the Somme, it is a remarkable recalibration with humanity amidst the carnage of conflict. It equalises men, their plight and their pity. As discussed below, 'Snow in France' is another good example of pity being shared equally amongst combatants.

Strachan also downplays the direct nationalist narrative of Mackintosh and others, calling it 'not so much flag waving and more home and hearth'. His citing of what is essentially environmental nationalism is of interest: 'the Scotland of these poets is overwhelmingly agricultural and rural, a Scotland of mountain and moor, not of munitions production and shipbuilding'.[32] Whilst they dreamed of home, did men consciously consider the land around them during the war? Mackintosh certainly did. 'Will you walk the heather?' he asks of the fallen of 'Beaumont-Hamel'.[33] Mackintosh brings places of the past, present and even afterlife into his poems. Place is important, but natural environment more so.

Goldie and Watson comment similarly to Strachan on a different type of nationalism in Scottish war poetry, not jingoistic or aggressive but quiet, rural and both reflecting and defining people and place together:

> There are forms of quiet pride and consolation in national and regional community, from the bucolic nostalgia of Mackintosh's 'Anns an Gleann'san robh mi og' (In the glen when I was young) to the pastoral elegance of Violet Jacob, and there are examples of steadfast courage and resolution, whether in the soldier's commitment to stand by his fellow sufferers as in Kerr's 'From the Line', or in his will simply to endure, seen in W.D. Cocker's 'Sonnets in Captivity'.[34]

Furthermore, Mackintosh, like fellow 'Scottish poet' Charles Hamilton Sorley, shared multiple identities. Sorley was born in Aberdeen and educated in England. Mackintosh was born in Brighton and Oxford-educated, but culturally awakened by the spirit of the Highlands that his ancestors inhabited. Mackintosh's biographers attest that his use of rhythm, whether from the poetry of the Highlands or from his piping experience, confirms his knowledge of Highland culture.[35] However, his mixed upbringing was evident in his poetry, 'Mallaig Bay' being cited as one example.[36] Mackintosh's biographers comment, 'the poem reveals dissatisfaction with the south, and a yearning for Scotland'.[37] Even in his formal education in England's top university, Scotland had an impact on him and his learning. His second tutor at Oxford had been born in Fraserburgh, Aberdeenshire. John Murray noted of Mackintosh 'both in terms of, and out term, he [Mackintosh] cultivated, above all, the sentiments and arts of the Highlands. He learned to play the bagpipes and speak Gaelic, things which later endeared him to his regiment.'[38]

Van de Pas suggests an increase in Scottishness as a result of the war, arguing that Mackintosh's 'Scots heritage [became] radicalized'.[39] However, poems like 'Mallaig Bay' were pre-war (this one written in Sussex in 1912) and demonstrate the tensions Mackintosh felt. Mackintosh wrote that he was 'sickened of the south and the kindness of the downs' and was 'weary for the islands' and 'weary for the faces that are sorrowful and stern'.[40] Despite the 'rain cloud over stormy Coolin's brow',[41] Scotland was certainly hame for Mackintosh. His wartime poetry also promoted his passion for Scotland, but again in a measured way. 'Snow in France' neither denigrates the enemy nor ennobles his own side, and describes Saxon and Scottish sentries looking out over the wasteland that separated them. Another poem, 'The Undying Race', aims to link the current conflict to those who had fought before. Whether Mackintosh's nationalism was 'radicalized' is debatable. The poem's references to Saxon hordes and those 'beside the Gael' certainly stir some emotion from previous conflicts – not, however, in any conspicuously 'radicalized' way:

> Year upon year of ancient sleep
> Have rusted on our swords
> But once again our place we keep
> Against the Saxon hordes.
> Since Arthur ruled in Brittany,
> And all the world was new,
> The fires that burned our history,
> Burn in our spirits too.[42]

Use of the past was something regularly deployed to make sense of and convey the present in his work. Mackintosh opens 'The Lost Lands' by asking, 'Oh where are the old kingdoms, Where is the ancient way?'[43] In particular, Mackintosh's beloved piper appears in many of his poems, usually piping men through the streets to war. Examples can be heard in 'Before the Summer' (1916) and 'In Memoriam: R.M. Stalker, Missing September 1916'. 'Cha Til MacCruimein' (subtitled 'Departure of the 4th Camerons') contrasts the pipes in the street playing the rallying call with the lonely pibroch recalling older wars and losses. 'Cha Til MacCruimein', though written in World War I, refers to the historic MacLeod of Skye's piper during The '45. MacCruimein taught *piobaireachd* on Skye but was captured at the Battle of Inverurie (December 1745). Tradition had it that Jacobite pipers refused to play again until their 'King of Pipers' was released. MacCruimein was later killed in the Rout of Moy (February 1746). It is believed that Mackintosh, in recounting this story in his 'Cha Til MacCruimein' poem, is foreseeing his own death during the Battle of Cambrai, 1917. No anger is shown to the enemy.

Death and Commemoration

Mackintosh had long seen his own death, 'Cha Til MacCruimein' being the most obvious example alongside 'The Creed'. This latter poem sees the speaker resigned to being 'strong in my pride and free' if death does come calling. The poems in *A Highland Regiment* focus predominantly on death: 'To a Dead Soldier' speaks to its title; 'To a Private Soldier' talks of his death; 'Anns an Gleann'san robh mi og' (In the glen when I was young) ends with Mackintosh seeing death and fighting men; in 'In No Man's Land' 'death or capture' lurks unseen; 'The Waiting Wife' has a tune of lament for the dead not dissimilar to the 'weary tune and sore' of 'MacCruimein'; and 'Miserere' tells of 'death unseen beneath our feet, Death above us in the sky'.

The Battle of Cambrai started on 20 November 1917, ten days after the close of Third Ypres, the hell that soldiers referred to as Passchendaele. The initial attack by General Byng's 3rd Army, with some 400 tanks being deployed, was an initial success – breaking through enemy lines near Cambrai and taking many German prisoners. However, the gains could not be capitalised on. In front of the 51st Highland Division, the tanks got too far ahead of the infantrymen at Flesquières. Mackintosh was attached to the 1/4th Seaforths, transferred from the 1/5th Seaforths days before his death. He wrote a note home on 19 November:

> My darling friend ['friend' written over the initial 'girl']
> We're going over to-morrow, so I'm leaving this in case I don't come back. Goodbye.
> No time for more.
> Your loving
> Alan[44]

Days of intensive fighting followed the initial attack on 20 November. In that period, the twenty-four-year-old Mackintosh died. His death has been a historical mystery since he fell at Cambrai. Mackintosh biographers Green and Campbell ask: 'How, precisely, did Alan Mackintosh die?'[45]

The 1/4 Gordon Highlanders and 1/4 Seaforth Highlanders were pinned down. Then the tanks arrived. Supported by infantry, the aim was to capture nearby Cantaing-sur-Escaut village early that afternoon. One account describes the Germans 'pouring machine gun fire down on them'.[46] Haldane's official account recorded: 'It is the first really big attack on the West Front, and I think everyone is really quite bucked about it.' It goes on to say 'What the 4th Seaforths can't hold, no one can hold.' However, despite that gusto before the action, the official account also notes:

> The losses were heavy:
> Killed: Captains A.K. Fraser and A.M. Macdonald, Lieutenants A.E. Mackintosh and N Sutherland, Second Lieutenant S.M. McMonnies.
> Wounded: Lieutenant Colonel J.S. Unthanks, Captain H.P. T. Gray, Lieutenant D.E.F. MacGregor, Second Lieutenants N.F. Swan and H. Paterson.
> Wounded and Missing: Captain T. H. Pervall.[47]

The official report related how:

> the situation was cleared up by the arrival of seven tanks, which moved forward to the 7th A.&S.H and the company of the 4th Seaforth Highlanders [. . .] Captain Gray was wounded, while Lieutenant E.A. Mackintosh was killed and Lieutenant MacGregor was wounded.[48]

Things did not settle down after these losses either. On St Andrews Day, the Germans made their great counter-attack and broke the British line.[49]

Mackintosh's tutor, John Murray, wrote a memoir of his late student in the posthumously published edition of *War: The Liberator, and Other Pieces with a Memoir*. Murray said of Mackintosh's death: 'He fell, shot through the head.' Meanwhile, *The Times* of 4 December 1917 did not give the detail of his death other than the circumstances in which he was killed, 'while observing enemy movement under heavy fire'.[50] This is partly corroborated by Lieutenant Coningsby Dawson, who noted that Mackintosh was 'killed recently [. . .] while observing enemy movements under heavy shell fire'.[51] Regimental diaries do not help much further other than giving the record of his death. Mackintosh's biographers, Campbell and Green, wondered whether he had potentially exposed himself to greater danger as a result of his bad eyesight.

The speculation could have continued were it not for a serendipitous connection between my father, Kenneth McLennan, and historian Colin Campbell. Recollecting the oral history of my great-grandfather Roderick McLennan Senior, fresh light can be shed on Mackintosh's death. Roderick McLennan did not often speak about the war. However, he had shared some insights with my father. Campbell used my father's oral history in a publication charting the history of the 51st Division during the Great War:

> Roderick McLennan was second man on a Lewis Gun. The Company were just beginning to prepare for a German counter attack during the Cambrai operations (as memory serves me this all happened near to or at a sunken road which had been fortified to receive the counter attack). Lt. Mackintosh was alongside my grandfather and the soldier who was firing the Lewis gun preparing to spot targets as they appeared. My grandfather had just placed a full 'pan' (magazine of Lewis Gun ammunition) onto the gun in preparation for the firing. The bullets were 'cracking' around them. Lt. Mackintosh who was alongside them and slightly forward lifted his head to get a better view of the oncoming Germans and was shot directly through the mouth into the head. He died instantly.
>
> He was an officer who was well loved by his men and remembered by my great grandfather with respect. He was a man who cared deeply for the soldiers under his command and sought the best for them on every occasion [. . .] the company moved forward later that day and I believe that the Germans were treated to a fair amount of cold steel [a rumour had circulated that no soldier wearing a kilt would be taken prisoner]. This was reciprocated in kind.[52]

This account corroborates aspects of eyewitness testimony, as Campbell notes. Bryn Hammond, historian of the Cambrai battle, notes an account from Private Frank Brooke (1/4 Seaforth Highlanders) which states that Mackintosh was killed by a shot between the eyes as the attack went uphill towards a heavily defended village, possibly Fontaine-Notre-Dame (we now believe this to be Cantaing-sur-Escaut, which sat before Fontaine-Notre-Dame).[53]

Campbell has a copy of a newspaper map of the Cambrai area from Mackintosh family sources with two crosses marked on it: 'one at Orival Wood Cemetery, where Mackintosh is buried, and one on a nearby sunken road uphill and south of Cantaing-sur-Escaut with a cross where he was killed, looking towards Cantaing Mill or the village'.[54] On 11 November 2017, Colin Campbell placed a poppy-adorned memorial cross at this site, approximately where he believed Mackintosh fell in action. Campbell was in France for the opening of a new memorial to Ewart Alan Mackintosh at the Saint Hubert Chapel at Cantaing-sur-Escaut. Almost two weeks later, my father, Kenneth McLennan, and I visited France for the 100th anniversary of the Battle of Cambrai and the anniversary of Mackintosh falling. At around midday, we laid a wreath at Mackintosh's grave, and we placed a cross at the site where Roderick McLennan and Ewart Alan Mackintosh were 100 years previously. The cross from Campbell and the cross from the McLennan family stood side by side. A small act of remembrance in an area with many, many poignant memorials.

Lieutenant A. E. Mackintosh MC is more permanently commemorated on the 4th Seaforth's Fontaine-Notre-Dame Memorial in Dingwall. That memorial is a stone cairn carrying the names of the five officers and thirty-five soldiers who fell on 21 and 22 November. Surmounted by a crudely made cross made from a tree trunk, this wooden cross memorial was originally erected in the village of Fontaine-Notre-Dame in France in November 1917. Colonel T. W. Cuthbert CMG DSO and the Seaforth Reunion Club brought it back to Dingwall in 1924 and sat it on a granite plinth from the Ardross Estate. It was unveiled on 12 March 1925 and refurbished in 2014.[55]

Mackintosh is also immortalised in a memorial in the centre of Edinburgh. The words in bold below, from his poem 'A Creed', are inscribed on the 'Scottish–American Memorial' in West Princes Street Gardens, Edinburgh, unveiled in 1927.

> Out of the womb of time and dust of the years forgotten,
> Spirit and fire enclosed in mutable flesh and bone,
> Came by a road unknown the thing that is me for ever,
> The lonely soul of a man that stands by itself alone.
>
> This is the right of my race, the heritage won by my fathers,
> Theirs by the years of fighting, theirs by the price they paid,
> Making a son like them, careless of hell or heaven,
> A man that can look in the face of the gods and not be afraid.
>
> Poor and weak is my strength and I cannot war against heaven,
> Strong, too strong are the gods; but there is one thing that I can
> Claim like a man unshamed, the full reward of my virtues,
> Pay like a man the price for the sins I sinned as a man.

> Now in the time of trial, the end of the years of fighting,
> And the echoing gates roll back on the country I cannot see,
> **If it be life that waits I shall live for ever unconquered,**
> **If death I shall die at last strong in my pride and free.**
> Vimy Ridge, 1916[56]

Mackintosh's words adorn this powerful memorial, situated in the capital under the shadow of the castle, that internationally recognised symbol of Scotland, antiquary and place. The memorial is down off the main thoroughfare of Edinburgh's Princes Street. However, his words perhaps sit, as he did when he fell, in a sunken road. In line with his leadership style, he is not dominant, not the overpowering hero of ardent glories. He is understated and still respected.

The 100th anniversary commemorations fuelled an interest in remembrance and commemoration on both sides of the Channel. In France in 2017, British and French officials, historians and interested parties gathered at Cantaing-sur-Escaut to open a new memorial close to the site that Mackintosh and his men were trying to take 100 years before. A replica of the wooden cross memorial in Dingwall was unveiled in France. Commemorating all the Seaforth Highlanders from that era, it stands alongside a specific memorial to Mackintosh, 'the Memorial Mackintosh'. This modern memorial blends a period site with modern memorialisation. Inside the restored Saint Hubert Chapel modern screen-printed information boards to Ewart Alan Mackintosh not only share his poems in print again, but also display his name, an image of him in uniform, a description of his life, and an overview of the final battle in which he took part. Original brickwork, once fallen away, stands proud again, strengthened by a new entrance to the restored chapel. Light floods on to the information boards, as the roof has not been replaced. The light-coloured stone façade of the new entrance looks similar to the Portland stone of Commonwealth War Grave Commission headstones. Perhaps unique, the memorial does not have the standardised and anonymous feel of those; nor does it have the standard form that post-war memorialisation took around Celtic crosses and the Cross of Sacrifice. This memorial, unveiled in 2017, is more akin to a public education site, helping educate for the future whilst remembering the past. Alan Bennett's *The History Boys* forces us to consider the purpose of memorialisation:

> It's not so much lest we forget, as lest we remember. Because you should realise so far as the Cenotaph and the Last Post and all that stuff is concerned, there's no better way of forgetting something than by commemorating it.[57]

For a poet, the best memorial must be that his words are published and printed. Seeing his words appear in Goldie and Watson (2014), MacGregor (2015) and in this publication goes some way to ensuring that we do not forget Mackintosh. Furthermore, this essay collection also keeps his place in history alongside the many Scottish Great War writers. They all deserve recognition, as much as the Generals and other notables who have dominated publications until recently. Mackintosh's 'To a Private Soldier' mused:

> Good-night, good sleep to you. But they
> Will never know good-night again,
> Whose eyes are seeing night and day,
> The humble men who died in vain.

One of Scotland's newest memorials was unveiled in Edinburgh in November 2018 during the Armistice centenary commemorations. The memorial remembers *all* Scotland's writers and poets of war, and indeed of anti-war, standing. They are remembered in Makars' Court, an evolving memorial place to writers in what is now UNESCO's first City of Literature. The granite Celtic Cross of Sacrifice, in itself a symbol of people of the past culturally connected across borders, is adorned with a long sword. Unlike the bronze ones of the Commonwealth War Graves, this granite sword turns into a pen near the bottom of the memorial.[58] The pen *is* mightier than the sword. Underneath the pen, words are inscribed representing all the war poets. Chosen in a national, public poll, they come not from combatants but from war journalist and writer Neil Munro, who lost his son in war. His words capture the loss but also connect us back to the land again:

> Sweet be their sleep now wherever they're lying,
> Far though they be from the hills of their home.

Mackintosh blended platonic nationalism with nature, patriotism with place. Patriotism, antiquary, servant leadership and environmentalism combined in Mackintosh. Whenever swords are drawn, sabres rattled and we come into conflict in this world, we might consider Mackintosh's words from 'Neil's Song' and the impact of conflict:

> When my dreams go down the hill
> Why should life remain?
> Now the world is burning out
> Mountain, glen and sea.

Notes

1. Colin Campbell and Rosalind Green, *Can't Shoot a Man with a Cold: Lt. E Alan Mackintosh 1893–1917: Poet of the Highland Division* (Argyll: Argyll Publishing, 2004).
2. Ibid. p. 208.
3. E. A. Mackintosh, 'In No Man's Land', in *The English Review* (June 1916), p. 515.
4. E. A. Mackintosh, *War, The Liberator, and Other Pieces with a Memoir* (London: John Lane, 1918) (publication adverts at rear of publication, unpaginated).
5. Ibid. (publication adverts at rear of publication, unpaginated).
6. Neil McLennan, qtd in Steven Brocklehurst, 'The Scottish War Poet Who Should Rival Wilfred Owen', BBC News (21 November 2017). Available at <https://www.bbc.co.uk/news/uk-scotland-42065875> (last accessed 15 May 2020).
7. *Forever: The Official Album of the World War One Commemorations* (Decca, 2014). Available at <https://www.youtube.com/watch?v=7cdxvZnsk2Q&feature=youtu.be> (last accessed 15 May 2020).
8. Available at <http://cerysmatthews.co.uk/reading-of-in-memoriam-armistice-day-the-cenotaph-whitehall-london/> (last accessed 15 May 2020).
9. Hew Strachan, 'Foreword', in *Beneath Troubled Skies: Poems of Scotland at War, 1914–1918*, ed. Lizzie MacGregor (Edinburgh: Polygon, 2015), pp. ix–xiii, p. xiii.
10. With thanks to Colin Campbell for this clarification.
11. Ewart Alan Mackintosh, *A Highland Regiment* (London: John Lane, 1917), p. 17.
12. For context's sake, but worthy of further consideration, publication was a year after the Second Iraq War began.
13. David Goldie and Roderick Watson, *From The Line: Scottish War Poetry 1914–1945*, (Glasgow: The Association for Scottish Literary Studies, 2014), p. xv.
14. Mackintosh, *War, The Liberator, and Other Pieces with a Memoir* (unpaginated Introduction by Lieutenant Coningsby Dawson).
15. Mackintosh, *War, The Liberator, and Other Pieces with a Memoir*, p. 29.
16. Robert Graves, *Goodbye to All That* (London, Jonathan Cape, 1929), p. 152.
17. Ernst Junger, *Storm of Steel*, trans. by Basil Creighton (London: Chatto & Windus, 1929), p. 250.
18. Brigitte Van de Pas, *World War One Through Scots Eyes: Scots and Identity in the British Army During the First World War* (thesis Leiden University, 2015), p. 49.
19. Alan Riach, 'Visions Beyond Violence: Alan Riach Examines Modern Scottish Literature's Response to War', *National* (21 October 2016).

20. Mackintosh, *War, The Liberator, and Other Pieces with a Memoir* (*Morning Post* advert, post-publication adverts, unpaginated.).
21. Strachan, 'Foreword', p. x.
22. Mackintosh, *A Highland Regiment*, p. 33.
23. E. Alan Mackintosh to John Lane, 2 November 1916, Harry Ransom Center, University of Texas at Austin, TXRC00-A11 – 30.3 f.16.
24. Robert K. Greenleaf, *Servant Leadership* (Mahwah, NJ: Paulist Press, 1964). Thomas Carlyle, *Heroes and Hero Worship* (London: James Fraser, 1840).
25. Neil McLennan, 'In Search of Leadership' *Teaching Scotland (General Teaching Council of Scotland)*, Vol. 28, January 2020, pp. 44–5.
26. Mackintosh, qtd in Lieutenant Coningsby Dawson, 'Introduction', in Mackintosh, *War, The Liberator, and Other Pieces with a Memoir* [unpaginated].
27. Mackintosh, *War, The Liberator, and Other Pieces with a Memoir*, pp. 141–2.
28. Mackintosh, *A Highland Regiment*, p. 92.
29. Dawson, 'Introduction', [unpaginated].
30. Campbell and Green, *Can't Shoot a Man with a Cold*, p. 13.
31. John Murray, in Mackintosh, *War: The Liberator, and Other Pieces with a Memoir*, p. 6.
32. Strachan, 'Foreword', p. xi.
33. John Lewis-Stempel, *Where Poppies Blow: The British Soldier, Nature, the Great War* (London: Weidenfeld & Nicolson, [2016] 2017).
34. Goldie and Watson, *From The Line*, p. xv.
35. Campbell and Green, *Can't Shoot a Man with a Cold*, p. 84.
36. Van de Pas, *World War One Through Scots Eyes*, p. 48.
37. Campbell and Green, *Can't Shoot a Man with a Cold*, p. 35.
38. Mackintosh, *War, The Liberator, and Other Pieces with a Memoir*, p. 4.
39. Van de Pas, *World War One Through Scots Eyes*, p. 61.
40. Mackintosh, *A Highland Regiment*, p. 59.
41. Ibid. p. 59.
42. Ibid. p. 27.
43. Ibid. p. 77.
44. Campbell and Green, *Can't Shoot a Man with a Cold*, p. 205.
45. Ibid. p. 208.
46. Lieutenant Colonel M. Haldane, *A History of the 4th Battalion Seaforth Highlanders* (London: Witherby, 1928), p. 241.
47. Ibid. pp. 253–4.
48. Ibid. pp. 241–52.
49. Ibid. p. 256.
50. *The Times* (4 December 1912).
51. Dawson, "Introduction', [unpaginated].
52. Colin Campbell, *Engine of Destruction: The 51st Highland Division in the Great War* (Argyll: Argyll Publishing, 2013), p. 202.

53. Bryn Hammond, *Cambrai, 1917: The Myth of the First Great Tank Battle* (London: Weidenfeld & Nicolson, 2008), pp. 218–19.
54. Campbell, *Engine of Destruction*, p. 202 n. 26.
55. 'Seaforths' Sacrifice "Not Forgotten" as Dingwall War Cross is Repaired', *Ross-shire Journal* (12 May 2014). Available at <https://www.ross-shire-journal.co.uk/news/seaforths-sacrifice-not-forgotten-as-dingwall-war-cross-is-repaired-170038/> (last accessed 15 May 2020).
56. Mackintosh, *A Highland Regiment*, p. 43.
57. Alan Bennett, *The History Boys: The Film* (London: Faber & Faber, 2006), p. 25.
58. War Poets' Corner Memorial, Makers' Court, Edinburgh. Designed by Annette MacDonald and Robin Duncan, produced by MacIntyre Memorials stonemasons and sponsored by Dignity Funerals.

Further Reading

Aberdeen University Review, vol. 2: 1914–15 (Aberdeen: Aberdeen University Press, 1915).
Aberdeen University Review, vol. 3: 1915–16 (Aberdeen: Aberdeen University Press, 1916).
Aberdeen University Review, vol. 4: 1916–17 (Aberdeen: Aberdeen University Press, 1917).
Aberdeen University Review, vol. 6: 1918–19 (Aberdeen: Aberdeen University Press, 1919).
Akers, Elizabeth, *The Sunset Song and Other Verses* (Boston: Lee and Shepard, 1902).
Alpers, Paul, *What Is Pastoral?* (London: University of Chicago Press, 1997).
Anderson, Benedict, *Imagined Communities: Reflections on the Origin and Spread of Nationalism*, revised edn (London and New York: Verso, [1983] 2006).
Anderson, R. D., *The Student Community at Aberdeen 1860–1939* (Aberdeen: Aberdeen University Press, 1988).
Atkin, Jonathan, *A War of Individuals: Bloomsbury Attitudes to the Great War* (Manchester: Manchester University Press, 2002).
Auden, W. H., *Collected Shorter Poems* (London: Faber, 1971).
Badsey, S. D., 'Battle of the Somme: British War Propaganda', *Historical Journal of Film, Radio and Television*, vol. 3, no. 2 (1983), pp. 99–115.
—, 'Cinema Chit-Chat', *Entertainer*, vol. 2 (September 1916).
Baldwin, Thomas, 'Cambridge Philosophers V: G. E. Moore', *Philosophy*, vol. 71, no. 276 (April 1996), pp. 275–85.
Bambery, Chris, *A People's History of Scotland* (London: Verso, 2014).
Bartlett, Niall Somhairle Finlayson, 'The First World War and the 20th Century in the History of Gaelic Scotland: A Preliminary Analysis' (unpublished MPhil thesis, Glasgow, 2014).
Belk, Patrick Scott, *Empires of Print: Adventure Fiction in the Magazines, 1899–1919* (Oxford: Routledge, 2017).
Bell, Henry, *John Maclean: Hero of Red Clydeside* (London: Pluto Press, 2018).
Bell, J. J., *Wee Macgreegor Enlists* (Edinburgh: Birlinn, [1915] 1993).

Bell, Stuart, '"Soldiers of Christ Arise": Religious Nationalism in the East Midlands During World War I', *Midland History*, vol. 39, no. 2 (2014), pp. 219–35.
Bennett, Alan, *The History Boys: The Film* (London: Faber & Faber, 2006).
Bernays, Edward, *Crystallizing Public Opinion* (Milton Keynes: Lightning Source UK, 2019).
Bhabha, Homi, 'Interrogating Identity', in *The Location of Culture* (New York: Psychology Press, 1994), <http://readingtheperiphery.org/bhabha/> (last accessed 4 June 2019).
Black, Ronald I. M. (ed.), *An Tuil: Anthology of 20th Century Scottish Gaelic Verse* (Edinburgh: Polygon, 1999).
— (ed.), *Eilein na h-Òige: The Poems of Fr Allan McDonald* (Glasgow: Mungo, 2002),
Blake, George, *The Path of Glory* (London: Constable, 1929).
Blunden, Edmund, *The Poems of Edmund Blunden* (London: Cobden-Sanderson, 1930).
Bold, Alan, *MacDiarmid: Christopher Murray Grieve: A Critical Biography* (London: Paladin, 1990).
Bond, Brian, *Survivors of a Kind: Memoirs of the Western Front* (London: Continuum, 2008).
Boyle, Andrew, *Only the Wind Will Listen: Reith of the BBC* (London: Hutchinson, 1972).
Broadie, Alexander, *A History of Scottish Philosophy* (Edinburgh: Edinburgh University Press, 2009).
Brooke, Rupert, *The Complete Poems* (London: Sidgwick and Jackson, [1933] 1945).
Brooks, John, *The Battle of Jutland* (Cambridge: Cambridge University Press, 2016).
Broom, John, *Fight the Good Fight: Voices of Faith from the First World War* (Barnsley: Pen and Sword Military, 2015).
Brown, Ian and Alan Riach, 'Introduction', in Ian Brown and Alan Riach (eds), *The Edinburgh Companion to Twentieth-Century Literature* (Edinburgh: Edinburgh University Press, 2009), pp. 1–14.
Brownlow, Kevin, *The War, the West, and the Wilderness* (London: Secker & Warburg, 1978).
Buchan, David (ed.), 'Introduction', in *Folk Tradition and Folk Medicine in Scotland: The Writings of David Rorie* (Edinburgh: Canongate Academic, 1994), pp. 1–16.
Buchan, John, 'The Allies Advance', *The Times* (29 September 1915).
—, 'The Battle of Festubert', *The Times* (29 May 1915).
—, 'The Battlefield of Loos', *The Times* (6 October 1915).
—, *Greenmantle* (London: Penguin Books, [1916] 1956).
—, 'The King of Ypres', in *John Buchan: The Complete Short Stories Volume Three*, ed. Andrew Lownie (London: Thistle, 1997).
—, *Memory Hold-the-Door* (London: Hodder and Stoughton, [1940] 1942).

—, *Mr Standfast* (Oxford: Oxford University Press, [1919] 1993).
—, *Nelson's History of the War*, vol. XXII (London, Edinburgh and New York: Thomas Nelson and Sons, 1919).
—, 'On a Flemish Hill', *The Times* (17 May 1915).
—, *Poems Scots and English* (London, Edinburgh and New York: Thomas Nelson and Sons, 1917).
—, *The Thirty-Nine Steps* (Ware: Wordsworth Editions, [1915] 1996).
—, 'Thrust for Lorgies', *The Times* (19 May 1915).
—, 'Ypres Today', *The Times* (22 May 1915).
Buchan, Ursula, *A Life of John Buchan: Beyond the Thirty-Nine Steps* (London: Bloomsbury, 2019).
Buitenhuis, Peter, *The Great War of Words: Literature as Propaganda 1914–18 and After* (London: Batsford, 1989).
Burnett, John and Kate Mackay, *John Buchan and the Thirty-Nine Steps: An Exploration* (Edinburgh: NMS Enterprises, 2014).
Burns, J. H., 'The Scottish Kantians', *Journal of Scottish Philosophy*, vol. 7, no. 2 (2009), pp. 115–31.
Burns, John, *A Celebration of the Light: Zen in the Novels of Neil Gunn* (Edinburgh: Canongate, 1988).
Cable, Boyd, *Action Front* (London: Smith, Elder, 1916).
—, *Between the Lines* (London: John Murray, [1915] 1917).
—, *Doing Their Bit: War Work at Home* (London: Hodder & Stoughton, 1916).
—, *Front Lines* (London: John Murray, 1918).
Caimbeul, Aonghas (Am Puilean), *Suathadh ri Iomadh Rubha* (Glasgow: Gairm, 1973).
Caimbeul, Aonghas Pàdraig, *An Oidhche mus do Sheòl Sinn* (Inverness: Clàr, 2003).
Caimbeul, Tormod, *An Naidheachd bhon Taigh* (An Teanga: Cànan, 1994).
Caird, Edward, *The Evolution of Religion*, vol. II (Glasgow: James MacLehose and Sons, 1893).
Calder, Angus, 'A Mania for Self-Reliance: Grassic Gibbon's *Scots Quair*', in D. Jefferson and G. Martin (eds), *The Uses of Fiction* (Milton Keynes: Open University, 1982).
Cameron, Ewen A., *Impaled Upon a Thistle: Scotland Since 1880* (Edinburgh: Edinburgh University Press, 2010).
Campbell, Colin, *Engine of Destruction: The 51st Highland Division in the Great War* (Argyll: Argyll Publishing, 2013).
Campbell, Colin and Rosalind Green, *Can't Shoot a Man with a Cold: Lt. E Alan Mackintosh 1893–1917: Poet of the Highland Division* (Argyll: Argyll Publishing, 2004).
Campbell, James, 'Interpreting the War', in Vincent Sherry (ed.), *The Cambridge Companion to the Literature of the First World War* (Cambridge: Cambridge University Press, 2005), pp. 261–79.
Campbell, R. W., *Private Spud Tamson* (Edinburgh and London: William Blackwood & Sons, 1915).

—, *Sergeant Spud Tamson, V. C.* (London: Hutchinson, 1918).
—, *Spud Tamson Out West* (London and Edinburgh: W. & R. Chambers, 1924).
Carlyle, Thomas, *Heroes and Hero Worship* (London: James Fraser, 1840).
Carr, E. H., *What is History?* (London: Penguin, 1961).
Costello, John E., *John Macmurray: A Biography* (Edinburgh: Floris, 2002).
Craig, Cairns, *Out of History: Narrative Paradigms in Scottish and British Culture* (Edinburgh: Polygon, 1996).
Crawford, Robert, *Scotland's Books: The Penguin History of Scottish Literature* (London: Penguin, 2007).
Crotty, Patrick, 'Swordsmen: W. B. Yeats and Hugh MacDiarmid', in Peter Mackay, Edna Longley and Fran Brearton (eds), *Modern Irish and Scottish Poetry* (Cambridge: Cambridge University Press, 2011), pp. 20–38.
Cunliffe, Barry, *The Extraordinary Voyage of Pytheas the Greek* (London: Allen Lane, The Penguin Press, 2001).
Dakers, Caroline, *The Countryside at War* (London: Constable, 1987).
Daly, Macdonald, 'Scottish Poetry and the Great War', *Scottish Literary Journal*, vol. 21, no. 2 (November 1994), pp. 79–96.
Darrow, Margaret H., 'French Volunteer Nursing and the Myth of War Experience in World War I', *The American Historical Review*, vol. 101, no. 1 (1996), pp. 80–106.
Das, Santanu, 'Ardour and Anxiety: Politics and Literature in the Indian Homefront', in Heike Liebau, Katrin Bromber, Katharina Lange, Dyala Hamzah and Ravi Ahuja (eds), *The World in World Wars: Experiences, Perceptions and Perspectives from Africa and Asia* (Leiden: Brill, 2010), pp. 341–68.
Davies, Owen, *Paganism: A Very Short Introduction* (Oxford: Oxford University Press, 2011).
Dawson, J. W., *The Origin of the World, According to Revelation and Science* (Montreal: Dawson Brothers, 1877).
Devine, Thomas M., *The Scottish Nation 1700–2000* (London: Penguin, 1999).
Dickie, J. L., *Peter Tamson: Elder o' the Kirk and Sportsman* (London: Country Life, 1915).
Domhnallach, Tormod Calum, *Call na h-Iolaire* (Stornoway: Acair, 1978).
Dougal, Josephine, 'Popular Scottish Song Traditions at Home (and Away)', *Folklore*, vol. 122, no. 3 (December 2011).
Ehland, Cristoph, 'The Spy-Scattered Landscapes of Modernity in John Buchan's *Mr Standfast*', in *John Buchan and the Idea of Modernity* (London: Pickering & Chatto, 2013), pp. 111–24.
Eksteins, Modris, *Rites of Spring: The Great War and the Birth of the Modern Age* (New York: Mariner Books, [1989] 2000).
Eliot, George, *Middlemarch* (London: Penguin, [1871–2] 1994).
Eliot, T. S., *T. S. Eliot: Collected Poems* (London: Faber & Faber, 2002).
Ellul, Jacques, *Propaganda: The Formation of Men's Attitudes*, trans. Konrad Kellen and Jean Lerner (New York and Toronto: Vintage Books, 1973).
Evan, Richard, *In Defence of History* (London: Granta, 1997).

Evola, Julius, *Pagan Imperialism*, trans. Cologero Salvo (n.p.: Gornahoor Press, 2017).
—, *Revolt Against the Modern World*, trans. Guido Stucco (Rochester, VT: Inner Traditions International, [1934] 1995).
Featherstone, Simon, *War Poetry: An Introductory Reader* (London: Routledge, 1995).
Ferguson, Andrew (ed.), *Ghosts of War: A History of World War I in Poetry and Prose* (Stroud: The History Press, 2016).
Ferguson, John (ed.), *Seven Famous One-Act Plays* (Harmondsworth: Penguin, [1937] 1950).
Fergusson, Niall, *The Pity of* War (London: Penguin, 1998).
Finkelstein, David, 'Literature, Propaganda, and the First World War: The Case of *Blackwood's Magazine*', in Jeremy Treglown and Bridget Bennett (eds), *Grub Street and the Ivory Tower: Essays on the Relations Between Literary Journalism and Literary Scholarship* (Oxford: Clarendon, 1998), pp. 91–111.
Fortner, Robert S., *Radio, Morality and Culture: Britain, Canada and Culture, 1919–1945* (Carbondale: South Illinois Press, 2003).
Fussell, Paul, *The Great War and Modern Memory* (Oxford: Oxford University Press, [1975] 2000).
Gaitens, Edward, *Dance of the Apprentices* (Edinburgh: Canongate, [1948] 1990).
Gallacher, William, *Revolt on the Clyde* (London: Lawrence and Wishart, [1936] 1940).
Gardner, Brian (ed.), *Up the Line to Death: The War Poets 1914–1918* (London: Methuen, 1964).
Garry, Flora MacDonald (interview with) [nee; Campbell, (1900–2000), (M.A. 1922), 4 January 1986, University of Aberdeen Special Collections, MS 3620/1/ 41. Quoted with the permission of Special Collections, University of Aberdeen.
Geddes, Patrick, 'The Scots Renascence' (1895), reprinted in *Edinburgh Review*, vol. 88 (1992), pp. 17–22.
Gelbart, Matthew, 'Allan Ramsay, the Idea of "Scottish Music" and the Beginnings of "National Music" in Europe', *Eighteenth-Century Music*, vol. 9, no. 1 (2012), pp. 81–108.
Gibbons, Thomas, '"Club Government" and Independence in Media Regulation', in Monroe E. Price, Stefaan Verhulst and Libby Morgan (eds), *Routledge Handbook of Media Law* (London: Routledge, 2013), pp. 47–65.
Gibbs, Philip, *Adventures in Journalism* (London: William Heinemann, 1923).
—, *Now It Can Be Told* (New York: Garden City Publishing, 1920).
—, *The Pageant of the Years: An Autobiography* (London: William Heinemann, 1946).
—, *Realities of War* (London: William Heinemann, 1920).
Gifford, Douglas, *Neil M. Gunn and Lewis Grassic Gibbon* (Edinburgh: Oliver and Boyd, 1983).

—, 'The Roots that Clutch: John Buchan, Scottish Fiction and Scotland', in Kate Macdonald and Nathan Waddell (eds), *John Buchan and the Idea of Modernity* (London: Routledge, 2016), pp. 17–33.
Gifford, Terry, *Pastoral* (London and New York: Routledge, 1999).
Goldie, David, 'Archipelagic Poetry of the First World War', in Santanu Das (ed.), *The Cambridge Companion to the Poetry of the First World War* (Cambridge: Cambridge University Press, 2013), pp. 159–72.
—, 'The British Invention of Scottish Culture: The First World War and Before', *Review of Scottish Culture*, vol. 18 (2006), pp. 128–48.
—, 'Hugh MacDiarmid, Harry Lauder and Scottish Popular Culture', *International Journal of Scottish Literature*, vol. 1, Autumn 2006, <http://www.ijsl.stir.ac.uk/issue1/goldie.htm> (last accessed 8 June 2019).
—, 'Romance by Other Means: Scottish Popular Newspapers and the First World War', in Chris Hart (ed.), *World War I: Media, Entertainment & Popular Culture* (London: Midrash, 2018), pp. 230–57.
—, 'Scotland, Britishness, and the First World War', in Gerald Carruthers, David Goldie and Alastair Renfrew (eds), *Beyond Scotland: New Contexts for Twentieth-Century Scottish Literature* (Amsterdam: Rodopi, 2004), pp. 37–57.
—, 'Scotland for Ever? British Literature, Scotland and the First World War', in Edna Longley, Eamonn Hughes and Des O'Rawe (eds), *Ireland (Ulster) Scotland: Concepts, Contexts, Comparisons* (Belfast: Queen's University Belfast, 2003), pp. 113–20.
Goldie, David and Roderick Watson (eds), *From the Line: Scottish War Poetry 1914–1945* (Glasgow: Association for Scottish Literary Studies, 2014).
Grassic Gibbon, Lewis, *A Scots Quair* (Edinburgh: Canongate, 1995).
—, *Smeddum: A Lewis Grassic Gibbon Anthology*, ed. Valentina Bold (Edinburgh: Canongate Classics, 2001).
—, *Sunset Song* (London: Penguin Books, [1932] 2007).
Gibbon, Lewis Grassic and Hugh MacDiarmid, *Scottish Scene, or The Intelligent Man's Guide to Albyn* (London: Jarrolds, 1934).
Graves, Robert, *Goodbye to All That* (London: Anchor, 1929).
Greenleaf, Robert K. *Servant Leadership* (Mahwah, NJ: Paulist Press, 1964).
Gregory, Adrian, *The Last Great War: British Society and the First World War* (Cambridge: Cambridge University Press, 2008).
Grieve, Michael and W. R. Aitken (eds), *Hugh MacDiarmid: Complete Poems 1920–1976*, vol. I (London: Martin Brien & O'Keefe, 1978).
Griffin, Roger, 'Series Editor's Preface', in Erik Tonning, *Modernism and Christianity* (Basingstoke: Palgrave Macmillan, 2014).
Gunn, Neil M., *Highland River* (Edinburgh: Canongate, [1937] 1991).
—, Dane McNeil [Neil M. Gunn], 'Padraic Pearse: I. The Man Called Pearse', *The Scots Independent*, vol. 4, no. 1 (November 1929).
—, 'Padraic Pearse: II. Poems, Plays, Stories', *The Scots Independent*, vol. 4, no. 2 (December 1929).

Gurney, Ivor, 'First March', in *The Complete Poems of Ivor Gurney*, ed. P. J. Kavanagh (Oxford: Oxford University Press, 1982).
Haldane, Lieutenant Colonel M., *A History of the 4th Battalion Seaforth Highlanders* (London: Witherby, 1928).
Hallett, Christine E., *Veiled Warriors: Allied Nurses of the First World War* (Oxford: Oxford University Press, 2014).
Hammond, Bryn, *Cambrai 1917: The Myth of the First Great Tank Battle* (London: Weidenfeld & Nicolson, 2008).
Hart, Francis Russell and J. B. Pick, *Neil M. Gunn: A Highland Life* (London: John Murray, 1981).
Hartley, Leslie P., *The Go-Between* (London: Penguin, [1953] 1961).
Haste, Cate, *Keep the Home Fires Burning: Propaganda in the First World War* (London: Penguin Books, 1977).
Hay, Ian, *Carrying On: After the First Hundred Thousand* (Edinburgh: William Blackwood & Sons, 1917).
—, *The First Hundred Thousand: Being the Unofficial Chronicle of a Unit of 'K (1)'* (Edinburgh and London: William Blackwood & Sons, 1915).
Hayward, Brian, *Galoshins: The Scottish Folk Play* (Edinburgh: Edinburgh University Press, 1992).
Herrick, Robert, 'Cherry-Ripe', in *The Oxford Book of English Verse 1250–1900*, ed. Arthur Thomas Quiller-Couch (Oxford: Clarendon Press, 1919), <http://www.bartleby.com/101/256.html> (last accessed 27 November 2018).
Hibberd, Dominic and John Onions (eds), *The Winter of the World: Poems of the First World War* (London: Constable, 2008).
Hughes, Annmarie and Jeff Meek, 'State Regulation, Family Breakdown, and Lone Motherhood: The Hidden Costs of World War I in Scotland', *Journal of Family History*, vol. 39, no. 4 (2014), pp. 364–87.
Humphrey, Christopher, 'John Watson: The Philosopher of Canadian Identity', Historical Papers 1993: Canadian Society of Church History, <churchhistcan.files.wordpress.com/2013/06/1993-7-humphrey-article.pdf> (last accessed 23 January 2018).
Hutchison, David, 'Scottish Drama 1900–1950', in Cairns Craig (ed.), *The History of Scottish Literature. Volume 4: Twentieth Century* (Aberdeen: Aberdeen University Press, 1987), pp. 163–77.
Hutchison, Hazel, *The War That Used Up Words: American Writers and the First World War* (New Haven, CT, and London: Yale University Press, 2015).
Huth, Kimberly, 'Come Live with Me and Feed My Sheep: Invitations, Ownership, and Belonging in Early Modern Pastoral Literature', *Studies in Philology*, vol. 108 (2011), pp. 44–69.
Hutton, Ronald, *Pagan Britain* (New Haven, CT, and London: Yale University Press, [2013] 2014).
—, *The Triumph of the Moon: A History of Modern Pagan Witchcraft* (Oxford: Oxford University Press, 1999).

Hynes, Samuel, *A War Imagined* (London: Pimlico, [1990] 1992).
Institute for the Study of Scottish Philosophy, 'Scottish Philosophy in North America', <http://www.scottishphilosophy.org/history/abroad/north-america/> (last accessed 1 June 2020).
Isherwood, Ian, *Remembering the Great War: Writing and Publishing the Experiences of the Great War* (London: I. B. Tauris, 2017).
Jacob, Violet, 'The Field by the Lirk o' the Hill', in *Beneath Troubled Skies: Poems of Scotland at War, 1914–1918*, ed. Lizzie MacGregor (Edinburgh: Scottish Poetry Library and Polygon, 2015), p. 77.
James, Henry, *Within the Rim and Other Essays* (London: Collins, 1915).
Jones, Henry, *Idealism as a Practical Creed* (Glasgow: MacLehose, 1909).
Junger, Ernst, *Storm of Steel*, trans. Basil Creighton (London: Chatto & Windus, 1929).
Kandinsky, Wassily, *Concerning the Spiritual in Art*, trans. M. T. H. Sadler (New York: Dover, 1977).
Kenyon, Sir Frederic, *War Graves: How the Cemeteries Abroad Will Be Designed* (London: His Majesty's Stationery Office, 1919).
Kern, Stephen, *Modernism After the Death of God: Christianity, Fragmentation, and Unification* (New York and London: Routledge, 2017).
Kirkwood, David, *My Life of Revolt* (London: George G. Harrap, 1935).
Klaus, H. Gustav, 'Individual, Community and Conflict in Working-Class Fiction, 1920–1940', in Scott Lyall (ed.), *Community in Modern Literature* (Leiden: Brill, 2016), pp. 43–60.
Korda, Michael, *Making the List: A Cultural History of the American Bestseller, 1900–1999* (New York: Barnes and Noble, 2001).
Kraus, Karl, *In These Great Times: A Karl Kraus Reader*, ed. Harry Zohn (Manchester: Carcanet, 1984).
Larkin, Philip, *Collected Poems* (London: Faber & Faber, 2003).
Lasswell, Harold D., *Propaganda Technique in the World War* (London and New York: Kegan Paul, Trench, Trubner, 1927).
Lawrence, D. H., *The Letters of D. H. Lawrence*, vol. 2, ed. G. J. Zytavak and J. T. Boulton (Cambridge: Cambridge University Press, 1981).
Lewis-Stempel, John, *Where Poppies Blow: The British Soldier, Nature, the Great War* (London: Weidenfeld and Nicolson, [2016] 2017).
Lindsay, A. D., 'Philosophy', in W. P. Paterson (ed.), *German Culture: The Contribution of the Germans to Knowledge, Literature, Art, and Life* (Edinburgh: T. C. and E. C. Jack, 1915).
Linklater, Eric, *Fanfare for a Tin Hat* (London: Macmillan, 1970).
Lloyd George, David, *War Memoirs of David Lloyd George*, vol. 1 (London: Odhams Press, 1938).
Lomas, Janis, '"Delicate Duties": Issues of Class and Respectability in Government Policy Towards the Wives and Widows of British Soldiers in the Era of the Great War', *Women's History Review*, vol. 9, no. 1 (2000), pp. 123–47.
Lucas, John, *Moderns and Contemporaries* (Sussex: Harvester Press, 1985).

Lumsden, Alison, '"Journey into Being": Nan Shepherd's *The Weatherhouse*', in Carol Anderson and Aileen Christianson (eds), *Scottish Women's Fiction, 1920s to 1960s: Journeys into Being* (East Linton: Tuckwell Press, 2000), pp. 59–71.

MacAmhlaidh, Fred (ed.), *Domhnall Ruadh Chorùna: Òrain is Dàin le Domhnall Domhnallach a Uibhist a Tuath* (Lochmaddy: Comann Eachdraidh Uibhist a Tuath, 1995).

Macbean, Lachlan, *The Celtic Who's Who* (Kirkcaldy: Fifeshire Advertiser, 1921).

MacCallum, Rev. Donald, *English Translation of the First Canto of Domhnullan* (Glasgow, 1927).

Mac Chalum, An t-Urr. Domhnull, *Domhnullan, Dàn an Ceithir Earrannan* (Glasgow: A. Mac-Labhruinn, 1925).

McCluskey, J. R., *The Works of James Wilson*, vol. I (Cambridge, MA: Harvard University Press, 1967).

McCulloch, Margery Palmer, *The Novels of Neil M. Gunn: A Critical Study* (Edinburgh: Scottish Academic Press, 1987).

—, *Scottish Modernism and its Contexts 1918–1959: Literature, National Identity and Cultural Exchange* (Edinburgh: Edinburgh University Press, 2009).

MacDhomhnuill, T. D., *An Déidh a' Chogaidh* (Glasgow: Archibald Sinclair, 1921).

—, *Dàin agus Dealbhan-Fhacail an Am a' Chogaidh* (Glasgow: Archibald Sinclair, 1918).

MacDiarmid, Hugh [C. M. Grieve], *Annals of the Five Senses* (Edinburgh: The Porpoise Press, 1923).

—, *The Company I've Kept: Essays in Autobiography* (London: Hutchinson, 1966).

—, *The Complete Poems: 1920–1976*, 2 vols, ed. Michael Grieve and W. R. Aitken (Manchester: Carcanet, 1993).

—, *Contemporary Scottish Studies*, ed. Alan Riach (Manchester: Carcanet, [1926] 1995).

— (ed.), *The Golden Treasury of Scottish Poetry* (London: Macmillan, 1946).

—, *A Langholm Lad Goes to War*, ed. Ron Addison (Langholm: Langholm Library Trust, 2014).

—, *Lucky Poet: A Self-Study in Literature and Political Ideas*, ed. Alan Riach (Manchester: Carcanet, [1943] 1994).

—, 'Nisbet, an Interlude in Post War Glasgow' (1922), in *Annals of the Five Senses and Other Stories, Sketches and Plays*, ed. Roderick Watson and Alan Riach (Manchester: Carcanet, 1999), pp. 104–13, p. 108.

—, *R.B. Cunninghame Graham: A Centenary Study*, in *Albyn: Shorter Books and Monographs*, ed. Alan Riach (Manchester: Carcanet Press, [1952] 1996), pp. 130–61.

—, 'Scottish Arts and Letters: The Present Position and Post-War Prospects', in *The New Scotland: 17 Chapters on Scottish Reconstruction* (Glasgow:

Civic Press and the London Scots Self-Government Committee, 1942), pp. 136–51.

Macdonald, Catriona M. M., 'Going Back to Yesterday: The Legacy of War', *History Scotland* (May/June 2019).

—, *Whaur Extremes Meet: Scotland's Twentieth Century* (Edinburgh: Birlinn, 2009).

Macdonald, Kate, *John Buchan: A Companion to the Mystery Fiction* Jefferson, NC: McFarland, 2009).

Macdonald, Malcolm and Donald John MacLeod, *Call na h-Iolaire: The Darkest Dawn, The Story of the Iolaire Tragedy* (Stornoway: Acair, 2018).

McFarland, E. W., 'A Coronach in Stone', in Catriona M. M. Macdonald and E. W. McFarland (eds), *Scotland and the Great War* (Edinburgh: Birlinn, 1999).

MacFhearghuis, Calum, *Suileabhan* (Glasgow: Gairm, 1983).

MacGill, Patrick, *The Great Push: An Episode of the Great War* (London: Herbert Jenkins, 1916).

MacGill-Eain, Somhairle/Sorley MacLean, *Caoir Gheal Leumraich/White Leaping Flame, Collected Poems in Gaelic with English Translations*, ed. Christopher Whyte and Emma Dymock (Edinburgh: Polygon, 2011).

—, *An Cuilithionn 1939 and Unpublished Poems*, ed. by Christopher Whyte (Glasgow: Association for Scottish Literary Studies, 2011).

McGregor, Lizzie (ed.), *Beneath Troubled Skies: Poems of Scotland at War, 1914–1918* (Edinburgh: Scottish Poetry Library and Polygon, 2015).

Mac Ill Eathain, Iain, *Cogadh Ruairidh* (Dingwall: Sandstone, 2009).

MacIlleathain, Ruairidh, *Còig Duilleagan na Seamraig* (Inverness: Clàr, 2019).

Mackay, Peter, 'Freedom from Judgement Above? Predestination and Cultural Trauma in Scottish Gaelic Poetry of World War I', in Gill Plain (ed.), *Myth, Memory and the First World War in Scotland: The Legacy of Bannockburn* (Lewisburg, PA: Bucknell University Press, 2016), pp. 187–204.

Mackay, R. L., *The War Diary of Lieut. R.L. Mackay, 11th and later 1st/8th Battalions, Argyll and Sutherland Highlanders, September 1916 to January 1919*. National Library of Scotland Acc.12350/18.

Mackenzie, Compton, 'Foreword to the 1949 Edition', in *Sinister Street* (Harmondsworth: Penguin Books, [1913] 1960), pp. 9–13.

MacKenzie, John, 'Essay and Reflection: On Scotland and the Empire', *The International History Review* (Simon Fraser University), vol. XV, no. 4 (November 1993), pp. 714–39.

Mackinlay, George A. C., *Poems: By George A.C. Mackinlay* (Glasgow: Lyon, 1919).

Mackintosh, E. A., *A Highland Regiment* (London: John Lane, 1917).

—, 'In No Man's Land', in *The English Review* (June 1916), p. 515.

—, *War, The Liberator, and Other Pieces with a Memoir* (London: John Lane, 1918).

McLean, Iain, *The Legend of Red Clydeside* (Edinburgh: John Donald, 1983).

McLennan, Neil, 'Standing on the Shoulders of Giants: Plaques Commemorating and Creating for Writers Warning About War', Royal Society of

Arts, 15 March 2019, <https://www.thersa.org/discover/publications-and-articles/rsa-blogs/2019/03/standing-on-the-shoulders-of-giants--plaques-commemorating-and-creating-for-writers-warning-about-war> (last accessed 12 May 2020).

—, 'In Search of Leadership', *Teaching Scotland (General Teaching Council of Scotland)*, Vol. 28, January 2020, pp. 44–5.

Macleod, Jenny, *Reconsidering Gallipoli* (Manchester: Manchester University Press, 2004).

MacLeòid, Dòmhnall, Iain Cailean MacIlleathainn, Morag NicLeòid, Anna NicSuain and Jo NicDhòmhnaill (eds), *An Cogadh Mór 1914–1918: The Great War* (Stornoway: Acair, 1982).

McLoughlin, Kate, *Authoring War: The Literary Representation of War from the Iliad to Iraq* (Cambridge: Cambridge University Press, 2011).

Macmurray, John, *Freedom in the Modern World* (Atlantic Highlands, NJ: Humanities Press, [1932] 1992).

—, *Persons in Relation* (London: Faber, 1961).

—, *The Self as Agent* (London: Faber, 1957).

MacPhàrlain, Murchadh, *An Toinneamh Dìomhair* (Stornoway: Stornoway Gazette, 1973).

Macquarrie, John, *Existentialism: An Introduction, Guide and Assessment* (London: Penguin, [1972] 1973).

Manson, John (ed.), *Dear Grieve: Letters to Hugh MacDiarmid (C. M. Grieve)* (Glasgow: Kennedy & Boyd, 2011).

Marsh, Edward (ed.), *Georgian Poetry: 1913–1915* (London: The Poetry Bookshop, 1918).

Massingham, H. J., *The Golden Age: The Story of Human Nature* (London: Gerald Howe, 1927).

Meek, Dòmhnall Eachann (ed.), *Mo Là gu Seo: Eachdraidh mo Bheatha le Tòmas M. MacCalmain* (Glasgow: Scottish Gaelic Texts Society, 2011).

Milton, Colin, '"A Sough o' War": The Great War in the Poetry of North-east Scotland', in David Hewitt (ed.), *Northern Visions: The Literary Identity of Northern Scotland in the Twentieth Century* (Phantassie: Tuckwell Press, 1995), pp. 1–38.

Moireach, Murchadh, *Luach na Saorsa* (Glasgow: Gairm, 1970).

Moireasdan, Dòmhnall Alasdair (ed.), *The Going Down of the Sun: The Great War and a Rural Lewis Community/Dol Fodha na Grèine: Buaidh a' Chogaidh Mhòir – Nis gu Baile an Truiseil* (Stornoway: Acair, 2014).

Moireasdan, Pàdruig, *Ugam agus Bhuam* (Stornoway: Acair, 1977).

Montague, C. E., *Disenchantment* (London: Chatto & Windus, 1922).

Morgan, Edwin, 'On John Maclean', in *The New Divan* (Manchester: Carcanet, 1977), p. 82.

—, *Twentieth-Century Scottish Classics* (Glasgow: Book Trust Scotland, 1987).

Motion, Andrew, 'Armistice', *The Guardian*, 4 October 2018, <https://www.theguardian.com/books/2018/oct/04/andrew-motion-poet-laureate-publishes-new-war-poem> (last accessed 13 November 2018).

Muirhead, J. H., *German Philosophy in Relation to the War* (London: John Murray, 1915).
Munro, Ian S., *Leslie Mitchell: Lewis Grassic Gibbon* (Edinburgh: Oliver & Boyd, 1966).
Murray, Charles, *Hamewith*, with Introduction by Andrew Lang (London: Constable, 1921).
—, *In the Country Places* (London: Constable, 1921).
—, *A Sough o' War* (London: Constable, 1917).
Murray, Isobel, 'Gibbon's Chris: A Celebration with Some Reservations', in M. P. McCullock and S. M. Dunnigan (eds), *A Flame in the Mearns: Lewis Grassic Gibbon – A Centenary Celebration* (Glasgow: Association for Scottish Literary Studies, 2003), pp. 54–63.
Murray, J. Clark, 'The Scottish Philosophy', *Macmillan's Magazine* (December 1876).
NicDhòmhnaill, Jo, Annella NicLeòid and Dòmhnall Iain MacLeòid (eds), *Cuimhneachan, Remembrance: Bàrdachd a' Chiad Chogaidh, Gaelic Poetry of World War One* (Stornoway: Acair, 2015).
NicLeòid, Mòrag (ed.), *Bàrdachd Scalpaigh* (Tarbert: Adhartas na Hearadh, 2014).
Nietzsche, Friedrich, *The Gay Science*, trans. Walter Kaufmann (New York: Vintage, [1882] 1974).
—, *Human, All Too Human: A Book for Free Spirits* (Cambridge: Cambridge University Press, [1878] 1996).
Niven, Alastair, 'New Diversity, Hybridity and Scottishness', in Ian Brown, Thomas Owen Clancy, Susan Manning and Murray Pittock (eds), *The Edinburgh History of Scottish Literature: Modern Transformations, Volume 3: New Identities (from 1918)* (Edinburgh: Edinburgh University Press, 2007), pp. 320–31.
Orwell, George, *Essays* (London: Penguin Books, [1947] 2000).
Owen, Alex, *The Place of Enchantment: British Occultism and the Culture of the Modern* (Chicago and London: University of Chicago Press, 2004).
Owen, Wilfred, *Wilfred Owen: The Complete Poems and Fragments*, ed. Jon Stallworthy (London: Chatto and Windus, Hogarth Press and Oxford University Press, 1983).
Passmore, John, *A Hundred Years of Philosophy* (London: Duckworth, 1957).
Paterson, W. P. (ed.), *German Culture: The Contribution of the Germans to Knowledge, Literature, Art, and Life* (Edinburgh: T. C. and E. C. Jack, 1915).
Peacock, Charlotte, *Into the Mountain: A Life of Nan Shepherd* (Cambridge: Galileo, 2017).
Pedersen, Sarah, 'Ladies "Doing their Bit" for the War Effort in the North-East of Scotland', *Women's History: The Journal of the Women's History Network*, vol. 2, no. 2 (2015), pp. 16–20.
—, *The Scottish Suffragettes and the Press* (London: Palgrave Macmillan, 2017).

Pennell, Catriona, *A Kingdom United: Popular Responses to the Outbreak of the First World War in Britain and Ireland* (Oxford: Oxford University Press, 2012).
Perloff, Marjorie, *Edge of Irony: Modernism in the Shadow of the Habsburg Empire* (Chicago and London: University of Chicago Press, 2016).
Peutan, Murchadh, *Sùil air Ais anns an Sgàthan* (Inverness: Clàr, 2018).
Pound, Ezra, 'Hell', in *Literary Essays of Ezra Pound*, ed. T. S. Eliot (London: Faber & Faber, [1954] 1960).
Pringle-Pattison, A. Seth, *The Idea of God in the Light of Recent Philosophy*, 2nd edn (London: Oxford University Press, [1915] 1920).
—, *The Idea of Immortality* (Oxford: Clarendon Press, 1922).
Ramage, George, *The Rather Tame War Experiences in Flanders 1915 of Lance Corporal George Ramage, 1st Battalion Gordon Highlanders*. National Library of Scotland MS 944–7.
Ramsay, M. C., 'Ian Stuart V. C.', *People's Friend* (23 November 1914), pp. 450–1.
Rayner, Jonathan, 'The Carer, the Combatant and the Clandestine: Images of Women in the First World War in *War Illustrated* Magazine', *Women's History Review*, vol. 27, no. 4 (2018), pp. 516–33.
Reeves, Nicholas, 'Cinema, Spectatorship and Propaganda: "Battle of the Somme" (1916) and Its Contemporary Audience', *Historical Journal of Film, Radio and Television*, vol. 17, no. 1 (1997), pp. 5–28.
—, 'Official British Film Propaganda', in Michael Paris (ed.), *The First World War and Popular Cinema: 1914 to the Present* (Edinburgh: Edinburgh University Press, 1999), pp. 27–50.
—, *Official British Film Propaganda During the First World War* (London: Croom Helm, 1986).
—, 'The Power of Film Propaganda – Myth or Reality?', *Historical Journal of Film, Radio and Television*, vol. 13, no. 2 (1993), pp. 181–201.
Reith, John, *Into the Wind* (London: Hodder and Stoughton, 1949).
—, *Wearing Spurs* (London: Hutchison, 1966).
Riach, Alan, 'Visions Beyond Violence: Alan Riach Examines Modern Scottish Literature's Response to War', *National* (21 October 2016).
Robb, George, *British Culture and the First World War* (London: Macmillan International Higher Education, 2014).
Rorie, David, *The Auld Doctor and Other Poems and Songs in Scots* (London: Constable, 1920).
—, *A Medico's Luck in the War* (Aberdeen: Milne and Hutchison, 1929).
—, *Folk Tradition and Folk Medicine in Scotland: The Writings of David Rorie*, ed. David Buchan (Edinburgh: Canongate Academic, 1994).
Rountree, Katharyn, 'Neo-Paganism, Animism, and Kinship with Nature', *Journal of Contemporary Religion*, vol. 27, no. 2 (2012), pp. 305–20.
Royle, Trevor, *Flowers of the Forest: Scotland and the First World War* (Edinburgh: Birlinn, [2006] 2007).
— (ed.), *In Flanders Fields: Scottish Poetry and Prose of the First World War* (Edinburgh: Mainstream, 1990).

— (ed.), *Isn't All This Bloody?: Scottish Writing From the First World* War (Edinburgh: Birlinn, 2014).
—, 'Literature and World War I', in Ian Brown and Alan Riach (eds), *The Edinburgh Companion to Twentieth-Century Scottish Literature* (Edinburgh: Edinburgh University Press, 2009), pp. 37–49.
—, *The Macmillan Companion to Scottish Literature* (London: Macmillan Press, 1983).
Ruddin, Lee P., 'The "Firsts" World War: A History of the Morale of Liverpudlians as Told through Letters to Liverpool Editors, 1915–1918', *International Journal of Regional and Local History*, vol. 9, no. 2 (2014), pp. 79–93.
Scott, Alex R., *Ours the Harvest: A Life of Charles Murray* (Aberdeen: Charles Murray Memorial Fund, 2004).
Scott, Sir Walter, *Redgauntlet* (Oxford: Oxford University Press, [1824] 2011).
Sedgwick, Mark, *Against the Modern World: Traditionalism and the Secret Intellectual History of the Twentieth Century* (Oxford: Oxford University Press, 2004).
Seth, Andrew, *Scottish Philosophy: A Comparison of the Scottish and German Answers to Hume* (Edinburgh: William Blackwood and Sons, [1885] 1899).
Shaw, Harry E., 'The Historical Novel', in M. Coyle, Peter Garside, Malcolm Kelsall and John Peck (eds), *The Encyclopedia of Literature and Criticism* (London: Routledge, 1990).
Shaw, Michael, 'William Sharp's Neo-Paganism: Queer Identity and the National Family', in Duc Dau and Shale Preston (eds), *Queer Victorian Families: Curious Relations in Literature* (New York: Routledge, 2015), pp. 77–96.
Shepherd, Nan, 'Charles Murray', in *Hamewith: The Complete Poems of Charles Murray* (Aberdeen: published for the Charles Murray Trust by Aberdeen University Press, 1979).
—, 'Descent from the Cross', in *Wild Geese: A Collection of Nan Shepherd's Writing*, ed. Charlotte Peacock (Cambridge: Galileo, 2018), pp. 1–38.
—, *The Quarry Wood* (Edinburgh: Canongate, [1928] 1996).
—, *The Weatherhouse* (Edinburgh: Canongate, [1930] 2010).
—, 'Women in the University Fifty Years: 1892–1942', *Aberdeen University Review*, vol. 29: 1941–42, pp. 171–81.
Shirey, Ryan D., 'Gibbon, Shelley and Romantic Revolutionary Renewal', in *The International Companion to Lewis Grassic Gibbon*, ed. Scott Lyall (Glasgow: Association for Scottish Literary Studies, 2015), pp. 89–104.
Sibley, Robert C., *Northern Spirits: John Watson, George Grant and Charles Taylor – Appropriations of Hegelian Political Thought* (Montreal and Kingston: McGill-Queen's University Press, 2008).
Sisson, Elaine, *Pearse's Patriots: St Enda's and the Cult of Boyhood* (Cork: Cork University Press, 2004).
Smith, G. Gregory, *Scottish Literature: Character and Influence* (London: Macmillan, 1919).

Sorley, Charles Hamilton, *The Collected Letters of Charles Hamilton Sorley*, ed. Jean Moorcroft Wilson (London: Woolf, 1990).
—, *Marlborough and other Poems* (Cambridge: Cambridge University Press, 1916).
Sorley, W. R., *Moral Values and the Idea of God* (Cambridge: Cambridge University Press, 1918).
Stevenson, Randall, *Literature and the Great War 1914–1918* (Oxford: Oxford University Press, 2013).
Stevenson, Robert Louis, *The Letters: Volume Three*, ed. Sidney Colvin (London: Heinemann [Tusitala edn vol. XXXIII], 1926).
Stewart, Karen A., *Scottish Woman Writers to 1987: A Select Guide and Bibliography* (Glasgow: Glasgow District Libraries, 1987).
Storey, Lisa (ed.), *D.M.N.C: Sgrìobhaidhean Dhòmhnaill Mhic na Ceàrdaich* (Inverness: Clàr, 2014).
— (ed.), *Litir chun an t-Saighdeir gun Ainm* (Inverness: Clàr, 2016).
Strachan, Hew, 'Foreword', in *Beneath Troubled Skies: Poems of Scotland at War, 1914–1918*, ed. Lizzie MacGregor (Edinburgh: Polygon, 2015).
—, 'The Scottish Soldier and Scotland, 1914–1918', in David Forsyth and Wendy Ugolini (eds), *A Global Force: War, Identities and Scotland's Diaspora* (Edinburgh: Edinburgh University Press, 2016), <https://edinburgh.universitypressscholarship.com> (last accessed 15 March 2019), pp. 1–19.
Stromberg, Ronald N., *Redemption by War: The Intellectuals and 1914* (Lawrence, KS: Regents Press of Kansas, 1982).
Tallis, Raymond, *Of Time and Lamentation: Reflections on Transience* (London: Agenda, 2017).
Taylor, David, *Memory, Narrative and the Great War: Rifleman Patrick MacGill and the Construction of Wartime Experience* (Liverpool: Liverpool University Press, 2013).
Thomas, Edward, *The Annotated Collected Poems*, ed. Edna Longley (Northumberland: Bloodaxe, 2008).
Thompson, E. P., *The Making of the English Working Class* (New York: Random House, [1963] 1964).
Urquhart, George, 'Confrontation and Withdrawal: Loos, Readership and *The First Hundred Thousand*', in Catriona M. M. Macdonald and E. W. McFarland (eds), *Scotland and the Great War* (Edinburgh: Birlinn, 1999), pp. 125–44.
Van de Pas, Brigitte, *World War One Through Scots Eyes: Scots and Identity in the British Army During the First World War* (thesis, Leiden University, 2015).
Wallace, Stuart, *John Stuart Blackie: Scottish Scholar and Patriot* (Edinburgh: Edinburgh University Press, 2006).
Watson, Alexander and Patrick Porter, 'Bereaved and Aggrieved: Combat Motivation and the Ideology of Sacrifice in the First World War', *Historical Research*, vol. 83, no. 219 (2010), pp. 146–64.

Watson, Janet S. K., *Fighting Different Wars: Experience, Memory, and the First World War in Britain*, vol. 16 (Cambridge: Cambridge University Press, 2004).
Watson, John, *The Interpretation of Religious Experience*, vol. I (Glasgow: James MacLehose and Sons, 1912).
—, *The State in Peace and War* (Glasgow: James MacLehose and Sons, 1919).
Watson, Roderick, *The Literature of Scotland: The Twentieth Century* (New York: Palgrave-Macmillan, 2007).
Watson, Rory, 'Introduction', in Nan Shepherd, *The Grampian Quartet* (Edinburgh: Canongate, 1996).
Webb, Simon, *British Concentration Camps: A Brief History from 1900–1975* (Barnsley: Pen and Sword Books, 2016).
Weil, Simone *An Anthology* (London: Penguin, 1994).
Wenley, Robert Mark, 'Edward Caird', *The Harvard Theological Review*, vol. 2, no. 2 (April 1909), pp. 115–38, <http://www.jstor.org/stable/1507019> (last accessed 3 May 2016).
Williams, Mark, *Ireland's Immortals: A History of the Gods of Irish Myth* (Princeton and Oxford: Princeton University Press, 2016).
Williams, Raymond, *The Country and the City* (London: Vintage, [1973] 2016).
Winter, Jay, *Sites of Memory, Sites of Mourning: The Great War in European Cultural History* (Cambridge: Cambridge University Press, [1995] 1998).
Wittig, Kurt, *The Scottish Tradition in Literature* (Edinburgh: Oliver and Boyd, 1958).
Woolf, Virginia, *To the Lighthouse* (Harmondsworth: Penguin, [1927] 1973).
Wordsworth, William, *The Collected Poems of William Wordsworth* (Ware: Wordsworth Editions, 1994).
Yeats, W. B., *The Collected Poems of W. B. Yeats* (London: Macmillan, 1971).
Zeiger, Susan, 'She Didn't Raise her Boy to be a Slacker: Motherhood, Conscription, and the Culture of the First World War', *Feminist Studies*, vol. 22, no. 1 (1996).
Zweig, Stefan, *The World of Yesterday: Memoirs of a European*, trans. Anthea Bell (London: Pushkin Press, [1942] 2009).

Index

An Deò-Gréine, 126
Auden, W. H., 205, 210, 212

The Battle of the Somme (film), 69, 72, 76
Bell, J. J., *Wee Macgreegor Enlists*, 47–8
Blake, George, *The Path of Glory*, 54–5, 58
Blunden, Edmund, 201–2
Brooke, Rupert, 206–8, 211
Buchan, John, 12, 29, 45–7, 218–37
   Greenmantle, 224–5, 229
   Memory Hold-the-Door, 47, 220
   Mr Standfast, 37–8, 46–7, 220–1, 224–5, 227, 229
   Poems Scots and English, 47
   The Thirty-Nine Steps, 218, 221, 225, 228, 231

Cable, Boyd, 70–7
   Between the Lines, 70–5
   Doing their Bit, 74
   Front Lines, 75
Caird, Edward, 144, 146–9, 152
Campbell, Angus Peter, 138
Campbell, Norman, 137–8
Campbell, R. W., *Private Spud Tamson*, 47–8

Cameron, William, 26
Clydeside, 4, 6, 37
Cocker, W. D., 8, 275
Commonwealth War Graves Commission, 7, 214

Eliot, T. S., 209, 242, 262

Fussell, Paul, *The Great War and Modern Memory*, 10, 49, 62, 67, 70, 81–2, 220–1

Gaitens, Edward, *The Dance of the Apprentices*, 55–7
Geddes, Patrick, 25–6, 30, 184
Georgian verse, 201–2, 204, 206, 210, 211–12, 214–15
Gibbon, Lewis Grassic, *Sunset Song*, 84, 87–8, 92, 170, 180–2, 184–7, 189, 191–3, 195, 242, 249–51, 257–65
Gibbs, Philip, 63–4, 68, 71, 232
Gunn, Neil M., *Highland River*, 180–3, 186–7, 189–91, 193–5
Gurney, Ivor, 207
Guth na Bliadhna, 126

Haig, Douglass, 4, 271
Hardie, Keir, 24, 127

Hay, Ian, *The First Hundred Thousand*, 1, 3, 35–7, 46, 66
Henderson, Angus, 126
high diction, 81–97
Hume, David, 143–4, 149
Hynes, Samuel, *A War Imagined*, 1, 57, 62

Iolaire, 6–7, 101, 118, 124–6, 134

Jacob, Violet, 23–4, 215, 275

Kerr, R. W., 8, 191, 275

Lawrence, D. H., 34, 185, 254–6
Lee, Joseph, 8, 27
Linklater, Eric, 2, 5

MacDiarmid, Hugh (Christopher Murray Grieve), 1, 8–9, 24, 28–33, 35, 37, 39–41, 158, 191, 215
MacDonald, Donald, 102
Macdonald, Norman Malcolm, 124–6
MacDonald, Thomas Donald, 110–12
MacFarlane, Murdo, 102–3
MacGill, Patrick, *The Great Push*, 67–9, 72–7
Mackenzie, Compton, 33–5, 39
 Sinister Street, 33–4
 Whisky Galore, 33
Mackinlay, George A. C., 200–17
Mackintosh, Ewart Alan, 9, 27, 212, 242, 268–85
 A Highland Regiment, 268, 273, 277
 War, the Liberator and Other Pieces, 268
Maclean, John, 4, 37–9
MacLean, Sorley, 115–18
Macmurray, John, 143, 157–8, 165, 172, 174–6
Mar, Roderick Erskine of, 23–4, 126
Modernism, 10, 23–32, 180–95, 210
Montague, C. E., 62–6, 75
motherhood, 87
Murray, Charles, 14, 27, 167, 215, 238–52
 A Sough o' War, 14, 26, 238–52
 Hamewith, 238, 240, 248–9
 In the Country Places, 238, 250–1
Murray, Murdo, 107–10, 122–4

Orwell, George, 24–5, 40
Owen, Wilfred, 35–6, 208–11, 218, 271

paganism, 180–99
pastoralism, 180–99, 200–17, 218–37, 242–3, 255, 262, 275
Pringle-Pattison, Andrew Seth, 149, 153, 156

Reid, Thomas, 143–6, 152
Reith, John, *Wearing Spurs*, 49–52
religion, 50–2, 82, 92, 146–8, 152, 156, 181, 184, 186, 228
Rorie, David, *A Medico's Luck in the War*, 52–4

Sackville, Margaret, 8
Salmond, J. B., 27
Sassoon, Siegfried, 261, 270, 273
Scottish Literary Renaissance, 8, 183
Scottish National Party, 22, 24, 35
Scottish National Players, 31
Shepherd, Nan, 165–79
 The Living Mountain, 165, 177, 189
 The Quarry Wood, 165, 168–9, 171, 173–4
 The Weatherhouse, 92, 165, 171–7

Sinclair, Donald, 113, 129
Smith, G. Gregory, *Scottish Literature: Character and Influence*, 2
Socialism, 24, 37–8, 55–6, 68, 84, 182, 193, 260–1
Sorley, Charles Hamilton, 26, 153, 201, 207, 209, 242
Sorley, W. R., 153–7
Stevenson, R. L., 22–3, 26, 33, 47
Symon, Mary, 8, 167, 215

Yeats, W. B., 184, 203, 248

EU representative:
Easy Access System Europe
Mustamäe tee 50, 10621 Tallinn, Estonia
Gpsr.requests@easproject.com